The Friar's Map of Ancient America
1360 AD

The Story of Nicholas of Lynn
and the Franciscan Map of America

by Gunnar Thompson, Ph.D.

English cog (1284)
Great Seal of Dover, England
source: Nansen (1911, 250)

From *Laura Lee Productions*
& Argonauts of The Misty Isles
Seattle, Washington

The Friar's Map of Ancient America
—1360 AD

Multicultural Heritage Series No. 3

by Gunnar Thompson, Ph.D.

Laura Lee Productions
P.O. Box 3010
Bellevue, WA 98009-3010
FAX (206) 455-1197; (206) 455-1053

also available:

American Discovery
by Gunnar Thompson
—400 page book on voyages 100,000 BC to 1500 AD;
  America's multicultural heritage; fully illustrated
  $20.95 post-paid; ISBN 0-9621990-9-5

ISBN 0-9621990-8-7
Library of Congress Catalog Card Number:
    96-78220

Recommended catalog entry:
Thompson, Gunnar   1946-
The Friar's Map of Ancient America—1360 AD
Bibliography
1. American History; 2. America—discovery and
exploration; 3. Cartography—history; 4. Multi-
cultural Studies; 5. Nicholas of Lynn; 6. Roger
Bacon; 7. Canada—history; 8. England—history; 9.
Astronomy—history; 10. Indians—history; I. Title.

printed in the U.S.A. on recycled paper

Dedication

Four individuals who deserve the most credit for this creation are:
Florence & Roy; Roger & Nicholas.

To Thor & Carolyn
Best Wishes,

Anna Thompson
1996

America's Oldest Map
Venetian Commercial Map
Albertin DeVirga, 1414
Facsimile by Thompson

The Friar's Map of Ancient America—1360 AD

abstract

When antique collector Albert Figdor purchased a 15th-century map in the Austro-Hungarian city of Sebenico, he didn't realize that he had acquired the most important map of American history. Like many scholars, he assumed that the value of the document as a collector's item exceeded its importance to historians. Fortunately, Mr. Figdor brought the map to Lucerne in 1932 where it was professionally photographed before being sold to an unknown collector. This precaution has provided scholars with an exact facsimile of the map; and it has enabled us to identify the earliest portrayal of North and South America on a map that existed almost a century before the famous Columbus voyage.

This 1414 map, by Venetian cartographer Albertin DeVirga, shows North America as a continent northwest of Norway; South America is portrayed as a continent southeast of Asia. DeVirga called his southern continent Ca-paru—which is the earliest mention of "Peru" in cartographical records. It is also the first time that New World continents appeared separate from Eurasia on a world map. Likewise, the map portrays Florida and the Antilles for the first time on a map.

Northern regions on the Venetian map were probably based on North Atlantic expeditions and geographical surveys undertaken by the English friar, Nicholas of Lynn, between 1330 and 1360 AD. The friar's expeditions, commissioned by King Edward III of England, sought to fulfill the dream of Roger Bacon who proposed the creation of a scientific map of the world. Bacon believed that such a map would be an invaluable aid to Christian merchants and travelers. The mapping effort of the Franciscan brotherhood resulted in an accurate map—the long lost "Friar's Map." Thus began a tradition of cartography that eventually involved Prince Henry The Navigator, Claudius Clavus, Andrea Bianco, Paolo Toscanelli, Fra Mauro, Henricus Martellus, and Martin Behaim. The friar's 1360 manuscript, Inventio Fortunatae, convinced the Portuguese to commit their maritime resources to a trans-South African approach to the Orient; even Columbus fell under the spell of the Franciscan cosmography.

As the earliest scientific map of America, the Venetian-Franciscan Map deserves a hallowed place in America's national shrine to knowledge and literature—the Library of Congress.

Acknowledgments

Many individuals in my world-wide network provided assistance and consultation. Dick Ibarra Grasso, an Argentine historian, provided copies of Roman and Medieval maps. Susan Matland, curator of a Norwegian museum, sent copies of Renaissance maps. Magne Bolstad sent copies of Scandinavian maps and interviewed a Norwegian heretic who was on the same path. Don Cyr—Stonehenge Viewpoint editor—added his material on ancient Chinese maps from the <u>Shan Hai Ching</u> geography. Fazi Khoury, Professor of Middle Eastern Studies at the University of Washington, helped translate Arabic and Persian maps from the 14th century. Marina Tolmachiva, a specialist in Arabian maps, and Afifi Durr of the Arabic Language Service in Seattle also assisted in Arabic translations and cartography. Robert Ness, a Seattle management and creativity consultant, contributed two volumes of 16th-century maps of America. W.R. Anderson, President of the Leif Ericson Society, added his collection of maps and articles on Norumbega. Paul Chapman, an Atlanta writer and Columbus biographer, offered his assessment of the location of Vinland and the maps of Columbus. Richard Nielsen served as a consultant on Norse runes and artifacts. Jo Curran provided access to English scholars. Susanne Thackray searched British sources for references about friar Nicholas and located a 19th-century biography about the friar. Thor Heyerdahl reviewed and commented on several manuscripts about ancient maps and pre-Columbian voyagers. The Huntington Museum in San Marino, California, provided an invaluable photograph of Ranulf Higden's map from the <u>Polychronicon</u>. Ross Togashi, manager of the University of Hawaii map collection, helped established contacts with international scholars via the internet. Toni Hammarlund and Devon Jung unlocked the vast resources of Powell's bookstore in Portland. Donne Florence, public relations officer at the University of Hawaii, helped with publicity. Laura Lee and Paul Roberts of Laura Lee Productions provided access to innovative theorists and writers in the Seattle area. Joel Fowler assisted in telecommunications. Michael Fredholm, Robert Ness, Don Cyr, and Vincent Mooney, Jr., read advance copies of the manuscript and offered valuable suggestions. Arthur Durst, Susanne Wegman of Switzerland and Helen Altonn wrote articles on the Friar's Map discovery. Sverre Kruger conducted an interview for broadcast on Norwegian Educational Television. Mark Privett assisted with printing and distribution. Rhude Thompson assisted with video and computer activities.

Some of the many individuals who have contributed ideas, time, and logistical support include: Tracey Baldwin, Maryann Ness, Claudia Snipes, Tom & Nancy Word, Glenda Carberry, Vernon Chester, Helen & Kenso Hamada, Steve Russell, Nathan Yellen, Charles Prazak, Ross Togashi, Mildred Marmur, John Jones, Donald & Joann Cyr, Ian Laundy, Florence & Roy Thompson, Rhude & Jennie Thompson, Jerilyn & Julie Thompson, Toni Hammarlund, Quinn Schenkel, David Haliday, Helen Achterman, Roger Aue, Sam Alvarado, Dave & Bonnie Dutton, Harry & Devon Jung, Jim Nelson, Dorothy Hayden, Wayne & Kris May, John Dolly, Kenneth Mortimer, Alexander Pickens, Aiko Oda, Jim Anderson, Joe & Judy Ferem, Sandy Landy, Dorothy Westby, Joseph Mahan, Rafique Jairazbhoy, Richard Nielsen, Larry Cruse, Reiko Fujikawa, Lyn Tebrugge, Harry & Joanne Barnhardt, Mike Greco, Karim & Laura Joard, David Childress, Jodi Lehman, Kathy Ryan, Wallace Bartholomew, Doug Easterling & Lucinda Brogden, Thor & Caroline Thompson, Shaine Silberstein, J.D. Brunier, Gloria Farley, Jean Hunt, Gayle Pollard, Frank Joseph, Martine Bohm, Tora Bohn, Roslyn Strong, and Geri Simmons.

Many others—unnamed but much appreciated—have given valuable assistance.

The Author extends to you his heartfelt appreciation for your support.

Contents

Navigator with Cross Staff
after a Dutch illustration in
The Light of Navigation by William Johnson
Amsterdam, ca. 1650

Forbidden Heritage

According to the traditional story of American discovery, the New World was virtually unknown until a Genoese sailor dared to cross the Sea of Darkness in 1492. If that is what you want to believe, don't read this book. And by all means, stay away from libraries, bookstores, and museums. You can never tell when the demons of heresy might jump out from behind the facade of traditional "history."

My discovery of the "Lost Friar's Map" happened because I enjoy solving puzzles; I am fascinated with mysteries; and I love finding answers to problems that experts declare are "impossible to solve."

My idea of a good time—on a rainy day—is to walk through libraries or second-hand bookstores. I'm particularly keen on entering areas where I've never been before. I usually scan the shelves for intriguing illustrations; and I'm mindful of derelicts—books with tattered covers that haven't been opened for decades. Sometimes, I find a volume written in a foreign language or cloaked by an icing of dust. That's when I'm sure to find long-forgotten gems of wisdom—or heresy. I'm intrigued by heresy because it provides a unique view of society from the perspective of the outsider, the malcontent, the mystic, and the visionary.

I studied two foreign languages—German and Spanish—and I've become familiar with a few critical words in Latin, Norwegian, and Danish. This knowledge helps in gaining access to writers with a different cultural perspective. But if the book has pictures—it doesn't matter what language the author used. Each time I open the cover, I find myself stepping into new worlds which can aptly be described as gardens of knowledge waiting to be harvested by the inquiring mind.

Back in the 1950's, when I had trouble adjusting to the boring and hostile environment of public education, I found solace in the maze of corridors at the city library. My passion for books, learning, and vicarious adventure has never ceased; that passion led me to a map that has been presumed lost for the past five centuries.

The map I found is a 14th-century relic—the legacy of an era when chivalry was in vogue, and European kings dreamed of world conquest. Plagues, famine, and warfare ravaged the continent and the British Isles. But those were not the only dangers: intellectuals and the curious had even more to fear from zealots of mind-control and moral purity. In those days, arrogant authorities in the Church hierarchy assumed the role of divine executioners. They extolled loyalty to dogma while roasting scientists, free-thinkers, and intellectuals in the fires of the Inquisition.

Historians tend to regard the 14th century as a backwater of human development—hence the expression: Dark Ages or Medieval Ages. But it

1

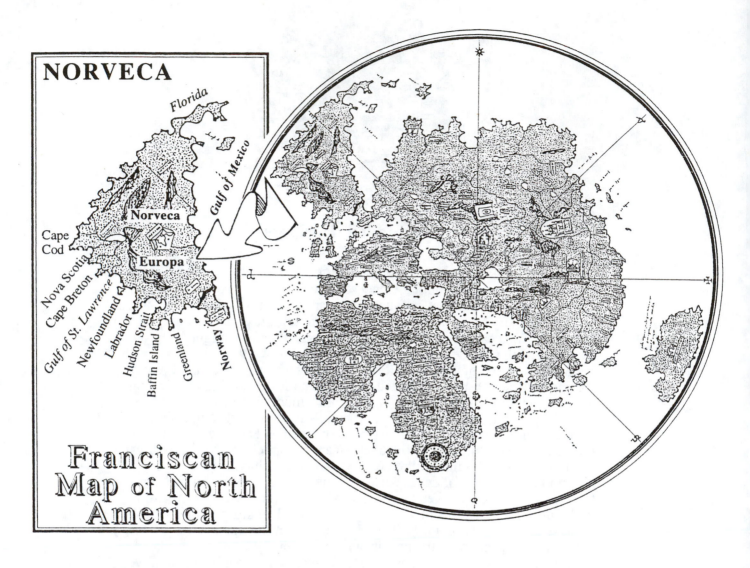

NORVECA

Florida

Gulf of Mexico

Norveca

Europa

Cape
Cod

Nova Scotia

Cape Breton

Gulf of St. Lawrence

Newfoundland

Labrador

Hudson Strait

Baffin Island

Greenland

Norway

Franciscan
Map of North
America

Venetian World Commercial Map of 1414

NORTH AMERICA is shown as a huge northwestern continent on Albertin DeVirga's world map of 1414. This map shows Venetian commercial interests throughout the world. It was compiled from numerous regional maps taken from ancient and contemporary sources. As frequent merchants traveling to London, Venetians were in a position to obtain English maps from the king who was heavily indebted to the Venetians for their services as importers of vital spices, ceramics, and textiles from the Orient.

The northwestern section of this map portrays a continental land reaching out from the side of Norway in the approximate position of North America as it appears on a modern globe. DeVirga has called this continent *Norveca Europa* or "Norway Europe." The term Norveca applied to Polar Regions (that is, North American territories) was only current during the span between 1261 and 1380—as these were the years when Norway claimed sovereignty over the Polar Regions. As Nicholas of Lynn and the Franciscan brothers were busy surveying the region during this period of time, it is reasonable to attribute this section of the Venetian map to English sources—as they would have identified the overseas land as a Norwegian kingdom.

Physical features of the Norveca continent enable identification of headlands along the North American coast—including Labrador, Newfoundland, Nova Scotia, Cape Cod, Florida, the Antilles, and the Gulf of Mexico.

Facsimile by Gunnar Thompson ©1995. Source: Marcel Destombes. *Mappemondes AD 1200-1500; Imago Mundi Supplement IV: A Review of Early Cartography.* Amsterdam: N. Israel, 1964.

was more than a period of urban misery and religious oppression: it was also the twilight of the Renaissance. The contents of ancient maps and travelogs prove that some daring individuals were trying to bring about an era of learning and science—even though most bureaucrats were not yet ready for a cultural transformation. Leading this effort in England were a group of Franciscan friars at Oxford University. Over the span of several decades, they traveled far-and-wide across the Atlantic Ocean; they compiled gazetteers of geographical reference points; and in the span of several decades, they produced an accurate map of the North Atlantic for use in maritime travel and commerce.

The "Friar's Map" is only one of several North Atlantic navigational charts which the Franciscans produced between 1335 and 1440. The earliest versions were understandably tentative and schematic. They portrayed western and northern lands in the shape of circles and rectangles—which by modern standards seem somewhat cartoonish and difficult to interpret. The names of the isles are often archaic forms of legendary or fantastic lands derived from the "Fortunate Isles" of Greco-Roman mythology. Later, these isles acquired more precise shapes as field explorers returned with gazetteers of relatively accurate geographical coordinates. By the late 14th century, Franciscan geographers were aware that lands across the Atlantic from Europe included an immense, wilderness continent with huge lakes and rivers. Some called it "Hyperborea;" others called it "Cathay." Travelers invariably came upon scattered European settlements—mostly aggregations of fur traders, whalers, lumberjacks, and even survivors of shipwrecks who decided to homestead in the lands where they had taken refuge. There were also pirates, wandering priests, and native hunters throughout the coastal regions. Farther inland, explorers found huge villages of the Micmac, Iroquois, and Beothuk tribes. In the far north, sailors encountered short people they called <u>pygnei</u> (the pygmy people) who modern historians have identified as the Eskimo (or, more properly—the Inuit people).

The Franciscan map that I came across in 1994 comes from the North American survey by an English friar called Nicholas of Lynn. The map was originally part of the friar's travelog called the <u>Inventio Fortunatae</u> which was completed circa 1360 and presented to King Edward III of England. It shows North America as continental land northwest of Europe. Both the shape and position of this New World continent are somewhat distorted due to the difficulty of crowding a huge overseas land into the confines of a circular map that was originally designed to show only the Old World continents of Europe, Africa, and Asia. Nevertheless, this "Friar's Map" portrays the distinct coastal features of North America from Greenland to the Gulf of Mexico. This is an astonishing achievement considering that most maps of the era were crude, allegorical creations that were totally useless for worldly travel.

The map of friar Nicholas is a wonderful document that finally fills in the missing pieces to the puzzle of New World discovery. Historians have characterized the 15th-century contact between Old World explorers and New World natives as a cathartic event that could happen only once. This singular event was supposedly one of the most-important turning points in the development of civilization, thus historians have promoted the one person who led the march as being "the most important individual since Jesus Christ." The glory of that so-called "discovery" was prematurely awarded to the European cavalier, Columbus, who—as a white, male, Christian—seems ill-suited for the role of superhero in a society that claims to be egalitarian. As it turns out, the Eurocentric story of New World discovery was the invention of romantic, 19th-century historians; it is almost pure fantasy.

Was this fantasy—the so-called "The Great Encounter"—simply the result of ignorance? Or did arrogance, incompetence, and outright deceit play a role in creation of the Columbus Myth? These are issues we should keep in mind as we expose the false assumptions that underlie the orthodox version of New World discovery.

Franciscan monks trained in surveying, mapping, and astronomy have left us clues of previously "lost" (or ignored) expeditions between the Old World and the New World in ancient times. The Franciscan mapping effort reveals that contact between the Eastern and Western hemispheres was gradual—not cathartic. It required many decades, if not centuries, to provide a foundation of cartography and geography that made possible the so-called "Age of Discovery" in the 15th and 16th centuries. Building this foundation is best conceived of as a process—not an event.

Some prophetic philosophers might even argue that the process is still under way. From their perspective, the so-called "New World" as a multi-dimensional conglomerate of dreams, ideals, and multi-ethnic achievements continues to evolve. And so must our conceptualization of the history of the New World evolve to fit newly-revealed facts about transoceanic voyages in ancient times.

The Friar's Map will forever change the way we think about the earliest days of America; and it may well challenge our cherished assumption that "history" as we know it is a reliable science. Although historians tell us that Columbus boldly sailed off towards unknown shores, the Friar's Map reveals that the mariner was quite honest—and sane—when he announced that his destination was already charted on his own map. Orthodox historians scoffed at that claim; and they scoffed at the accounts of friar Nicholas which they characterized as unimportant fables of non-existent isles. This gross misconception has endured these many years due to the prevailing assumption that the friar's map along with his travelog were forever lost in the depths of antiquity.

However, the time has come to reassess where we have been and where we are going as a society. The historians were wrong about the friar; they were wrong to assume his map was "lost;" and they were wrong to assume that Columbus engineered the first significant contact between the hemispheres. Those assumptions stemmed from a mistaken belief that history could be interpreted as a divine mandate for European domination of the New World.

Now that "The Lost Friar's Map" is finally out of hiding, our cherished history—and our cherished mythology—will have to be revised to better reflect the way events really happened.

Trail of The Phoenix

My discovery of the Lost Friar's Map is a story in itself.

The actual event—which occurred in November of 1994—was an astonishing, personal triumph. However, it was not the kind of "glamorous" event we often associate with such a grand achievement. There was no band and no thunderous applause from an arena of eager spectators. In fact, I was alone with a book in the dimly-lighted corridors of a university library. The book was not some exotic travelog; it was a collection of ancient maps. Indeed, it was the kind of book that would likely plunge most ordinary folks into the depths of narcolepsy.

What I found was a photograph—or rather, a copy of a photograph made of an ancient map in 1912. This wasn't even the first time I had seen such a photograph—although the first specimens I remember were of such poor quality that it would have been impossible at that time to comprehend what was before my eyes.

On the other hand, I wasn't mentally prepared in the beginning to understand the importance of the map. In essence: the formula, or recipe, for discovery just wasn't sufficiently refined to yield a favorable outcome. And that is one of the lessons of discovery. As Louis Pasteur—the famous biologist—observed so long ago: "Discovery favors only the mind that is prepared."

Once I was puzzled by those words; now I understand what they mean.

Preparation of The Mind

Why on Earth would I spend several years of my life looking for maps that most historians have declared couldn't possibly exist? That is a question I have often pondered in the late hours of many nights as I sat in front of a computer or found myself being chased from a library. It hasn't been unusual for a custodian to find me still reading books after closing time—as though I was oblivious to the rest of the world. And honestly, I was oblivious to everything but my stacks of books.

I still have dreams where I see lights flashing in the library—telling me that the building is about to close. The impending closure causes great anxiety; and the flashing lights are annoying, because I am desperately trying to make copies from a stack of books that seems endless. In such hectic moments, I often loaded books on a library cart and hoped they went unnoticed until I had a chance to return the next day.

The reason why I was able to identify the missing map when scores of professors and college students have looked at the 1912 photograph without seeing anything remarkable is a consequence of the way our educational system conditions us to think. We are essentially taught from birth by our parents, by teachers, by the implicit design of the language we use, and by cultural dictates of our environment to perceive our world in an orthodox manner. In a sense, our culture, traditions, and language condition us to actually "see" things in a certain way; and anything that doesn't fit this rather limited framework is essentially beyond our sight. Something very important might be standing right before our eyes—yet we are unable to see what it is. In a very real sense—we are blind.

Poet Marcel Proust accurately observed a truth that cultures by their very nature try to conceal from us: "The real voyage of discovery consists not in seeking new landscapes—but in having new eyes."

According to Proust, I had no hope of making a real discovery—until I acquired "new eyes." Proust wasn't suggesting corneal implants or radial keratotomy. By "new eyes" he had in mind a new way of seeing or a new way of thinking that wasn't bound up by cultural expectations and conditioning. Essentially, before I could be free to find something new and important, I had to unlearn the way I was taught to think.

I wasn't consciously aware at the time, but ever since I was a child, I was a suitable candidate for acquiring new eyes. As a youth, I was suspicious of the culture around me. There were too many contradictions, too many discrepancies, too many hypocrisies for me to absorb what I was being told without having a healthy dose of disbelief and skepticism.

To begin with, the whole scenario about America's origins seemed hopelessly confused—or contrived. Grade-school teachers instructed us that Columbus "discovered America." But how was that possible when the native peoples were already present in the land when he arrived? Some teachers even praised Columbus for bringing "civilization" to the New World. That was ridiculous! I soon learned that there were native civilizations in the form of huge, advanced cities. By comparison, European explorers who reached the native shores of Turtle Island (America) were probably like most boaters who have been away from civilization for several weeks—they stank and looked like lost puppies. Furthermore, was not the goodwill that native tribes showed Columbus and the Pilgrims evidence that the aboriginals were civilized?

The more I learned about the official version of American History, the more I came to believe that it was all a sham designed to uphold the monolithic facade of Anglo superiority. At some point during my high school years, I committed my life to finding out the secrets that were hidden behind the veil of mythology that was advertised as "history."

My quest for the truth about America's multicultural origins continued as a graduate student in anthropology at the University of Wisconsin in Madison—the state capitol. I was elated to find that this center of politics and education offered two major libraries for me to explore. The possibilities for finding the objective of my quest seemed endless.

Before long, I found evidence in various books concerning the great cavalcade of voyagers who had come to America before Columbus. Asians, Hindus, Africans, Egyptians, Celts, Phoenicians, Romans, Jews, and Vikings all made their way to America in ancient times. They traded with Native Peoples; sometimes they fought with belligerent tribes; they left ideas, artifacts, and diseases; they took home native plants and resources; and they told of their travels in legends and historical accounts.

I was excited to learn about such ancient voyages; however, my graduate advisors were appalled. Unknowingly, I had crossed over the boundary of "acceptable scholarship" into the realm of heresy—a region I have come to call the "forbidden history" of America.

I parted ways with the doctoral program when I encountered the all-too-familiar backwater of establishment dogma. My new independence freed me from the curse of paradigm myopia that is common among orthodox academicians, and it allowed me to open many doors of interdisciplinary research that otherwise would have been out of bounds. My unfolding path of independent scholarship introduced me to a host of maverick authors and inquisitive pioneers. I have gained through this experience an education that would have been impossible under the tutelage of hidebound academics.

Within a few years, I was back in school. Although I remained skeptical about the American educational system, I completed a Ph.D. in counseling psychology at the University of Wisconsin. I did this because I realized the economic and social importance of learning advanced skills and joining a professional association.

Meanwhile, I continued my research on America's multi-ethnic origins. In 1986, I came across new evidence that Asian voyagers had crossed the Pacific in ancient times. This led to my first book on American cultural history called: Nu Sun (1989). My book enumerated evidence of Taoist religious symbols that were brought from China to Mexico circa 500 BC. These symbols and Taoist religion were adopted as the core of Mayan religious belief and artistic expression. With this book, I succeeded in proving that Old World voyagers played a significant role in the early development of the native Mayan culture. Interest in my book led to growth of a world-wide network of informants—many of whom were amateurs practicing outside their own professions. In this manner, I became part of a fellowship of heretics and individualists. The efforts of this fellowship were significantly advanced in 1986 when I founded the Multicultural Discovery Project which was dedicated to revealing the truth concerning America's multi-ethnic heritage.

For ten years, I lived a bipolar existence: during daylight hours, I worked at various jobs—as a counselor, as an educator, as a commercial artist, and as a carpenter; in the evenings, I became a detective of ancient history—searching for clues to America's hidden past. Trips to libraries, museums, and archeological field sites, as well as meetings with independent scholars contributed to the unfolding story of pre-Columbian voyagers. The growing mountain of evidence painted a picture of America as a multicultural society—long before Europeans began the so-called "Age of Exploration." The old paradigm praised European superiority; reality exposed that paradigm as an ethnocentric fantasy.

During our many hours invested in libraries and museums, my colleagues and I noticed references on old maps concerning ancient voyagers. A Ming dynasty map from China was said to have been based on trans-Pacific voyages during the 3rd millennium BC; a Roman map by Claudius Ptolemy in the 2nd century featured a city called Cattigara—which Spaniards claimed was located in South America; and numerous Medieval European maps showed the Isles of Paradise—"The Fortunate Isles"—west of Africa. These intriguing documents inspired us to expand our research into map libraries. As soon as we entered the realm of cartography, we encountered a new universe of knowledge. It was a universe that contained many secrets about America's true heritage.

Over an interval of five years, I had an opportunity to acquire "new eyes." My skills in cartography improved substantially as a consequence

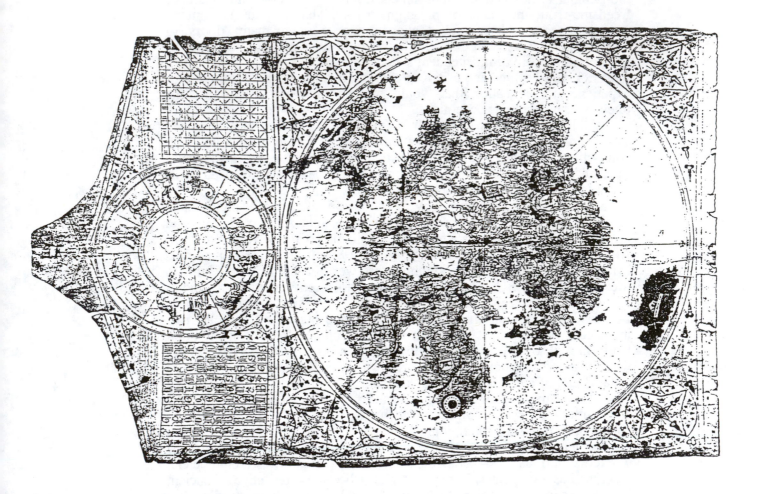

Albertin DeVirga World Map, Venice, ca. 1414 AD

This map by Venetian cartographer Albertin DeVirga was compiled from numerous sources between 1411 and 1415. Most scholars date the map at 1414—although the last Roman numeral on the original manuscript is illegible. Collector Albert Figdor obtained the map in 1911. There was sufficient writing on margins of the map for the Austrian Franz von Wieser to verify authenticity in 1912. Figdor brought it to Lucerne in 1932. The present whereabouts of the map is unknown. All subsequent reproductions and textbook illustrations are based on either this 1912 photograph or another version taken at the Lucerne auction in 1932. A copy of the 1932 photograph appeared in a March 1995 edition of the journal *Cartographica Helvetica*. This article by Arthur Durst was in response to the author's publication of a technical report on the discovery of the Friar's Map.

Source: Marcel Destombes. *Mappemondes AD 1200-1500; Imago Mundi Supplement IV: A Review of Early Cartography.* Amsterdam: N. Israel, 1964 (LC # GA 101.I6, Supplement #4).

of effort and perseverance. I perused every book I could find on ancient maps—even books in Japanese and Arabic. When I again had an opportunity to examine a photograph of the mysterious Friar's Map—I was prepared to actually see what was before my eyes.

A Treasure Map in Sebenico

The Friar's Map took a long and torturous route from Oxford, England, to the place where it was eventually identified—in Honolulu, Hawaii. During the Late Middle Ages, copies of the Inventio Fortunatae including the Friar's Map circulated among groups of Franciscans, English sovereigns, and wealthy merchants. Those who were most concerned with the origins of the map were wool merchants who traveled yearly between England and Venice. During the early 1400's, a Venetian cosmographer named Albertin DeVirga set to work on a world map for use as an illustration of Venetian commercial enterprises. Like all of his associates in the mapmaking craft, DeVirga was dependent upon numerous sources to provide regional information on distant lands. He chose for the northern section of his map the Franciscan portfolio of gazetteers (or map coordinates) from the Inventio. The Venetian Commercial Map was finished circa 1414 and given to one of DeVirga's patrons. This was how the Friar's Map found its way into the hands of Venetian merchants.

Because the 1400's were a time of expanding commercial ventures and international travel in the North Atlantic, new knowledge concerning the size and shapes of Atlantic isles was recorded at a rapid pace. DeVirga's map was soon outdated. Why it was not discarded when better maps became available is entirely speculative. Perhaps it just got stuffed away someplace where it went unnoticed for many decades. Who knows? At any rate, the map was unimportant enough in its own time to be left in a place where it was neither used nor damaged. And this seems to have been its fate for approximately five hundred years. Eventually, the map became old enough to gain some value as part of the clutter of history that collectors regard as "antiques."

By the early 1900's, the Venetian map found its way onto the shelves of an aging antique shop in Sebenico—a coastal port on the Adriatic Sea which was then part of the Austro-Hungarian Empire. How many years the map lay sheltered among stacks of decaying books and correspondence—we cannot say. It could have easily succumbed to the ravages of war, fire, or natural disaster—but that was not to be.

In 1911, a visiting Austrian named Albert Figdor entered the antique shop in search of bargains. This Austrian tourist was a career speculator in old letters and memorabilia, thus he was accustomed to spending hours rummaging through the crumbling pages and envelopes of long-forgotten correspondence. While thus engaged, he was ever mindful of the potential diamond lying hidden within mountains of worthless trash.

At first glance, the parchment bundle containing the map must not have seemed very impressive. Doubtless, it had the appearance of many discarded papers that had passed through Figdor's hands over the years. The parchment had been folded several times cloaking the critical surface of the map. This careless treatment revealed that previous owners had not regarded the document as something worthy of great care. However, once the parchment was unwrapped, Figdor suspected its potential worth.

This was no ordinary map: it was a remarkably well-preserved masterpiece of Renaissance craftsmanship. The whole world as it was known to Medieval geographers was portrayed in faded pastels. The continents of Europe, Asia, and Africa were colored green; and there were two extra lands "Norveca" and "Ca-paru." These must have struck Figdor as oddities whose significance only ancient cosmographers could have possibly understood.

At last, the years of tramping through dusty old shops had brought the Austrian his just reward. Figdor must have felt like shouting for joy; but that would have been a mistake. Any premature sign of excitement would have betrayed his interest in the document and resulted in a higher price; so his strategy must have been to express only minimal interest until the purchase was final. It must have taken him only a brief moment to examine his prize, calculate a reasonably low bid, and settle the deal.

Once the map was in his possession, he was free to dream about the importance of his prize and the profit he would gain at a future auction. The 15th-century date on the map was sufficient to suggest that it was a valuable artifact from the dawn of the Renaissance. This was the Golden Era of Oriental commerce that brought silk, spices, and the latest Arabic inventions into Medieval Europe. Figdor knew that if the map happened to have unusual historical importance, then its value would increase accordingly. Perhaps the map had once belonged to a famous prince? Or, it might be the key to some great enigma of history?

Such questions must have intrigued the speculative Austrian as he boarded a steamer heading north to Rijeka. Around him, the world was rapidly disintegrating: hostilities had already broken out between Italy and Turkey; flotillas with marines had set out across the Adriatic. All of Europe was at the brink of war: within three years, the assassination of Austria's Archduke Franz Ferdinand, the so-called "Balkan Incident," would engulf the region in an extended war—the "First World War." Sebenico was devastated; the antique shops were left in ruins. Some priceless treasures managed to find their way abroad; some were buried in vaults. However, the 1414 map would not have qualified as such a treasure at the time. Who knows what might have happened to the priceless map if Albert Figdor had waited for more peaceful times?

The antique dealer left no journal of his travels; nevertheless, the general features of his return to Vienna by ship and train are not hard to imagine from what we know of the regional culture and history. Trains between the seaport of Flume (Rijeka) and Vienna had to traverse mountains in Croatia and Hungary; there were stops in Zagreb and Budapest. The trains were slow—but dependable; Figdor had plenty of time to ponder the fate of his investment. One thing was certain: he needed the endorsement of a highly-regarded historian to assure an inflated selling price for his Renaissance artifact. Whether the document found its way to a museum or into the hands of a private collector was of little consequence to the veteran speculator.

We know that Figdor promptly took his antique to the Austrian State University in Vienna. He must have been anxious for a positive appraisal; but the examination of the artifact was slow and methodical. The scholar who undertook the task was none other than the highly-esteemed Her Doctor-Professor Franz Von Wieser. He was a true aristocrat—one of Europe's leading historians and a specialist on ancient maps. Like Figdor, the professor had spent numerous years examining antique collections in search of "gems," and he had personally located several valuable 16th-century maps. These were now the pride of the Austrian State Museum. As an esteemed Germanic academician, Von Wieser was duly pompous and arrogant; he was also impatient with those who did not belong to his elite profession; and he was contemptuous of those who hoped to profit from the sale of historical documents. In short, he was the wrong authority for the likes of an antique speculator.

Von Wieser examined the specimen from his lofty perspective as dean of European Academia—steeped in the values of Western Civilization, inspired by Christianity, and armored with orthodox traditions of professional loyalty. It was readily apparent to Von Wieser and his colleagues that the map belonged to a defunct, Medieval branch of cartography characterized by mappamonds or "wheel-maps." Western scientists held these maps in disrepute because they were often saturated with mythological themes, and they generally lacked geographical reliability (Kimble, 1938, 187). This mappamond pedigree was evident from the circular shape of the map and the lack of longitude or latitude lines. These lines, which are often referred to as "meridians" and "parallels," enable accurate location of geographical features such as cities, lakes, mountains, and rivers. They are an essential component of what professional geographers call "scientific" maps.

Seemingly fabulous isles on the Venetian map seemed to confirm Von Wieser's diagnosis of a Medieval heritage. He regarded the northwestern territory—"Norveca"—as a grossly-distorted Norway. A huge extension of land north of Europe seemed to represent the mythical "Hyperborea" of Roman tradition. And the huge isle southeast of Asia—"Ca-paru"—seemed like an inaccurate representation of Japan or Java. Von Wieser had never seen an isle in that location on a Medieval map. This apparent departure from the mappamond tradition was a sure sign that the ancient cartographer had burst the bounds of conventional geography.

The professor devalued the map for another reason: it had obvious connections to Arabic culture. The map's portrayal of Africa as a bifurcated continent followed Arabic traditions; and it was centered on Mt. Ararat—symbolizing the importance of the Moslem patriarch, Noah (whose Ark was presumed to have landed on the mountain peak in Armenia). Furthermore, the exaggerated size of the Persian Gulf and adjacent Arabian territories accentuated the importance of Moslem domains at the expense of Christian Europe. These distortions, along with Arabic designs along the map's border, indicated a strong Moslem heritage for the Venetian document. These shortcomings led Von Wieser to conclude that the map was part of an alien tradition that had fallen by the wayside of Western scientific development in the early 15th century.

Perhaps Von Wieser's evaluation was unduly influenced by his concern that a favorable assessment would bring the speculator unjustified wealth; or he might have resented the idea that a non-academic hoped to gain fame by promoting an unimportant document. Regardless of his reasons, the professor summed up his negative views in a short treatise— Die Weltcarte des Albertin DeVirga (1912). Although he certified that the map was genuine, he insisted that it was nothing more than an anomaly of little historical importance.

Unfortunately, Von Wieser's assessment totally missed the broader context of world exploration, and it nearly condemned the Venetian masterpiece to oblivion. The passing decades witnessed little scholarly interest in the Venetian Map—though some allowance must be made for the social disruption that resulted from the First World War that raged across Europe for five years.

Leo Bagrow, History of Cartography (1951), Plate No. CXVII

CXVII - Albertine de Virga
Manuscript world map. c. 1414

1. WORLD UPSIDE DOWN & BLURRED

Vanishing Isles

It is only natural to wonder why New World continents on DeVirga's 1414 Venetian Commercial Map were not noticed until 1995. The answer is that other scholars have not been sufficiently interested in a critical re-examination of orthodox beliefs concerning the history of cartography. Leo Bagro's popular book, *History of Cartography* (1951) used a copy of the 1912 photograph of DeVirga's map (Plate No. CXVII—#1—above). His illustration shows the map upside down—making it difficult to comprehend; and the resolution is so poor that the northwestern continent, Norveca, is illegible.

Another example of DeVirga's map accompanied an article which the Canadian scholar Philip Stooke wrote for the journal *Cartographica* (Vol. 29, 1992—right). In this case, Stooke erased both the northwestern continent and the southeastern continent (Peru) because they were of no importance to his article.

The author's facsimile (3) aligns the map with north at the top—per Western convention; and both overseas continents (Norveca—North America and Ca-paru—South America) are clearly shown.

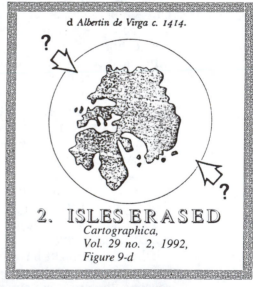

d *Albertin de Virga c. 1414.*

2. ISLES ERASED
*Cartographica,
Vol. 29 no. 2, 1992,
Figure 9-d*

3. ISLES REVEALED

Albertin DeVirga, 1414
Facsimile by Thompson

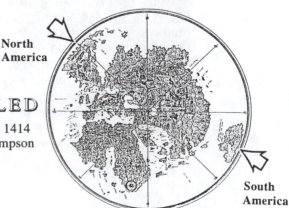

North
America

South
America

Meanwhile, the disappointed and humiliated Austrian speculator waited twenty years until 1932 before offering his map for sale. He chose a public auction in hopes of gaining a meager return for his investment. Even that effort proved a disappointment. In spite of the remarkable age and beauty of the document, it failed to draw the opening bid; such was the fate of an antique scorned by academia. Figdor withdrew his albatross and disappeared. That was the last time the Venetian Map has been seen in public; its present whereabouts are unknown.

Finding the "Hidden" Map

Franz Von Wieser's thoroughness as a scientist inspired him to include an excellent photograph of the Venetian Map in his 1912 book. This single, compulsive act has earned him the respect of future generations—for it preserved an exact copy of the original document for examination by later scholars.

An even more precise photograph accompanied the sales brochure used for the 1932 auction. A copy of Von Wieser's photo appeared in a 1964 publication as one of several mappamonds in a French-language supplement to Imago Mundi—the international journal of the history of cartography. At that time, scholars still held the opinion that Von Wieser's original assessment was accurate: the map was a Medieval stepchild of Arabic extraction that had little importance to the history of Western science. The Imago Mundi publication assured the inevitable resurrection of the Venetian Map and the subsequent identification of North American lands from the missing Franciscan document—the Inventio Fortunatae.

Another 30 years passed before the map again found its way to a favorable audience. Meanwhile, copies of Leo Bagrow's popular text, The History of Cartography (1951), circulated in Europe and America. This text featured a miniaturized copy of the 1912 photograph; but it was printed upside down and in such poor resolution that the mysterious overseas continents of Norveca and Ca-Paru were virtually unintelligible (Bagrow, 1951, fig. 67). Thousands of college students and scores of map historians must have glanced at the photograph in Bagrow's book without noticing anything of great importance. Indeed, their assumptions that such Medieval mappamonds are of little importance must have been confirmed. A 1992 issue of the journal Cartographica (Vol. 29, No. 2, fig. 9) presented another miniaturized version of the map. In this illustration, Old World lands were clearly visible, however the mysterious overseas isles of Norveca and Ca-Paru were completely erased—presumably so as not to confuse readers with irrelevant information (Stooke, 1992, 20). The net result of such publications was to reinforce the common perception among scholars and students that orthodox paradigms were accurate. If maps showing New World lands prior to Columbus were either concealed or illegible, then the belief that Columbus was first to reach America was seemingly beyond reproach.

I entered the drama rather late in the final act. My heroes were the mavericks of New World scholarship—Robert Von Heine-Geldern, Gordon Ekholm, Betty Meggers, and Thor Heyerdahl. They regarded historical orthodoxy in the same manner that an innocent child pities a surrey horse with blinders. My talents were primarily in the visual arts, so I brought highly-refined, visual-spatial skills to the task of deciphering old maps. As a Boy Scout, I had used a compass and topographic maps to find my way through the wilderness. As a sailor and kayak enthusiast,

I was familiar with sea charts and coastal navigation. And after spending several years reviewing the mapping styles and idiosyncrasies of innumerable ancient cartographers, I was uniquely prepared for the unexpected opportunity that came about one early Saturday morning in November of 1994.

The air was crisp; morning doves were cooing love songs to the sun; palm trees and eucalyptus were swaying in the breeze. It was a great day to be outdoors. But as I walked past Hamilton Library, I felt compelled to go inside. This was a surprising sensation because I had no intention that morning of stopping at the library; other errands were on my mind. Nevertheless, I have learned to follow my intuition (inner voice, or guardian angel—if that is your fancy), and this time the reward that awaited me inside was beyond my wildest imaginings.

I followed the pathway of my intuition like a guided missile seeking out the broadcast of a radio beacon. Soon, I found myself in the geography section where I noticed the collection of journals by Imago Mundi—an international consortium dedicated to the history of cartography. I actually doubted the sanity of my quest for a brief moment: after all, I had examined the entire collection in another library—at least I thought I had seen the entire collection. However, a sudden realization came over me that there was one volume I had not seen before: it was an oversized copy of a special, supplemental edition on Mappamonds. As this was an extra edition that involved additional cost, it was not available in most libraries that subscribed to the regular map journals.

This book stood out from the shelf like a crown jewel on a beach of black sand. (They have black sand beaches in Hawaii.) I noticed a layer of dust on the top edge of the book; then I opened the back cover and looked at the status card for the record of borrowers. It was blank: the book had never been checked out of the library. This wasn't surprising since the text was in French and the publisher was Dutch. Nevertheless, these were sure signs that something valuable might be inside.

I visually scanned the pages. Simultaneously, I found myself mumbling doubts that anything really important could have gotten past the scholastic censors. Their role in publishing is to assure that only relevant (that is, orthodox) material is made available for public viewing. I was already familiar with the maps it contained. Even the Venetian Map was not new. I had seen several miniaturized versions that were either doctored by the author so that nothing unusual was revealed or too small and fuzzy from the photographic screening process to enable identification of anything significant. Such photographs were typically printed upside-down (supposedly in accordance with Medieval traditions), and this further concealed important details from those who are used to seeing maps oriented with North at the top. However, this supplement (Volume V.) contained a twelve-inch enlargement of the 1912 photograph. The resolution was nearly perfect: Norveca and Ca-Paru were clearly visible.

Although perfect clarity and large scale were vitally important for the photograph to be intelligible—they were only part of the equation. Mental preparedness was also essential, and this time, I had my "new eyes." I nearly screamed when I saw the entire, unadulterated map. My mind saw, compared, and digested the entire illustration in an instant. Five years earlier, such a feat would have been impossible.

I realized immediately that I had found a document of great importance to our understanding of America's "hidden history." According to leading scholars, this map wasn't supposed to exist.

Time and again, historians had declared that the existence of such a map was "impossible." Yet, the impossible was happening, and I had the lead role in the unfolding drama. In my hands was a document showing North and South America at least a century before Columbus. This map provided clear and convincing evidence that two previously undisclosed continents (comprising the New World) had been surveyed prior to the early 15th century. These were not the kind of amorphous isles commonly found on cosmological <u>mappamonds</u> and referred to in the scholarly literature as "fabulous" or "mythical isles." Indeed, the level of accuracy of coastlines could have been achieved only through an extensive, scientific surveying effort. That much was certain; although at the time, I had no idea who might have been responsible for such a survey. Standard texts offered no clues—as their authors naturally assumed that such surveys were impossible before the advent of Spain's super-hero of exploration, Christopher Colon (a.k.a. Columbus).

Unlike many other relics of pre-Columbian voyagers, authenticity was not an issue with this document. The Venetian pedigree had been established by Von Wieser in 1912; and historians had accepted the map's validity without complaint for the past eighty years. Unfortunately, Von Wieser's examination of the map was prejudiced by doctrine and lacked the artistic vision which I was able to provide. He had viewed the map with "old eyes" and saw what he expected to see. Now, "new eyes" examined the hidden jewel.

My new vision enabled me to see what was really there. The land area reaching out from the northwest side of Norway—though labeled "Norveca"—was in the right position for North America; and it had about the right size and coastal outline for the East Coast. The rubric on the southeastern isle—"Ca-paru"—immediately suggested an early representation for the coastline of South America in the region of Peru. Subsequent research confirmed that both hunches were accurate.

Several more months of intensive study brought to light more unexpected wonders. Examination of 15th-century Danish maps revealed a similar pattern of headlands to those portrayed on DeVirga's northwestern continent. This was the first indication that the unknown surveyors who provided the field data or gazetteers for the Venetian commercial map were part of a larger mapping effort that had established a mapping tradition for the North Atlantic. This tradition lasted for more than two centuries. The level of precision on DeVirga's northwestern continent (Norveca) were astonishing: an island along the east coast was in the right position for Newfoundland; a peninsula jutting out into the Atlantic Ocean clearly represented Florida; near the peninsula were three isles in the right place for the Antilles; a great gulf adjacent to the peninsula was an early version of the Gulf of Mexico; below that was coastline in about the right place for Venezuela and Brazil.

Eventually, we found sufficient clues to name the English friar, Nicholas of Lynn, as the likely candidate for the earliest-known survey map of North America. His gazetteer of geographical locations—his <u>Inventio Fortunatae</u>—was produced at the right time and place to serve as the source for DeVirga's mysterious, northwestern continent of Norveca. However, before we could identify the source of DeVirga's map, we had to examine all available clues regarding ancient voyages and mapping of the Atlantic Ocean.

Lands of Myth & Lands of Legend

Tales of Atlantic isles are common in the folklore of ancient Europe. Greek and Roman storytellers identified distant isles across the western ocean: the Hesperides, the Gorgades, and the Fortunate Isles. There were also overseas continents: Antichone (south of Africa), the Antipodes (west of Africa), and Epirios Occidentalis (west across from Europe). The Irish believed in a paradise across the Atlantic called Hy-breasail; Welsh bards sang the praise of Avalon in the western Atlantic; and Nordic seafarers told stories about the wondrous beaches of Wineland the Good.

Orthodox historians dismiss these legends without hesitation: the lands are "fabulous"—merely fantasies of the Medieval imagination. Drunken sailors, they say, were forever conjuring up isles that never existed. Numerous captains, including Columbus, witnessed visions of distant isles that disappeared into the twilight haze when ships were sent to investigate. He also saw a mermaid and the Earthly Paradise; but such visions haven't compromised his glory as the champion of discovery. Of course, Columbus also ran into some very real islands that emerged from the western mists: one of these sank his flagship on Christmas Eve, 1492.

Medieval European maps were often plastered with mythical lands— including the Earthly Paradise or Garden of Eden from the <u>Book of Genesis</u>. This paradise was typically located east of China. It was also known as "The Land of Promise" which was the destination of an Irish monk named Brendan of Clonfert in the 6th century. In later years, his voyage was commemorated by the naming of an isle, "St. Brendan's Isle," which was supposedly located someplace south of Ireland. Brendan's Isle is a classic example of a mythical place often seen on Medieval maps—but never in reality. At least, it wasn't found where the maps suggested it should be found—in the middle of the Atlantic Ocean.

When considering how the ancients viewed their world, there is a need to distinguish between mythical lands, fabulous isles, legendary isles and what the Romans called <u>terra firma</u>—meaning "firm land" as in a real continent. Historian Raymond Ramsay (1972) wrote a book on the subject of "Places That Never Were." Unfortunately, his orthodox training prevented him from seeing any other kind of ancient isle in the Atlantic besides "Never-Never Lands" of fantasy. In his eyes, all overseas isles named in legends before 1492 were "fantastic"—and this is essentially the credo of orthodox historians. Ramsay's treatise on the subject was partially correct: there were mythical places. One of these was the magnetic mountain of the north said to lie beneath the pole star and offered as an explanation for why compass needles point north.

One mythical isle that has perplexed historians is the mysterious land called "Ophir." This land was mentioned in the <u>Bible</u> as the source of King Solomon's gold mines. Since most orthodox scholars dare not question divine revelation, they have acknowledged the existence of such a land—someplace in Africa or Asia—but insist that it has been lost to antiquity. As long as it isn't found someplace in the New World, they don't have to worry about legends of Ophir being mistakenly associated with unorthodox theories of transoceanic voyagers. Yet shameless heretics have suggested the unthinkable—that Ophir was located in Peru.

Not all legendary isles vanished into sea mist. In northern latitudes, where ice crystals in the atmosphere reflected the distant shores of continents, sailors reported seeing "floating islands." These reflections of actual lands were called <u>icebliks</u>. Among Norwegian sailors, the iceblik effect was one of the most important aids to navigation. The fact that Europeans eventually found the so-called "fabulous" lands of Arcadia, Avalon, Antilia, Albania, Brazil, and Wineland—all in America—would seem to add some credence to the theory that legends were often based on actual places and events. Orthodox historians are being a bit too hasty when they presume that all legends of idyllic lands before Columbus are "merely fables."

Long before the days of Romans, folk cultures passed along stories of real lands across the seas. Homer's <u>Odyssey</u>, written between the 12th and 6th centuries, told of a land in the Western Sea called <u>Elysium</u>—or the "Isle of The Blest." In the 5th century BC, Greek philosophers Herodotus and Avienus speculated about Phoenician colonies across the Atlantic; and in the 3rd century BC, Plato tantalized audiences with tales of an island civilization called Atlantis. This fantastic civilization presumably sank beneath the Atlantic Ocean following a 10th-century BC cataclysm. Thereafter, the region of the Atlantic where Atlantis rested was known from Plato's tale as "The Sea of Darkness."

In the 4th century BC, Theopompus and Aristotle mentioned a western continent having forested lands and navigable rivers. By the 1st century, Sicilian geographer Didorus Siculus claimed that Phoenicians had already established a colony across the Atlantic:

> There lies in the deep off Libya (Africa) an island of considerable size. It is situated across the ocean by a voyage of a number of days to the west. The land is fruitful, much of it being mountains and not a little being a level plain of surpassing beauty. Through it flow navigable rivers which are used for irrigation. The island contains many parks planted with trees of every variety and gardens in great multitudes which are traversed by streams of sweet water. (Bailey, 1973, 37)

Romans and Greeks believed in a western continent across the Atlantic called <u>Epeiros Occidentalis</u>—The Western Land. This continent was commonly known to later Romans and Medieval writers as <u>India Occidentalis</u>—the "Western India." Philosophers believed this land extended along the border of the Atlantic Ocean. It could be reached by sailing north to Thule (Iceland), then over the Glacial Sea to Ogygia—the home of Calypso (Greenland), past the wastes of Cronos (Baffin Island) and on to the western mainland. A cache of Roman coins found on Iceland suggests to some writers that Romans actually sailed along the route of legend to North America—although orthodox historians have assumed such a voyage was impossible.

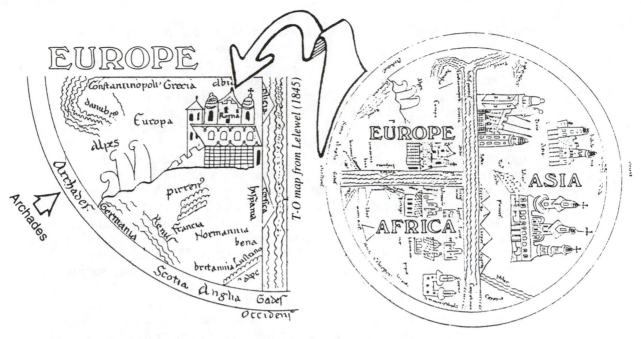

T-O map from Lelewel (1845)

Arcadia—Legendary Land in the New World

In ancient Greece, Arcadia was a region of the central Peloponnesus that was noted for its wines and easy life-style. Therefore, it was only natural for ancient seafarers to apply the name "Arcadia" or variations thereof to meadows and vineyards found in North America. A 1340 cosmographical map (above) has "Archades" situated to the distant north of Scotland. On a map that fails to mention Ireland—this does not represent the Orkney Islands as historians have assumed. By 1375, Catalan maps (below) show "Archania" (i.e., Arcadia—**A**) and Chatanes (Cathay?—**C**) north of Iceland, while the Orkneys (which are hardly arcadian in character) lie adjacent to Scotland. Another legendary isle, Brazil (**B**) is shown west of Ireland. Verrazano identified the region of Chesapeake Bay as "Arcadie" in 1524. By 1566, Zalteri located "L'Arcadia" between Nova Scotia and Cape Cod on his map of the New World.

Catalan map from Lelewel (1845)

18

Hyperborea

Myths of people living near the North Pole were very popular during the Middle Ages. The name "Hyperborea," which appears along the northern border of many Medieval maps, can be translated as "Land Beyond the North Wind." Since Boreas—the North Wind—was presumed to originate at the North Pole, the Hyperboreans could be thought of as residents of a land beyond the North Pole. According to Roman legend, Hyperborea was a northern land above Europe that had a temperate climate, wheat fields, orchards and vineyards.

Most Classical, Medieval, and Renaissance scholars scorned the possibility of habitable lands near the North Pole. There were two divergent views among Classical writers regarding the climate of the Polar Regions:

> By astronomical speculations, the Greeks had come to the conclusion that north of the Arctic Circle, there must be midnight sun at midsummer and no sun at midwinter. The general view was that the polar regions, north and south, belonged to the uninhabitable frozen zones; while according to a less-scientific notion there was a happy region north of the north wind (Boreas), where the sun was always shining and the Hyperboreans led a peaceful life. (Encyclopedia Britannica, 1955, Vol. 2, 294)

During the 5th century, "zonal maps" of the Macrobius tradition indicated that the polar zones were too frigid for habitation, while equatorial zones were deemed too hot for survival. Superstitious Europeans believed that at the Equator, water boiled and mortals were quickly burned to charcoal. This hypothetical barrier of heat supposedly prevented migration to the Antipodes—a land said to lie beneath the equator. It was for this reason that superstitious Portuguese sailors during the early days of Renaissance seafaring were reluctant to make voyages near the Equator.

Modern historians also mocked the Hyperborean legend as "pure fantasy." Scandinavian historian Fridtjof Nansen (1911, 383) compared Norse legends of Wineland (or Vinland) to tales of Hyperborea and the Fortunate Isles—which he assumed were mythical. Ramsay's 1972 encyclopedia of supposedly "mythical isles" continued the theme that any Atlantic isle associated with an idyllic climate had to be "a fantasy."

Among the more influential supporters of the legend was the Roman author Pliny The Elder who claimed that such a land actually existed near the North Pole. A 13th-century English historian, Roger Bacon, cited the testimony of ancient writers who had said that such a land was visited by numerous sailors. In his 1275 treatise On The Habitation of The Earth, Bacon reported that:

> How far habitation extends north, Pliny shows through actual experience and by various authors. For habitation continues up to that locality where the poles are located; and where the day lasts six months and the night for the same length of time. Martin, moreover, in his description of the world, agrees with this statement; whence they maintain that in those regions dwells a very happy race.

There is some evidence from remote times that one Roman expedition might have reached Hyperborea. According to Antonio Galvano (a 16th-century historian), it was reported that the Romans had sent an army by

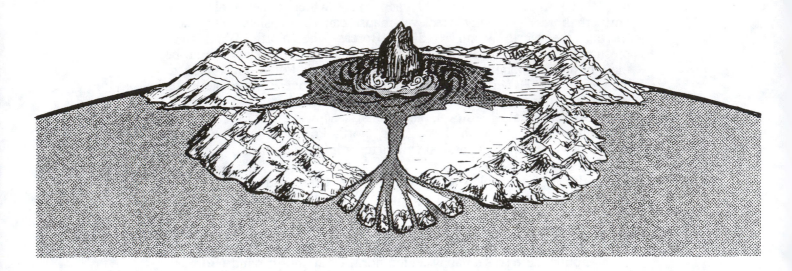

The Polar Regions—Realm of Myth and Controversy

Many Roman philosophers believed that Earth was divided into climactic zones: frigid—near the Arctic Circle; temperate—near the tropics; and torrid—near the equator. Both the Arctic and Equatorial zones were thought to be uninhabitable. Many also believed that a huge magnetic mountain was situated at the very center of the Polar Regions. This magnetic mountain explained to Romans why magnetized needles rubbed with lodestone always pointed north. Directly above the magnetic mountain was the Pole Star—or Polaris—around which the celestial sphere was thought to rotate. Thus, the magnetic mountain was thought to be the geographical location of the North Pole. Philosophers also theorized that the mountain was surrounded by four frozen islands and a whirlpool fed by four rivers.

This concept was popular during the 15th and 16th centuries—as seen in Mercator's map of the North Polar Regions (1595—below).

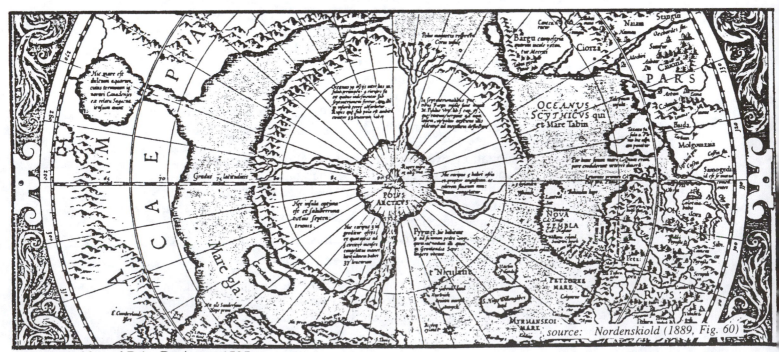

source: Nordenskiold (1889, Fig. 60)

Mercator's Map of Polar Regions—1595

sea to "India" against the khan of Cathay in 200 BC. The shortest route to this so-called "India" was across the North Atlantic. Keep in mind that the region we customarily refer to as East Asia was known to the ancients as <u>India Occidentalis</u>. This voyage beyond the Straits of Gibraltar took the Roman sailors northwest across the Atlantic to isles called "the Cassiterides." Galvano says they were located "opposite Cape Finnisterre" in northern Spain (Kerr & Eden, 1811, 39). The word "opposite" in such tales usually refers to the latitude of overseas lands—which in this case would place the expedition somewhere in the vicinity of Newfoundland or Nova Scotia. Ships returning from this expedition brought back tin—probably from the British Isles (a.k.a. the "Tin Isles"). This tale could refer to a voyage to England (the choice of orthodox historians) or to the New World as Galvano contends was the case.

Orthodox historians call the legend of Hyperborea a "fantasy" because they assume that Hyperborea was in the Arctic region where idyllic habitations were impossible. However, North America might qualify as the inspiration behind the Roman legend. Indeed, North America lies "beyond" the north wind and has the appropriate accouterments of orchards, wheat fields, wine grapes, and a temperate climate.

Medieval Europeans who were unfamiliar with the location of the New World assumed that Hyperborea was located near the North Pole. Some supporters of the legend, such as the eminent English scholar Roger Bacon, believed that habitation was reasonable due to the testimony of witnesses who said that they had traveled to the North Pole where they saw wheat fields and orchards first-hand. This apparent impossibility can be resolved by the realization that there are two North Poles: 1) the Geographic Pole whose environs are very cold; and 2) the Magnetic Pole whose climate is fairly temperate in Summertime. Another line of argument followed logic: the 16th-century English philosopher and merchant, Roger Thorne, debunked the theory of a "torrid zone" at the equator by citing Portuguese voyages to South Africa. Therefore, Thorne suggested that since proponents of the climatic zone theory had erred with respect to equatorial habitation, they might also be incorrect regarding habitation in the far north. This kind of reasoning helped support the concept of a northwest passage through the Arctic regions of Canada to the Pacific Ocean. Unfortunately for many sailors who died seeking the trans-Arctic passage, Thorne's reasoning was flawed.

The Hesperides

One of the more colorful Greco-Roman myths told of idyllic isles in the Western Ocean that were dedicated to the Goddess Hera. The most acclaimed feature of her realm was an orchard of golden apples. Greeks called this land the "Hesperides"—after the maidens who guarded the orchard. Hera's paradise was also known as "The Land of Golden Apples." This title appears in legends from many European countries.

Was the isle "pure mythology" as orthodox historians have claimed? Or were the Hesperides another name for America? Diffusionists are quick to point out that Spanish explorers in the 16th century found natives growing yellow tomatoes. The Spaniards called these tomatoes <u>pomos de oro</u>—or "golden apples" (Thompson, 1992, 171; Schwartz, 1991,58).

An Iberian version of the legend tells of a king of Spain named Hesperus who sailed far-and-wide circa 2350 BC and discovered some isles in the western sea. These were named the Hesperides in his honor. Renaissance geographers assumed that the legendary isles referred to the

EUROPE

ASIA

Sinus Magnus

AFRICA

Cattigara

INDICVM

PTOLEMÆUS ROMÆ 1490.

Claudius Ptolemy
after Ruscelli's Geography
Italy, 1574

Ptolemy's World

This map is a 15th-century copy of an original by Claudius Ptolemy in the 2nd century. There are no lands indicated north of England—with the exception of the isle of "Thule" which was the Roman name for Iceland. The Indian Ocean is shown here extending from Africa to the "Sinus Magnus" (meaning Great Gulf). This was the Roman name for the Pacific Ocean. Along the eastern edge of this Sinus Magnus was land reaching all the way to the south. Historians call this a "fictional land," but it actually represents an early concept of South America and Antarctica. According to the Romans, there was a major town and bay called "Cattigara" in the far-eastern land. This bay can be identified on 15th and 16th-century maps as the Bay of Guayaquil between Peru and Ecuador.

The Mediterranean region was accurately surveyed by Julius Caesar—although the length was overestimated. Ptolemy, shown at left using a quadrant to measure the height of the sun, grossly underestimated the span of the Sinus Magnus (Pacific). His associate, Marinus of Tyre, was closer to the mark. Marinus placed the eastern border 45 degrees farther east—bringing the land on Roman maps much closer to the actual position of South America.

22

Cape Verde Islands; however, in the 16th century, Spanish historian Gonsalvo Ovido insisted that the real Hesperides were the West Indies (Kerr & Eden, 1811, 30).

The Fortunate Isles

Among Romans, a more popular designation for the western paradise was the Insula Fortunatae, or "The Fortunate Isles." According to the ancient philosophers, these isles were located "in the farthest recesses of the Atlantic Ocean." Modern historians have mocked legends of "Fortunate Isles"—insisting that there was no such land of apple orchards, wheat fields, and eternal life. Claims of immortality were an obvious fantasy in scientific circles; historians complained that apple orchards in America were a post-Colombian phenomenon.

According to the isolationist argument, apples (an Old World fruit) were not imported to America until the 17th century. Records confirming those imports are available in Colonial archives, however they are not the oldest reports of apples in America. French-Venetian explorer Giovanni Verrazano reported apples growing along the East Coast in 1524. That report was included as part of Richard Hakluyt's Diverse Voyages (1582). Hakluyt's disclosure of apple orchards in America comes more than 50 years before the earliest documented account of colonial imports of apples into New England (ca. 1633). Indeed, Hakluyt listed apples as one of the principal "native" resources of North America.

French explorer, Jacques Cartier, also reported apples growing near the St. Lawrence Gulf in 1535. Apples, grapes and figs were among the items listed in his compendium of native foods (Florio, 1966, 46).

New England historical accounts dating to the 17th century reveal that "old-growth" orchards were already being cultivated near native villages at the same time that the first European saplings were imported; the traveler John Longstreth reported "thousands of apple trees near Annapolis" in the 1690's (Price, 1954, 38). These orchards were several generations too early to be reasonably attributed to New England traders. Colonial militias, including soldiers who participated in General Sullivan's 1779 march against Cayuga and Seneca tribes in western New York, reported seeing native villages with horses, cows, and apple orchards. According to S.A. Beach, author of The Apple (1905), Sullivan's men found orchards that were "bending with fruit." Historical reports of apple imports are of unquestioned authenticity; but so is the fact that native Americans had apple orchards prior to the 16th century.

When Portuguese sailors found Madeira and the Azores west of Africa during the mid-14th century, many European geographers assumed these were the Fortunate Isles of legend (Hale, 1965, 51). This belief is apparent from most Medieval and early Renaissance charts which identify the Azores and Canary Isles as the "Fortunate Isles." However, some Renaissance scholars objected to the popular nomenclature by noting that Roman writers had specified that the legendary isles were actually situated "in the farthest reaches of the western Ocean." And it was apparent that the Ocean continued far beyond the Azores and Canary Isles for a considerable distance. It seemed reasonable, therefore, to believe that the real Fortunate Isles were still mysteriously hidden somewhere in the west.

Ptolemy & The Three Indias

The nature of continents across the Atlantic was another matter of speculation. Ptolemy's 2nd-century world map left the issue open for

source: Thompson (1994)

After a map in the Huntington Library, San Marino, California.

Perusta

Antipodes

The Roman World of Macrobius

By the 5th century, Romans believed that Earth had two principle parts: the "Known World" (a.k.a. the *Oecumene*) and a huge southern continent. During the 18th century, explorers searched in vain for this "Terra Australis" not realizing that it was the old Roman concept of a continent in the location of South America. The map shown here is a 1483 copy of a map by Macrobius in the 5th century—about 440 AD. This zonal map of Earth is divided into 5 parallel climates: FRIGID at the poles; the habitable regions called TEMPERATA; and the TORRID equatorial region which was believed to be too hot for habitation. Lands north of the equatorial ocean are Europe, Africa, and Asia—comprising the *Oecumene* or Known World. Below the equator lies *Antipodum*—the Antipodes. The southern continent was also known as Antichone, the 4th Part of Earth (or 4th Continent), and also *Alter Orbis*—or "The OTHER WORLD." That was what Columbus called South America when he landed in Venezuela in 1498—because he believed he had reached what the ancients described as the Antipodes. This continent conforms to the major characteristics of South America by its location south of the equator and across the ocean from both Africa and Asia.

This map shows the earliest use of the Roman word *Perusta* in reference to Peru. The Latin *perusta* means hot or parched territory—which is an accurate description of the northwestern coastal region of Peru. This interpretation is confirmed by the 1436 mappamond by Andrea Bianco which names a huge land southeast of Asia as the Isle of Pir-land. Pir was an abbreviated form of Peru.

source: Nansen (1911, 86)

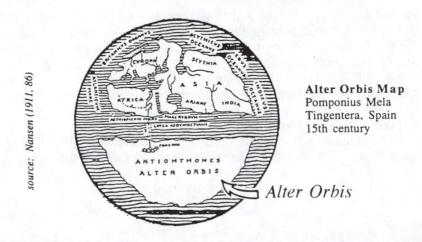

Alter Orbis Map
Pomponius Mela
Tingentera, Spain
15th century

Alter Orbis

debate: his map shows the "Known World" (or Oecumene) from the west coast of Europe and Africa to the Sinus Magnus—a large eastern gulf which is his equivalent of the Pacific. There his map stops at about 180° east of Europe. Along the border of his map, he indicates land continuing eastward to an undetermined extent. His geography, however, suggests that land continues for a considerable distance; and this terra incognita occidentalis was known to his contemporaries and to Medieval geographers as "India Tercer" (the Third India). This terminology followed a tradition among Roman geographers that the land beyond India's eastern border at the Ganges (Indochina) was the Second India. Beyond Indochina and across the Western Sea (or Sinus Magnus) was a third India (India Tercer). Since the Sinus Magnus represented the Pacific Ocean (in a highly compressed form on Ptolemy's map), this third India across the ocean corresponded to America. Among Hindus, the distant land south of the equator was known as India Patala—or India Beyond the Ocean. This India Patala corresponds to South America on most Medieval and Renaissance maps. Romans called lands north of Patala "India Superior" (or India of the Higher Region). Thus, Romans had two names for North America—India Superior and India Tercer.

Medieval Europeans believed that lands across the Atlantic were part of this Third India. In accordance with Roman geography, the northern region of the Far East (across the Atlantic) was called India Superior; the southern region was referred to as the Antipodes (and occasionally as India Patalis. When people from India Superior (North America) were cast ashore in northern Europe in 57 BC, 1160 AD, and in 1477, they were called "Indians" because it was apparent that they had come from the continent across the Atlantic—India Tercer (Newton, 1932, 221). Columbus saw native Americans who had been cast upon the shore near Galway, Ireland, in 1477; his associates called them "Indians." It is therefore evident that the European practice of calling the inhabitants of lands across the Atlantic—"Indians"—was established long before Columbus sailed to the Caribbean in 1492. Indeed, Columbus cited Classical authors, Pliny The Elder and Pomponious Mela, to justify his belief that India was situated across the Atlantic from Europe.

In his treatise On The Heavens, Aristotle affirmed that India was not far distant from Spain across the Atlantic: "Cadiz is only a few days sailing" (Keen, 1959, 17). This view was shared by Averroes, Seneca and other Classical cosmographers (Newton, 1932, 102). Aristotle maintained that the ocean of India was contiguous with the Atlantic; Seneca maintained in his treatise, Natural Questions, that with a fair wind, a ship could sail west from Spain to the Indies in a few days; and Pliny wrote that the ancients had reached India via a northwest passage (Newton, 1932, 214). This India of the ancients was not the subcontinent of India but "India Superior" (that is, North America). A legend on the Genoese planisphere of 1457 states that: "Pomponius (Mela) and many others say that many have passed through these parts from India to Spain. (Kimble, 1938, 197). According to Ferdinand Colon, his father decided to sail west to the Indies on the authority of Classical writers who claimed that India was within easy sailing distance to Europe and that many voyagers had already accomplished the voyage (Dor-Ner, 1991, 76).

The Antipodes

Phoenicians, Romans, and Greeks had legends of continents across the southern Atlantic. The Greek geographer Macrobius in the 5th century

Irish Curraugh

The common coastal trading vessels of the Gaelic Isles of Ibernia (a.k.a. Ireland) were made of wood frames covered by thin strips of wood (lath) and oxhides. The oxhides provided the principle water-repellent skin. They were stitched together and covered with grease. Such vessels, called "curraughs" or skin boats, were very light and very durable. The modern British adventurer, Tim Severin, sailed such a vessel from Ireland to Newfoundland in 1977. The famed Brendan of Clonfert used such a vessel when traveling between the isles of Ibernia.

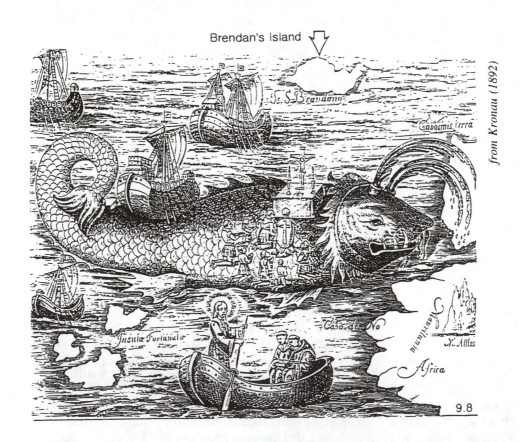

St. Brendan's Voyage—565 to 573 AD

Of the many Irish legends of trans-Atlantic voyagers, none is more romantic than the tale about Brendan of Clonfert—who was later immortalized as Saint Brendan the Navigator. This 19th-century engraving of a Medieval painting shows a band of Irish monks celebrating mass on the back of Jacimonus—the whale. Above the whale is a caption next to the "Isla St. Brandano"—Brendan's Island. An isle of this name on Medieval and Renaissance maps ranges from the North Atlantic to the Caribbean. Also on this map are the "Fortunate Islands" of Greco-Roman legend. Medieval geographers assumed these were the Canary Isles and Azores which Arabian mariners discovered west of Spain.

26

identified a "Fourth Continent" apart from the customary Europe, Asia, and Africa which comprised the <u>Oecumene</u> or "Known World." Macrobius referred to this continent as "The Antipodes" or the "Alter Orbis"—the Other World. This wasn't the first time the Antipodes were identified on a map. Crates of Mallos, a 2nd-century geographer said that the Antipodes was a huge continent situated across the ocean from Africa in the southern hemisphere. Of course, that is the location of South America on the world globe.

Subsequently, 16th century historian Peter Martyr identified South America as the Antipodes of legend; he also called it "Alter Orbis" (the Other World) as it was similarly known to Columbus and to Nuremberg cosmographer Martin Behaim. The mutual designations "Antipodes" and "Other World" were used by the Spanish cosmographer Pomponius Mela of Tingentera. Likewise, explorer-cartographer Bartholomew Colon made a map showing South America as the Antipodes. Regardless of this testimony, orthodox historians continued to assume that the Antipodes (or "Southern Continent") was simply a "fable" (Morison, 1971). This so-called "fable" reappeared in the 15th century on the Venetian Commercial Map of 1414 as <u>Ca-paru</u> (i.e., Peru)—a huge island continent southeast of Asia. By the early 16th century, the land in this region was known as the <u>mondo novo</u> or "New World." Within a few decades, mapmakers designated the southern continent as "South America."

Celtic Voyagers: to Mag Mel, Hy-Breasail, & Albania

Legends of overseas lands are most common in Irish folklore. According to Celtic mythology, there was a paradise across the Atlantic called <u>Mag Mel</u>. This was the sanctuary of Ireland's original inhabitants who fled Germanic invasions. The land was also known as <u>Tierna Nog</u>—the Land of Eternal Youth.

Many Irish folk heroes are said to have undertaken voyages to the overseas paradise and returned. In Cormac's adventure to "The Land of Promise," the king of Ireland is said to have made a seven-month journey in 248 AD. In an epic tale, "The Voyage of Bran," our hero sailed to a land across the Atlantic that was said to be 150 times the size of Ireland. This was either a poetic reference to a new continent—or pure fantasy. The Formorian clan is said to have taken refuge in this western land following their defeat in battle. In another folktale, a 10th-century hero, Cuchulain, sailed west to Mag Mel in search of a fairy princess to be his bride. In "The Voyage of Tergue," Sean was lost at sea for nine weeks before reaching sanctuary in the far west. Others followed in the "Voyage of O'Corra," the "Colloquy of The Ancients," and "The Voyage of Maeldun." Lots of Irish heroes sailed west; they all found some sort of idyllic land. This wondrous land was the same place that poets and romantics called "The Land of Opportunity"—i.e., America.

Native American legends confirm the arrival of Celtic voyagers. An Abnaki historiographer, Bernard Assiniwi, spoke to the Sagamore—a native elder—who told him that:

> Our chiefs speak of these strangers who came to us by boat from the sea about two thousand years ago. They established their colonies on our territories trying to take us by force. But after they had destroyed their vessels, our Algonquian fathers convinced them to live with us. They called themselves "Kelts."
> (Assiniwi, 1973)

Eastern Albania or Albania Magna

This is the St. Severus version of the 8th-century Beatus map. Completed circa 1050, it shows a land called "Albania" in northeastern Asia. On the Beatus maps, this Albania is close to the Caspian Sea—suggesting that it might represent the Mediterranean Albania known to the Romans. However, Medieval maps such as the English Psalter Map ca. 1250 and the Borgia Map ca. 1450 refer to "Albania Superior" or "Albania Magna" in the same region. As Europeans believed that this region of northeastern Asia was situated across the Atlantic, the eastern Albania on the St. Serverus map might be another instance where European cartographers placed any overseas isle along the northern region of maps above Europe or Asia. Thus, Albania on the 8th-century maps might refer to a "White Man's Land" located across the Atlantic in the New World.

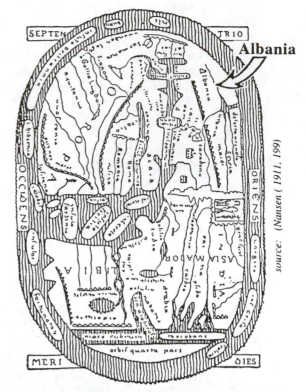

Albania

source: (Nansen 1911, 199)

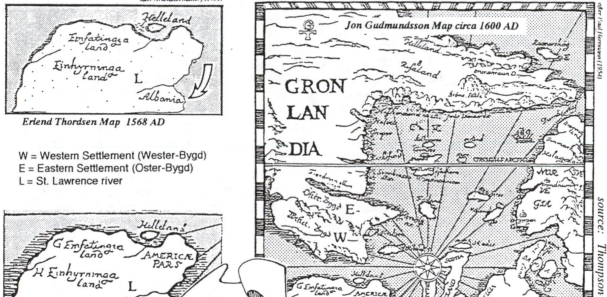

after Arlington Mallery (1951)

Erlend Thordsen Map 1568 AD

W = Western Settlement (Wester-Bygd)
E = Eastern Settlement (Oster-Bygd)
L = St. Lawrence river

section from the Gudmundsson map

Jon Gudmundsson Map circa 1600 AD

after Paul Hermann (1954)

source: Thompson (1994)

Western Albania or Great Ireland

Two 16th-century maps confirm the location of a western Albania in the New World. These maps also support the theory that territories called "Albania" on Medieval mappamonds and on 11th-century Arabian maps in the region of the North Pole also represent New World settlements. Jon Gudmundsson's map (above—circa 1600-1650) shows Albania situated in the region of Nova Scotia in North America. An earlier map which Erlend Throdsen brought to Iceland in 1568 is said to date from the 14th century (Mallery, 1951). This map also shows Albania in the vicinity of Nova Scotia. This is the same region where Icelandic sagas reported a "White Man's Land" (Hvitramannaland) which was also known as "Irland Mikla" or Great Ireland. Thus, historian Bjorn Jonsson concluded that Albania and Great Ireland were alternative names for the same, Celtic settlement in America.

These "Kelts" left megalithic structures in the New England region; they marked strange symbols called "ogam" on rocks; and they gave new words to the native language. Among the Algonkians, the Celtic word segomaros (victor) became the word for chief (sagamore); the Celtic word for mountain (monadh) became the Algonkian monaden; the Celtic village (dun) became the Algonkian odana (Boutet, 1996, 63).

The land had various names in Irish folklore denoting numerous qualities associated with paradise. There was Tir-nam-ban (the Land of Women), Airctech (the beautiful land), Ciuin (the mild land), and Imchiuin (the very mild land). Inis Subai was the isle of gladness where all people lived in a state of continuing joviality. Tir-na-ningen was a land of amorously aggressive women. Tir-nam-ban was said to lie beneath the sea. Tir-na-nog was the land of youth; and Tir-nam-buadha was a land of virtues. They were all in the west, they were all beautiful, and as far as most historians are concerned: they were all fables.

Regardless of what modern historians think of the "fabulous" character of Irish folktales, stories of overseas lands motivated countless brave souls to undertake voyages across the Atlantic Ocean. In 565 AD, the Irish Abbot Brendan of Clonfert decided to seek out the western paradise on one of his many evangelical expeditions. After several years of mystical experiences in various parts of the Atlantic, including an overnight stay in a distant monastery, and a landing on the back of a whale, his entourage of monks finally found "The Land of Promise." They traveled far inland before deciding that the land was so huge that they would soon become lost in its vastness. After seven years, they returned home where the oral traditions of their exploits were finally recorded in the 8th century. There are two versions of this colorful journey: Vita Brendani—The Life of Brendan; and Navigato Sancti Brendani—The Voyage of Saint Brendan. A 9th-century manuscript of this legend is said to be in the Vatican Library (Babcock, 1922, 36).

The Book of Lismore which also describes the monk's life was compiled in the 12th century (Ashe, 1962, 63). It was recovered from a walled-up closet in 1814. According to this version of the legend, Brendan learned of the location of the Land of Promise from brother Barinthus—a monk from Ardfert who had made an earlier trip across the ocean. St. Brenainn (or Saint Brendan) failed in early attempts to cross the Atlantic in a curraugh, and he eventually built a large wooden vessel in Connaught which was manned by sixty religious men. This wooden ship carried them to the "Promised Land" and back to Ireland (Babcock, 1922, 35). In another version of the tale, Brendan sails west in as the "Apostle of The Orkneys" with a crew of 75 monks (Lehner, 1966, 9).

Perhaps the most sought-after land of Irish legend was Hy-Breasail (The Blessed Isle). It was also called the Great Land and a variety of other names often associated with an earthly paradise. Medieval maps had a circular symbol for this isle that was placed southwest of Ireland. It was said to be the location of brazilwood (a.k.a. brasilium) which was an exotic wood that contained a valuable red dye. Brazilwood was known to Europeans by the 14th century, although the source of the wood was unknown. During the 1480's, English merchants sought Hy-Breasail (and its forest of brasilwood) in the northwest Atlantic; eventually, the trees were found growing in South America; and the land where the trees were found soon acquired the name "Brazil." A similar kind of wood, called "sapan," was imported into Europe via Mecca. This wood originated in the East Indies.

When Norse voyagers reached the East Coast of North America in the early days of the 11th century, they found habitations and farms of Europeans who had preceded them. Some of these earlier voyagers were identified as Irish in Icelandic sagas and maps. Karlsefni's Saga told of a land of white people living near the forests of Markland. The colony was identified as a settlement of Irish called "Hvitramannaland" or Ireland the Great. This was said to be the same place where Ari Marsson landed in an episode of the Icelandic Landnamabok. The Eyrbiggja Saga (1250) relates that a trading party from Dublin sailed to a land west of Iceland where they met a stranded Norse sailor, Bjorn of Iceland, who was living with a village of people who spoke Irish (Sauer, 1968, 180). Bjorn had been rescued by a band of Irishmen riding horses who took him to their camp and required him to be baptized.

A common name for Celtic settlements in the New World was "Albania"—designating a colony of immigrants from Albion (Old England). There were two Albanias on Medieval maps; both have been identified as "lands of white people." The Albania most people are familiar with, the southern Albania near Greece, was commonly placed near the Adriatic Sea. A second Albania was introduced on 8th-century maps in the Beatus tradition where it is found in northeast Asia. Al-Idrisi's 1154 map shows Albania north of Norway. On the Borgia Map of 1458, this northern Albania is referred to as "Albania Magna" or (Great Albania); on the Psalter Map circa 1250, it is called "Albania Superior."

The earliest mention of the northern Albania is in Arthurian legends possibly dating to the 6th century in which "Albenne" was regarded as one of Arthur's kingdoms. It is so identified in a 14th-century manuscript copy of an earlier document by Peter Langtoft—The Chronicle of England (British Library document MS Royal 20 AIIf-4r).

In 1605, Bjorn Jonsson identified Hvitramannaland (Land of Whites) as the long-lost Albania (Land of Whites) of the north. As recently as 1492, German cartographer Martin Behaim had shown the "Land of Whites" (weises volck) north of the Arctic Circle. Besides the similarity of names, Erlend Thordsen had found a 14th-century map which identified the region of Nova Scotia as "Albania." Since the sagas had referred to the Irish settlement west of Vinland as "Hvitramannaland" (or "Irland it Mikla") and since Vinland was believed to have been situated in this same area, Jonsson reasoned that Albania of the north and Hvitramannaland referred to the same region of Celtic Irish settlements.

Welsh Voyages

During the Norman invasion of Wales in the 11th century, beleaguered Welsh clans fled to a land across the western sea called "Avalon." The Welsh phrase for Avalon—Ynys yr Afallon—means Land of Apples. Modern historians have taken this as a simple copy of the Greek isle of the Hesperides—also a land of apples.

Legends of this western paradise were common at least as early as the 5th or 6th century when King Arthur is said to have sent expeditions across the North Atlantic. A legend called "The Spoils of Anwin" recounts the Arthurian voyage; and a subsequent tale recorded by Geoffrey of Monmouth called the Gestae Arthuri (Legend of Arthur) eulogized the fallen Arthur who was carried back to Avalon on the shoulders of three fairy princesses. A priest in the court of Norse King Haakon VI Magnusson (1355-80) told the Flemish traveler Jocobus Cnoyen that Arthur's colonies were located in the "northern regions" beyond Greenland. Historian Richard Hakluyt (1599, 100) identified this territory as "Norumbega" on 16th-century maps. The modern name for this region is Nova Scotia.

Historian Elizabeth Jenkins (1975, 27) assures us that the legendary Arthur was a real person—although many of the fabulous achievements attributed to him in later centuries are certainly mythical. A 6th-century document in the British Museum called Historical Miscellany contains several references to Arthur as a successful general in battles against the Romans and Saxons. And the Anglo-Saxon Chronicle in 488 AD mentions that "Arthur fought against them in those days with the kings of the Britons" (Jenkins, 1975, 30).

Orthodox historians once assumed that apples were not present in America until the 1630's, however historian Richard Hakluyt (1582) and several others have provided testimony that apple orchards were relatively common near aboriginal villages. A New England traveler named Longstreth reported finding apple orchards in what had been regarded as an aboriginal wilderness near Annapolis in the 1690's.

The most popular Welsh traveler was Madoc ab Owain Gwynedd—whom legends call the "discoverer of America" in 1170 AD. This Prince Madoc is said to have sent three expeditions across the Atlantic: the first to reconnoiter the ocean passage; the second to scout for a suitable land; and the third comprising a fleet of ten ships carrying settlers, cattle, and farm animals. They may have landed in the Carolinas, Florida, or Alabama—from where they proceeded inland. Their fate is unknown, although Colonial archivists reported numerous encounters with Welsh-speaking tribes along the East Coast. Some settlers claimed Mandan tribes of South Dakota included Welsh descendants with red hair.

Madoc's voyages were recorded in Historia Cambria—the Medieval Welsh history—compiled by Cardoc of Llancarfan. British historian David Powel edited the manuscript in 1584 as part of the English effort to justify access to North America. Although Spanish historians claimed the document was a fraud, they still acknowledged prior English settlements in North America. Physical evidence forced them to do so: Spanish soldiers reported the remains of stone forts in Florida which they attributed to ancient Welsh inhabitants.

Although modern historians have scoffed at reports of Welsh-speaking natives and Madoc's alleged voyage, Welsh incursions into aboriginal America are corroborated by native testimony and archeological remains. Native tribes reported numerous legends of encounters with whites who sailed up coastal rivers and disembarked. According to a report in Henry Schoolcraft's book, Indian Tribes of North America (1851), Shawnee Chief Blackhoof claimed that an ancient legend told of a white race that lived in Florida and used iron tools before the Spanish arrived. Chief Oconostota reported a Cherokee legend of whites sailing up the Alabama river and building a stone fort near the Highwassee river. Alabama natives informed Benjamin Bowen in 1854 that a tribe of whites called the "Welegens" (a Welsh clan) had lived along the Conesauga Creek. Ohio tribes had a legend that a battle with a tribe of whites had taken place near the Falls of The Ohio river long before the arrival of English and French colonists (Thompson, 1994, 204).

Frontier tales of encounters with Welsh speaking natives are commonplace. Colonial settler John Hawkins reported a meeting with a Welsh tribe called the Monacans in 1568 (Covey, 1975, 13). Captain Peter Wynne of the Jamestown militia reported Welsh-speaking natives

31

near the James river falls in 1600. Virginia colonist Morgan Jones reported an encounter with Tuscarora natives in the Carolinas and claimed that he used Welsh to gain his safe release (Deacon, 1966, 110). Another Welshman captured in the Carolinas described Welsh-speaking natives who said their ancestors came from an island across the Atlantic—presumably from Wales (McGlone and Leonard, 1986, 8). In 1738, French explorer Pierre Gautier deVarennes visited a city of Welsh-speaking Mandans in North Dakota. Maurice Griffith called the Mandans "white men in red men's dress who understand Welsh" (Mallery and Harrison, 1979, 29). Frontier artist George Catlan and James Girty both compiled lists of words that had the same meanings in Welsh and Mandan. In 1770, Captain Abe Chaplain reported a conversation with Welsh-speaking natives (Hope, 1983, 201). Similar accounts are found in frontier chronicles until the early 1800's when an epidemic of smallpox decimated the Mandan population.

News of America's Welsh-speaking natives inspired the London researcher John Evans to explore the frontier in 1792 seeking evidence for patrons in Europe. Perhaps his effort some 300 years following the Anglo invasion of the New World came too late? At any rate, Evans reported no evidence of white natives speaking Welsh. Subsequently, his supporters declared that all the frontier reports were either part of a conspiracy to defraud Columbus of his rightful glory, or they were the consequence of an enduring mass-hysteria (Gardner, 1986, 36).

Modern historians have also voiced skepticism regarding Welsh-speaking natives, however they can't deny that the many testimonials formed part of the official colonial record long before the controversy over the Columbus discovery became an issue.

Artifact or Artifancy?

More than legends and frontier testimonials greet the serious scholar who searches the fields and library stacks for evidence of ancient voyagers to America. Engineer and antiquarian enthusiast Arlington Mallery (1951) identified scores of Celtic iron-smelting furnaces in the Eastern United States during field surveys in the 1940's. Josiah Priest, author of <u>American Antiquities and Discoveries in The West</u> (1833), reported numerous artifacts that substantiated his theory of pre-Colonial settlements of Europeans in the Ohio valley. His antiquarian relics included metal helmets, bottles, ceramic dishes, swords, and mirrors recovered from Celtic mounds. But the most impressive evidence has been the discovery of ancient masonry walls found buried beneath Colonial-era habitations. Joseph Gardner and associates (1986, 36) reported that:

> Archeological support for the tales of Welsh-speaking Indians has centered upon three ruined forts, apparently of pre-Columbian origin, on sites near Chattanooga—Old Stone Fort, Tennessee; DeSoto Falls, Alabama; and Fort Mountain, Georgia. Considered to be unlike native construction in the region, they seem to date back to the 12th century, a few centuries before the Age of Exploration. The Tennessee site, in particular, with its walls and single gateway and moat fed by the Duck River, resembles ancient remains that have been studied in Wales.

Medieval Voyages to The Polar Regions

During most of the Middle Ages, lands near the Arctic Circle were barely habitable. Greenland, Baffin Island, and Labrador were occupied only by Inuit (or Eskimo) bands. The Orkney Islands, the Faeroes, and Iceland played refuge to Catholic hermits, outlaws, and families that survived on fishing and hunting during the summer. By the 9th century, the Gulf Stream shifted to the north bringing warmer waters to the Arctic. Wild wheat fields returned to the lower fjords of Greenland—hence the name "Green Land"; Norway grew unseasonably warm. Fish and game were abundant—more abundant than they had been for centuries. Human populations grew rapidly—so fast that the youth of Scandinavia were compelled to seek farmlands in adjacent territories of the Baltic and North Seas. Unfortunately, these lands were already occupied.

Norse immigrants set sail in all directions. In the east, the Varangian Rus from Sweden sailed up the Volga to the Black Sea and Constantinople. Their descendants became known as "Russians." Danes invaded Ireland in 795 AD; Norwegian raiders descended upon the Scottish coast in 802 AD. In 865 AD, a Danish army invaded England and settled in the Province of Northumbria. The growing Scandinavian territory came to be known as the "Dane Law" because that was the region where Danish law prevailed. Norse immigrants invaded the Rhineland and northern France—giving their name to the region called "Normandy."

The most adventurous and desperate raided and settled in northern Spain; they conquered cities along the north African coast and attacked Italy. A band of "Northmen" settled near Luna in the Gulf of Genoa. Others conquered Sicily and Cyprus. Their fleets were the most powerful in all of Europe.

The vanguard of Scandinavian migrations were "Viking" bands that burned cathedrals, terrorized peasants, and absconded with gold and jewels. Viking raiders earned the title of "the scourge of Christendom." They were often followed by immigrant farmers who settled peaceably near Christian villages. Norse farmers converted to Catholicism; they learned the language and customs of their neighbors; and before long, their ethnic and cultural identity merged with those of local inhabitants.

Voyagers sailing west were equally daring and equally destructive towards native populations. Norwegians chased Celtic hermits from Iceland (ca. 865 AD); within a century, the Norse population grew to nearly 60,000 inhabitants. This place that Norse seafarers called "Island" served as a launching platform to the next habitable land to the west— Greenland. An expedition led by Eric Roda (Eric The Red) landed on the southwestern tip in 981 AD and established the settlement of

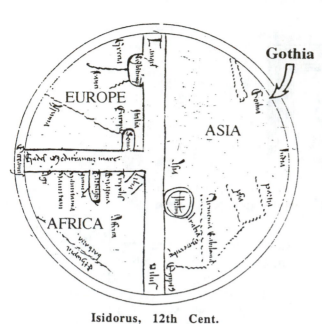

Gothia

Isidorus, 12th Cent.

source: Imago Mundi (Destombes; 1964, Pl. C)

Borgia Carte
1458 AD

*Al-Idrisi section source: after Lelewel (1857)
Borgia Carte from antique Russian Ms.*

Albania

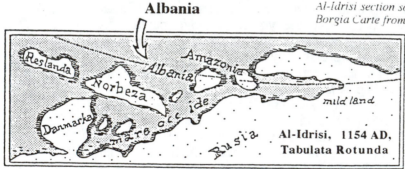

Al-Idrisi, 1154 AD,
Tabulata Rotunda

*Thompson (1994, 198)
after Paul Herman (1954)
source: Torfaeus (1706)*

Jon Gudmundsson 1600 AD

Albania

Gothia Orientalis or Northern Albania

Medieval maps in the circle & tau-cross tradition (T-O, above left) from a 12th-century geography by Isidorus show Gothia Orientalis in northern Asia above China. The same land, variously referred to as Albania Magna or Great Ireland, can be seen on the Borgia Carte of 1458 (above right) and Al-Idrisi's Tabulata Rotunda of 1154 (center). On Al-Idrisi's map, Albania is shown as an island adjacent to Amazonia—Land of Women. Amazonia represents the Hesperides of Greek legend. In the 1600 map by Jon Gudmundsson (bottom right), Albania is shown on the east coast of North America below "America Pars" or Labrador. This region corresponds to East Coast regions where 16th-century explorers such as Giovanni Verrazano and Martin Behaim reported pre-existing resident populations of white people.

"Herjolfsness." Less than a decade later, explorers from Greenland sailed south in search of new lands to conquer and new places to hunt and fish. Sometime between 998 and 1003 AD, Leif Ericson's party reached a place they called "Wineland." This Wineland, or Vinland, was a region of lush vegetation located someplace between Newfoundland and New York. They were followed by several other expeditions seeking financial gain from lumber, fish, furs, and grapes. At this point, the story of the sagas becomes murky—partially due to the lack of archeological field work and partially due to the stranglehold of academic dogma.

Orthodox historians claim that natives with bows and arrows chased out the armored Vikings. The climate of the North Atlantic then grew colder, and the settlers in Greenland supposedly succumbed to disease and the ravages of longer winters. Presumably, Norse inhabitants of Greenland neglected to sail a few hundred miles south to temperate lands of the East Coast. Here the orthodox version of "history" ends with the extinction of Norse inhabitants who never quite succeeded in establishing a permanent settlement in the New World (Gardner, 1986, 65). Although Norse artifacts have been found in Minnesota, Massachusetts, New York, and Nova Scotia, they are typically regarded with disdain in academic circles. By proclaiming such artifacts as "frauds" or "hoaxes," orthodox historians seek to convey the image of Native America as a "virgin wilderness" in time for the arrival of Christopher Columbus and John Cabot in the late 15th century. As far as they are concerned, Norse expansion to the west ended at Greenland; knowledge of their exploits was lost by the time of Columbus; and that is the end of the story of Nordic discoveries in the west—period!

However, reality paints a vastly different picture of the Norse-Germanic role of New World discovery during the Middle Ages. As early as the 6th century, Germanic historians recorded tales of voyages across the Western Ocean. Following Icelandic sagas of the 12th century that reported an abundant supply of lumber, furs, fish, and gold in arcadian lands across the North Atlantic, numerous fishermen and merchants sailed northwest with dreams of making huge profits from the overseas paradise. Most voyages went unrecorded; but occasional reports have survived in ancient manuscripts. Such accounts are customarily ignored in modern textbooks which serve the function of screening out undesirable information that runs counter to established dogma.

Gothic Tales: Gothia Orientalis

Among the more bizarre testimonials of the Middle Ages is an account in Jordanes' 6th-century <u>History of The Goths</u>: "This same ocean (the Atlantic) has in its western region certain islands known to almost everyone by reason of the great number of those who journey there and return" (Ashe, 1962). Other documents provide confirmation of western voyages. Maps of the 13th century—some of the oldest surviving maps of Medieval Europe—show lands called "Gothia Orientalis" west of Europe across the northern ocean. On oval maps and circular maps of the tau-omega (T-O) tradition, "Gothia Orientalis" (or Gothia of The East) is typically shown as a northeastern region of Asia—so it is simultaneously east of Europe by land and west by sea. The term "Orientalis" designated Gothia as part of the Orient—that is, part of the Far East. There was another Gothia which was variously referred to as Gothia, Gothia Major, or Gothia Occidentalis (Gothia of The West). This Scandinavian country was typically located on maps of the Baltic Sea in Europe. Thus, there were two Gothias—one the European territory and the second an overseas colony frequented by Gothic voyagers (Danes and Germans).

The overseas land was reached by sailing west across the North Atlantic in what was erroneously presumed by Europeans to be in the direction of Asia on the world globe. Maps by Donnus Nicolaus Germanus (1470), included an archaic version of Scandinavia that placed Arctic isles such as Engroneland (Greenland), and New World territories such as Vinland adjacent (and north of) Norway and Sweden. On these maps, Gottia Occidentalis (of the West) is shown northeast of Gothia (a Swedish territory) on the Baltic; Gottia Orientalis (of the Far East) is shown farther north beyond Engronelant and Venthelant (Vinland). Some later versions of this map show a "Greenland" in place of Gottia Orientalis—as though confirming speculation that Gottia of The East was later absorbed into a generic western territory—"Greenland Province" or "Terra Verde"—that was later named North America. References to Gothia Orientalis (Gothia of Asia) can be found on copies of maps by Donnus Nicolaus Germanus as late as 1525.

Thus we can see that Jordannes' claim of Gothic voyages to the west is corroborated by contemporary maps which identify a Gothic territory in that direction. Later maps of the 15th century moved this Gothia Orientalis to a position north of Norway—and this was due to the advent of the magnetic compass and the resulting confusion between the Geographic North Pole and the Magnetic North Pole.

Navigation on North Atlantic Seas

Prior to the advent of the compass, sailors set their course by the sun and prevailing winds. Routes to simple destinations were learned by rote from those who had sailed before; the learned kept sailing books (called "peripli") or scrolls that recorded wind directions and landmarks. These were the precursors of Medieval sailing maps called "portolanos."

Once the compass was introduced, Norse charts show Greenland directly north of Norway—for that was the magnetic direction of Greenland with the compass needle pointing towards Hudson Bay which was the site of the Magnetic North Pole. All the lands mentioned in the sagas, including Iceland, Greenland, Helluland, Markland (or Skraelingland), Wineland, and Hvitramannaland (a.k.a. Albania or Gothia Orientalis) were typically said to be situated between Norway and the North Pole, thus sailors presumed they were all "northern territories," and they are portrayed accordingly on Medieval maps. An archaic form of the North Atlantic saga-map is preserved in the Donis Kort (1470) which shows Engronelant (Greenland) and Ventelant (Wineland) along the north coast of Norway—presumably where they would be encountered on the way to the North Pole.

Modern historians have erred by assuming that lands shown on Medieval maps near the Geographic North Pole were simply "fabulous" (read non-existent) islands. The problem arose because Medieval geographers did not know that the geographic pole and the magnetic pole were not in the same location. Because they assumed that compass needles pointed towards the geographic pole, mapmakers mistakenly placed western isles beside the Geographic North Pole on their maps.

Compass use was common by the end of the 13th century in northern European waters. Earlier Christians may have avoided the device due to its association with magic and pagan cultures. Invented in China by the 2nd millennium BC, it was known to the Phoenicians, Greeks and

Romans.   Phoenician legends told of a north-pointing metal which Haracles used in a golden cup; the Greek poet Homer told of a device which enabled sailors in the <u>Odyssey</u> to find their way through fog and darkness without fear of shipwreck (Bailey, 1973, 323).   Classical writers explained the north-pointing characteristic by supposing the existence of a huge magnetic mountain at the Geographic North Pole.

Heinrich Winter (1937, 102) notes that early sagas of the Faeroe Isles (9th century) mention Viking use of lodestones "floating" in containers, gnomons or sundials, and water-clocks which enabled sailors to determine their location at sea.   Use of these devices by pagan Vikings predates later accounts during the Christian era in which use of such magical arts was apparently condemned by Church authorities.   As Vikings settled in Mediterranean towns during the 9th century, and King Roger II of Sicily established a university at Salerno in 1100 AD, Norse sailors were in a position to acquire the compass from Arabian mariners. Most historians don't believe the compass reached the West until the end of the Crusades in the 13th century. But this is simply the time at which it became acceptable to mention compass use in Christian documents.

It has been presumed that Christian Europeans learned of the device via Crusaders who had returned from the Holy Lands.   These Crusaders presumably took home instruments that they had obtained from their conquest of Moslem-held territories (Fiske, 1920, Vol. I, 313).   The earliest references to use of the compass in European literature are found in the 12th-century writings of Alexander Nekam and Jacques de Vitry. Historian George Kimble (1938, 222) noted that the compass had been in use in China and Arabia for a considerable time before it reached the West.   He believes the device may have been used secretly in European waters due to its association with the magical arts: "It is just possible that one reason why the compass was not in common use in Christendom until the 14th century was that those in possession of the secret of it were afraid to reveal it lest they should be suspected of magic or that sailors were equally afraid to employ the new device for the same reason" (Kimble, 1938, 222).   Those who were suspected of practicing magical arts were subjected to torture and execution at the hands of civil authorities in cahoots with the Inquisition. Church bureaucrats devised this abominable institution as a means of enforcing authority and exterminating dissent. By some estimates, millions of heretics, scientists, free-thinkers, and Jews lost their lives to this instrument of spiritual and mental "purity." It is no wonder, then, that judicious mariners might conceal use of a device that was condemned as "magical."

The Oxford friar, Roger Bacon, showed a magnetic needle to his associate, Brunetto Latini, who was attending parliament in 1270. Latini noted in a letter to a friend that:

> This discovery, which appears useful in so great a degree to all who travel by sea, must remain concealed until other times; because no master mariner dares to use it lest he should fall under the imputation of being a magician; or would the sailors venture themselves out to sea under his command, if he took with him an instrument which carries so great an appearance of being constructed under the influence of some infernal spirit. A time may arrive when these prejudices, which are of such great hindrance to researches into the secrets of nature, will be overcome; and it will be then that mankind shall reap the benefit of the labors of such learned men as Friar Bacon, and do justice to that industry and

Norse Polar Region

*source: Bagrow (1951, Pl. 47)
State Library, Zeitz*

Norway's Polar Regions

A circular map from a Ptolemaic Atlas of 1470 shows Norwegian territory reaching to the North Pole. This region was claimed by King Haakon in 1261. A legend on the polar land proclaims that it is part of the Norwegian realm. Other maps of this period called the territory "Hyperborea Europa," "Norveca Europa," or "Septentrionalis."

*artist's reconstruction
of ancient mariners' chart*

source: Thompson (1995)

Magnetic Saga Map or Sea Card

The earliest "map" of the North Atlantic was an oral description of sequential land areas—which corresponds to geographical accounts in Icelandic sagas recorded in the 12th and 13th centuries. The sagas tell of a sequence of headlands or promontories projecting into the seas beyond Iceland. These were: 1) Greenland; 2) Helluland; 3) Markland; and 4) Wineland. Helluland (or "slab" land) is thought to represent the flat rocks of Baffin Island or northern Labrador; Markland was a land of forests (southern Labrador or Newfoundland); and Vinland was a temperate, fertile land where Leif Ericson found grapes and abundant salmon—probably someplace near the Gulf of St. Lawrence. The "Promontorium Winlandia" shown on 16th-century North Atlantic maps is thought to represent Newfoundland Island—though not necessarily the Wineland of Leif's original camp nor the location of the later colony—Vinland det Goda. Headlands on the sea cards were probably oriented like those shown above during the 13th century when magnetic compasses were used in maritime travel. At that time, all of these lands were regarded as being on the way to the North Pole—that is, the Magnetic North Pole of Hudson's Bay. The great strait—Ginnungagap—was later known as "Christian Strait" or "Bering Strait." Compass symbol marks the location of the Magnetic North Pole.

38

intelligence for which he and they now meet with no other return than obloquy and reproach. (Fiske, 1920, Vol. I, 314)

For this and other crimes of "unorthodox thought," Bacon was thrown into prison for 14 years; the sentence was mild considering the severity of the offense. By the end of the 13th century, Bacon was dead—but the compass was in common use.

Norse Voyages to America

Testimonials of Norse voyages to North America's East Coast in pre-Columbian times are numerous. Icelandic sagas tell of four expeditions from Greenland Island to North America during the 11th century for purposes of exploration, trading, and settlement.

The North American continent was first sighted by Bjarny Herjolfsson circa 996 AD while on a trip from Iceland to Greenland. This sighting led to Leif Ericson's expedition between 998 and 1003. The sagas relate that Ericson's company gave names to the different lands they passed as they sailed south along the East Coast of North America. As they passed the barren rocks of Baffin Island (and perhaps northern Labrador), they named the place Helluland. Next, they came to a forested land (Labrador) which they named Markland. Eventually, they landed someplace between Newfoundland Island and New York. Leif called the region of his base camp "Wineland" (a.k.a. Vinland) because they found abundant wine grapes growing wild.

Commercial enterprise was a primary interest of Norse voyagers. Ericson's fruitful discovery of Wineland was followed by his brother Thorvald's excursion in 1004. Thorvald's men withdrew after a skirmish with natives; but the venture turned a profit in wine, lumber, and furs. Thorfinn Karlsefni's expedition took place in 1010. Within two years time, his company of 160 men and women explored much of North America from Hudson Bay to Florida. Their exploits were reported in Icelandic sagas. Thorfinn's group departed from their encampment after a battle with natives whom they called skraelings (savages). This expedition also turned a profit. Historian Adam of Bremen's Description Insularum Aquilonis of 1073 reported that the Wineland colony was noted for its wines. If the Norse produced wines for import to European monarchs as late as three generations after Leif's expedition to the wine country, it is apparent that Greenlanders succeeded in establishing a North American colony that was later known as "Vinland det Goda."

Norse historian Fridtjof Nansen once ridiculed the sagas as "fairy tales"—presuming that grapes, an Old World plant, were not introduced into New England until the 1600's. However, several early explorers, including Giovanni Verrazano, Jacques Cartier, and Samuel Champlain reported finding wild grapes along the Gulf of St. Lawrence. Hakluyt's Diverse Voyages (1582) mentions wine grapes as one of the principal fruits of Norumbega (or Morumbega in the East Coast region of Nova Scotia). Hakluyt also noted that French Captain John Ribault reported grape vines growing in northern Florida in 1562. French explorer Nicolas Denys reported grape vines growing in the hinterlands of Nova Scotia in 1672—a mere 40 years after grapes were supposedly "first imported" by New England colonists (Nansen, 1911, 3). Is it possible that so many explorers could be mistaken about the nature of a fruit that was commonly known to European society?

Thorlaksson's map from Torfaeus (1706)

Ginnunga Gap (later Hudson Strait)

Bishop Thorlaksson's 1606 map of the Atlantic (above) shows "Pars America extrema Versus Gronlandiam" or "The closest American province near Greenland." Presumably, he made this notation in order to differentiate Labrador (**A**) and Estotelandia (**E**)—lands which earlier geographers often referred to as "Gronelandia"—from the Arctic isle of Greenland (**G**). The waterway between Labrador and the Arctic isle was known to Norwegians as "Ginnunga Gap" centuries before Eric The Red established a settlement on Greenland. This waterway was once thought to lead directly north of Norway to the North Pole. And it does head due north by compass bearings to the Magnetic North Pole at Hudson Bay. By geographic coordinates, the direction of sailing from Iceland to Ginnunga Gap was almost due west.

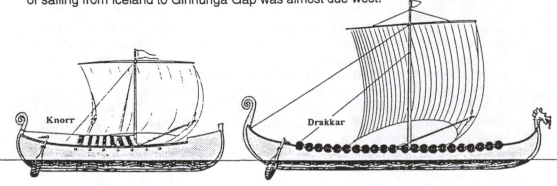

40

Over the course of several centuries, a characteristic pattern of exploration, immigration, and commerce dominated Nordic life in the North Atlantic. Contrary to orthodox assumptions, there is substantial evidence from artifacts, traditions, historical accounts, and maps that Norse voyagers and other Europeans established thriving settlements along the East Coast of North America. Orthodox historians have wrongly assumed that the sagas, once thought to be mere fables, represented the "only" testimony of unproductive Nordic voyagers. That is a gross misconception. Indeed, archeologists Thomas Lee (1979), Eben Horsford (Stromsted, 1974, 148), and Arlington Mallery (1951) found numerous remains of Norse settlements along the eastern seaboard of North America. Another misconception of orthodox historians is the belief that colonies on Greenland Island were overrun by Inuit warriors and that the few survivors merely succumbed to the increasing severity of northern winters.

Mystery of The Greenland Settlements

During the 12th and 13th centuries, there were two principle settlements on Greenland: Ostribygda—the Eastern Settlement (which included Herjolfsness, and Vestribygda—the Western Settlement. The two settlements had separate fates. According to the testimony of Deputy Bishop Ivar Bardarson in 1350, inhabitants of the Western Settlement voluntarily abandoned their dwellings and sailed south to America. Presumably, this move was in response to the increasing severity of winter storms and Inuit raids. At any rate, when an armed guard from the Eastern Settlement arrived at Vestribygda, they found the place abandoned. They assumed the move was voluntarily as there was no evidence of warfare. Numerous cattle and sheep that had been left behind continued to graze beside deserted homesteads. Inuit legends about a massacre of a Norse village (recorded by Henry Rink in 1890) probably relate to a remote village called Nordsetr which is variously thought to have been situated in northern Greenland or "north" near Hudson Bay.

The Eastern Settlement (actually located on the southwestern tip of Greenland) seems to have endured until the early 1500's. Historian G.J. Marcus (1981) notes that a theory of isolation, desolation, and famine expounded by C.C. Hansen in the 1930's is now defunct. Hansen surmised from the frail condition of a few skeletons unearthed near Herjolfsness that the last inhabitants of the Eastern Settlement had died of malnutrition. However, his sample size was small, thus his conclusions were premature. Unfortunately, Hansen's dire analysis led many subsequent authors to conjure images of beleaguered settlers gradually starving to death as the winters grew longer and ships ceased to arrive from the East. More recent excavations have uncovered numerous 15th-century burials of individuals who were apparently well-fed, well-clothed, and in reasonably good condition at time of death. Burial clothes of the 15th century were reasonably similar to those of contemporary European fashions. Thus, the evidence hardly supports a theory of isolation even though the population was declining throughout the 15th century.

Residents of the Eastern Settlement had more pressing concerns than foul weather and starvation: historical accounts of the 14th and 15th centuries tell of numerous pirate raids on Iceland, Greenland, and Finmark. According to the Historia de gentibus septentrionalibus (Rome, 1555), King Haakon Magnusson commanded an expedition of his battle fleet into the waters of Greenland as part of a campaign against natives

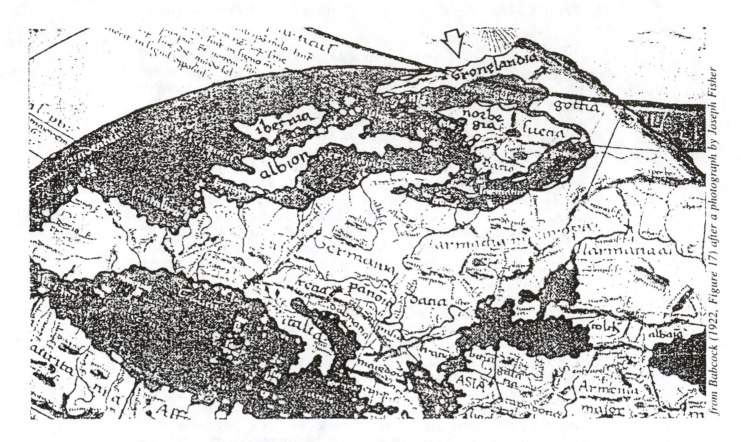

from Babcock (1922, Figure 17) after a photograph by Joseph Fisher

Greenland & The Polar Regions

This map of the North by the German cartographer Donnus Nicolaus Germanus (circa 1485) shows Greenland as a slender peninsula reaching out from central Europe. The map is at least partially based on a scientific survey of northern waters as the tip of Greenland is accurately located at the 60th parallel. The distorted shape of the region—here shown rising out of the surface of the map into the air—reflects the difficulty of showing polar lands on maps using the Ptolemaic configuration of longitudes and latitudes. This method of showing distant lands, like the cylindrical projection technique, has the greatest distortion at the extreme north and south. This is the very region where most New World voyages occurred. However, the Germanus map, because of its distortions, helped convince modern historians that Greenland was too far north to play a significant role in New World discovery.

Greenland & The Church

The rising status of Greenland and Iceland are evident in this cosmological "map" circa 1300 AD. This is the earliest known map to mention Greenland which by this time was a thriving colony and the center of a diocese that included Wineland in North America. Already, the island has been identified as being situated near the North Pole.

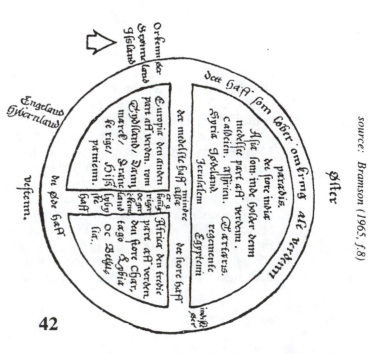

source: Bramson (1965, f.8)

42

and pirates between 1355 and 1380—or about the time that Venetian traveler Antonio Zeno reported naval conflicts in the western Atlantic. Haakon also fought with ships from the Hanseatic League in 1363 (Holand, 1940, 147).

Antonio Zeno's account of barbarian raids in the North Atlantic during the 1380's was reported by the Italian Ramusio in Viaggi (1558) and a translation appeared in Richard Hakluyt's Diverse Voyages (1582). Kidnapping and pirate raids during the 1420's were the subject of a treaty between the king of Denmark and the king of England in 1432. Following the treaty, Norse slaves living in the British Isles were repatriated to their homelands. A 1448 letter from Pope Nicholas V to Bishop Marcellus bemoaned an attack on Greenland in 1418 by a fleet of barbarian ships from the neighboring coasts of the heathen. The letter mentioned that only nine parish churches escaped plunder, while many inhabitants were carried off into slavery. This was not a native Inuit raid.

The Pope referred to these pirates as non-aligned "barbarians" who came in a fleet of ships from "the neighboring coasts of the heathen." This coast—indicating lands farther west—could only have been Labrador or the isles of the Newfoundland archipelago. According to Nicholas, the "sword-wielding" barbarians carried off many women and children who were forced into slavery.

Modern historians assumed that the assault was an Inuit (or Eskimo) raid, and it has been cited as evidence of the deteriorating relationship between Greenlanders and natives (Cameron, 1965, 122). However, the Inuit did not sail in ships nor did they carry swords. Indeed, another Inuit legend tells the story of a pirate raid on the Greenland colony not by natives but by people of European stature (Marcus, 1981, 162). The Historia de gentibus septentrionalibus of Olaus Magnus notes that King Haakon's battle fleet was off the coast of Greenland sometime between 1355 and 1380. The fleet captured two skin boats on this expedition. We also know that explorers in the St. Lawrence Gulf region identified white-skinned "natives" with blond hair and blue eyes as the makers of deerskin boats—much in the fashion of the old Celtic curraughs. These may have been the "pirates" who attacked European traders, Greenland settlements, and Haakon's fleet. A 16th-century letter from Burgermeister Carsten Grip of Kiel to King Christian III mentioned that two commodores, Pyningk (a.k.a. Pinning) and Poidthorsth (a.k.a. Pothorst), were sent by the king's grandfather to "explore new countries and islands in the north" (Nansen, 1911, 126). The Burgermeister noted that the region where Pinning and Pothorst sailed was notoriously infested with pirates—and this was a reference to European brigands, not natives.

Historian J.G. Marcus (1981) reports that the parish churches at Gardar and Herjolfsness in Greenland's Eastern Settlement were destroyed by fire and presumably looted since none of the usual Catholic relics were recovered in archeological excavations. He also relates an Inuit legend that a Norse village was attacked by pirates: some survivors fled in a ship; others escaped with Inuit benefactors. In the early 1500's, Portuguese raiders stalked the East Coast of the "New Land" for slaves. These raids might have contributed to the depopulation of Greenland.

It is uncertain whether the "Greenland" mentioned in the letter of Nicholas V refers to Greenland Island or to the larger Greenland Province (North America) located to the southwest. Nevertheless, it is clear that as late as 1418 there existed a thriving Catholic settlement in a place called "Greenland" that was adjacent to territories occupied by European pirates.

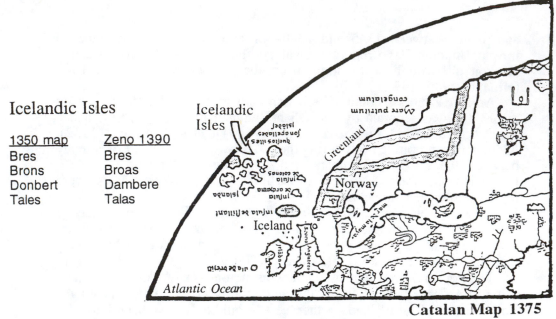

Icelandic Isles

1350 map	Zeno 1390
Bres	Bres
Brons	Broas
Donbert	Dambere
Tales	Talas

Icelandic Isles

Atlantic Ocean

Catalan Map 1375
source: Nansen (1911, 233)

The Icelandic Isles—or Newfoundland Archipelago?

During the mid-14th century, maps of the North Atlantic show a group of seven or eight isles north of Iceland. The legend on the maps indicates that these islands are known as "The Icelands." On both maps shown here, the isles are situated northwest of a larger, oblong-shaped island representing the traditional Iceland. A similar pattern of isles can be seen on the Catalan Este map of 1450, on the Florentine Planisphere of 1447, on Toscanelli's Planisphere of 1457, and on the Juan De LaCosa Map of 1500. On the planispheres, the Icelandic Isles are situated directly west of England at the approximate latitude of the Gulf of St. Lawrence. This suggests that the Icelandic Isles are an early representation for the Newfoundland archipelago and the isles of the Gulf of St. Lawrence. The Zeno narrative of 1380 or 1390 mentions several isles in the Polar Region which have the same names as this group of isles (see chart above). Zeno described these isles as being near Frisland—whose abundant salmon suggest the region of Newfoundland. Charters from English kings for voyages to "Iceland" may have sought to conceal trips to Newfoundland.

Icelandic Isles

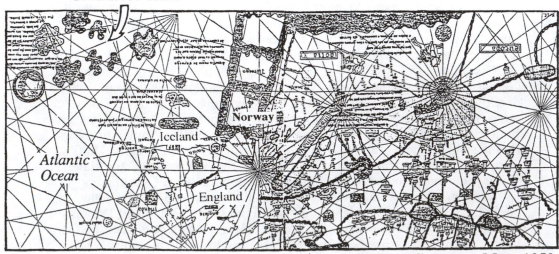

Modena Compass Map 1350
source: Nansen (1911, 231)

It is also apparent that this mysterious Greenland was of great significance to the Vatican throughout the 15th and early 16th centuries: bishops were assigned to serve Greenland's parishioners in 1492 and again in 1520. Whether or not the bishops ever reached their appointed diocese is speculative. However, it was not the practice of popes to appoint bishops to deserted islands. We can only assume that wherever Greenland was located, it was inhabited with at least a few Catholic parishioners.

Naming the Lands: Deceptive Clues on Ancient Maps

Ever since the "Great Age of Exploration" in the 15th and 16th centuries, scholars have been perplexed by inconsistent reports from explorers. It seems that captains filed grossly different navigational charts of the same areas, and they often gave the same places different names in order to please their sovereigns back home. Thus, Columbus declared that the largest island in the Caribbean was henceforth to be known as Isabella—after the Spanish monarch, Queen Isabel. By so naming the island, he hoped to gain favor with his royal benefactor. He also ignored the native name, Cuba, out of an ethnocentric belief that native names were unimportant. On a subsequent voyage, he insisted that the land was known to the ancients as India—and he had his men swear an oath to that effect. However, a 16th-century historian, Peter Martyr, deduced that the place Columbus had landed was actually known to the Portuguese as Antilia—a term that had been used since the early 1400's to designate a large island ante (or in front of) Asia which was thought to lie across the seas from Europe. Later geographers agreed with Martyr: the Caribbean isles are known today as "The Antilles."

Native terms for tribal homelands were invariably lost as Europeans pushed back the frontier and named the lands after their own favorite saints or sovereigns. When European settlers moved from one place to the next, they often carried along the name of their previous residence. And to make matters worse for latter-day historians, explorers from many different European nationalities gave different foreign names to the same native lands on their navigational charts, or they used the same name to refer to several different territories.

The Roman designation for the northern frontier, "Thule," was first used as a name for Iceland and later—North America. A Roman explorer named Pytheus is said to have found a large isle called Thule north of England. On the Rudimentium Novitorium Map (Lubeck 1475), Thule is shown as a land situated east of Asia. Yale's Vinland Map has "Ultima Thule" situated northwest of Europe as an alternative for Hyperborea. The name "Island" (for Iceland) was similarly applied to several different places. During the 15th-century, the name identified Denmark and lands north of Norway as well as representing an island north of England which is now called Iceland. In the 14th century, the name was also used to identify an archipelago of isles in the vicinity of the Gulf of St. Lawrence. Presumably, these "Icelandic Isles" were so-named because they were situated near Icelandic fishing territories. Another reason for naming the isles "Icelands" is that people from Iceland had migrated to these isles.

The "Islads" (a cluster of 8 Icelandic Isles) are shown northwest of England on the Modena Este world map of 1450 (in the Biblioteca Estense, Modena; Kimble, 1938, Plate 9). A cluster of seven Icelandic Isles is represented on the Henricus Martellus map of the north (ca. 1480) now in the Biblioteca Mediceo-Laurenziana, Florence (Pl. 29.25). The Juan de LaCosa map of 1500 shows ten Icelandic Isles north of Frislanda,

Tille (Thule), and Ysla de Eshlanda (Iceland). Since there are no such lands in this part of the North Atlantic, historians have assumed that they represent fictitious isles. However, as there are accounts from the late 1300's of mariners traveling to these isles (as in the Zeno narrative), it is apparent that on the maps they represent archaic isles whose location became confused over the passing decades as sailing routes changed and surveying technology improved.

Likewise, the name "Greenland" designated a variety of lands. It was used to represent a Norwegian realm (Hyperborea) north of Norway; it was the name of a mysterious isle (Isla Verde) in the mid-Atlantic; and it represented an Arctic island that was settled by the Icelandic felon—Eric The Red. During the 15th and 16th centuries, a group of similar names including Terra Verde (Green Land), Isola Verde (Green Isle), Groenlandia Province, and Greenland were used to identify North America. Thus, identification of territories solely on the basis of their names in historical accounts can be deceiving. On the other hand, there are traditions in cartography which can enable the skilled researcher to accurately identify the places indicated and to trace the progress of European exploration across the Atlantic to the Americas.

It is now apparent from cartographic traditions found on antique maps that the Americas were visited and incorporated into European charts more than a century before Columbus. And they are often referred to in bona fide historical accounts—even though the names of these New World lands may seem illusive and legendary.

Norway's Polar Territories—
Norvega Europa & Septentrionalis

The 11th-century German historian Adam of Bremen noted in his Descriptio insularum aquilonis (1067) that "Harold, Prince of Nortmanni, explored the breadth of the Northern Ocean to the boundaries of the Earth." Such a voyage would have taken the Prince of the North Men to the Ginnungagap Strait south of Greenland as far as Hudson Bay. This is the only place in the North beyond Greenland and Baffin Land that a Norse prince would have regarded as the "boundary of Earth."

In the 13th century Swedish historian, Olaus Magnus (a.k.a. Olaus Magnusson) mentioned that Norway's King Haakon IV Haakonson had sailed "to Greenland and beyond." These travels, combined with an appeal for protection on the part of Norse settlers in the distant lands, and the growing importance of overseas commerce led Haakon to declare sovereignty over lands reaching from "Norway to the North Pole." This declaration came in 1261—barely three years after the king had crushed an uprising in the northern territories of Greenland, Iceland, and "Landanu"—the New Land. Haakon's "North Pole" was not some fabulous region at the top of the world; it was the temperate regions of Hudson Bay and the East Coast of North America—then known as the "New Land." Two centuries after this declaration, the Icelandic songwriter Sturle Tordsson wrote in the Norges Konge Sagaer:

> Farther toward the north—even under the leading star—you (Haakon) like to increase your power. There, good men look with pleasure on your reign. No earlier king has secured or claimed the area. People bring you honor in lands farther than the sun shines. (Knut Mykland, Norges Historie, Oslo, 1976.)

Haakon's 1261 AD territorial claim encompassed lands from Greenland Island to Markland (Labrador), Nyaland (Newfoundland), Wineland (Nova Scotia), Florida and much of the continental region between New England and Hudson Bay (which the Norse called "Christian's Bay"). This territory, much larger than Norway itself, was known by several names. The northern regions (including Greenland Island and Hudson Bay) where sunlight was absent for three months each year was known as "Dusky Norway;" the common name for the New England region appears to have changed from "Vinland det Gode" (Greater Vinland) to "Norvega," or "Norvega Europa." This may have been the source of a similar name, "Nor(um)bega," which was a pre-Colonial name for New England. Another popular name for the whole region of eastern North America seems to have been simply "the New Land." This "Landanu" is mentioned in Haakon's contract of 1262 with Greenland and Iceland.

Most Medieval maps leave no doubt regarding the extent of territory comprising the realm of Norse kings: it was immense. Sometimes, it was referred to as the "Great Realm," and it appears on maps as a huge territory reaching from the Baltic Sea to the North Pole. A classic example is Joachim von Watt's 1534 world map published in Zurich. Watt's map shows a huge land area reaching from the Hyperborean Mountains northeast of Norway to the North Pole. This archaic map reflects traditions of Norway's northern realm.

Maps by Battista Agnese (c. 1543) show the archaic concept of the ancient Norwegian territory reaching from the Scandinavian peninsula to the North Pole. On his planisphere map (now in the Medicea-Laurenziana Library, Florence) the northern territory is called Terra Nova or "New Land." This map seems to reflect the 13th through 14th-century Norse claim of sovereignty over habitable lands from "Norway to the North Pole" (Portinaro & Knirsch, 1987, Pl. XXIII to XXV).

Since no habitable lands really exist near the North Pole, it is not surprising that most historians regard the so-called "northern regions" as a Nordic fantasy. However, if we realize that sailors and cartographers were referring to lands between Norway and the Magnetic North Pole, it becomes readily apparent that the "Northern Regions" were simply misplaced western territories. Nordic sagas and historical accounts confirm that this is what happened. In the King's Mirror (1250 AD), Archbishop Einar Gunnarson reported that: "Greenland lies on the outermost edge of the Earth towards the north;...the land has beautiful sunshine and is said to have a rather pleasant climate." The bishop was surprised by the temperate climate, because most scholars believed northern lands were too frigid for habitation due to climatic zones encircling the Earth.

The Two Greenlands—Magnetic versus Geographic Maps

During the mid-15th century, cartographers produced maps having two "Greenlands" (usually some variation of spelling such as "Engroenland," "Grunland," or "Grvtlad"). The 1539 pictorial map by Olas Magnus, for example, has two peninsulas of land marked "Grvtladie Pars" and "Grvtlandie Pars" across the northern border.

There are two plausible reasons for the portrayal of two Greenlands. The first rationale is that there were two different places known as Greenland: one of these, often called "Engronelant" was an island—the modern "Greenland;" the other was a huge Norwegian territory—

Geographic Greenland

Magnetic Greenland

Olaus Magnus (ca. 1539)

source: Nordenskiold (1889)

Olaus Magnus—TWO GREENLANDS

The 16th-century cartographer Olaus Magnusson (a.k.a. Olaus Magnus) produced some maps which had characteristics of both magnetic and geographic traditions. The position of Grvtlandie Pars (Greenland Province) directly north of Norway on the map shown above (circa 1539) is based on magnetic coordinates. Here, Greenland is in the same relative position where it appears on Martin Behaim's 1492 globe. Sailors who traveled north from Norway by compass bearings actually sailed towards the Magnetic North Pole at Hudson Bay. Sailors believed they were heading North—towards the geographic pole—so this location north of Norway is where Greenland is indicated on maps based on compass bearings. Grvtladie Pars or the second Greenland Province (top left) is in the approximate geographical location of territories collectively referred to as the Danish province of Greenland in the 15th century. This province seems to have included Labrador and Nova Scotia.

48

Greenland Province—extending from Northern Norway to the Hudson river in North America. The second rationale is that cartographers occasionally sought to please two different kinds of consumers: politicians and sailors. Politicians wanted maps that reflected true geographical relationships, and for this they demanded geographically correct maps (or "G-maps"). Sailors wanted maps that conformed to compass bearings—so they demanded maps based on magnetic coordinates (or "M-maps"). Due to the high disparity between magnetic and geographical coordinates in the northwestern North Atlantic—resulting from magnetic declination—maps of this region typically show the greatest variability.

Greenland is portrayed as a long peninsula reaching out from Northern Europe in a map by Claudius Clavus (1424). This transcontinental land bridge goes across the North Atlantic and down the western side of the map. Use of the logo "Gronlandia Provincia" reveals that Clavus intended to include northern and western territories in addition to the island commonly referred to as "Engroenland." Confirmation of this interpretation is found in a 1532 map by Jacob Ziegler. This map is similar to the one by Clavus, however it clearly shows that "Gronlandia" refers to North American territory: beneath the term "Gronlandia" is a region called "Terra Bacallaos"—the Portuguese term for Newfoundland.

The portrayal of a land bridge across the North Atlantic conforms to mariners' accounts of a continuous shoreline or "land bridge" between Norway and the North American mainland (Nansen, 1911, 358). Jacopo Gastaldi portrayed this geographical concept of continuous land between Europe and America in an atlas called the Strassburg Ptolemy in 1548. Such a trans-continental "bridge" of ice and land was a reality for ancient travelers who began their treks across the Atlantic in Springtime.

Some geographers based their interpretation of northern lands on travelers' reports from late Summer months when broad seas separate Greenland from both Labrador and Norway. Other maps show Greenland as continental land comprising much of North America. Pietro Coppo's 1528 world map portrays a huge isle or continent north of Florida called "Isola Verde"—the "Green Isle." This serves to represent North American mainland. Coppo's map also shows a peninsula north of Norway in the common location of Greenland Island on European maps. This is another case of two Greenlands being shown to differentiate between Greenland—the Island, and Isola Verde—a continent.

Another map showing the use of "Groenlan" to represent North American territory is Nicola Van Sijpe's 1589 world map. On Sijpe's map, "Groenlan" includes Greenland Island, Canadian provinces, and East Coast territories as far as Chesapeake Bay. Sijpe's "Groenlan" is portrayed as a temperate land of abundant trees, even though it extends far above the Arctic Circle. This portrayal provides further confirmation of ancient beliefs that Greenland was a huge northern land with a temperate climate comparable to "Hyperborea" of Roman legend. It wasn't an "imaginary land" as orthodox historians have assumed: in fact, the land was actually located further south and west beyond the Magnetic North Pole—that is, "beyond the North Wind" as the ancients had always claimed. This land was North America.

Portrayals of Greenland as continental land on Coppo's map and Sijpe's map clearly contradict previous assumptions by historians that "Greenland" referred only to settlements on the North Atlantic Island of Greenland. If we realize that Greenland often referred to a trans-continental "province," then many conflicting accounts in historical

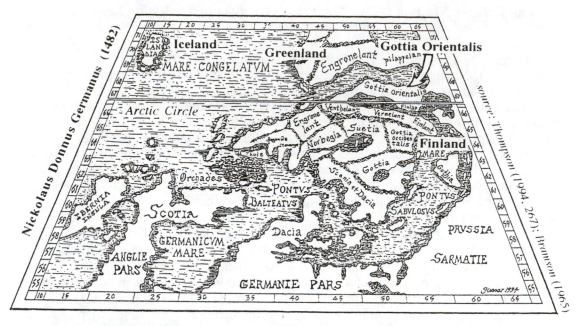

Nickolaus Donnus Germanus (1482)

source: Thompson (1994, 267); Bramson (1965)

Magnetic Maps of The North Atlantic
Gottia Orientalis

The "Donis Kort" (above) portrays Engroneland (Greenland) directly north of Norway which is how it would seem using magnetic compass coordinates. Likewise. Islandia (Iceland) is shown north of Scotia (Scotland). Both land areas are actually situated to the northwest. The Donis Kort shows two Gottia's— Gottia Occidentalis east of Suetia (Sweden) and Gottia Orientalis farther north above the Arctic Circle. Donis shows two Engronelants: the one adjacent to Norbegia (Norway) represents the archaic location of Greenland on older maps. Likewise. beside this archaic Greenland is Ventheland (Vinland), and farther north is Gottia Orientalis—the Gottia across the seas near Vinland. Schedel's map below calls this same region "Grvnland" (Greenland)—confirming that Gottia Orientalis was considered as part of the "northern region" of Greenland. Schedel's map has the Mediterranean Albania in its correct position. This was not the same Albania which Medieval maps placed north of China.

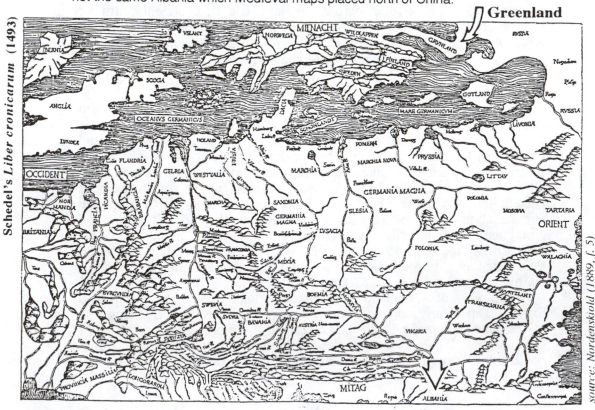

Schedel's Liber cronicarum (1493)

source: Nordenskiold (1889, f. 5)

narratives begin to make sense. Norwegian records of <u>taxes in natura</u> sent from "Greenland" include beaver pelts, elk skins, sable, ermine, wolverine, lynx, and black bear furs. These items which were sent to Norway as payment of the king's tax and the Church tax during the 14th and 15th centuries couldn't possibly refer to imports obtained on Greenland Island, because these fur-bearing mammals were only present on the North American mainland (Winge, 1902, 322; Gibson, 1974, 173). Thus, reports of fur shipments actually correspond to transoceanic trade from "Greater Greenland"—that is, the Greenland Province that included eastern Canada. These furs must have been obtained from European settlements in North America or from native tribes near the St. Lawrence Gulf.

It is apparent that numerous ecclesiastical and merchant reports relating to "Greenland" may refer to either the Arctic island or to North America; so it is important to seek further information to clearly distinguish the intended location (Thompson, 1994; Nielsen, 1994). In 1567, Absalon Beyer of Bergen wrote that: "Greenland is a country rich in wild game, white bears, sable and marten; there are marble, crystal, fish, wadmal, butter, mighty forests, deer and reindeer." Beyer's mention of "sable, marten, and mighty forests" reveal that the Greenland of which he speaks is actually North America (Gibson, 1974, 173).

Historical Accounts—
Greenland Province, Markland, and Vinland

The impression conveyed by modern historians is that Norse contact with North America ceased following the early voyages of Leif, Thorvald, and Thorfinn during the early years of the 11th century. However, runic inscriptions, travelogs, port records, maps, and archeological evidence paint a picture of ongoing contact through the 16th century.

Written testimonials pertaining to Norse settlements in North America are numerous. Runes on a monument in Honen, Norway, referred to "Vinland" in the year 1050: "Far and wide they were driven from the coast of Vinland and were cast on the ice of the uninhabitable regions needing food and clothing. Evil fate may overtake one so that he dies early" (Gibson, 1974, 175). This reference to Norse voyagers "from Vinland" substantiates that settlers from Greenland or Iceland had established colonies in North America in spite of the difficulties encountered by the earliest explorers.

As mentioned previously, Adam of Bremen commented on the wines of "Wineland" (Vinland) in his <u>Description Insularum Aquilonis</u> of 1073. His <u>Geography</u> says that "Winlandia is a country along the mountains of Norway on the east extending on the shore of the ocean" (Nansen, 1911, 190). Adam noted that his source was Svein Estridsson, King of Denmark, whose testimony—however fantastic it might seem to modern historians—was regarded as beyond reproach by his contemporaries. According to Svein, merchant voyages to the Wineland colony were frequent during the 11th century.

"Vinland" was mentioned as part of the first diocese of Bishop Jon of Ireland in 1053. Icelandic historian Ari the Learned (a.k.a., Are Frode) mentioned "Vinland" four times in his 1120-1130 account of Norse settlements—the <u>Islendingabok</u>. He noted that settlers in Greenland found stone implements and the remains of habitations that were similar to ruins in Vinland. Ari assumed that the tools once belonged to <u>skraelings</u> or natives (Holland, 1940, 62). Another explanation suggested by

Magnetic Greenland

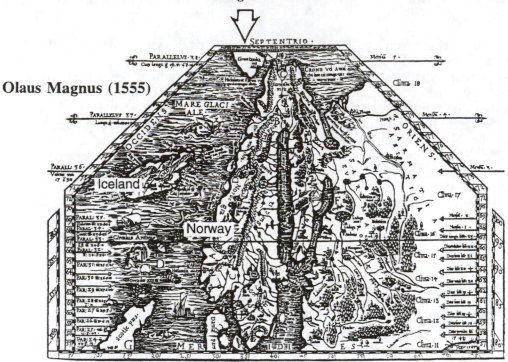

Olaus Magnus (1555)

source: Thorkild Hansen. *The Way to Hudson Bay.* New York: Harcourt, Brace, 1970.

Magnetic versus Geographic Greenland

A map by Olaus Magnus (variously dated between 1530 to 1555—above) shows Greenland Island north of Norway in the position it occupied on charts made using magnetic bearings. Martin Waldseemuller's 1513 map shows an alternative concept of Greenland. On this map, Greenland appears as a peninsula reaching out of the top of Europe and extending northwest of the British Isles. As this is the approximate geographic location of Greenland Island, we can assume that this map is based on geographic as opposed to magnetic coordinates. Directly west of England and Ireland is an unnamed land which was variously referred to as New Found Land (**NFL**) Baccalaos, Isle of Seven Cities, or Wineland.

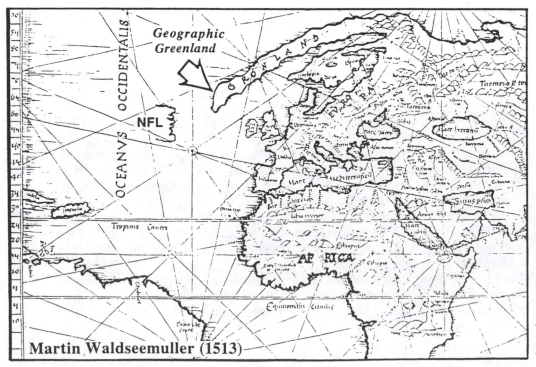

Geographic Greenland

Martin Waldseemuller (1513)

source: Nordenskiold (1889)

historian Ian Wilson (1991, 19) is that the pre-Norse Vinland ruins might have belonged to earlier Celts who once inhabited Greenland.

In 1112, Pope Paschal II appointed Erik Gnupsson bishop of Greenland in partibus infidelium—that is, Greenland and "adjacent territories." Holland believes this reference to "adjacent territories" confirms that Vinland was still occupied and not abandoned as isolationist historians have claimed (Holand, 1940, 75). Indeed, Ari Frode reported Bishop Gnupsson's 1112 AD voyage to visit "Wineland" in Libellus Islandorum (the Icelandic Annals) of 1121. Hauk Erlendsson's Landnamabok uses the spelling "Vind-land." French historian Ordericus Vitalis referred to "Wineland" in his Historia Ecclesiastica of 1120 (Skelton, 1965, 233). This comes only three years after Bishop Gnupsson's second voyage from Greenland to Vinland in 1117 AD—as reported on the 1440 Yale Vinland Map (Skelton, 1965). Considering that most Church archives were lost during fires in Iceland's cathedrals, it is reasonable to assume that only a few accounts of the bishop's travels have survived. Indeed, the Vinland visit of 1117 was unknown until publication of R.A. Skelton's 1965 report on Yale's Vinland Map.

Three Norse sagas, now widely regarded as oral historical accounts, were recorded in Iceland during the 12th and 13th centuries and preserved in Catholic monasteries. Two of the sagas mention "Wineland" as a region of the northeastern coast of a huge land extending far to the north, west, and south. In other words, this Wineland was situated along the coast of a continent. The Kristni-saga (1245) and the Heimskringla Saga (1250) casually mention that Wineland was discovered by Leif The Lucky. The Eyrbyggja-saga (1250) identifies "Wineland The Good" as a place where Norse merchants traded with and fought the native skraelings. Eric The Red's saga (1260) gives a detailed account of voyages to "Wineland." The "Wineland" colony was mentioned by name in the Icelandic choreography of Abbot Thing-eyrar in the 13th century.

In the Icelandic annals of 1285 it is written "fandz land vestr undan Islande"—that is, a new land has been found west of Iceland. The Annals identified the discoverers of this land as two priests—Adalbrand and Throvald. This marks the entry of Icelandic sailors into the arena of New World exploration previously dominated by voyagers from Greenland Island. German historian Gebhardi's Kongfriget Norges historie (1778) identified the new lands as Nyaland (New Land) and Duneyar: "A remarkableness in the lifetime of King Erik is the discovery of a new shoreline in northern America, which an Icelander, Rolf, was the first to discover in 1258" (Tornoe, 1965, 49).

The land in question is probably Newfoundland or one of many isles in the Gulf of St. Lawrence. These show up in later charts as the "Icelandic Isles" located in the Atlantic vaguely west or north of Iceland. An entry in Bishop Gissur Einarsson's journal (1548) says that the direction of sail to New Land or "Nyaland" is southwesterly from Iceland (Nansen, 1911, 285). Are Frode's Landnamabok also informed sailors that the new land was situated southwest of Iceland: Hafa vitrirmen sagt at sudvester skal til Nyaland undan Krysuvikur Bergi—"Well-informed men have said that the course from Cape Bergi to the Newland is southwest" (Tornoe, 1965, 48). This direction of sail from Iceland would take voyagers to North American territories somewhere between Newfoundland and Cape Cod. Norwegian King Eric organized an expedition to this new land under Landa-Rolf in 1289. This date probably marks a rising tide in Norse colonization of mainland south of the St.

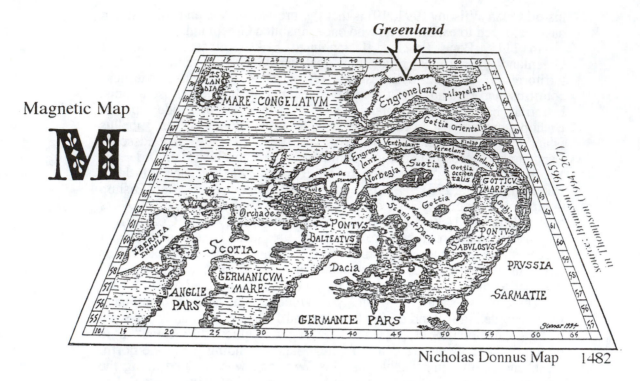

Magnetic Map

Greenland

source: Brauwers (1994, 267)
in Thompson (1965)

Nicholas Donnus Map   1482

North Atlantic Mapping Traditions—Magnetic vs. Geographic Maps

European maps based on Ptolemaic measurements were fairly accurate as far north as the Scandinavian territories. At this point, the curvature of Earth's surface combined with limited geographical data led to excessive distortion. Mapmakers used one of two traditions to plot the position of Greenland Island, Iceland, and other lands of the Northern Regions. The Magnetic method (top) placed Greenland directly north of Norway, because that was the direction sailors followed when using the magnetic compass. However, as early as 1350, celestial measurements taken at the southern tip of Greenland indicated that the land was actually situated west of Norway in the approximate position shown on the Geographical map of 1467. These traditions coexisted until the early 1500's.

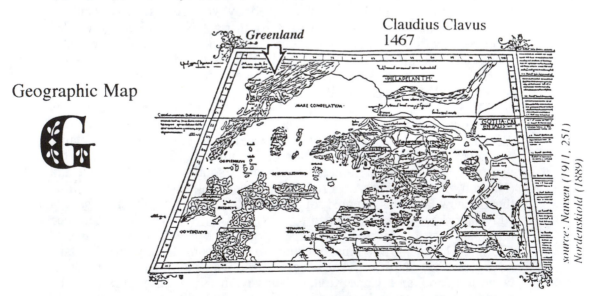

Claudius Clavus
1467

Greenland

Geographic Map

source: Nansen (1911, 251)
Nordenskiold (1889)

Lawrence Gulf. Due to the reliance on compass coordinates for travel and mapping, these newly settled territories were conceived of as being located in the Polar Regions north of Norway.

The Flateyjarbok (Gronlendinga saga) of the 14th century describes the 10th-century discovery of Greenland and "Wineland." A rhyming cosmography from England in 1385 placed "Veneland" (Vinland), Iceland, Greenland, Maydenland (Amazonia), Hakesland (fishland), and Friesland north of Europe. The French priest, Guillaume de Filastre, argued that the temperate climate of Greenland was sufficient evidence to confirm that it was situated south of Iceland (Ramsay, 1972, 195). Guillaume's 1427 treatise is most likely a reference to Norse colonies in the region of Nova Scotia—a region that European cartographers later identified as "Greenland Province." A Medieval Faroese fairy tale placed "Vinland" in the far west across the Atlantic.

The Icelandic Annals for 1347 reported that a Norse ship from Greenland which had been blown off course by foul weather had arrived with a cargo of lumber taken from the Markland forests (in Newfoundland or Nova Scotia). The importance of this event is that it confirms merchant contact between Greenland and Labrador at a time when the absence of any historical records of such activity might imply isolation of the Greenland settlements. On the contrary, incidents such as a lost ship reaching Iceland suggest that voyages to the East Coast for lumber were common; thus, other kinds of voyages to hunt, trade, or for purposes of migration must be regarded as probable—if not commonplace.

In 1350, the English monk Ranulf Higden wrote a geography called Polychronicon which included northern lands such as "Iceland" and "Wineland," and he produced a map showing "Wineland" north of Europe. His geography described "Wyntlandia" together with the Fortunate Isles as islands in the outer ocean. Many copies of Higden's map and geography circulated in the monasteries of Europe, so it is reasonable to conclude that most learned people were aware that Vinland existed and that it was situated somewhere north or northwest of Europe.

Two contemporary Icelandic geographies held that Wineland was an extension of Africa. Although historians have featured these accounts as examples of Norse geographical misconceptions, they may be regarded as exceptions rather than the rule. One example of this concept is the Catalan-Este map (ca. 1450) that has a new-world continent attached to the tip of South Africa. The western extremity of this continent represents Vinland; the eastern extremity represents Brasil—in this case spelled "Basera." This map comes only ten years after the Yale Vinland map and probably reflects a Franciscan concept that Vinland included tropical lands south of the equator. In other words, Franciscan geographers regarded Vinland as the equivalent to what modern geographers identify as North and South America combined.

King Magnus Eiriksson dispatched a search party to Greenland in 1355 under the command of Paul Knutson. The expedition traveled to lands then regarded as part of Greenland Province—a Norse territory which encompassed large areas of North America from the Gulf of St. Lawrence to Christian's (later Hudson's) Bay. Several guards in the Knutson party may have died in Minnesota in 1362. A runic memorial with that date was found in 1898 near Kensington, Minnesota. This rune stone bears an epitaph to Swedes (Goths) and Norwegians who died in battle during an exploratory venture "west from Vinland." Although once called a fraud, the Kensington inscription has been vindicated following

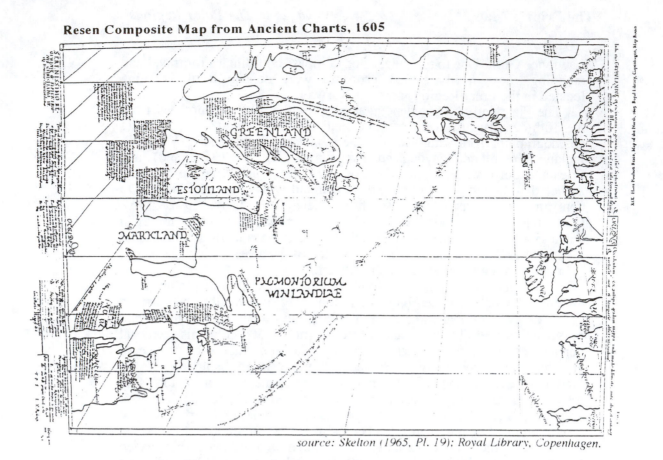

source: Skelton (1965, Pl. 19); Royal Library, Copenhagen.

Geographic Saga Maps: Danish & Hungarian

Bishop Hans Resen (a.k.a., Christian Fresio) compiled a chart from maps that he called "many centuries old" in 1605. Norse archeologist Helge Ingstad (1965) found a similar map by an anonymous Hungarian cartographer. The map was one page of an atlas of sea charts in the state library at Tyrnavia. As was the case with Yale's Vinland map of 1440, this map shows Greenland as an island.

Hungarian Vinland Map, 1599

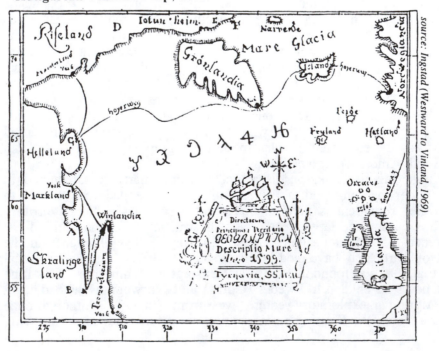

source: Ingstad (Westward to Vinland, 1969)

the most exhaustive examination by America's leading runeologist—Richard Nielsen (1994). The return date of the expedition is presumed to be about 1364, although there are no historical documents to verify this speculative conclusion (Holand, 1940, 143). Eva Taylor reported a passage in Mercator's Cosmographic implying that only eight men from the expedition returned to Bergen (Holand, 1959).

By the mid-14th century, Norse settlements had spread far into North America. The French writer Philippe de Mezieres (1327-1405) recorded a letter from Norse King Peter of Cyprus concerning the vast Norwegian territories in the Northern Regions. According to a passage in Mezieres' Songe du Vieil Pelerin (1369): "The king of Norway had an enormous realm. Parts of his domain were in the ocean so far from Norway and beyond Godeland that his emissaries sent on ships to collect taxes from his subjects required three years to complete their rounds and return home again" (Gibson, 1974, 179; Nielsen, 1994, 3). "Godeland" is probably a reference to Vinland det Gode on the East Coast near Nova Scotia.

The Historia Norvegiae and the Rymbegla both describe inhabited lands to the north of Norway beyond the North Sea and beneath the pole star—i.e., at the North Pole (Nansen, 1911, 263). These were the lands which Norse kings claimed as part of their extended overseas realm. Two 14th-century Icelandic manuscripts, one by Abbot Nikulas Bergsson, recorded the "modern" geographical conception of Norse territories in the North Atlantic (Nansen, 1911, 237). These lands followed the traditional sequence of the sagas but recognized that Markland and then "Vinland hit Goda" were situated south of Greenland—whereas the earlier concept placed Wineland near the North Pole. It is evident that some unknown geographer—perhaps the English friar Nicholas of Lynn—had begun to influence archaic beliefs about the location of Norse territories. This change was reflected in the earliest map of the region in the 14th century.

Continental land northwest of Norway bears dual titles "Norveca" and "Europa" on the Venetian Commercial Map of 1414. Other geographers called the extended territory "Greenland Province"—a title that appears on a map by Danish cartographer Claudius Clavus Swart in 1427. The Dane claims to have visited Greenland sometime between 1412 and 1423:

> The peninsula of the island of Greenland stretches down from land on the north which is inaccessible or unknown on account of ice. Nevertheless, as I have seen, the infidel Karelians daily come to Greenland in great armies, and that, without doubt, from the other side of the North Pole. (Nancy Ms. in Nansen, 1911)

If Clavus saw "Karelians" (Skraelings), he was probably near "Skraelingeland"—or Labrador—and not on the Island of Greenland. "Skraelings" was a term that usually referred to the native inhabitants living near the St. Lawrence Gulf; the "North Pole" he refers to was most likely in the vicinity of Hudson Bay—where it is conceivable that Claudius might have encountered "great armies" of natives.

An anonymous letter to Pope Nicholas V in 1450 mentions "the forests of Gronolonde" (Nansen, 1911, 270). Since there are no forests on Greenland Island, it can be inferred that the author of the letter is writing about conditions on the East Coast of North America in a region that in earlier years might have been referred to as "Markland" (i.e., forest land). "Vinlandia" is mentioned in a Lubeck manuscript of 1486 as an island reaching as far as Livonia—northern Russia (Nansen, 1911, 32; Nordenskiold, 1889, 3).

source: Thompson (1994); Herrmann (1954); Nansen (1911, 34) originally in Torfaeus (1706)

B   = Baffin Land
D   = Davis Strait
E   = Oster Bygd (Eastern Settlement)
GP = Ginnungagap
L   = Labrador
W   = Wester Bygd (Western Settlement)

Joint Headlands: Gronlandia—Baffin Land

The combined northern territories of Greenland and Baffin Island are shown in a map by Jon Gudmundsson (circa 1600). A nearly identical map which Erlend Thordsen copied from an earlier chart was brought to the Staden monastery in 1568. The tip of Greenland is marked on this map by a long inlet reaching northwest from Frisland and below the Arctic Circle. This inlet corresponds to Davis Strait which separates Greenland from Baffin Island. The northern section of the strait is frozen in winter—thus the perception that Baffin Land and Greenland were joined together. On the southwestern coast is the name "Wester-Bygd" which is the name of the Western Settlement of Old Greenland. Traditions and archeological remains confirm that this settlement was originally located on Davis Strait north of Oster-Bygd (the Eastern Settlement). It is possible that the name has been misplaced on this map; alternatively, people of the Western Settlement could have migrated farther west to the far side of Baffin Island and facing Ginnungagap or Hudson Strait. Such a move would explain why Ivar Bardeson mentioned the "twelve days journey by sail" needed to reach the Western Settlement by sailors from the Eastern Settlement. Had they merely been sailing up the west coast of Greenland, the journey would only have taken a couple of days.

English Voyages

Ever since the days of the legendary King Arthur, fabled lands to the west attracted English seamen. Most came to fish along the Grand Banks of Newfoundland; some came as pirates to prey upon Greenland's settlements; and others came to explore and enjoy nature's wonders. Voyages of fishermen and traders were largely unrecorded—unless they came across English or Norse coast-guard vessels sent on patrol for tax evaders.

Sometime in the 12th century, one hundred monks from the Breton monastery of St. Matthew sailed westward to discover Elysium in the Atlantic (Fingerhut, 1994, 56). What became of their mission is unknown. They were among the many explorers, merchants, and immigrants who rarely warrant mention in the chronicles of their day, yet their passing from one land to another transfers knowledge, culture, and the fruits of the earth across the oceans.

By some accounts, English knight Sir John Mandeville almost circumnavigated Earth after sailing east to China and west to northern Canada in 1320 (Hakluyt, 1582). Danish cartographer Claudius Clavus confirmed the knight's travels in the Nancy Manuscript (1427) saying that Mandeville had sailed from the "Indian Seres"—that is, the East Coast of North America—across the Atlantic to Norway (Nansen, 1911). By Mandeville's own account, he had traveled to Cathay via the Middle East. There is no evidence that he crossed the Pacific Ocean, thus romantic claims by his contemporaries that he circumnavigated Earth probably resulted from the erroneous belief that the "Indian Seres" which was thought to lie across the Atlantic was adjacent to Cathay. However, the knight made no such claim though he reported knowledge of an Englishman of Norse ancestry who had gone all the way around the globe—presumably across the "northern regions."

Orthodox historians call the Mandeville story a fraud—citing numerous similarities to other literary accounts of the age. He is generally presumed to be a French plagiarist, Jean de Bourgogne, or an Englishman named John Burgoyne (Fiske, 1920, Vol. I, 290). In spite of doubts raised by modern historians, the knight had a respectable following in the 16th century; nor was he regarded as any more eccentric than the "fabulous" Marco Polo—who has since been exonerated.

During the mid-16th century, European kings argued over who had bona fide access to New World territories. Papal bulls in 1484 and 1493 (the Inter caetera) awarded control of the Atlantic first to the Portuguese and then to Spanish authorities. Popes wisely left the door open for other monarchs who could prove that their subjects had prior settlements across the Atlantic. Queen Elizabeth assigned her personal advocate, John Dee, the task of defending England's claim to New World territories, and it is in Dee's manuscripts that we find the earliest credible references to ancient voyagers from England.

Advocate Dee compiled summaries of ancient trans-Atlantic voyages in his Great And Rich Discoveries (1580-1583) which still survives though in badly mutilated condition. Among his sources, Dee mentions a 16th-century version of Gestae Arthuri—or "The Legends of Arthur." He also tells the tale of a Catholic priest who was presumably a descendant of Arthur's 6th-century colony on the east coast of North America; he provided a summary of the Inventio Fortunatae which was compiled by the English friar, Nicholas; and he gave and a translation of Ramusio's Viaggi (Number 7) which reported the tale of a Venetian—Nicolo Zeno.

Modern historians have assumed that most of these sources are either fabulous or irrelevant, however Dee regarded them as credible, and he built a case upon the fact that information from widely different sources provided cross-confirmation of their content.   Most of Dee's contemporaries also regarded the sources as fairly accurate—although the argument has been advanced that they were biased towards the English cause.   The Gestae Arthuri and the Inventio have been lost, so it is difficult to gauge their level of accuracy.

According to Gerhard Kramer (Mercator), the Gestae Arthuri told of the king's voyage to Scotland and Iceland in 530 AD before heading far to the north.   He left settlers on an island called "Grocland" (or Great Land—as in a huge island or continent).   This island was located near the edge of the surrounding ocean where indrawing seas streamed towards the North Pole.   Numerous 16th-century maps have a large island (Grotland or Grocland) located in the Arctic regions west of Greenland Island—so it can be assumed that most people thought of Arthur's colony as a northern isle near the North Pole and beyond Greenland. Of course, there is no habitable land in that area.   Baffin Island or Labrador are plausible locations—given that "northern regions" or "polar regions" in Medieval manuscripts typically referred to lands west rather than north. According to the Gestae, Arthur sent a second fleet of 12 ships with 2,200 men and women into the northern regions the following year.   Five ships are said to have been lost in a storm; the remainder reached their destination. Was this land later known as the northern "Albania?"

Iceland was a common destination for English merchants and fishermen during the 14th century as Hakluyt points out in Principal Voyages (1599, 101).   Edward III had a special contract with fishermen from Blakeney in Norfolk to service Icelandic markets.   In this regard, it should be kept in mind that what we regard as Iceland—a large isle in the mid-North Atlantic—was not necessarily synonymous with what 14th-century English sailors called "Iceland."   The Catalan mappamond from Florence (ca. 1350) identifies seven islands in the northwest Atlantic as "Icelands" in addition to the usual island of that same name north of England. The Modena compass chart (circa 1350) has eight "Icelands" in the northwestern Atlantic region.   These Icelandic isles probably correspond to the Newfoundland archipelago of the Gulf of St. Lawrence. It is apparent from these maps that royal charters allowing sailors access to Iceland may have concealed actual North American destinations.

Historian Arthur Newton (1932, 205) notes that as early as the reign of Edward III (1327-1377), English merchants had free access to the dominions of the Norse king.   That is, they had free access as long as they avoided their primary rivals—the Hanseatic merchants from Lubeck, Novgorod, Bergen, and assorted enclaves in England at King's Lynn and at London's "Steelyard."   Merchants from Lynn, England, who were trading in Norwegian ports were assaulted by Hanse merchants in 1394 as part of an increasingly hostile trade war.   English King Henry IV was asked to intercede on their behalf.

During the 15th century, English trade was often held hostage to political and economic conflicts in Scandinavia. There had been a long-standing Norse monopoly on trade with Greenland (North America), and this was extended to Iceland at various times. Presumably, ships heading west were required to register at Bergen, however as English historian G.J. Marcus (1981, 140) points out, both English and Danish kings issued licenses for special ships that were exempted from the monopoly.

King Eirik issued such a license to an English merchant vessel in 1413, and King Henry V authorized five special voyages in 1414. In 1429, the king of Denmark issued an edict prohibiting the Icelandic voyage, and this was confirmed by an act of the English parliament the following year. Even so, kings of England and Norway granted at least forty licenses for voyages between England and Iceland during the next 14 years. Marcus (1981, 140) notes that numerous merchants risked the voyage without the appropriate documents because of the great profits that were expected:

> Judging from the numerous cases of arrest, forfeiture of ship and cargo, imprisonment, etc., that we meet with in the national archives during the next decade or so, there must have been many who determined to dispense with the formality of a license, and to follow the more economical, if riskier, course of sailing direct to Iceland. At any rate, by 1436, many English ships were unable to get a cargo and had to return home with empty holds.

In 1431, the Danish king complained to his English counterpart that illegal traffic with Iceland, Greenland, and "other isles" had reached such an extent that it had severely impinged upon Denmark's tax revenues. England and Denmark established a treaty in 1432 to stop the illegal trade, however clandestine voyages seem to have continued unabated. Historian Marcus cites numerous ships whose cargoes and profits were confiscated over the next thirty years because they violated the ban. Several ships whose manifests were described in port records (such as the *George* and *Trinity* in 1481) are known to have carried supplies suitable for fish processing. Marcus infers that the vessels sailed to the Newfoundland fisheries—thereby circumventing both taxation and the added costs of purchasing processed cod from Icelandic merchants.

English historian Arthur Newton (<u>Great Age of Discovery</u>, 1938, 206) noted that sailing restrictions in the North Atlantic were more a formality than they were an effective barrier to commerce:

> It is perhaps more pertinent to note that restrictions on the movements of English merchants to Iceland, Helgoland and Finmark appear only to have been enforced in the 15th century, which becomes therefore a period of fading English knowledge of the North. Nor is it to be forgotten that restrictions upon fishermen, as opposed to merchants, are almost impossible to carry into effect, and the whale fisheries of Greenland, described in Ivar Bardsen's 14th-century narrative, may have attracted Englishmen thither.

Vinland Maps

Contrary to what most orthodox historians believe, the Norse American colony of Wineland is mentioned quite frequently on Medieval and early Renaissance maps confirming that it was well-known during the 15th century. Sometimes variations of the name are used such as "Winlandia," "Vinland," "Winiland," and "Venthelant." Vinland is shown as an island with a castle northwest of Europe on two versions of the Rudimentium Novitorium published in Germany during the 1470's and 1480's. In the earliest version from Lubeck (ca. 1475), the name is spelled "Winlad." Another version by Hans Rust (ca. 1480) was published at Augsburg. On Rust's map, the spelling of the isle northwest of Europe is "Vinlad" (Nordenskiold, 1889). Although some orthodox historians have posited that "Winlad" on the Lubeck map is a

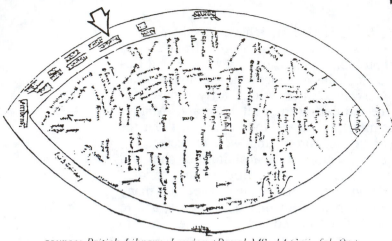

Svinlandia

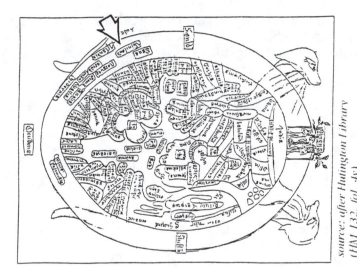

Winiland (Wineland)

Widland (Vindland)

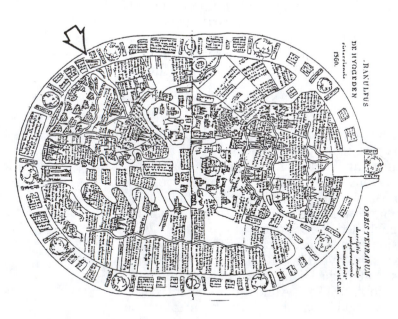

Vinland Maps from *Polychronicon* Ranulf Higden, 1350 AD

These elliptical or ark-shaped world maps are of schematic and cosmological design. They were used to illustrate Latin manuscript copies of Higden's geography—*Polychronicon*. They typically have 10 isles northwest of Europe. The second or third isle from the top (north) is called "Svinlandia," "Winiland," "Wineland," or "Widland" in reference to a land of grape vines. None of the 21 copies of this map known to geographers is spelled with an "F" at the beginning so there is no indication that the isle was confused with Finland. Furthermore, the placement and spelling are consistent with Vinilanda Insula on Yale's Vinland Map of 1440.

"misspelling" for Finland, the spelling on the Augsburg map—in which a "V" is clearly used—confirms that cartographers intended for the isle to represent the Norse colony of Vinland.

Vinland was also mentioned in perhaps hundreds of manuscript copies of a geographical treatise—the <u>Polychronicon</u>—by the 14th-century English monk, Ranulf Higden. Most of these manuscripts also included copies of Higden's schematic world map. His ark-shaped map (from the Huntington Library) shows ten "isles" northwest of Europe including "Winiland" and a vague notation that looks like "Thule" dribbling off the edge of the North Atlantic. Of course, Winiland is a clear reference to the Nordic Vinland colony. "Win" is the Old English term for grape wine; and "Vin-land" or "wine-land" was Leif Ericson's designation for the Nordic American colony that he pioneered circa 1000 AD.

Higden's map is of importance for several reasons. First, it is of <u>bona fide</u> pre-Columbian vintage. The dating of this map is universally accepted by historians, although few have acknowledged that Vinland was among the islands portrayed northwest of Europe. Secondly, Higden was one of the most prolific authors of his time. This popular Medieval reference book was duplicated by numerous scribes and translated from Latin into English by 1482. Over 100 manuscript copies of the text are known to exist—attesting to its common availability throughout Europe. Twenty-one manuscript copies of the world map have survived in public archives; others are sequestered in private collections. The maps use several variations of the name for Vinland, including "Winiland," "Widlad" (or Vindland), "Svinlandia," "Wyndlond," and "Wineland." These variations resulted from the personal styles of different monks who produced manuscript copies. Since Columbus was a frequent visitor to monastic libraries, it very likely that he was familiar with <u>Polychronicon</u> and knew of the northern isle of Vinland. A third reason why Higden's maps are important is the unusual spelling of "Win-i-land." This spelling is consistent with "Vin-i-landa" found on Yale's Vinland Map—providing further confirmation of authenticity for the Yale map because forgers could not have predicted this peculiar, 14th-century spelling.

An archaic Danish or Dutch designation for Viniland—spelled "Venth-e-land"—endured on European maps of the 15th century by the cartographer Donnus Nicolaus Germanus. His 1457 map (presumed to be a copy of a map by Claudius Clavus) showed Venthelant as a region beyond Engronelant (Greenland). Numerous versions of this map were produced as late as 1525. Thus, Vinland (or some variation of the name for Leif Ericson's colony) persists on maps from 1350 to 1525. Some of these maps even include the eastern Scandinavian territory of Finland—putting the kibosh to isolationist theories that Vinland on Medieval maps was simply a "misspelling" for Finland.

Historian James Fiske (1920, Vol. I, 209) notes that: "There is a passage in Ordericus Vitalis (<u>Historia Ecclesiastica</u>, 1140, Vol. 4, 29) in which Finland and the Orkneys, along with Greenland and Iceland, are loosely described as forming part of the dominions of the kings of Norway. This <u>Finland</u> does not appear to refer to the country of the Finns, east of the Baltic, and it has been supposed that it may have been meant for Vinland." Fiske says that during the 17th century, Scandinavian scholars read Adam of Bremen's accounts of a Vinland (or Wineland) near the Arctic Circle and assumed that Adam must have been referring to Finland because they were not familiar with sagas of a Vinland in North America. In 1689, the Swedish writer Ole Rudbeck

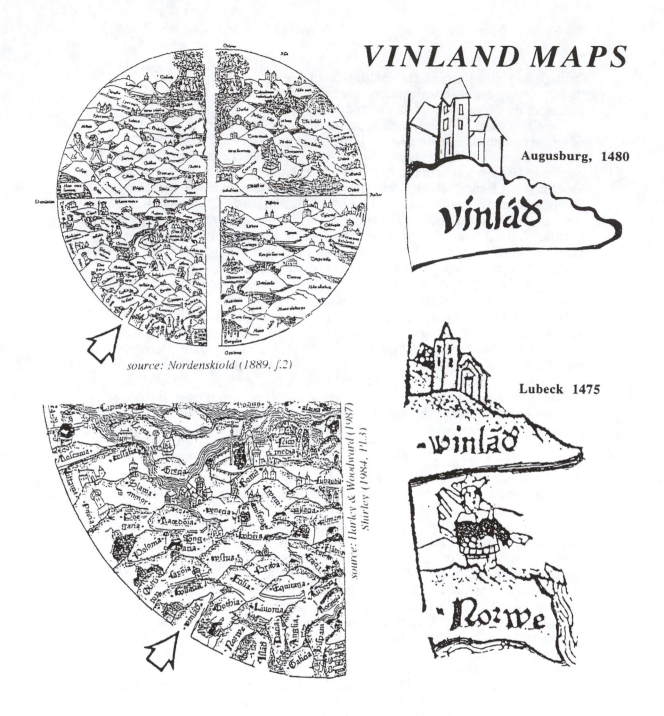

source: Nordenskiold (1889, f.2)

Augusburg, 1480

Lubeck 1475

source: Harley & Woodward (1987)
Shirley (1984, Pl.3)

The Rudimentium Novitiorum, Lubeck 1475 & Hans Rust, Augsburg, ca. 1480

At least two versions of a map in the anonymous Lubeck geography called *Rudimentium Novitiorum* show the Norse colony of Vinland northwest of Europe on an island that extends into the Atlantic Ocean. The two spellings (Vinl'ad, and Winl'ad) are variations of Vinland. Historians and geographers have claimed that "Winlad" on the Lubeck map is a misspelling for "Finland." However, the spelling is consistent with contemporaneous historical and geographical references to Wineland and Vinland as well as the Higden maps which consistently use "W" or "V" for Wineland. Furthermore, as the later Augusburg map distinctly has the spelling "Vinland" (where the ' represents "n"), we can be certain that use of a "V" for Vinland was not a mistake. Such maps confirm that Vinland was a well-known location to 15th-century Europeans as thousands of copies of the Lubeck map were printed.

could not understand Adam of Bremen's allusion to Vinland, so he assumed that Adam was referring to Finland. Thus Rudbeck's writings and those of his contemporary, Sturleson, mistakenly use "Finland" in place of "Vinland" (Fiske, 1920, Vol. I, 387).

Later historians continued the error of earlier writers, thus the assumption that maps referring to Vinland were misspellings for "Finland" became something of a tradition in the history of cartography. Fiske (1920, Vol. I, 387) believed that: "The absence of any reference to Vinland in the Zeno narrative is an indication that the memory of it had faded away before 1400, and it was not distinctly and generally revived until the time of Torfaeus in 1705." Likewise, historian Joseph Fisher (1903, 80) assumed that 15th-century cartographers omitted Norse colonies in North America because the colonies had been abandoned. Apparently, neither Fiske nor Fisher—nor most modern historians for that matter—bothered to examine the evidence of cartography to any great depth. Actually, there are numerous references to Vinland in historical accounts and maps—although most writers assumed that the legendary wine country was situated <u>north</u> of Norway in the mythical realm of Hyperborea.

Several 16th-century and 17th-century copies of ancient Vinland maps are on deposit in Icelandic and Danish archives. Most historians regard these copies as "vain attempts" to defraud Columbus of his rightful glory as Discoverer of America. The result is that important historical documents have been ignored by the academic community.

The most commonly known Nordic map is a 17th-century copy of Sigurdur Stefansson's 1570 (or 1590) sea card. It shows the approximate sea route between Bergen, Iceland, Engroneland (Greenland), Helluland (Baffin Island), Markland (southern Labrador), the St. Lawrence Valley (Skraelinge Land), and <u>Promontorium Winlandia</u>—the gateway to Vinland. Most scholars of Norse exploration have identified the "promontorium" as the long peninsula on the northeast side of Newfoundland. Helluland—literally "flat-rock land"—was derived from the Norse image of hell as a frozen waste of rock and ice. This term seems to have applied equally to northern Labrador which on some maps has the designation "Estotilant" (possibly a variant of Escotiland—i.e., Scotland). Historians generally believe that the date on Stefansson's map is a later copyist's error for 1590—since it is commonly thought that he was only a teenager at that time. However, a second version of Stefansson's map also has the 1570 date suggesting that it was not an accident (Nansen, 1911, 7; Storm, 1887, 28; after Torfaeus, 1706).

Another version of the basic Vinland sea card surfaced in Hungarian archives bearing runic inscriptions and a copy date of 1599. Major ports along the way between Bergen and Winelandia are called "Yorks"—an Old Germanic word for port. This map is significant for several reasons: first, it demonstrates that copies of the Vinland sea card were commonplace throughout northern Europe; second, it suggests that the overseas destination had become an international attraction—not just a Norwegian possession; and third) Engroneland or Greenland is shown as an island with numerous fjords—which is a fairly accurate portrayal of the actual geography. This is of importance because one of the major objections which orthodox scholars raised against the authenticity of another Vinland map in the possession of Yale University was that Yale's map showed Greenland as an island with fjords.

Danish Bishop Hans Resen incorporated numerous copies of ancient charts into a North Atlantic territorial map produced in 1605. His map includes land areas that are similar to those in Stefansson's map along with notations showing subsequent French and Portuguese discoveries. A notation on Resen's map informs us that it was based on charts "several centuries old." In other words, Resen claimed that some of his original charts dated from the period 1200 to 1500 AD—establishing a pre-Columbian pedigree for the Norse sea card. Orthodox historians cried "foul." Since Resen's composite map was not produced until 1605, it was conceivable that Resen—a Protestant—was part of a conspiracy to defraud Columbus—a Catholic—of his rightful glory as discoverer of America.

It was not until 1965 that Yale University acquired a map of North Atlantic territories from an earlier age—circa 1440. The map's author was thought to be an anonymous Franciscan living in Switzerland. If authentic, this map would provide evidence that 15th-century mariners were familiar with the location of the ancient Norse colony in North America. Presumably, such knowledge might have influenced subsequent New World voyages; while Norwegians might claim that their ancestors preceded Columbus. A legend on the map relates that Greenland's Bishop Eric visited Vinilanda in 1117 AD. This the earliest historical reference of a Catholic prelate visiting America; it also suggests that Vinland—the region between the St. Lawrence Gulf and New York—was occupied by European colonists. Contrary to orthodox claims that Norse explorers had been chased out of North America by native skraelings, it would substantiate theories that settlers from Greenland continued to prosper in the New World.

An outspoken champion of orthodox history, Nigel Davies (1986, 232) claims that tales of Wineland and of Norse voyages did not survive into the mid-15th century at which time they might have influenced the Columbus voyage. Accordingly, Davies says that they were virtually irrelevant to the unfolding course of history. In order to sustain that belief, he embraced theories that Yale's Vinland Map was a fraud.

The argument against authenticity for Yale's Vinland map stemmed from the identification of microscopic traces of the chemical anitase which McCrone & Associates found on the map in 1974. According to Walter McCrone (1988, 1009), the chemical was not developed until the 1920's in German research laboratories. McCrone also noted a yellow stain alongside the borders of continents on the map; he believed these were evidence of secondary outlines which the presumed forger used in an attempt to mimic the fading and separation of ancient inks. Based on this assessment, McCrone branded the document a "plain forgery."

Orthodox historians attacked Yale's sponsors of the Vinland map with exceptional vehemence—perhaps out of disgust that competent scholars had dared to approve such heretical material. Samuel Morison—famed Columbus biographer led the charge with his declaration that the forger had erred by showing Greenland as an island: "Note that Greenland is an island. It was never so depicted on any map prior to 1650, but as a peninsula of Asia" (Morison, 1971, 69). This so-called "error" was also the leading complaint of Eva Taylor:

> The most forthright condemnation came from one of England's leading cartographists, the late Professor Eva Taylor. Her rejection of the Map rested largely on the depiction of Greenland, which was drawn as an island—a fact which no one could possibly have

known before it was established by explorations late in the 19th century; in addition, Greenland was drawn with such accuracy that Professor Taylor had no hesitation in saying that it had simply been traced from a modern school atlas. (Magnusson, 1980, 237)

Far from being conclusive "proof" of forgery, complaints raised by Samuel Morison, Eva Taylor and Walter McCrone are best considered in a broader context of evidence. Yale's "Vinland Map" has been the subject of unprecedented scientific examination including chemical analysis, proton-beam scans, and numerous scholarly studies. Presently, the weight of evidence favors authenticity: researchers Tom Cahill and Dick Schwab (1987) at the Crocker Nuclear Laboratory (University of California—Davis) found that the map produced a proton reflection pattern that was similar to authentic 15th-century documents such as the Gutenberg Bible. There was neither more nor less anatase than was present in ancient specimens: ergo, the chemical was found in nature.

Unfortunately for the cause of historical orthodoxy, there exist numerous pre-19th century maps that portray Greenland as an island; there are also historical texts that tell of Greenland as an Arctic isle. Adam of Bremen in his Descriptio Insularum Aquilonis (1076) was convinced that Greenland was an island located either west or north of Norway. "Adam's idea of oceanic insulation was accepted in many quarters, as the maps disclose" (Babcock, 1922, 95). Greenland was portrayed as a separate island with bays on the Andrea Bianco map of 1436. This comes four years prior to the presumed date of Yale's Vinland map. The Laon globe of 1493 also portrays Gro'landia (Greenland) as an island.

Many 16th-century cartographers also shared the conviction that the Arctic Greenland was an island. Oronce Fine's 1534 map has Greenland as an island (Portinaro & Knirsch, 1987, Pl. XV). The Ortelius map of 1564 has Greenland as an island. Paulo Forlani's 1565 map has Greenland as an island next to the North Pole which follows somewhat the position on Behaim's globe (in Portinaro & Knirsch, 1987, p. 95). Andre Thevet's 1575 map has Greenland or "Groenlant" as a separate island (Weiss, 1884). Greenland appears as an island on Ortelius map of 1570. Michael Lok's map of 1582 has Greenland as an island. Humphrey Gilbert's 1585 map has Greenland as an island near the North Pole. A map by Cornelius Judaeus in 1593 shows Greenland as an island. It is similarly shown as an island on the "Orbis Terrae" by Peter Plancius in 1596 (Portinaro & Knirsch, 1987, Pl. LVII). Theodore DeBry's map of 1599 shows Greenland as an Arctic island as does the Hungarian Vinland map of 1599 (mentioned above). Clearly, a substantial number of cartographers regarded Greenland as an island prior to the 19th century. Thus, we can readily see that the principle argument advanced by Taylor and Morison regarding the supposedly fraudulent nature of the Yale Vinland map is simply wrong.

The "forger's trick" that chemist Walter McCrone pointed out in his examination of Yale's Vinland Map has an alternative explanation: among map copyists, it is a common practice to do a preliminary tracing using a lighter color or stain. If a mistake is made at this stage in the process of making a map, it can be corrected much more easily than if a dark ink had been used from the outset.

A unique linguistic feature on Yale's map also favors authenticity. Use of the archaic Danish version of "Vin-i-landa" on the map instead of the common Vin-land or Wineland is about as close to fool-proof evidence

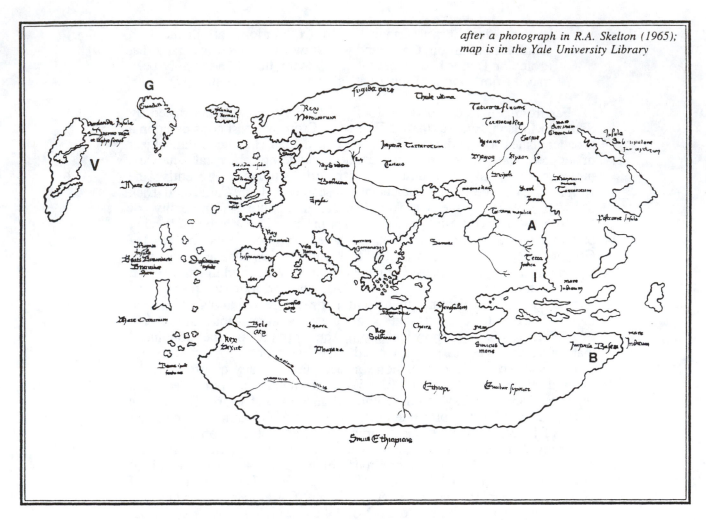

after a photograph in R.A. Skelton (1965);
map is in the Yale University Library

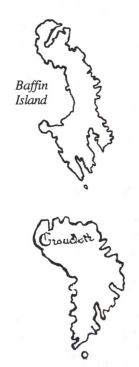

Baffin Island

Yale's "Vinland Map" of 1440 A D

This anonymous map by a Swiss Franciscan has been the focus of heated debate because of claims that it confirms European knowledge of Norse discoveries in the western Atlantic. Originally described by R.A. Skelton (1965) as an illustration for friar John of Plano Carpini's mission to the Tartars, it fell under the specter of academic doubt when a modern chemist found what he thought was a 20th-century synthetic compound of titanium dioxide or "anatase" in inks used on the map. Now, scientists say that the substance occurs naturally—so the latest ruling after proton beam scans at the University of California (Davis) holds that the document is authentic.

This map is famous for showing the Norse colony of "Vinilanda Insula" (**V**) or Wineland as an isle west of Europe. The spelling of Vin-i-landa is a peculiar Danish version that was current only during the 15th century. Some scholars believed that the insular portrayal of Greenland (**G**) was evidence of fraud as Greenland was most commonly regarded as a peninsula of Europe during the early Renaissance. On the other hand, earlier historians identified it as one of the islands in the Atlantic, and the shape of the isle—with two bays on the east coast and the top half bending westward— is more in accord with the shape of Baffin Island. Indeed, Baffin Island was sometimes known as "Greenland" or "Groetland;" and it is situated far enough south to enable easy circumnavigation. The truncated coast of Asia (**A**) is indeed peculiar: it shows a southeastern peninsula (**I**) representing "India Terza"—the third India. This seems strange because the other two Indias which should appear in central Asia have been eliminated as a result of the shortening of Asia. The offshore isles to the east represent Sakhalin, Japan, and the Philippines. "Imperia Basera" (**B**) to the south of India Terza is in accord with Andre Bianco's 1436 identification of Brazil as "Basera." On Giovanni Leardo's map of 1442, the same region is called "Balsera."

as can be that the document is authentic. At the time the map was produced, circa 1440, the Wineland region of the western continent (North America) was under Danish sovereignty. On most 15th-century Danish maps of the north, Vinland is typically situated directly north of Norway on the Scandinavian peninsula where it is called "Venth-e-lant"— which was the archaic Danish version of Vinland. This archaic spelling and location of Vinland is commonplace on maps by Donnus Nikolaus Germanus circa 1482. Vinland was placed north of Norway because the map was plotted using magnetic coordinates: compass bearings from Bergen to Greenland and North America in the 15th century indicated that these lands were due north. It is unlikely that a 20th-century forger would have used the spelling "Vin-i-land" instead of the common form— Vinland. Indeed, most modern-day historians are still unaware of the Danish variant; and it is not unusual for orthodox historians to misspell the name from the Yale Vinland map as "Vin-land"—leaving out the extra "i." Presumably, this is done in hopes of not confusing readers. As it turns out, these helpful historians are the ones who are confused.

Yale's map has another striking peculiarity that a modern forger would not have conceived: the coast of Asia is truncated and has a peculiar peninsula projecting out from the southeast corner. On later, 15th-century maps, this peninsula has been identified as "the horn of Asia." In the published account of a scholarly review of the map, R.A. Skelton (1965, 120) commented on the peculiar shape of the Asian coast and the absurd inland sea—"The Sea of Tartaria"—that was created as a result. Skelton noted that: "the eastern coast of the mainland fringing the Sea of the Tartars has no counterpart in any known cartographic document." This unprecedented coastline is hardly the kind of invention a forger would concoct if he expected his map to pass as authentic.

The coastline that so puzzled Skelton and his associates is one of the earliest representations of the North American coastline; the peninsula or "horn" represents Florida (as will be demonstrated in later chapters). As far as we know, this so-called "horn" actually occurs for the first time on the Venetian Map of 1414 which was derived from an earlier Franciscan gazetteer or map of the North Atlantic. Far from being a "peculiarity," Yale's Map is actually a plausible representation of the evolving knowledge of American shores as they were known among Franciscans during the 15th century. And it occurs within the historic context of more than eight related maps having similar features.

Discovery of so many Vinland maps during our search of map archives came as a shocking revelation, because the cornerstone of orthodox history has always been an assumption that Nordic-American colonies were "never mentioned" on ancient maps. Historians often reiterate a truism that "if Nordic colonies in the New World had been important, then they would have been mentioned on Medieval maps." Here we encounter a classical example of circular reasoning and self-fulfilling prophesy. Historians failed to distinguish between their assumption and reality. The assumption that Nordic colonies weren't mentioned on Medieval maps dissuaded them from bothering to check ancient sources in order to verify the accuracy of their theories Meanwhile, they summarily dismissed as "unimportant" historical accounts of Nordic voyages to Vinland which were reported in Icelandic, Danish, and Vatican archives.

The mistaken assumption also led to <u>a priori</u> determinations that runestones, ancient fortresses, house foundations, iron-smelting furnaces,

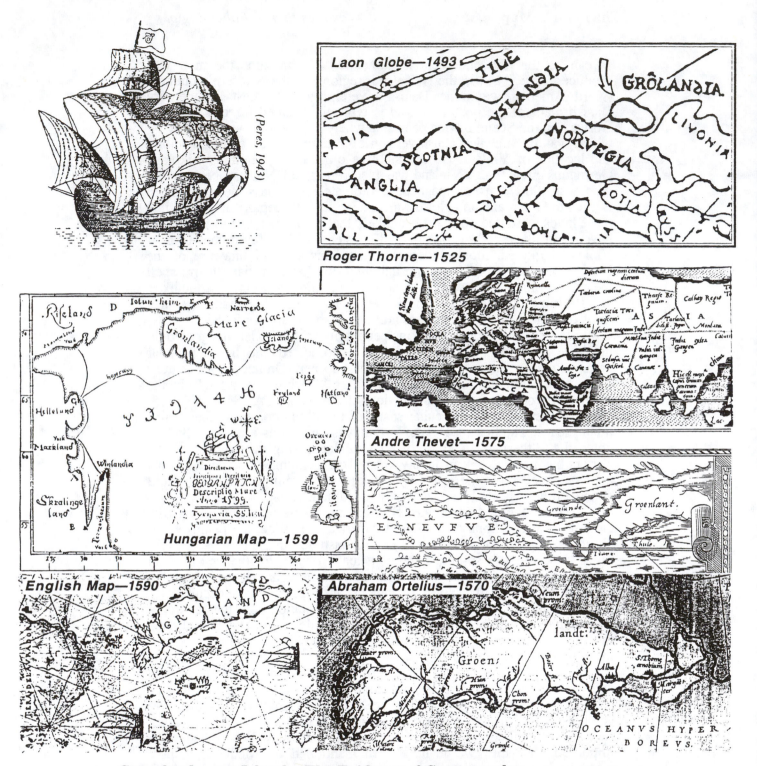

Greenland as an Island—The Evidence of Cartography

Some Medieval cartographers held that Greenland was a long peninsula reaching out of Europe or that it was part of continental Europe via land and ice in the north. This view conformed to biblical doctrine that there were only three continents and these were all connected in a way that enabled the animals and children of Noah to inhabit the globe. Another view held that Greenland was an island. This viewpoint was reflected in the portrayal of Greenland in Yale's "Vinland Map." Samuel Morison and Eva Taylor voiced the popular criticism that this portrayal was evidence of fraud—as they believed that Greenland wasn't shown on maps as an island until the 18th century. However, that belief was only an assumption without support of evidence. That assumption was false—as six ancient maps (above) will verify.

and other pre-Columbian artifacts found in North America <u>must</u> be fraudulent because they were, by definition, "impossible." The result of the inviolability of orthodox doctrine has been a wholesale misinterpretation of early American history.

Physical Evidence of Thriving Colonies

Ancient fortifications and iron-smelting furnaces which Arlington Mallery (1951) identified along the St. Lawrence river, the Ohio river, on Newfoundland and along the East Coast correspond to Nordic and Celtic settlements in the Eastern United States and Canada. Canadian archeologist Thomas Lee (1979) found similar ruins in Labrador. The antiquarian Josiah Priest (1834) identified abandoned fortresses and earthworks in the Mississippi and Ohio valleys. And archeologist Eben Horsford (1880) identified Norse ruins near Boston. Norse historian W.R. Anderson (1994) has amassed an encyclopedia of Norse relics found in farms and valleys from Maine to Minnesota. Orthodox historians and anthropologists have presumed that the Nordic artifacts found at these sites, including iron and bronze tools, axe-heads, glass bottles, beads, swords, boat rivets, and stones inscribed with runes are either colonial-era relics or frauds. However, contrary to what orthodox historians might believe, such assumptions do not constitute evidence.

America's leading runeologist, Richard Nielson (1994), has confirmed the authenticity of 14th and 15th-century runestones in Minnesota and Maine by virtue of exhaustive comparisons with original rune texts in Scandinavian museum collections. The most controversial artifact he has examined is the Kensington Runestone—a 200-lb., yard-long slab of granite that was found beneath a tree in 1898 near Kensington, Minnesota. Although it was once on exhibit in the nation's museum, The Smithsonian, in Washington, D.C., orthodox historians eventually convinced the museum curator that the artifact was a hoax. They claimed that the lengthy rune inscription included "modern" expressions and letters.

Historian Robert Hall (1994, 82) with Richard Nielsen and Rolf Nilsestuen conducted the most-recent examination of the Kensington Runestone by means of a thorough linguistic analysis. Noting that orthodox historians had compromised the validity of the artifact by associating it with other so-called "Viking hoaxes," they reasonably declared that the controversy over authenticity of other artifacts found in Minnesota was irrelevant to the issue of the Kensington text:

> It is on the basis of the language of the stone, and that alone, that our verdict must rest. It has been our main thesis that its language is purely medieval, with no modernisms and indubitable archaisms, and that we must therefore consider both the language and the artifact as genuine. ... It is a major historical document in its own right as a prime witness to Scandinavian penetration into the interior of North America between the time of Leif Eiriksson and that of Columbus.

Arlington Mallery's search for artifacts of ancient European colonies in America resumed following his service as a military officer and engineer. In 1946, he scoured the St. Lawrence river valley and the isles of the Gulf where he found an abundance of artifacts. He identified fourteen Norse habitation sites on Newfoundland and many others along the shores of Sop's Island.   His successful endeavor anticipated the Ingstad excavation at La Anse Aux Meadows by more than a decade:

> For proof of a Vinland in Newfoundland, I went to that island. There, on the raised beaches, I found hitherto unidentified ruins of long central hearths like the hearths in the longhouses of the Norse in Norway and Greenland after 1300 AD.   In and around these ruins, I found scattered iron chisels, boat spikes, clinch nails, and a battle axe side-by-side with stone tools, arrowpoints, and spearheads exactly like those found in all the areas of northern Europe once occupied by Scandinavians. (Mallery and Harrison, 1979, 56)

In order to answer valid concerns of skeptics and his own curiosity, Arlington Mallery (1979, 31 & 56) had iron tools from Nordic archeological sites in the eastern United States and Nova Scotia tested at Battalle Laboratories.   The judgment of the metallurgists at Battalle was that the artifacts were made by a pre-colonial process called "cladding" in which iron was built up in successive layers by hammering on peatbog ore.   Cladding iron was common among ancient Celtic and Nordic cultures but absent after the 15th century by which time foundries produced molten iron.   Mallery (1979, 56) noted that iron artifacts of Newfoundland's Nordic sites were made from "carburized wrought iron like the Viking iron which archeologists have found in Norse ruins in Scandinavia and Greenland."   Over the course of four years of field excavations, he identified remains of twenty Nordic iron-smelting furnaces along the Ohio Valley, and he located scores of Nordic habitation sites along the St. Lawrence.   His associate, James Howe, found remains of sixteen Norse iron-smelting furnaces in Virginia's Roanoke Valley where he collected 400-lbs. of iron artifacts.

The Catholic Mission—
Bishopric of Greenland and Wineland

Medieval history and Renaissance exploration had a common theme: world evangelism.   Leif Ericson's initial mission in 999 AD was to spread the Gospel from Norway to Greenland.   Once that mission was completed, he pursued his personal ambitions to discover new lands.   His voyage south to Wineland figured prominently in subsequent colonial expansion into the Western Continent.   However, it was not the discovery of new lands that earned Leif a place in Church chronicles, it was his success as an evangelist.

The first bishop of Greenland and adjacent territories, Jon of Ireland, took office in 1053.   According to the <u>Biskupa Sogur of Hkongrvaka</u> (1856), Jon undertook an evangelical mission to Vinland where he was martyred.   Subsequent commercial enterprise and migrations brought settlers from Greenland to Leif's gateway settlement.   It was not long before Catholic settlers needed an official of the Church to establish ecclesiastical authority in the colony.   Icelandic historian Ari Frode reported Bishop Eric Gnupson's voyage to Wineland in <u>Libellus Islandorum</u> (the Icelandic Annals) of 1121.   Some scholars interpret the voyage as a visit to existing parishes in America; skeptics assume the trip was merely a passing fancy to investigate the location of Leif's "lost colony."   If the bishop was seeking after phantoms of old Norse voyagers, then he went on such an outing twice!   A caption on Yale's Vinland Map reported that Bishop Eric visited Vinland four years earlier.

Taxation of Norse settlements was an important source of income for the Church. That the size of Norse territories in the west had grown considerably beyond the Island of Greenland was evident from a letter that the archbishop of Nidros sent to the pope in 1276. At that time, the archbishop (who was based at Trondheim, Norway) was responsible for collecting taxes from northern England, Scandinavia, Iceland, Greenland—and the regions beyond. The archbishop informed the pope that it would take five years to collect the tax from Greenland (Sauer, 1968, 146). As there were only two major settlements on Engronelant—it seems apparent that the archbishop had in mind settlements farther west.

By the 14th century, the population of Greenland Island reached an estimated 6,000 people. There were 280 farms, 17 parish churches, 2 monasteries, and one cathedral. However, as the climate grew more severe, settlers in the Western Settlement of central Greenland were forced to abandon their homesteads, and they left to an unknown destination. In 1350, Deputy Bishop Ivar Bardarson of Greenland's Eastern Settlement reported that the inhabitants of the Western Settlement had voluntarily left their farms. The fact that they had taken along most of their farm animals suggests that they migrated south to Nova Scotia or Newfoundland. Icelandic Bishop Gisle Oddson in 1637 reported that the 14th-century inhabitants of the Western Settlement had left the faith and joined the natives of the Western Continent which he identified as America.

This exodus of Christian subjects shocked King Magnus Eiriksson into sending a search party from Bergen in 1355. The expedition, under the command of Paul Knutsson, did not return until 1364. Presumably, they followed the renegades from Greenland to their new homesteads in the southwest; certainly, Knutsson's force did not sit in desolate Greenland for nine years before returning home. Some writers connect Knutsson's band with the Kensington Runestone left in Minnesota in 1362 (Holand, 1968).

Papal archives of July 9, 1492, note that Innocent III accepted the resignation of Jacob Blaa as Bishop of Gardar, Greenland. The Pope appointed Mathias Knutsson as a replacement. Historian Tryggvi Oleson (1964, 120) believed this appointment was sufficient evidence that a significant Catholic congregation still survived in the most-northern outpost of Christianity.

English Mercantile Trade in The Northwest Atlantic

England's role in North Atlantic shipping continued to grow throughout the 1300's. During this century, merchants expanded their territories beyond Iceland to include the maritime provinces of Canada—also known as the "Icelandic Isles." Norwegian markets from Bergen to Iceland were open to Christian ships—although licenses were required to assure that the ruling authorities received adequate revenues from taxation of cargoes. Historian Richard Hakluyt (1599) noted that during the mid-1300's, King Edward III granted special privileges to the merchants of Blakeney to assure that nothing interfered with their voyages to Iceland. This special status exempted Blakeney's ship owners from the usual service required of merchant vessels in coastal defense or in maritime expeditions against France. Trade with Greenland Province—a huge territory that extended from Labrador to Chesapeake Bay—was restricted officially to vessels commissioned by the king of Norway. Nevertheless, some English investors risked losing their ships and cargoes in efforts to circumvent taxes and license requirements. These confiscations have been recorded in harbormasters' records at Bergen and Bristol.

In those days, "Iceland" consisted of the isle situated between Norway and Greenland as well as an archipelago farther west called the "Icelands" or Icelandic Isles. One of these was "Frisland"—an isle which Frisian nobles had colonized in the 11th century. Hanseatic merchants competed in this region with those of the English. Venetian captains, whose ships brought Oriental goods to England, coveted the lucrative North Atlantic trade in codfish, furs, whale oil, narwhal ivory, wine, and lumber.

London's shipping magnates became increasingly more concerned that Venetian entrepreneurs might soon join forces with arrogant Hanseatic merchants in the North Atlantic. Like their English competitors, the Hanse sailed beyond Iceland to lucrative markets in Norse territories of Nyaland, Norveca, and Iceland. Though claiming no interest in piracy, Hanse agents had been known to raid English warehouses in foreign lands; English trawlers near Iceland and merchants in Greenland were also vulnerable to attacks by Hanse ships. Indeed, each passing year brought increasing complaints from merchants in Bristol and Lynn that their overseas markets were being compromised.

It was during this time of extensive maritime activity in the North Atlantic that an English friar undertook a royal commission to survey the "Northern Regions." His travelog provides authentic documentation of early European commerce and settlements in North America.

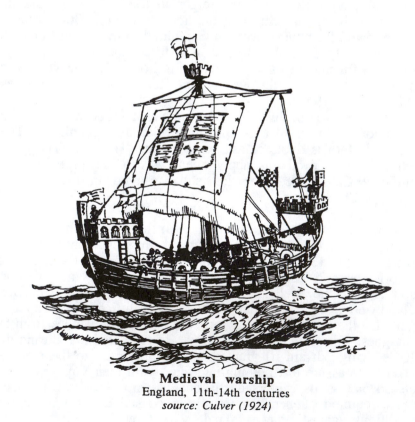

Medieval warship
England, 11th-14th centuries
source: Culver (1924)

The Franciscan Survey of the North Atlantic

Maritime travel during the 13th century took place in a cauldron of religious superstition and political drama. Cogs, carraks, and galleons—the great vessels of European maritime trade—were adequate to the task of riding out storms on high seas. It was the mariners who had difficulty reconciling their superstitious notions of sea dragons and ill-winds with the very rational demands of international commerce.

Religious dogma added to the difficulties that confronted mariners. Useful devices, like the compass, were initially banned on Christian ships—out of fears that the devil was responsible for the "magical" properties of magnetic needles. Cartography and cosmography—the sciences of mapmaking—were poorly developed due to ages-old dogma that defined Earth in biblical terms as a flat disk surrounded by an abyss. According to Church authorities, the only destination people really needed to be concerned about was on the final journey to Paradise—and that couldn't commence until death, anyway. Meanwhile, biblical scholars produced cosmological maps—called <u>mappamonds</u> showing the location of Paradise near Asia—but mortals were forbidden to go there due to the sins of Adam & Eve. Common sailors lived forever in fear that their ships might sail too close to "the Edge of the abyss" or crash into uncharted reefs. Sailors who strayed from the beaten path were literally "at God's mercy." Even in so-called "friendly waters" they might be attacked by pirates. English merchants called these roaming brigands "sea-monsters"—a term that came into use in the 9th century when Vikings in drakkars or "dragon boats" terrorized the North Sea.

Into this world ruled by fate and tradition came a young boy who was destined to change the course of world history. The youth, who was born into a wealthy English family, was named Roger Bacon. He was a curious lad who was blessed with the financial and intellectual resources to indulge in travel, literature, and education. Upon his enrollment at Oxford University, young Bacon joined the Franciscan Order of mendicant friars. His skill as an orator earned him a post at the University of Paris. It was at Paris that he befriended Guy Fulcodi—a local cardinal who became Pope Clement IV in 1265. The success of this friendship and a personal request from Pope Clement led Bacon to write his most famous work, the <u>Opus Majus</u>, in 1266.

This was the creative spark that led English Franciscans to conduct a geographical survey of the North Atlantic in 1330 AD. The products of that survey—a map and travelog by friar Nicholas of Lynn—served as the foundation for North Atlantic cartography for over 200 years. It also paved the way for trans-Atlantic voyages in the early 15th century.

Pope Clement IV 1265-1268

Cardinal Guy Fulcodi reluctantly answered the calling of his associates to head the Catholic Church. During his brief tenure, continuous wars in Italy prevented him from giving serious attention to an interest from more peaceful times in Paris where he had become enthralled with the ideas of Roger Bacon.

Roger Bacon 1214-1292

Franciscan friar and Oxford Scholar, Bacon proposed creation of a world map based on scientific principles. He was imprisoned for "unorthodoxy" from 1278 to 1292 as a result of his proposal to improve Christian education with scientific subjects.

Bacon's View of Polar Regions

Roger Bacon compiled a world map in 1266. This schematic representation shows his belief that India (or Asia) was separated from Europe by an ocean of 2,000 to 3,000 miles distance. He conjectured that Polar Regions were surrounded by open seas.

source: Roger Bacon, Opus Majus, 1266

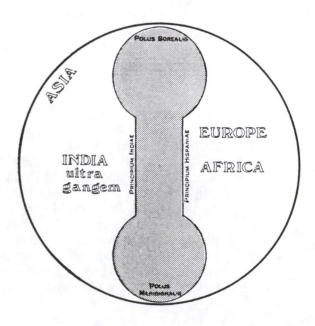

The Universe of Roger Bacon

Roger Bacon (1215-1292) is considered one of the leading thinkers and scientific pioneers of Western Civilization. Trained in the arts and religion at Oxford University, Bacon was invariably drawn into the liberating worlds of literature, astrology, alchemy, magic, and science. Among the subjects he mastered were music, mathematics, astronomy, optics, and surveying. He became an avid reader, an inventor, and a philosopher; he thereby lost his innocence as a disciple of Church authority. Bacon studied Latin, Greek, and Arabic; and he amassed his own library of foreign books. Most of these costly manuscripts were scorned by Church authorities; yet these so-called "pagan" documents led to Bacon's experiments with optics, gunpowder, and magnetism.

The maverick friar also studied world geography and the physical laws governing celestial navigation and maritime travel. He was among the first Europeans of his Age to recommend a voyage westward across the Atlantic to the overseas continent. His contemporaries argued over what they might find; Bacon assured them that the only way they would know the truth was by sending out expeditions to visit the overseas lands. Had the friar actually had the opportunity to make such a voyage, he would have been able to settle the issue on the basis of empirical evidence. He was the right man at the right place—but at the wrong time. Unlike most of his contemporaries, Bacon was a man sufficiently educated and insightful to have the capacity for viewing the world from the perspective of scientific experimentation. Had the dreaded Inquisition not prevailed in 1268, it would have been Roger Bacon who earned the title "Discoverer of The New World."

During Bacon's lifetime, European society was ruled by men whose minds and vision were ruled by superstition and dogma. Even Pope Clement realized that his esteemed associates, the cardinals and bishops, were not ready for innovative ideas to be incorporated into one of the greatest bastions of orthodoxy—the Catholic Church. So he instructed Bacon to proceed with extreme caution—to keep his writing project a secret. This was indeed a cumbersome order, for it was also the edict of Bacon's superiors that Franciscan friars were forbidden to write books. This edict was intended to "protect" friars from creating anything that might detract from their adherence to scripture. Thus, Bacon was simultaneously charged by the pope to keep his mission secret while breaking his sacred oath to his superiors not to engage in such projects.

Bacon's goal in writing the Opus Majus was to explain to the pope his proposal of reforming Christian education through incorporation of scientific principles and equipment. It was Bacon's belief that scientific education could help improve the minds of individuals and thereby make them better, more effective servants of God.

One of the areas of study where Bacon believed the most important improvements were needed was geography. His Opus Majus was a daring departure from contemporary geographical wisdom—if there was such a thing in the Middle Ages. The book contained the earliest practical description of geography available in Medieval Europe. Bacon accurately described habitable lands in the North Atlantic; he accurately identified the southern continent across the Atlantic as a land known to the Hindus as Patalis; and he accurately calculated the size of the Atlantic Ocean which separated western Europe from the continents across the sea.

As a scientist during an era of Church conflict with intellectuals, Bacon was often considered a heretic. He believed in the unity of scientific pursuits and the importance of multi-disciplinary research: multiple perspectives, he advised, could increase the accuracy of observations. He believed that theories regarding the forces of nature should be subject to observation and experimentation. This proposal was in direct opposition to the practice of his peers and Church officials who typically relied upon scriptural interpretations—and the wisdom of so-called "authorities." When empirical evidence contradicted traditional beliefs, Bacon argued for adopting new theories in order to explain the phenomenon as it was observed in nature. This argument posed a serious confrontation for prelates who were accustomed to interpreting life solely on the basis of faith and scripture.

Bacon's manuscript on Earth and the Heavens, the Opus Majus, arrived by courier at Pope Clement's residence at Viterbo, France, sometime in 1267. At the time, the pope seems to have been preoccupied with devastating wars and political conflicts in Italy. Whether or not enemies in his own entourage prevented him from examining the document is a matter of speculation; at any rate, there is no indication that Clement ever knew the manuscript had arrived. He died suddenly, and mysteriously, from a fever in 1268.

Loss of this ecclesiastical patron drastically reversed the fortunes of England's consummate scientist. Although Bacon's intentions were motivated by the highest ideals, his proposal represented a serious threat to established doctrine. The Minister General of the Franciscans, Jerome of Ascoli (later Pope Nicholas IV), promptly condemned Bacon's Opus and ordered the Franciscan friars to repudiate his teachings. Bacon was subsequently interred in an English prison for 14 years. He died shortly after his release in 1292.

In spite of Jerome's order of condemnation, Bacon's world map and his manuscript inspired later geographers of the Franciscan Order. Among these was a Spanish Franciscan who traveled on Atlantic seas in the 14th century. The Spaniard's travelog, The Book of Knowledge, was an accounting of Atlantic isles—a guidebook of sorts to aid Christian merchants in commercial endeavors and evangelism. Franciscan monks from England to Italy studied Bacon's writings on the astrolabe and the scientific method.

English historian Austin Poole (1958, 592) credited Bacon with preparing the way for the study of astronomy at Oxford:

> Roger Bacon observed the heavens with instruments and discussed astronomical theories at length in various writings; his emphasis on measurement seems to have helped to build up both the Parisian school of astronomy at the end of the 13th century and the school associated with Merton College, Oxford, in the 14th century.

Poole notes that Merton College went on to become the leading center of teaching and research on astronomy in the early 14th century. He notes that: "William Rede and Simon Bredon constructed astronomical almanacs for Oxford which gave this city something like the modern position of Greenwich" (Poole, 1958, 593). Such almanacs were essential for the calculation of geographical coordinates using trigonometry. Equally important, Rede and Bredon wrote manuscripts describing the method for constructing astronomical instruments such as the astrolabe. Mass production of accurate instruments was an essential part of training and equipping cadres of surveyor-astronomers. Chaucer's popular treatise on the astrolabe was another important consequence of the training provided at Oxford. Thus by the third decade of the 14th century, England had the most highly-trained corps of friar astronomers in all of Christendom.

Following master Bacon's lead, Franciscan friars succeeded in conducting a geographical survey of North Atlantic territories by the mid-14th century. Under the direction of an English Franciscan, Nicholas of Lynn, they compiled an accurate map of the Atlantic that was included in Lynn's book—the Inventio Fortunatae. During the early 15th century, a Swiss Franciscan illustrated the travels of friar John De Plano Carpini to Tartary with a world map that included the Atlantic isles of Greenland and Vinland. This map is now popularly known as "Yale's Vinland Map." Bacon's Opus also inspired a leading geographer of the early 15th century, Cardinal Pierre D'Ailly, whose treatise Imago Mundi convinced Paolo Toscanelli and Columbus that a voyage was feasible across the Atlantic Ocean. D'Ailly even copied passages verbatim from the Opus without giving credit to his source—thus Columbus was oblivious to the unknown debt he owed to the 13th-century Franciscan master (Fiske, 1920, Vol. I, 372).

Bacon's World Map

Bacon mentions a map in the Opus that was based on both current and ancient sources. Among the sources Bacon mentioned were the 2nd-century Roman Ptolemy, the Arabic cosmographer Alfraganus, John DePlano Carpini, and William Rubruk. Friar John was a Franciscan who Pope Innocent IV sent to Mongolia in 1245. Friar William (a.k.a. DeRubruquis) was another Franciscan who went to visit the Tartars at Karakorum on a mission for King Louis of France in 1253. Both papal emissaries described Cathay as a country on the eastern sea of Asia.

Bacon's map was made in the form of a cylindrical projection using longitudes and latitudes to locate the relative positions of nations, cities, major rivers, mountains, and oceans. He thereby anticipated similar Ptolemaic maps of the 15th century. Although no map under Bacon's signature has been found, it is possible to reconstruct the principle features from his written account in the Opus and from a small, schematic diagram of the Atlantic which accompanied his treatise on mathematics. The most important feature of this map is the Atlantic Ocean which is described as a relatively narrow sea of perhaps 2,500 miles separating Europe and Asia. Along the Asian shore, Bacon placed "Great Cathay" (China) in the region that was commonly known as "Farther India," and to the south he indicated a land called "India Pathalis" (or Patala). Although his placement of Cathay was a major error, he realized that Cathay was known as "Seres" to Classical writers. He was the first European on record to report that the people of Cathay used paper money. The land he called "Pathalis" was subsequently identified as South America. Furthermore, the land was situated precisely where he suggested about 2,500 miles west of Africa and below the Equator. Bacon called northern Africa "Hisperia" or "Farther Spain."

Bacon's concept of the size of the Atlantic Ocean can be calculated from the length he gives to the known world—about 18,000 miles based on the writings of Ezra and Aristotle and his own calculation of the circumference of Earth at 20,428 miles. It was Ezra's belief that "six parts of the Earth are habitable and the seventh is covered by waters" (Burke, 1928, 311). This yields a figure of about 2,500 for the expanse of the Atlantic. Although Bacon was dependent upon Classical writers for his concept of Earth and its oceans, he was also convinced that his ancient

Scenes from The Inquisition

From the 10th century through the 18th century, orthodox Christians systematically exterminated anyone suspected of holding different beliefs from those sanctified by Church authorities. Scientists such as Roger Bacon and philosophers such as John Wycliffe were particular targets of a Church tribunal called the Inquisition. Those who were condemned suffered torture and public execution. Bacon was prominent enough to get by with 15 years in prison; Mercator's associates were buried or burned alive. When Church authorities called Wycliffe before a tribunal in 1377, King Edward III's son, John of Gaunt, intervened with an armed guard.

sources were guided not by mere hypotheses and speculation but by the crucible of experience:

> Aristotle maintains at the end of the second book of <u>The Heavens and The World</u> that more than a fourth is inhabited. And Averroes confirms this. Aristotle says that the sea is small between the end of Spain on the west and the beginning of India on the east. Seneca in the fifth book on <u>Natural History</u> says that this sea is navigable in a very few days if the wind is favorable. And Pliny teaches in his <u>Natural History</u> that it was navigated from the Arabic Gulf to Cadiz. (Burke, 1928, 311).

Realizing that his calculations of the size of the Atlantic ran counter to the beliefs of most cosmographers, Bacon (1266) stressed the dependability of his sources:

> Aristotle was able to know more (than Ptolemy) because on the authority of Alexander, he sent 2,000 men to investigate the things of this world, as Pliny states in the eighth book of the <u>Natural History</u>. . . Therefore, Aristotle could attest more than Ptolemy could. And Seneca likewise; because the Emperor Nero, his pupil, in similar fashion sent him to explore the doubtful things in this world, as Seneca states in the <u>Questions on Nature</u>. Therefore, according to these facts, the extent of the habitable portion (of Earth) is great and what is covered by water must be small. (Burke, 1928, 311).

Another feature of Bacon's map which has mystified modern historians is the location of navigable seas surrounding both North and South Geographic Poles. Bacon was somewhat perplexed by conflicting theories and the reports of mariners who claimed to have sailed to inhabited isles in temperate lands near the poles. The Greek philosopher Aristotle had surmised that the midnight sun in polar regions would render them uninhabitable due to prolonged exposure to the heat of the sun; and Bacon's own calculations suggested that the oblique angle of the sun's rays would render the polar regions too cold for habitation (Burke, 1928, 154). Nevertheless, Bacon observed that the testimony of reputable scholars held otherwise: "When Pliny in his <u>Natural History</u> and Martianus in his description of the regions of the world found by certain experience that the regions beneath the poles are the most temperate in this world, as they themselves state, and they allege that experience of men who were there, we cannot deny that the regions there are the most temperate" (Burke, 1928, 155). Thus, Bacon was forced to concede that the Polar Regions must be temperate—in spite of the zonal maps of ancient Rome that showed the Arctic as frozen wasteland. Furthermore, Bacon knew from numerous reports current during his lifetime that the northern land of Hyperborea was a peaceful place that had served as a refuge for Europeans (Burke, 1928, 377). The scholar-monk was faced with a dilemma: in the polar regions, scientific hypotheses conflicted with the unimpeachable evidence of actual observation. And it was Bacon's belief that actual observation of empirical evidence must supersede theories based on logic alone. Therefore, he revised his own theory by calculating the presumed effects of heat trapped by the Hyperborean mountains and Riphean mountains that reportedly surrounded parts of the Arctic. In those parts of the polar regions, where high mountains absorbed the heat of the sun, Bacon theorized that human habitation was to be expected:

> How far habitation extends north, Pliny shows through actual experience and by various authors. For habitation continues up to that locality where the poles are located; and where the day lasts six months and the night for the same length of time. Martian, moreover, in his description of the world, agrees with this statement: whence they maintain that in those regions dwells a very happy race where people die only from satiety of life, attaining which point they cast themselves from a lofty rock into the sea. These people are called Hyperboreans on the European side and Arumphei in Asia. (Burke, 1928, 327)

It was Bacon's belief that creation of an accurate world map was essential for Christian evangelism and for the success of Christian merchants. According to Bacon: "This knowledge of the places in the world is very necessary to the state of the believers and for the conversion of unbelievers and for opposing unbelievers and the Antichrist. . . For the most vigorous men sometimes through their ignorance of the places in the world have destroyed themselves and the business interests of Christians" (Burke, 1928, 321).

Bacon also voiced his disgust with the Medieval mappamonds which were practically useless for navigation and often jeopardized the lives of travelers and merchants:

> He who is ignorant of the places in the world lacks a knowledge not only of his destination, but of the course to pursue. Therefore, whether one sets forth to convert unbelievers or on other matters of the Church, he should know the rites and conditions of all nations in order that with definite aim he may seek the proper place. . . For very many have been foiled in the most important interests of Christian people because they were ignorant of the distinctions in regions. (Burke, 1928, 321)

Bacon established the western coast of Africa (which he called Farther Spain) as the location of a "prime meridian" from which to measure all other points of longitude. This meridian could then be used to calculate relative positions on Earth. Cartographers had made this task difficult because every principality used its own set of so-called "prime" coordinates. Bacon's map, with its emphasis on geographical coordinates, served as the foundation for a 14th-century Franciscan survey of nations bordering the Atlantic Ocean. This survey prepared the way for European expansion in the 15th century.

Another obstacle to world-wide mapping was the "Julian" calendar which was then in use. According to Bacon's calculations, every 130 years, this calendar gained one extra day from the accumulated effect of Leap Years. This error rendered celestial tables inaccurate and forced periodic recalculation of all prior coordinates in order to compensate for the accumulating errors. Such computations made accurate surveying difficult if not impossible; construction of scientific charts was also cumbersome because of the frequent calculations. Therefore, Bacon urged a modification of the calendar that was eventually adopted in 1582.

Friar Bacon was well-aware that preparation of an accurate map was an impossible task for any one individual—regardless of how many ancient sources he had to draw upon. His treatise on geography was therefore an appeal to Pope Clement to marshal the resources of scientific men of the Church in order to produce reliable maps for commerce and evangelism. "Greater labor is here needed," he stressed, at the end of his description of the regions of Earth in 1266 (Burke, 1928, 324).

Bacon's proposal to exploit the full potential of science for the benefit of Christian enterprise was initially condemned as blasphemy. In the eyes of Church authorities, God needed no assistance from the lowly friar Bacon to achieve His own divine objectives. Bacon was jailed for heresy; however his allies in the Church prevented the physical tortures and burning at the stake that were common fare of the Inquisition. The irrepressible monk continued writing, but he lost the convenient access to his library of foreign books and the companionship of creative thinkers from abroad. These had been the vital fuel of his creative enterprise.

Controversy over the monk's writings raged in England for several decades until the gradual forces of new technology and the demands of commerce eventually tipped the balance in favor of England's most-maligned priest. Posthumously, the Franciscan Order endorsed Bacon's proposal for a scientific curriculum in Christian education. Oxford University embraced the new sciences with a fervor that belied their former contempt. Historian Edward Lutz (1936, 69) noted that: "Repentant Oxford had once more received friar Roger back into the family by the 15th century, because from then on the undergraduates quoted its celebrated alumnus as an authority in their public debates." His writings inspired the Oxford Franciscan William of Alnwick who became a professor at the Royal University in Naples (ca. 1330)—thus his scientific principles and writings were passed on to scholars and collegians in southern Italy. Another protégé, William Herbert became a famous scholar at Oxford where he promoted Bacon's scientific method. Over the years, Bacon's Perspectiva on optics was carried abroad in manuscript copies which influenced the writings of numerous scholars of the Renaissance (Lutz, 1936, 69). His writings on the astrolabe and its use in making maps became part of the Oxford curriculum that trained Nicholas of Lynn in the skills he needed to make the first scientific map of North America.

The King Commands: "Make a Map!"

During the early years of his long and glorious reign, King Edward III of England faced a threat in the Northern Regions beyond Iceland. Privateers sailing from hidden harbors devastated merchant fleets and raided distant colonies. To make matters worse, Venetian galleys had begun to sail past Scotland to join the Hanseatic League in the North Atlantic. Edward knew that he had to act with deliberate speed, however he lacked sufficient foreign intelligence to design an effective strategy. The navy was adequate to tackle any adversary in northern waters—if only they could by located. Alas, the isles and hidden harbors of the Northern Seas were largely unknown to the king's closest advisors.

Edward III had all the charming graces and manly skills that exemplified an ideal monarch of the Middle Ages. He took the throne in 1327, and he built his kingdom into a thriving nation. He established overseas provinces in northern France that remained loyal until the culmination of his reign in 1377. Edward was generally successful in battle; although his armies were driven from Scotland. He master-minded some impressive military victories in France during the mid-1340's. These campaigns provided a grand opportunity for knightly feats, as his

King Edward III, England and Normandy (1327-1377)

Edward ruled from 1327 to 1377. Fond of chivalry and Arthurian legends, the king hosted Medieval tournaments and sent mendicant friars in search of Avalon—the legendary resting place of King Arthur. Likeness, above, is from a 15th-century stained glass panel; the official shield included a field of fleur-de-lis representing Edward's claim of sovereignty over territories in northern France.

own son, the Black Prince, proved to be a commander of the utmost cunning and courage. As a result of successes in continental wars, lords, knights, and merchants enjoyed prosperity that came from expanded commerce with English provinces in Normandy. Victorious knights also looted French cities and brought home to England hoards of gold and jewels. This wealth circulated throughout the kingdom and contributed to the economic revival. At the height of his campaigns, Edward's fleet of converted merchant vessels numbered over one thousand. Such awesome power and several major victories in naval engagements inspired Edward to declare England's "dominion over the seas" (Myers, 1982, 44). Once this proclamation was made, Edward was suddenly held accountable for protecting English merchant vessels from pirates.

Enchanted by victories and surrounded by hereditary lords, Edward's vision for the realm was to bring about a Renaissance of 6th-century heraldic traditions. He drew his inspiration from the legendary exploits of King Arthur and the Knights of The Round Table. Thus, he created his own retinue of champions called "The Order of The Garter." He revived traditions of chivalry and the old tournaments of knightly combat that had once been the hallmark of feudal Europe. The castles of England, as well as towns and villages, were once more decked out with bold banners proclaiming an era of social pride and merrymaking.

It was only natural for a king who was so obsessed with Medieval traditions to glorify the founders of English royalty. He revived interest in the legendary Avalon that was known as King Arthur's paradise across the western sea. It was often retold among the bards and scholars of the 14th century and confirmed by ancient manuscripts, such as the Gestae Arthuri or "Legends of Arthur," that the old king's resting place was in a land near the North Pole. This nostalgia for the revered Arthur was but one of many reasons why Edward decided to send an agent, friar Nicholas of Lynn, to investigate the Northern Regions beyond Iceland.

Even at this early date, merchants and kings throughout northern Europe pondered the nature of lands in the western Atlantic. Who among the upper class were not aware of Marco Polo—the famed Venetian traveler and aide to Kublai Khan?

Polo returned from his China Odyssey in 1295. Initially, the patricians of Venice ridiculed his fabulous stories about the vast expanse of China with its golden pagodas and thousands of ships. Some of these "giant junks," he had said, "were powered by six huge masts and carried hundreds of passengers." "The Khan's harem," he had said, "numbered in the thousands; his army in the tens of thousands." "Books and even money were printed on paper using a printing press that eliminated the need for monks to make individual copies laboriously by hand." Who could believe such incredible tales?

Most skeptics thought him mad; but a few loyal friends suspected that there might be an element of truth in some of his less-bizarre adventures. Nevertheless, they all found him very entertaining. Had he been born a few centuries later, he might have had the inclination to become a travel writer. But this was still in the time of monasteries and scribes: writing was reserved for the important affairs of nobles and manuscript copies of the Bible. Only after his capture during a naval engagement with arch-rival Genoa, and the enforced boredom of a jail cell, did Marco have an opportunity to compose his memoirs of the China experience. A fellow-inmate served as secretary while the seasoned traveler retold episodes of the mysterious Far East.

Medieval Ships

Merchants

The Beauchamp Pageant
15th century

**English merchant vessel
in the Icelandic trade**

Pirates

Pirates attack an English merchant vessel.

14th-century manuscript; source: after Hallum (1995, 201)

Sea monsters

after Olaus Magnus, circa 1530

His popular book, Marco Polo's Travels, inspired many Europeans to dream of voyages to the Orient. This was a land of abundant gems, gold, spices, silks—all the riches that were coveted by Medieval Europeans. One of his accounts told of a journey to a Land of Women across a northern sea to the east. King Edward was among those who suspected that Polo's northern journey had taken him to the same Northern Regions that were located northwest of Europe. These regions were portrayed— though with poor clarity—on monastic mappamonds. Edward reasoned that if Polo's journey had taken him northwest of Europe, then the rich and exotic land of Cathay with all its gold and spices might be reached by sailing north across Arctic seas.

However, the attraction of Cathay was a paradox for the English: although Asian markets might be a bonanza, the region was widely-regarded as a potential threat. Edward wasn't concerned about the Khan's vast army. Indeed, the Khan had requested missionaries from the pope, and that was a sure sign that Chinese officials were anxious for peaceful relations with Catholic Europe. The principal threat arose from the fantasies of cosmographers and the Book of Revelations.

Ever since time immemorial, monastic mappamonds had contained vivid warnings about the supernatural allies of Satan who were said to be lurking on the northern fringe of Asia. Two huge statues of the giants Gog and Magog stood in the London Guildhall as a potent reminder of a prophesy in Revelations about Armageddon when Gog and Magog would lead the forces of Satan against the Kingdom of God. If Magog's monstrous horde of voracious cannibals was north of China (as it was shown on cosmolographical maps), then the forces of Satan were entrenched in the Northern Regions across the Atlantic. Some cosmographers believed these satanic armies were the skraelings, or "savages," that Norse sailors had mentioned in 10th-century sagas. Every time a monk produced a manuscript copy of the archetypal mappamond or the aging geography upon which it was based, the fearsome legend of Gog-Magog was passed on to the next generation. The expected threat from these giants and their patron, Antichrist, was one of the reasons Roger Bacon gave in support of his urgent proposal to make a map of the North Atlantic: it was one way to calculate the potential threat of Gog-Magog to the British realm (Encyclopedia Britannica, Vol. 2, 1954, 891).

Medieval mappamonds included an assortment of real and imaginary lands, and it was often difficult to tell them apart. Amazonia (a land of women), Gothia Orientalis, Albania, and Wineland (a land of vineyards) were placed near the North Pole. Sailors reached these lands by heading due north from Scotland and north from Iceland; accordingly, they occupied the Northern Regions of maps like the 13th-century Psalter Map. Mappamonds were always centered on Jerusalem, and they included religious anecdotes and points of reference based on biblical themes such as the tower of Babel and Mt. Ararat—landing site of Noah's ark. These mappamonds also featured an Earthly Paradise (the Garden of Eden) situated along the coast of China. Mortals were forbidden to approach this paradise because of the enduring punishment demanded of the descendants of Adam and Eve. In this manner, mappamonds portrayed Earth as a stage for the divine drama of salvation, conquest, and world evangelism; simultaneously, they discouraged curiosity.

Cosmological in nature, mappamonds changed little over time as scribes in monasteries relied on the "authorities"—that is, earlier archivists—for their sources. Intended primarily as props for religious

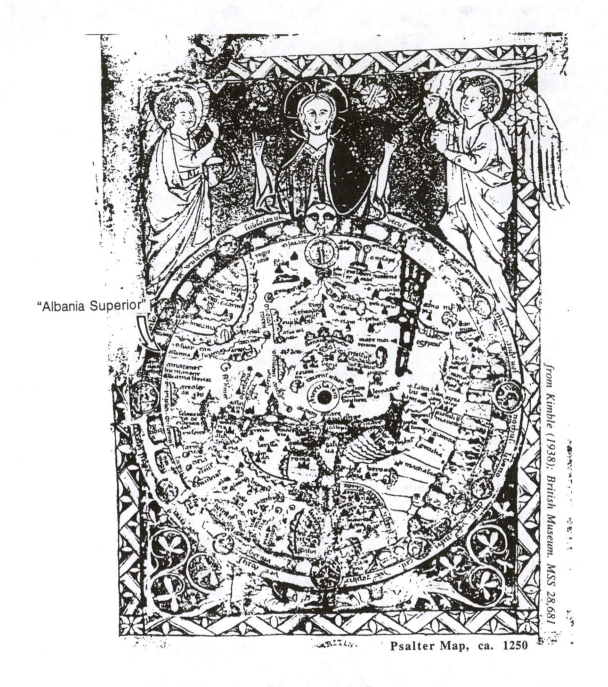

"Albania Superior"

from Kimble (1938); British Museum. MSS 28,681

Psalter Map, ca. 1250

Medieval Mappamond—13th Cent.

This English map, called the "Psalter Map," is an example of the kind of cosmographical devices which were called "maps" but actually had little value for geographical reference or travel. In accordance with scriptural interpretation, Jerusalem was placed at the center. The map has a circular shape—which is in accord with knowledge that Earth was round. Various captions and symbols on the map, such as the landing place of Noah's ark and the location of paradise in the far east were intended primarily to illustrate biblical concepts. In the far north is the territory of "Albania Superior" (arrow) which might represent King Arthur's colony from Albion (England) in the 6th century.

88

studies and the preservation of doctrine, <u>mappamonds</u> were of no value in navigation or travel between cities. Meanwhile, sailors kept their own booklets of sailing directions between ports. Their navigational booklets (sometimes called a <u>peripli</u>) and sea cards or mariners' charts were crude but adequate for seasoned pilots.

Unfortunately, none of the <u>mappamonds</u> and mariners' charts available to King Edward III were satisfactory for the needs of a head of state. Monastic <u>mappamonds</u>, though useful for biblical studies, lacked sufficient accuracy for geo-political interests. And mariners' charts—though accurate with respect to landmarks and routes of travel—were too limited in scope to serve as aids in planning wide-ranging military or commercial strategy. Edward was undoubtedly familiar with the most commonly available world "map" in England: Ranulf Higden's <u>mappamond</u> from the geography <u>Polychronicon</u> circa 1325. This <u>mappamond</u> didn't even include Marco Polo's Cathay, although it had the classical "Fortunate Isles" of antiquity west of Spain. Another fortunate isle—Wineland—was in its usual position near the North Pole. For a king who was vitally concerned about worldly affairs—such as conquest and commercial expansion, Higden's "map" must have seemed like a cruel joke. However, the <u>mappamond</u> was not intended to help travelers negotiate the English channel—its only purpose was to aid the faithful in their search for salvation.

King Edward was disturbed by the fact that his royal predecessors had neglected the importance of scientific maps as a tool for conducting official policy and foreign intelligence. He must have looked with jealousy upon the first <u>portolanos</u> which Venetian sailors brought on their yearly trips from the Mediterranean. These newly devised mariners' charts were crafted by highly skilled cosmographers who were specialists in mathematics, astronomy, and geometry. <u>Portolanos</u> were based on accurate measurements; they provided graphic portrayals of the relative positions of lands and seas; and they included reference markers for determining compass bearings and wind directions. Because they were wholly utilitarian in design, they lacked irrelevant biblical themes and monsters that confused and terrorized ordinary seamen.

The king's interests and the financial concerns of the nation had grown considerably in recent years, and accurate maps had become essential for effective management. Ministers of commerce and defense needed to be aware of the home ports, trade affiliations, and the cargoes of ships engaged in overseas commerce, however harbormasters often had no idea where many of the ships came from nor where they were going when they left. Port authorities made copies of ship's manifests to assure fair taxation; however, even they were often only vaguely aware of the vessels' points of origin and destinations. Maps were needed in order to monitor the movements of these vessels and thereby provide some assurance that overseas ventures did not infringe on the prerogatives of other monarchs. Such infringements might lead to confiscations of cargoes or even naval battles—which happened frequently. Protection of sea-lanes from pirates and the planning of new commercial ventures also required accurate maps; but alas, such maps were not available in Medieval England.

With all of these concerns weighing heavily upon his shoulders, King Edward came to the realization that England desperately needed an accurate nautical map of the North Atlantic. As Edward III was born at about the same time that Oxford scholars instituted the scientific

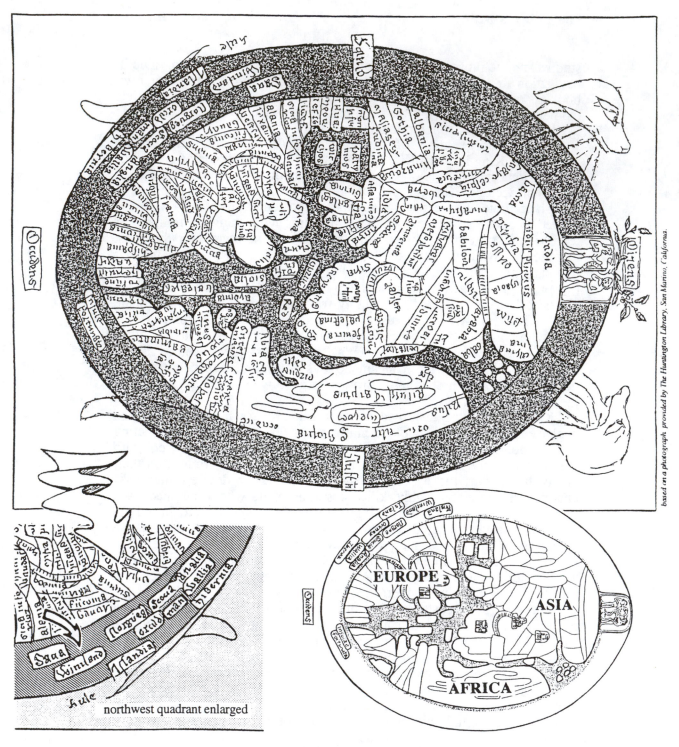

based on a photograph provided by The Huntington Library, San Marino, California.

northwest quadrant enlarged

key:

Anglia	—England
Walia	—Wales
Hibernia	—Ireland
Scocia	—Scotland
Man	—Isle of Man
Orchd	—Orkneys
Norgveg	—Norway
Islandia	—Iceland
Winiland	—Wineland
Saua	—Finland (?)

Ranulf Higden's Map from *Polychronicon* 1350 A D

Numerous monks issued manuscript copies of Higden's original geography and map. This version, circa 1350, has ten isles northwest of Europe. The second isle from the north is here called "Win-i-landa" which was the Danish spelling for Wineland—the Norse colony near Cape Cod. This placement and spelling are consistent with "Vin-i-landa" on Yale's "Vinland Map." Other copyists used such spellings as Wyondlond, Svinlandia, Widland, and Wineland. Twenty-one maps and over one-hundred manuscript copies of the geography are known to exist—confirming that this was a popular book in Medieval Europe. Albania in the northeast quadrant probably represents the North American territory once known as Irland Mikla—or Ireland the Great. East of India (far right) is a frame representing the biblical Garden of Eden.

90

curriculum championed by Roger Bacon, he couldn't help being influenced by the rising popularity of Oxford's most-prominent alumnus. Bacon's Opus was a common topic of conversation—as was the challenge he had given to Christian popes and kings to produce a scientific map of Earth. Bacon's research on magnetism, gunpowder, and optics had brought obvious rewards to English merchants: mariners now used the compass without fear of being punished for reliance on magic; gunpowder was being adapted to the needs of defense; and telescopes made possible long-distance observation.

A scientific map—as Bacon had proposed—would certainly meet both the needs of commerce and the requirements of the navy for overseas intelligence. Bacon had also stressed the importance of knowing the distribution of Christian and pagan peoples in order to prepare for the Day of Judgment and the anticipated onslaught of the legions of Antichrist. It was also apparent that Oxford University was now producing graduates with skills—not just in theology—but in mathematics, astronomy, and surveying. For the first time in the history of the British Isles, there were sufficient resources of skilled specialists to actually achieve the goal that Bacon had proposed. All that was needed to begin the process was a royal command—and someone sufficiently smitten with the mystique of royalty to accept the delegated responsibility.

In times of crisis, English monarchs often turned to the friars of Oxford University whose dedication to God was the only thing that surpassed their loyalty to king and country. (One might also add that in an era of tight budgets, royalty often took advantage of mendicant priests as a reliable source of free labor.) We don't know precisely when Edward informed the chancellor of Oxford about his plan to have the cadre of Franciscans make a map of North Atlantic seas and isles. Perhaps it was in 1329 or 1330 that the search was begun in earnest to find a suitable candidate to lead the project.

The search for a project director soon focused on residents of the friary at King's Lynn in Norfolk. This dormitory and sailor's hall was renowned throughout the realm as a gathering place for Oxford's most daring travelers. (In those days, of course, almost anyone boarding a ship bound for foreign ports could be considered "daring.") Edward appointed a youthful friar, Nicholas of Lynn, to supervise the mapping of the Northern Regions. The friar's mission was to explore unknown lands and make a chart showing the disposition of friendly colonies and pirate lairs. His destination—in 1330 AD—was North America.

Historical Sources on The English Friar

One name stands out among all others as the most important contributor to the foundation of New World cartography: that name is Nicholas of Lynn. This seasoned traveler, Franciscan friar, and Oxford mathematician is the person most often mentioned by Renaissance cartographers regarding lands in the polar regions. The friar prepared a written account of northern territories, The Inventio Fortunatae, which he presented to Edward III of England circa 1360. Copies of this manuscript and an abbreviated account by a Flemish explorer named Jacob Cnoyen eventually circulated among the leading explorers and cartographers of Europe in the 15th and 16th centuries.

Extant documents regarding the life of friar Nicholas consist of short notations scattered about the personal correspondence of cartographers, merchants, and kings. The most important document is a letter that

Astrolabes

12th century English astronomer
after Bodleian MS. Bodley 614, British Library

13th century Spanish astronomer s
after Psalter of St. Louis of Blanche, Castile

Astronomical Surveying Instruments

An Egyptian, Chinese, or Middle Eastern invention called the astrolabe was the principle astronomical and surveying tool of the Middle Ages. The device consisted of a circular base and a pivoting arm with mounted sights at either end. The base was calibrated to enable measurement of the angle of elevation of celestial objects. More sophisticated models had additional wheels for calculation of corresponding angles of constellations. By comparing the angles obtained from field sightings with tables showing the measurements for a given point of reference (prime meridian), it was possible for English friars to pinpoint approximate geographical positions at remote locations in the Northern Hemisphere. The Merton astrolabe (lower right) is probably similar to the one that Nicholas of Lynn used to map the "northern regions."

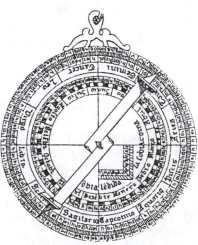

13th century Portuguese astrolabe
from Peres (1943)

English astrolabe ca. 1350
after photograph, Merton Col.

Gerhard Mercator sent to an English advocate—John Dee.   Another valuable source is the Norfolk Biography which included a biographical sketch on the friar as a man of historical importance. Added to these are several brief references on 15th and 16th-century maps and travelogs of New World explorers. There is also and a single paragraph in John Bale's biographical sketches of 1558. These are sufficient to reconstruct only the barest outline of the monk's travels and accomplishments.

According to the official Norfolk county record (in Stacy's Norfolk Biography of 1829, 450), Nicholas was born at King's Lynn, Norfolk. Although the date of the friar's birth is not established in the biography, sometime circa 1305 is plausible given the known period of the friar's service to the king of England.

As a young man, he entered the Franciscan Order. (Members of this Catholic organization of priest-educators are sometimes called "Greyfriars" in reference to the color of their robes; they are also known as "Minorites.") The Norfolk Biography mentions that the friars of King's Lynn had gained some notoriety for their world travels and frequent missions in the king's service. In this respect, they served similar roles to their Franciscan brothers in France and Italy who sometimes traveled great distances on diplomatic missions deep into Asia.

Nicholas attended Oxford University—probably sometime between 1320 and 1330. He studied music, mathematics, astronomy, and use of the astrolabe. His glowing reputation as an accomplished musician and surveyor brought him to the attention of King Edward III. It seems that Edward was in need of a competent surveyor to chart the Northern Isles.

The Norfolk Biography reports that the friar's first expedition in the king's service was to the "northern regions" in 1330 (Stacy, 1829, 450). This territory included the most distant regions of the north and western Atlantic which were becoming increasingly more important as outposts for England's overseas trade. The biography mentions an unidentified report that Nicholas "went as far as the pole itself where he discovered four in-draughts of the ocean." Biographer John Stacy mocked this "imaginary discovery" as a fantasy—though he acknowledges that the friar was highly honored and respected in his own time. The poet Geoffrey Chaucer, he says, called him "Freere N. Linne—a reverend clerk." This reference occurs in Chaucer's book—Treatise on The Astrolabe (Gibson, 1974, 177).

The friar's subsequent voyages are not discussed in the biography, although the friar's book of travels is identified as the Inventio Fortunatae which was presented to Edward III in about 1360. The Inventio was subsequently mentioned by numerous influential people including John Day, Columbus, Ferdinand Colon, John Ruysch, Abraham Ortelius, John Dee, Jacob Cnoyen, Gerhard Kramer (a.k.a., Mercator), and Bartholomew Las Casas.

During his long and productive career, the friar completed another work that merited comment in Chaucer's chronicles of the age. This book, Kalendar Astronomy, was one of the early sourcebooks on practical navigation which were essential for captains to accurately plot their positions at sea (Gibson, 1974, 178).   Chaucer's account of Medieval life in The Miller's Tale praised the young Nicholas as a creative and intuitive person who was skilled in mathematics, geometry, music, and astrology. Both the poet and the friar were protégés of John of Gaunt—Duke of Lancaster and one of the most influential princes of

England. Through his association with the duke, the friar's influence eventually reached Portugal's College of Navigation at Sagres.

Nicholas seems to have joined a second Catholic order towards the end of his career. Although most historians characterize him as a Franciscan, two early 16th-century writers mentioned that he was also known as a Carmelite. John Bale believed this was true, and he cited the 1557 testimony of a contemporary historian named Fuller as his source (Stacy, 1829). It seems likely that Nicholas joined the Carmelites—or "Whitefriars"—fairly late in life—after he had settled back into the routine of being an author and educator at Oxford University. Thus, friar Nicholas is known to some writers as a Franciscan; others declare that he was a Carmelite; and some acknowledge that he probably switched affiliations as he grew older. This apparent ambiguity concerning the friar's membership in religious organizations has caused great discomfort and confusion for orthodox historians. They have few clues regarding the "true" identity of England's most mysterious explorer.

The Norfolk Biography estimates the friar's death at sometime after 1360—followed by burial at King's Lynn. According to John Bale (in the Scriptorum illustrium, 1558), a renowned Oxford scholar identified as "Nicholas of Lynn" wrote a treatise called De usu astrolabii or "use of the astrolabe" circa 1370. He also mentioned that a famous Oxford mathematician was named "Nicholas." However, it is not known if this was the same Nicholas who surveyed the Northern Regions. Oxford had several prominent scholars with the first name of Nicholas, so it is possible that another Nicholas was the "famous" mathematician in Bale's reference. Bale's text also suggests that the friar lived to be at least 65-years old. He was then about the same age as his patron, King Edward III, who died in 1377.

English historian Richard Hakluyt knew of the friar's travelog by virtue of examining correspondence between the advocate John Dee and Gerhard Kramer (a.k.a. Mercator). Kramer had once had in his possession a manuscript by Flemish explorer Jacobus Cnoyen of Herzogenbusch—a man who had gained some fame as an explorer in the northern regions during the mid-1300's. Cnoyen's manuscripts about northern lands included summaries of conversations with a Norwegian priest in 1364. Four years earlier, the priest had talked at length with a person that Cnoyen identified as an English "Minnebroder" (or Minorite) from King's Lynn, Norfolk. According to the Norwegian priest, this Minnebroder was skilled as an astronomer, and he carried an astrolabe on his travels which he used to survey the lands. He traveled to Bergen on one of these expeditions in 1360 and was the guest of King Magnus Eiriksson of Norway. It was at the Norwegian court that the Norse priest heard the Minnebroder's tale of exploration in the Polar Regions. Cnoyen's manuscripts were subsequently obtained by Abraham Ortelius, a famous Flemish cartographer, who lent them to Mercator at Duisburg circa 1565. John Dee sought the manuscripts from Mercator in 1577, however they had already been returned to Ortelius and subsequently lost. Meanwhile, Mercator sent Dee his memoirs relating to the manuscripts in a letter dated 1577.

Hakluyt printed excerpts from Mercator's memoirs in Principal Voyages in 1582. It was at this time that he identified the mysterious Minnebroder of Cnoyen's tale as the English Franciscan—Nicholas of Lynn. This identification is important because none of the friar's contemporaries actually identify him as the author of the travelog—

Inventio Fortunatae. One of Hakluyt's sources, John Bale, had mentioned in his Scriptorum-Catalogus of 1558 that an Oxford scholar named "Nicholas of Lynn" had written a treatise on the astrolabe. This fact, along with the popularity of the Kings' Lynn friary as a gathering place for Franciscan travelers led Hakluyt to conclude that the Oxford friar was the same anonymous priest who Cnoyen mentioned as the author of the Inventio Fortunatae.

No contemporary documents are known to have survived at Oxford or in royal archives which might reveal that a map of the North Atlantic was ever officially sanctioned. Those mariners and cartographers who referred to the Inventio Fortunatae during the early 1500's never identified the author. It may well be that the original work was a confidential project undertaken solely for the benefit of Edward III; and for that reason, manuscript copies of the original travelog were also anonymous. Considering that the instigator of the North Atlantic survey—Roger Bacon—had languished in a religious prison for his unorthodox views, it is not unreasonable to suspect that Edward III and his son, John of Gaunt, thought it wise to keep the identity of the author in confidence. Indeed, both Edward and John had their own difficulties with Church authorities. The Inventio was probably not widely circulated during the time it was originally completed because it was regarded as a state secret. In later years, copies of the travelog surfaced long after the friar's map and book on navigation were superseded by more accurate versions of the North Atlantic cartography. By the time of Columbus, the Inventio was probably regarded more as a curiosity than as an important geographical reference—although Mercator thought it was the only reliable source for a place that no one else seems to have visited: the Polar Regions.

Hakluyt might have had access to other sources in 1582 that are no longer in existence. As an Oxford-trained geographer (and therefore an alumnus of the same university where Nicholas was a scholar), he was in an excellent position to learn about the oral traditions of the university and to review documents that have since been lost. Nevertheless, orthodox historians have questioned his objectivity regarding the friar's role in New World discovery.

Two well-informed biographers (Ferdinand Colon and Bartholomew Las Casas) mentioned that Columbus had seen or heard of the Inventio Fortunatae prior to his voyage in 1492. They were of common opinion that the travelog played a role in the mariner's favorable assessment of trans-Atlantic travel in the Polar Regions. In 1496, he was again in need of the Inventio, and he wrote a letter to the Bristol merchant, John Day, to request a copy of the manuscript. The response from John Day is the earliest historical reference to the friar's book that is still in existence:

> Your Lordship's servant brought me your letter, and considering what you instructed me therein, which I would wish to do in accordance with my desire and duty, I do not find the book Invincio Fortunati. I thought I had brought it with my effects and am greatly annoyed that I can not find it. (Morison, 1971, 206)

John Day ended his letter to Columbus by promising to lend him a copy of the Inventio as soon as one could be found. As this correspondence took place just a few months before Columbus sailed off toward unknown lands south of Hispaniola, we might surmise that the Spanish mariner was after some kind of nautical information concerning the southern continent or the land of brazilwood trees which the friar mentioned in his travelog.

Many 16th-century cartographers claimed the Inventio as the source of their impressions of the Polar Regions. Johann Ruysch cited the Inventio Fortunatae as a source for polar regions on his world map of 1507— although it is believed that his source was the Cnoyen manuscript and not an actual copy of the Inventio. Likewise, Gerhard Kramer (a.k.a., Mercator) credited the Inventio as his source for the Polar Regions on his world map of 1569. When John Dee questioned Mercator about this reference in 1577, the cartographer acknowledged that the section of his map attributed to the Inventio was actually based on a Classical legend that was simply reported in the travelog. Mercator admitted that the English friar had only "heard about" the Classical legend from other sources. This Classical concept of the Polar Regions as an ice-bound region seems to have been confused with the friar's report of navigable seas near the Magnetic North Pole. Only Martin Behaim's 1492 globe seems to include lands in the Northern Regions that were actually based on survey information; other maps of the era follow closely a mythical Greco-Roman concept of the Arctic as a magnetic mountain surrounded by four uninhabited islands of ice. Historian Fridtjoff Nansen surmised from the accuracy of Behaim's portrayal of Greenland that the 15th-century cartographer had examined the Inventio Fortunatae and based his concept of the Arctic on the friar's actual map or gazetteer of the region (Skelton, 1965, 175).

George Best, who traveled with Frobisher's voyage to Baffin Island in 1578, prepared a narrative of the voyage which included a short quotation that is said to come from the Inventio Fortunatae describing a region of raging currents carried towards a gulf where there was little wind. Historian Hjalmar Holand (1959) and others believe this was an accurate description of Hudson Bay in Springtime. That belief is buttressed by another passage from Cnoyen's account of the Inventio which identifies the "Pygnaei" or Inuit natives in a land towards the northeast, while lands toward the southwest were characterized by "fruitful and wholesome soil." Such a description is best suited to eastern Canada someplace between the tundra of Baffin Island and the forests of Labrador or Hudson Bay. Similarities between the quotation in Best's narrative and Mercator's version of the Cnoyen manuscript suggest that Best derived his information from Mercator and not from the lost Inventio Fortunatae.

John Dee's summary of Mercator's memoirs was published in his Great And Rich Discoveries (ca. 1580). This manuscript still survives though in badly mutilated condition. In his role as judicial advocate for Queen Elizabeth, Dee used this summary of the Inventio as part of his evidence supporting the English claim to lands across the North Atlantic in the New World. Dee's account was included in two publications by the Oxford scholar Richard Hakluyt; these were Divers Voyages Touching the Discoverie of America (1582) and Principal Voyages of the British Empire (1599). The objective of these publications was to support English claims upon New World territories and to promote the search for a northwest passage to Asia.

Since Richard Hakluyt provides our principal information on Nicholas of Lynn, we should briefly consider his veracity as an accurate source. Hakluyt was born in 1551 in London; he studied at Oxford and was ordained in 1578 to the Church of England. He died in his mid 60's in

1616—the year of Shakespeare's death. Historian David Hawke (1972, xiii) characterized Hakluyt's <u>Divers Voyages</u> as "a propaganda." Nevertheless, Hawke says of the author's other works that:

> He had for the most part been a scrupulous editor, presenting a report or narrative as he had found it, with few excisions or interpolations. He made no effort to scrub away failures or exaggerate successes. He let the reader evaluate for himself the quality of an account, and where research had revealed discrepant versions, he would present them without comment. (Hawke, 1972, xv).

Historian Jack Beeching (1972, 11) describes Hakluyt as a reliable source: "Hakluyt's intention as archivist and editor was consciously historical." Beeching regards Hakluyt's <u>Divers Voyages touching the discovery of America</u> as "a response to a need of practical politics" used to support the planting of a colony in the new land to harass Spanish treasure galleons, as a base for taking the northwest passage to Cathay, and as a source for vital commodities at cheap rates. He has genuine praise for the "sober scholarship" of the English author:

> Hakluyt was only a part-time spy. He was primarily a scholar in the magnificent Renaissance tradition—a man for whom the gratuitous pursuit of knowledge for its own sake was life's most important end. ... He has accepted the roles of archivist and editor, but does both superlatively. ... He will go to great lengths to get the facts. (Beeching, 1972, 19)

Beeching notes that Hakluyt once traveled 200 miles in order to take the testimony of the last survivor of an expedition to Newfoundland in 1536. "To sailors of the time," he says, "the <u>Principal Navigations</u> were simply their own account of themselves." Other critics praised his veracity: Hakluyt's documents—in the words of English historian Ben Jonson—were "registered for truth" (Beeching, 1972, 28).

Friar Nicholas of Lynn & The <u>Inventio Fortunatae</u>

Edward's selection of Nicholas for the assignment of mapping the Northern Regions was largely due to the friar's reputation as a skilled surveyor, his knowledge of astronomy, and his familiarity with the astrolabe. According to Richard Hakluyt, another factor in Edward's choice was the notoriety of the Franciscan monastery at Lynn as a house of world travelers. By selecting a friar from such an establishment, the king was assured that his servant was well-prepared to deal with the difficulties and deprivations of overseas travel. A section from Mercator's 1577 memoirs provides a summary of the friar's first expedition:

> The priest who had the astrolabe related to the king of Norway that in 1360 AD, there had come to these Northern Islands an English Minorite from Oxford who was a good astronomer, etc. Leaving the rest of the party who had come to the Islands, he journeyed further through the whole of the North etc., and put into writing all the wonders of those islands, and gave the king of England this book, which he called in Latin <u>Inventio Fortunatae</u>, which book began at the last climate, that is to say latitude 54° continuing to the Pole. (translated by E.G. Taylor, 1956, 58.)

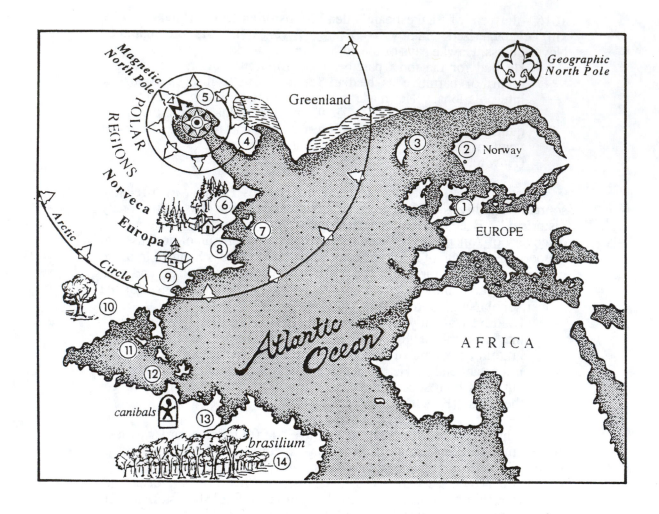

The Friar's Map—New World Expeditions 1330-1365

Cylindrical projection of ancient maps reveals Medieval English concept of Western Atlantic territories ca. 1360 as they were described in the friar's book—*Inventio Fortunatae*. The western half of the map above is derived principally from the northern or Arctic section of DeVirga's 1414 World Commercial Map. DeVirga's source has been identified as the English Franciscan, Nicholas of Lynn, who traveled to the "Polar Regions" between 1330 and 1365. The northeastern quadrant is from a 1424 map by the Dane, Claudius Clavus Swart; the southeastern section is from DeVirga's map.

Chronology of The Friar's "Polar" Expeditions

Highlights of 35-years of travel include the following: 1) Expedition sets out from Norfolk; 2) friar's visit with Norway's King Haakon VI in Bergen; 3) Iceland—staging area for Polar voyages; 4) friar observes ice on eastern shores of Baffinland and Greenland; 5) friar identifies magnetic pole—Foxe Isle—at 66°; 6) observation of forests in southern Labrador; 7) visit to Icelandic Isles of Newfoundland archipelago; 8) deserted towns and ships; 9) Norveca (a.k.a., Norumbega) is identified as habitable region of Arctic circle; 10) forests along the gulf; 11) mapping the great gulf; 12) observation of floating isles (the Antilles) west of Spain; 13) cannibals and a great river (the Amazon) along an east-west coast; and 14) identification of brasilwood forest—source of valuable red dyewood.

Map reconstruction and chronology are based on accounts by: Ferdinand Colon (1530), Martin Behaim (1492), Jacobus Cnoyen (ca. 1370), Bartholomew Las Casas (1563), Richard Hakluyt (1552 & 1599), Albertin DeVirga (1414); and Claudius Clavus Swart (Nancy Ms., 1427).

Over the span of three decades, while his patron battled foes in France, friar Nicholas traveled repeatedly to the distant isles of the "Northern Regions." Hazards surrounded the brave voyager at every turn: pirates, plagues, whirlpools, and hurricanes threatened his mission and tested his faith. In spite of such adversities, Nicholas lived a long and fruitful life.

The friar's associates observed that he was somehow protected from evil and the elements by what they called his "magical arts." Probably they had in mind his curious ritual using astronomical paraphernalia, reference books, and a compass. When he was in a hurry, he simply held an astrolabe in front of his face in order to ascertain the angle towards the appropriate constellation. When time permitted, the device could be suspended from a tree. There followed a period of time in which the priest gazed into the eye-piece of this device; he made numerous adjustments to the dials; then he had to record his angular measurements of sun, moon, or stars. He made this recording using parchment and a pen with an inkpot. The parchment contained the friar's gazetteer of longitudes and latitudes which estimated the geographical coordinates of the places he had visited. Anyone watching this ritual—in an era when science and mathematics were totally alien to ordinary people—must have been amazed by the friar's behavior and equally impressed by the precision of his craft.

The friar's humble appearance was another factor in the success of his mission. The friar's shaved head, cumbersome robes, and strange behavior must have added an element of humor to the life of this homeless wanderer. The religious symbols he carried and his "magical" equipment identified him as a man of God—and a wizard of some unknowable power. At times, his merriment and musical talents invested him with the aura of a jester or a buffoon. None regarded him as a threat; he gave no one cause for alarm. As a mendicant priest, he was used to traveling alone and begging for food when that became necessary. Sailors were always happy to have a man of God on board; settlers and natives were always anxious for entertainment and news of other lands. Whether the natives regarded him with reverence or disdain, it didn't matter to the priest whose only concern was service to God, king, and fellow men. His personal safety was equally of no concern: he was protected by faith and humility. In any case, the friar had no significant hairlock to tempt a warrior who needed trophies.

According to Richard Hakluyt (Principle Voyages, ca. 1599, 100), Nicholas initially traveled with an expedition that headed for Iceland. Most historians have assumed that the first trip took place between 1355 and 1360, however Stacy's (1823) biography gives a firm date of 1330. In those days, Iceland was a common destination for English ships heading "north," and it was from this dreary outpost of Medieval European civilization that the friar commenced his survey. Voyagers from Norfolk typically made the crossing in less than two weeks:

> From the haven of Lynn in Norfolk to Iceland, it is not above a fortnight's sailing with an ordinary wind, and it hath been of many years a very common and usual trade: which further appeareth by the privileges granted to the fishermen of the town of Blackney in the said county of Norfolk by King Edward the IIIrd for their exemption and freedom from his ordinary service, in respect of their trade to Iceland. (Hakluyt, 1599, 100)

From Iceland, the friar's company headed north by compass (but actually west by geographical bearings). According to brief excerpts that survive from Mercator's memoirs, they headed to the "northern regions" beneath the North Pole. Nicholas estimated longitude by recording days of travel, compass bearings, and celestial observations. Calculation of longitude in those days was a much more difficult task than determining latitude—so early measurements are often very inaccurate particularly near the Arctic Circle where compass declination, converging meridians, and the midnight sun were significant variables. Nicholas was a highly-skilled mathematician and astronomer, as well as a very intelligent man, so it is probably no coincidence that the accuracy of latitudes for northern territories on European maps improved considerably following the friar's first expedition (Nansen, 1911, 261). The earliest scientific chart of the North Atlantic—the Medici Marine Atlas of 1351—came twenty years later. This chart is notable for being the earliest portolan map showing Greenland in its correct geographical position west of Norway.

Friar Nicholas devoted thirty years of his life to subsequent voyages to the northern regions. According to the traveler Jacobus Cnoyen, the Minnebroder from Lynn (presumably friar Nicholas) visited lands first colonized by King Arthur in the 6th century (Hakluyt, 1600, 100; and Newton, 1932, 203). These lands included Grocland, Estotiland, and Frisland. English historian Hakluyt had no doubts that these lands included the East Coast of North America both north and south of Norumbega (the modern Nova Scotia). Grocland (or Great Land) is often shown on 16th-century maps west of Greenland—but it probably represents North America. Estotiland (or Estland) appears south of Greenland on several North Atlantic charts of the 16th century and probably represents Labrador. Frisland is shown on a map by Arabian cartographer Al-Idrisi (1154); he calls it "Resland" and places it north of England and west of Norway. Most Medieval and Renaissance maps show Frisland southwest of Iceland.

Orthodox historians have branded Frisland a "fabulous island," however the consistent position it occupies southwest of Iceland on early Renaissance charts suggests that it was an early version of Newfoundland or lands nearby that were originally reached and charted by sailors using compass bearings. Later, when navigators surveyed Newfoundland using geographical coordinates that enabled accurate placement of the "new-found" isle on maps, cartographers failed to remove the archaic Frisland that they assumed must be farther east. An account by Nicolo Zeno reported that numerous European fishing boats sailed to Frisland in order to take advantage of the abundant codfish and salmon. This description of the natural resources of the island suggests that Newfoundland is a likely candidate for being the Frisland of the ancients. The land was also known to Columbus who sailed there in 1477.

Cnoyen's manuscript reported that the friar's account of northern lands corresponded to tales of the same region that a priest from Dusky Norway told the Norse king in 1364. Thus, we can assume that the lands were fairly well known in northern Europe even though most geographers were unaware of their precise location. The names of those places also changed over time—making it difficult for historians to accurately follow the travelogs of ancient mariners. Cnoyen's source can be regarded as a knowledgeable informant: he claimed to have lived in Dusky Norway (Hudson Bay or Greenland) for many years, and he mentioned that he was a descendant of Arthur's original colony. This testimony was recorded by Cnoyen—whom the respected Gerhard Mercator called "a man of good judgment."

We can be certain that the friar traveled to the region of Hudson Strait—the Norse Ginnungagap—for he accurately described northern lands where the seas froze each winter along the eastern shores—yet remained open to commerce from the west. This characteristic is typical of Baffin Island and Greenland where offshore currents along the western shores keep the pack-ice from closing off the bays for most of the year. Some of the lands were inhabited by short people which the friar described as being only four feet high. These were the Inuit natives of northern Labrador, Baffin Land and Greenland. Maps of the 15th century often describe these "pygmies" living in Arctic regions.

The friar mentioned seeing deserted houses and the remains of huge ships that had been built using iron tools. Use of iron tools for fabricating massive beams and bulkheads identifies the habitations as European settlements. Fridtjof Nansen (1911) surmised that the friar had encountered the deserted Western Settlement of Greenland. However, Nicholas also told of visits to forested lands that were situated far beyond Greenland, and he mentioned that two of the isles near the North Pole were occupied by people other than pygmies.

Deserted villages might have been the remains of colonies located in Nova Scotia, Newfoundland, or Labrador. The maverick historian and iron engineer Arlington Mallory identified numerous European settlements along the East Coast:

> My detailed examination of a Newfoundland beach for remains of Scandinavian settlements has turned up evidence, though indirect, in support of the theory that settlements there were destroyed by the plague. Since the land there has been rising at the rate of 4 feet every century, it is possible to date various artifacts by their location in relation to the advancing shoreline. Proof of Norse occupancy during the period 1250 to 1400 exists in the form of artifacts, but there is no evidence of any settlement for any period subsequent to 1400. (Mallery and Harrison, 1979, 165)

John Dee's notes on the Cnoyen manuscript stated that Brother Nicholas traveled past forested lands—such as those described in Norse accounts of Markland (or Labrador) on the East Coast of North America. Therefore, we can be certain that the friar traveled to North America as he conducted his survey of northern regions: there are no forested lands northwest of Iceland—except those regions of North America that sailors reached by following compass bearings towards the Magnetic North Pole. Richard Hakluyt indicates that the friar's travels took him to Hudson Bay, southern Labrador, Nova Scotia and Newfoundland.

European immigrants from Germany, Greenland, Iceland, Ireland, Scotland, and Norway once occupied small villages and fortress communities in these regions. When Bubonic Plague (or The Black Death) spread to the region (circa 1350), many of the villages must have been devastated as badly as similar communities in Europe. Some towns lost more than half of their inhabitants; social order collapsed and survivors fled to rural areas or the wilderness to escape the rat-infested cities. The friar might have come upon some of these deserted villages late in the years of his survey of the Northern Regions. Of course, other hazards such as warfare, piracy, and famine could account for the abandoned settlements.

The Arctic Regions on Martin Behaim's 1492 globe indicate that at least two of the western lands were inhabited by Europeans as recently as the early 15th century. The most reliable reconstruction of Behaim's globe is the 1730 version by J.G. Doppelmayer. On this reconstruction (which Adolph Nordenskiold praised for its accuracy), there are four Arctic lands. Directly north above Norway is a contiguous land comprising Greenland and Baffinland (which on the globe is labeled "Wildt Lapplant"). The northwestern tip of Baffinland reaches almost to the North Pole—and in this manner mimics the close proximity of Baffinland with the Magnetic North Pole of Hudson Bay. During the 14th century, the magnetic pole was near Prince Charles Island in the Foxe Basin directly northwest of Baffinland. This close association between the location of the pole and Baffinland establishes beyond any doubt that Behaim derived his configuration of the Polar Region from a gazetteer of geographical coordinates for the very polar regions that friar Nicholas claimed to have visited. However, Behaim placed these lands around the Geographic North Pole more than a thousand miles northeast of their actual location. This misplacement has caused modern historians great confusion; and that confusion has been compounded by the fact that historians have relied on more recent reconstructions of Behaim's globe. The most often illustrated version—the one by G.E. Ravenstein in 1908—is also the least accurate.

Behaim's globe has an open, navigable sea over a thousand miles wide around the North Pole. If we consider that the distance separating the geographic pole from the magnetic pole is also over one thousand miles to the south, and if we adjust the position of these "polar isles" on Behaim's globe by that distance southward, these isles suddenly assume the approximate position of lands bordering Hudson's Bay. The fact that Columbus wrote a book about the feasibility of traveling across polar seas to China suggests that he had seen Behaim's prototype that portrayed the route across the pole as accessible to oceangoing ships. This is also what we would expect from the friar's travelog concerning his visit to the region of the magnetic pole of Hudson Bay where the sea is a thousand miles across and navigable in Summer.

Lands shown adjacent to the polar sea on Behaim's globe can be equated with territories named on 16th-century Danish maps. West of Greenland is Helluland (representing Baffin Land or northern Labrador). Next comes an island—Newfoundland, followed by two more large isles representing Norumbega and New York. Behaim identifies the last two as occupied by white Europeans. A caption for these two isles on his globe reads: <u>Hir findet man weises volk</u>—that is, "White people (Europeans) are found living here." The isles beside the caption lie in the same location later identified as "Norveca Europa" on the Venetian Map and as "Norbeca" or "Norumbega" on most 16th-century maps. Thus, we find a direct correspondence between the friar's map and the location of "white natives" encountered by early Portuguese and French explorers in the 16th century.

Nicholas eventually reached South America after crossing the Gulf of Mexico. This incredible achievement in the friar's travels is evident from Cnoyen's manuscript, for Dee states that Nicholas visited the land of brasilwood trees that produced a red dye (Newton, 1932, 205).

There is only one place in America that was identified during the 16th century as a source for brasilium (or brasilwood) and that was Brazil. John Cabot searched for the valuable tree along the coast of North

America in 1497, but he had to return with the discouraging report that there was no brazilwood along these shores (Newton, 1932, 134). Portuguese diplomats often lamented that French raiders trespassed on their private preserve (Brazil) and absconded with shiploads of the valuable dyewood. Such acts of piracy deprived Portuguese officials of taxes which they believed were due their own treasury in accordance with papal decrees and the Treaty of Tordesillas. Of course, France was not included in the treaty which was between Spain and Portugal—two countries which assumed they had exclusive rights to Atlantic exploration. Meanwhile, the French regarded the New World as an open market that was available to anyone willing to risk a trans-Atlantic voyage. When Portuguese diplomats complained about French privateers in the Atlantic, Francis I, King of France, sarcastically commented: "I should very much like to see the passage in Adam's will that divides the New World between my brothers, the Emperor Charles V (of Spain) and the king of Portugal" (Hale, 1966, 57).

Historical accounts of the 15th century suggest that the French may have learned about the source of brazilwood from the Irish. Carpenters at the Louvre in Paris used brazilwood paneling for the palace interior. The raw materials were imported on ships sailing from Irish ports; but the lumber didn't come from the forests of Ireland. It must have originated in Brazil (Ashe, 1962, 140; Chretien, 1993, 203; Thompson, 1994, 211).

The commodity, brazilwood, was so inextricably linked to northeastern South America that attempts to give the land an official Portuguese name failed. Pedro Alveres Cabral officially discovered and named the region Terra de Sanctae Crucis—"Land of The True Cross"— in 1501. However, much to the chagrin of Portuguese authorities, sailors and cartographers renamed the land "Brazil" as a testament to the valuable brasilwood trees that were common in the tropical forests. The friar's mention of this resource in the Inventio Fortunatae is one reason for believing that he crossed the Gulf of Mexico and traveled along the northern coast of South America. (Another reason is that this region also appears on the Venetian Commercial Map of 1414 AD.) Perhaps the friar's travelog motivated sailors from Bristol to seek out this pristine land in the early 1480's?

Confirmation that the friar's travels took him to the East Coast of North America and to tropical regions of the Caribbean can be found in the accounts of Bartholomew Las Casas (the Columbus biographer) and Ferdinand Colon (the mariner's son). In his book, Historia de las Indias, Las Casas reported that Islas de lo mismo se hace mencion en el libro llamando Inventio fortunata—that is, "islands are indicated across the Atlantic westward from the Azores and from the Cape Verde Islands in a book called Inventio Fortunata" (Quinn, 1974, 108). Islands west of the Azores along the North American coast include Newfoundland and the islands of Chesapeake Bay; west from the Cape Verdes are the Antilles and Cuba. In Le Historie de la vita e dei fatti di Cristoforo Colombo, Ferdinand Colon makes the statement that E Juvenzio Fortunato narra, farsi menzione di due altre Isole volte al-l'Occidente a piu australi che le Isole di Capo Verde le quali vanno sopra l'acqua nuotando—that is, "the Inventio Fortunata says that two floating isles lie west-southwest of the Cape Verde Islands" (Quinn, 1974, 108). South America lies in that direction. In the translation Ferdinand's book by Benjamin Keen (1959, 25), Colon adds his observation that: "Cases of this kind may explain why many people on the islands of Ferro, Gomera, and the Azores

103

assured the Admiral (Columbus) that every year they saw some islands to the west, and many persons swore it was so."

There is some evidence besides the friar's own testimony that he reached the Magnetic North Pole and Hudson Bay. This bay was probably known to earlier voyagers as "Christian's Bay" and a variety of other terms including the Glacial Sea of The West. Sailor-historian George Best (1578) in his narrative of Frobisher's voyage to Baffin Island quoted friar Nicholas as saying that "The land on the southwest is fruitful and a wholesome soil; the northeast is inhabited with a people called pygnaei" (Holand, 1959). The sailor attributed the friar's assessment to the region of Hudson Strait—but it could equally apply to Hudson Bay farther west. It is possible that George Best took this information out of Mercator's correspondence—or else he had heard folktales about the friar.

On his way back to England circa 1360, Nicholas visited the court of Norse king Magnus Eiriksson in Bergen. We can assume that this "courtesy call" was the result of the mendicant friar's habit of catching a ride on any available ship. Merchants made frequent voyages between Frisland, Iceland, and Bergen in those days—so finding a vessel for transit would not have presented an insurmountable obstacle. Superstitious sailors might well have fancied having a holy person along on the trip across the North Atlantic. The priest had good reason to visit the reigning monarch since many of the territories he visited were within the realm of Norse kings—ever since the 1261 proclamation of sovereignty over all the regions "from Norway to the North Pole." Regardless of his reasons, Nicholas remained in Bergen long enough to befriend a visiting priest from Dusky Norway (probably a Greenlander) to whom he presented his astrolabe in exchange for a testament. Jacobus Cnoyen, the Flemish writer who also traveled to Bergen, learned of the friar's travels from the priest who got the astrolabe.

It seems likely that the friar also visited the seat of the archbishop at Nidrosia (Trondheim). In the 13th century, Nidrosia ("Rose of the River Nid") was the site of a huge, gothic cathedral and numerous buildings required for Church business. The archbishop was responsible for clerical affairs in the northern region that included all of Scandinavia, northern England, Iceland, Greenland, and the western territories of Landanu (New Land) and Norveca (North America).

Nicholas is said to have traveled to the northern regions numerous times after his first expedition (Hakluyt, 1600, 101). Cnoyen's account stated that five trips took place after Nicholas wrote the Inventio circa 1360. If the frequency of the friar's visits to the northern regions seem excessive, keep in mind that making a map of the North Atlantic region had become the friar's chief responsibility. Other explorers made repeated trans-Atlantic voyages: Champlain, for example, sailed twenty-three times between Honfleur and the Gulf of St. Lawrence (Florio, 1966).

Although historians speak of the surveying expeditions of friar Nicholas as though he acted independently, it is more accurate to consider him the leader of a surveying effort undertaken by the Franciscan Brotherhood. It seems apparent from the Norfolk Biography that Nicholas continued his relationship with Oxford throughout his adult years, and he also produced a text on use of the astrolabe. The account of the friar's travels reported by the Flemish writer Cnoyen tells us that the Minnebroder sometimes traveled with companions who may have assisted in his surveying mission. On at least one occasion, Nicholas gave an astrolabe to a fellow priest from Dusky Norway. Historian Ralph Skelton (1958) surmised that this priest might have conducted an independent survey of Greenland. Although somewhat speculative, this conclusion rests on the appearance of several 15th-century scientific charts of the North Atlantic; Skelton theorized that the extent of new knowledge represented by these charts was beyond the capacity of a single individual. One of these maps, Yale's "Vinland Map" of 1440 includes fairly precise details of New World topography including Greenland, Lake Ontario, the St. Lawrence river, Florida, and Brazil. As an esteemed educator and foreign minister for the popular King Edward, Nicholas was in a position to marshal assistance from his Franciscan brothers at Oxford where initiates were just beginning to learn the surveyors' art.

The friar's book, Inventio Fortunatae (ca. 1360), was produced late in his career—perhaps after he retired to Oxford as a professor. As a summary of the Franciscan Brothers' North Atlantic mapping effort, it might have included gazetteers from numerous sources spanning several decades. Copies of the manuscript might have been revised substantially over the passing decades as later copyists added the most current geographical information. This practice wasn't at all unusual: a comparable volume, the Polychronicon by English geographer Ranulf Higden, was up-dated at numerous times during the 14th century.

The "Northern Regions" of English Seas

Medieval Europeans used such terms as "Northern Regions" or "Polar Regions" to designate isles in the vicinity of the Arctic Circle, because that was the direction of travel indicated on magnetic compasses on ships bound for Iceland and Greenland. Even when vessels sailed on towards the East Coast of the Western Continent (North America), they still had to sail on a northerly compass course for the first portion of their voyage. This common approach to western lands via the far North Atlantic created the impression that western voyages ultimately led to isles in the vicinity of the North Pole. Sailors who passed by Hudson Strait (which early mariners called "Christian Strait" or "Ginnungagap") and then traveled southwards along the East Coast to warmer climates still believed that these temperate lands were situated near the North Pole. Indeed, their own nautical charts showed these lands thousands of miles north of Europe—because the geographic pole above Europe was their frame of reference on current maps. When they started heading south past Hudson strait, compass needles still pointed towards the Magnetic North Pole of Hudson Bay. From this point on, the apparent direction of travel by compass seemed to be west. This gave the impression that they were heading above Russia towards Siberia and Cathay—when in fact, they were actually heading due south. Although friar Nicholas was aware of the problem and discussed it in his travelog, few cosmographers were able to rectify the discrepancy on world maps until the late 15th century.

Europeans who did not travel far from home were not likely to be aware of the mapping problem caused by reliance on the compass. The most traveled sea-lanes along the coast of Portugal are in close alignment with the Geographic North Pole, the Pole Star, and the Magnetic North Pole. This alignment created the false impression that the magnetic pole and the geographic pole were located in the same place at the top of the Earth. The problem was compounded by tradition: Classical geographers had argued that the geographic pole was the site of a magnetic mountain. When transoceanic travelers reported discrepancies between the direction

Polar Regions on the Paris Map of 1490

The Paris map which is sometimes attributed to Columbus shows a global view of Earth. The center point is Mt. Ararat in Turkey—the traditional focus of Jewish cartographers who followed the tradition of honoring the patriarch, Noah. The South Pole is situated near the tip of Africa; the North Pole is actually located inside the northern mainland between Europa and Asia—approximately at the symbol for "Geographic North." The location of the Geographic North Pole can be ascertained by noting the position of Greenland—whose bottom in reality points South. Since Greenland in this model points towards the top of the map, we can determine that the top of the map is actually South from a true geographical perspective.

The confusion regarding the orientation of the top of the map arises because of the failure of Medieval cartographers to distinguish between the geographic and magnetic poles. Modern historians have the same problem. Most scholars assume that maps and accounts of voyages beyond Greenland are either "fictitious" or they refer to trans-Arctic travels to Asia. Actually, voyages beyond Greenland or Iceland to the "Polar Regions" refer to travels to temperate lands near the magnetic pole at Hudson's Bay—indicated by the fleur-de-lis. These lands included Labrador, Newfoundland, and Nova Scotia. The Zeno narrative of 1380 or 1390, for example, told of a Venetian voyage to Frisland—which the author placed in the Polar Regions. Norse Sagas of the 11th century told of voyages to Wineland and Great Ireland (a.k.a. Albania—**A**) which were thought to be someplace north or northwest of Europe. We have subsequently identified the St. Lawrence Gulf as the region where Wineland was situated. This was the location of the "Polar Regions." Placement of Albania north of China on Medieval maps was a consequence of geographical naiveté. Thus, ancient cartographers welded North American territories to the apparent northern rim of Europe and Asia.

106

after a photograph of map in National Library, Paris

of compass needles and the Pole Star, they were invariably informed that something was wrong with their compasses—or their eyesight! Heinrich Winter noted mariners' reports about magnetic declination as early as the 13th century in Europe, but no one seems to have proposed that the magnetic pole was someplace other than where Classical writers said it should be—at the top of the globe (Kimble, 1938, 236).

Meaning of The Title—Inventio Fortunatae

Seers (1923, 132) translates the title of the friar's book, Inventio Fortunatae, as "The Fortunate Discovery." However, the preferred translation for the Latin word inventio is "to invent" or "to define scientifically." In this sense, the word indicates a scientific description of something. That "something" is the fortunatae—which happens to be a plural noun. But what are "the Fortunates?"

We will return to the meaning of the title after examining the context in which it was used. As a protégé of Roger Bacon, friar Nicholas was concerned with the scientific description of natural phenomena or places, and this description was best derived from observation and practical experience. This approach to the understanding of nature was in opposition to the practice of conventional geographers who deduced the nature of Earth through use of logic, scripture, or dogma. In Classical times, logic had served Greek philosophers who deduced that the polar regions were uninhabitable due to the frigid climate. Bacon had criticized this deduction because it was based solely upon logic without the benefit of objective experience. On the contrary, he knew and so stated in his Opus Majus, that the north polar region had a temperate climate. Of course, Bacon was thinking only about the reports of mariners who had traveled to the magnetic Polar Regions and who had reported that the climate was temperate and the seas navigable. Thus, friar Nicholas was faced with explaining a phenomenon of nature that had been wrongly addressed by Classical scholars and misinterpreted by Medieval monks.

The word Fortunatae in the title of the friar's book is plural—thus it refers to more than one thing or event. During the friar's time, the word fortunatae in geographical terms most often refers to Classical isles of Roman legend which were said to lie across the western sea. Most Medieval geographers assumed these isles were the same off-shore islands west of Africa—the Canary Islands—which are called Insulae Fortunatae on Medieval and early Renaissance charts.

Given that the friar was writing a geographical account, it is quite possible that his use of the term Fortunatae refers to his belief that he had found out the secret location of the Roman isles across the western sea. It was his finding—based on practical experience and use of scientific instruments—that the Fortunate Isles were actually situated in the Polar Regions—at least the polar regions relative to Europe. With this background in mind, a more-accurate translation of the title of the friar's book would be: "A Scientific Description of The Classical Isles of Greco-Roman Legend Known as The Fortunate Isles."

Scholastic Inquisition
—Controversy About The Friar's Identity

Skeptics among the ranks of orthodox historians have complained that historian Richard Hakluyt was biased towards the British cause. Presumably, this bias influenced the validity of his report in Principal Voyages that an English friar visited North America. His quotations from

Mercator's manuscript are perfectly accurate; we know this because the manuscript still exists—though in damaged form—much as it was when examined by Hakluyt circa 1582. Nor can there be any dispute regarding the existence of a book called the <u>Inventio Fortunatae</u> because it is mentioned by too many 16th-century writers.

Due to the controversial nature of the friar's expedition to North America—coming two centuries before the "official" discovery by Columbus—many historians have been reluctant to acknowledge the friar's important achievements. Foremost among these are the following: 1) the first historical survey of North America; 2) discovery of the Magnetic North Pole; 3) the first scientific map of the North Atlantic based on geographical as opposed to magnetic coordinates; 4) identification of North America as a continent; and 5) the first map of the Gulf of Mexico from Florida to Brazil. All of these achievements were alluded to in 16th-century maps and historical accounts.

However, modern historians discounted the impact of the friar's survey due their own confusion between the friar's expeditions to "Polar Regions" and Roman legends about a northern land called "Hyperborea." Since most historians regard the Roman territory as a "fable," the friar's travelog was also branded as a work of fantasy. By declaring the friar's work "fabulous," historians believed they had a reasonable excuse for consigning the friar and his travelog to the infamous "dustbin of history." It was a convenient way to dispose of an enigma that threatened the orthodox paradigm of the Columbus discovery in 1492.

Given that the <u>Inventio</u> was mentioned so often, it seemed reasonable to 16th-century historians that it wouldn't be too difficult to find a copy. Consequently, several English scholars, undertook an extensive search for the friar's manuscripts. But they found nothing. Should we be surprised? That search came nearly two centuries after the original manuscript had been written—and that version was probably regarded as a state secret. We also know that the manuscript didn't mention the author's name. Probably, portions of the document were incorporated into later works on navigation by other authors until they became increasingly more out-of-date and lost their practical value.

Some skeptics concede the existence of a book called <u>Inventio Fortunata</u> but claim that it was nothing more than a fantasy based on Classical mythology. Historian Samuel Morison (1971, 206) calls it a "Ghost Book." Others have challenged the identification of the friar who wrote the book, the reputation of John Dee as a witness to the Cnoyen manuscript, the veracity of Jacob Cnoyen, the scruples of Richard Hakluyt, and the location where the survey took place. Some critics have gone so far as to suggest that the survey was a total fabrication and that friar Nicholas never even existed.

Eva Taylor (1956, 67) noted that the only historical account of Oxford Franciscans, A.G. Little's <u>The Greyfriars of Oxford</u> (1892), failed to mention a specific Franciscan called "Nicholas of Lynn"; although she found another reference to a famous Oxford mathematician named Nicholas who was a Carmelite. She also speculated that Nicholas had become confused over the years with a certain Irish Minorite named "Hugh of Ireland." It turns out that Hugh happened to write a travelog in 1360—the same year that the <u>Inventio</u> was produced. From this scanty evidence, Taylor surmised that there never was an Oxford Franciscan who traveled to the Northern Regions. Instead, she concluded that it was Hugh of Ireland who sailed north—but he only got as far as Greenland where he recorded folklore about distant lands which he heard from local mariners. According to her theory, careless nationalists such as Hakluyt and Dee confused the legends of the Irish Minorite with an unimportant Oxford friar named Nicholas who they erroneously credited with the Irish travelog. And this travelog was only a compilation of hearsay and mythology—it was not a compendium of places from first-hand observation. Taylor ultimately dismissed John Dee as a charlatan who wound up "overseas chasing the will-o'-the-wisps of alchemy and crystal-gazing in Prague." Thus the accuracy of the friar's manuscript was suspect as was Dee's claim that England had sovereignty over ancient, North American territories. Both Dee and Hakluyt believed that friar Nicholas had visited English settlements in a region of the East Coast that was later known as "Norumbega." Hakluyt described Norumbega as a city and province someplace near modern-day Nova Scotia.

Tryggvi Oleson (1964, 106) ridiculed Dee's account of the Minorite by pointing out the obvious fact that the so-called "Polar Regions" and the North Pole are inaccessible due to the frigid climate. His criticism echoed the complaint of a 16th-century skeptic, Thomas Blundeville, who declared: "Neither do I believe that the frier of Oxford, by virtue of his art magic, ever came so nigh the Pole as to measure with his astrolabe those cold parts—unless he had some cold devil out of the middle region of the air to be his guide" (Oleson, 1964, 106). Blundeville, like many of his outspoken associates, assumed that the friar's account of "polar" travels in the Inventio referred to the Geographic North Pole. He was thus ignorant of the friar's travels near the magnetic pole where the climate is temperate in Summer. Based on this gross misconception, Blundeville and Oleson condemned the Inventio as an obvious fable. Oleson, like his colleague Eva Taylor, concluded that the only Nicholas known to historians was a Carmelite—not a Franciscan: "It may be stated conclusively that Nicholas of Lynn was not the author of the Inventio Fortunatae. The author is always described as a Franciscan or a Minorite, and Nicholas was a Carmelite" (Oleson, 1964, 106). Unfortunately, Oleson was also unaware of the Norfolk Biography which more than adequately explains the confusion over the friar's fraternal affiliations.

During the hoopla over the Columbus Quincentennial celebration, historian John Keay (1991, 39) called Nicholas "a Carmelite who worked in and may never have strayed far from Oxford." Keay's brief dismissal doubtless seemed sufficient for an ancient English friar who claimed the impossible: his travels to the North Pole, New England, and Brazil more than a century before Columbus. As an eminent historian, Keay contributed the force of his prestige to the mountain of disbelief concerning the friar's legacy. His conclusions were the result not of using the scientific method to find the truth—but of relying upon Orthodox assumptions and basing judgments on limited or faulty "evidence." Meanwhile, Keay's new book, World Exploration, lauded the accomplishments of the doctrinaire hero—Christopher Columbus.

So easily do hidebound historians brush aside one of the most enterprising, daring, and productive surveying efforts ever undertaken. And this by a friar who is described in Stacy's 1829 biography as both a Carmelite and a Franciscan. If we didn't have the friar's map, the issues of whether or not Nicholas ever existed, and whether or not he was a Franciscan or Carmelite, and whether or not he attended Oxford or Yale would all be academic questions of little importance. However, we have scientific survey maps of the North Atlantic and North America that were

Claudius Clavus (1424)

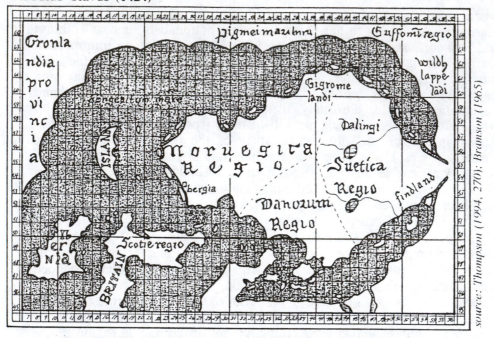

Newfoundland on Geographic Maps of The North Atlantic

Two maps demonstrate the continuation of North Atlantic cartography that seems to have begun with the Medici Atlas of 1351. These maps by Claudius Clavus (1424) and Jacob Ziegler (1532) show Greenland as part of a continuous land reaching across from northern Norway or Europe. The Clavus map implies that more than just the island Greenland is indicated in the narrow peninsula, because the legend calls this "Greenland Province." This interpretation is confirmed by the Ziegler map which identifies the southern extremity of Gronlandia as "Terra Baccalaos." This is the name given to Basque-Portuguese settlements near the Gulf of St. Lawrence; it is most often identified as Newfoundland. Thus we have confirmation that the name "Gronlandia" and particularly "Gronlandia Provincia" represented a transcontinental territory that included at least the northeastern region of North America.

Jacob Ziegler (1532)

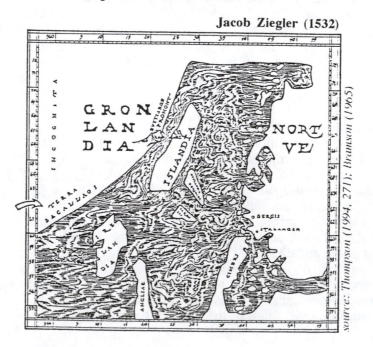

made at the very time Cnoyen's account said that the friar traveled to the Northern Regions. Orthodox historians may argue as they will over the veracity and reliability of Cnoyen, Bale, Hakluyt, or Stacy—but they will have to settle for the fact that a fairly accurate survey of North America was conducted between 1330 and 1360 by some very obstinate Franciscan friars. The most important map from that survey has been preserved and incorporated into the Venetian Commercial Map which Albertin DeVirga crafted circa 1414.

Early Franciscan Cartography of The North Atlantic

Historians have no documentation for what took place on most of the friar's expeditions, however the increasing accuracy of North Atlantic maps and creation of a standard Scandinavian map of the route from England to Wineland may derive from the friar's growing knowledge of the northern regions. Extant reports indicate that friar Nicholas presented his completed manuscript, Inventio Fortunatae, to King Edward III in 1360. But the exact date is uncertain, and the configuration of the 1360 map is also unknown. We know that the friar returned from the field on numerous occasions to deposit his gazetteers and replenish his spirit through companionship with Franciscan Brothers. Most likely, one or more of his Oxford associates assisted with the actual translation of field measurements into geographical coordinates for use in preparing maps. The friar's close association with King Edward and the royal family as well as frequent contact with sailors must have resulted in the gradual dissemination of kowledge about overseas territories.

During the thirty-plus years of field expeditions, several regional charts must have been issued to merchants and the king's favorites. And this is precisely what seems to have taken place with regards to the scientific mapping of the North Atlantic. Historians now have at least fourteen differing versions of North Atlantic maps based on scientific information: 1) Steffanson's copy of ancient Nordic maps—date unknown; 2) Medici Marine Atlas—1351; 3) Bishop Resen's copy of ancient charts—date unknown; 4) *DeVirga—1414; 5) *Claudius Clavus—1424; 6) *Yale's Vinland map—1440; 7) *Florentine planisphere—1447; 8) *Genoese Planisphere—1457; 9) *Fra Mauro—1459; 10) *Donnus Nickolaus Germanus—1482; 11) Henricus Martellus—1489 and 1490; 12) *Behaim—1492; 13) *Roselli—1508; and 14) *Mercator—1569. Of these, nine (*) can be traced to Franciscan cartographers, to relatives of Edward III (who we can reasonably assume had access to Franciscan maps), or directly to the Inventio. It was also common in the Middle Ages for disciples to revise the works of their predecessors—so we can also assume that the Inventio might have been up-dated with more recent information after 1360.

Friar Nicholas may have been the first cosmographer to correctly locate Greenland Island west of Norway instead of north or northeast where it appears on many Medieval maps and even several maps of the 16th century. Aside from cosmological maps of the Middle Ages, only two extant maps show Greenland Island prior to the Inventio Fortunatae. These are the Medici Atlas of 1351 and the Medicean Marine Atlas of 1351—both are within the lifetime of Brother Nicholas and may have been based on his northern voyages. On the Medici Atlas, Greenland Island is shown as a narrow peninsula on the western side of the map with the name "Alogia"—which is probably a derivative of the Medieval Latin or Old High Germanic word "alodium"—meaning freehold or non-

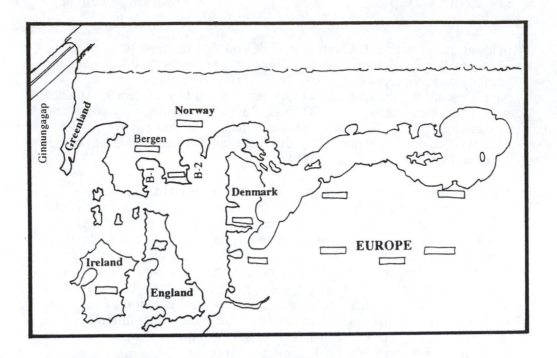

Geographic Maps of The North Atlantic

These maps from the Medici Atlas (1351) are the earliest known European maps using geographical coordinates. As they follow the proposal of Roger Bacon to construct a world map using the geographical plan of Ptolemy (which was based on longitudes and latitudes), they may represent the earliest work of the Franciscan mapping effort. They are recognizable as "geographic" maps because Greenland (here called Alogia) is shown as a narrow peninsula in its approximate geographical position west of Norway and northwest of England. On maps constructed using compass bearings, Greenland would have been positioned directly north of England. The Medici map includes the earliest mention of an Atlantic isle called "Salvagia" which is thought to stand for a forested land—the Markland of Norse sagas. On these maps, Norway has two bays facing south—Bergen (B-1) and Oslo (B-2). Bergen was the principal port city serving routes to England, Iceland, and Greenland.

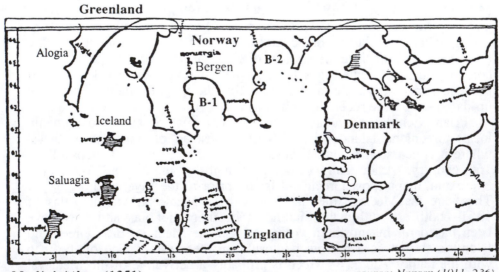

Medici Atlas (1351)   *source: Nansen (1911, 236)*

feudal estates. A variation of this name is "Alolanda." As both Medici maps show the island northwest of England, we can surmise that they were based on geographic as opposed to magnetic coordinates. It is the geographic tradition of mapping the North Atlantic that we presume was introduced by Nicholas of Lynn. This tradition was continued in the Venetian Map of 1414 which shows Greenland Island as a narrow peninsula north of England; and it follows on maps by Nicholas Martellus in 1467, 1489, and 1490 which show Greenland Island as a long narrow peninsula reaching out above Norway to a terminus north of England.

These are the first geographically-based or "scientific" maps of the North Atlantic. The accuracy of these maps reveals that navigators using astrolabes surveyed the Northern Regions. Had the navigators used magnetic compass bearings instead of astrolabes for their surveys, they would have reached the common—though mistaken—conclusion that Greenland was situated north or northeast of Norway. The Atlas is dated about twenty years after the first surveying expedition of friar Nicholas—giving plenty of lead time for the friar's survey notes in the form of gazetteers to reach Genoa. It was in this Italian city where the Medici Family based its mercantile empire; and it was under Medici sponsorship that the atlases were produced.

The Medici maps are illustrative of the "errors" that sometimes occur when cartographers convert geographical coordinates from gazetteers to the flat surfaces of parchment. In this case, the maps shows a peculiar orientation for the west coast of Norway—which oddly seems to have been laid on its side (that is, the west coast has assumed a horizontal, east-west orientation above Scotland). As the west coast typically has a north-south orientation when the Geographic North Pole is used as a point of reference, the 90° rotation of the coastline to the west—so that the northern border of Norway faces due west instead of due north—suggests that the cartographer decided to orient the Norway section of the maps to the Magnetic North Pole of Hudson Bay. Such an "accident" might have resulted from a misinterpretation of coordinates in a gazetteer of Northern Regions in which the surveyor identified the western North Pole (the magnetic pole) as the point of reference. If the cartographer assumed that the western point of reference also applied to Norway, then "north" for that section of the map would have been shifted 90° west.

Historians have no idea who conducted the accurate survey of the North Atlantic that resulted in the Medici maps. Brother Nicholas and his Oxford peers would be reasonable candidates for the honor: after all, they are the only skilled astronomers we know of historically who had an official assignment to conduct such a survey prior to 1351. If the Gray Friars included Norway in their gazetteers of Polar Regions and identified the magnetic pole of Hudson Bay as the point of orientation, then there is a good reason why Medici cartographers erred in orienting the west coast of Norway towards the Magnetic North Pole of Hudson Bay. We know from the testimony of Jacob Cnoyen that Nicholas visited King Magnus in Bergen and he gave an astrolabe to one of the priests at the king's court. By including Norway in his travels, and perhaps in his gazetteers, Nicholas may have introduced the misconception that Norway's coast had the same alignment as lands near the Magnetic North Pole.

Fridtjof Nansen (1911) believed that friar Nicholas had charted the coast of Norway in addition to Greenland. He based this conclusion on the grounds that geographical coordinates mentioned by Claudius Clavus in the Nancy Manuscript of 1427 were unusually accurate and provided sufficient evidence that skilled surveyors with astrolabes had visited those shores. The Clavus map of 1424—a.k.a. the "Nancy Map"—shows the tip of "Gronlandia Provincia" west of Ireland at the correct latitude of 60°. Of course, someone else trained in use of the astrolabe could have determined the location of the southern tip of Greenland; it didn't have to be Nicholas. Regardless of who actually took the measurements and produced the gazetteers, we have reason to acknowledge the importance of Franciscan surveyors, such as friar Nicholas, whose pioneering efforts began the process of scientific mapping in the North Atlantic.

Friar Nicholas and the Franciscan Brothers are the most likely candidates for beginning the scientific traditions of Danish cartography. The Atlantic coast of "Norveca Europa" on the Venetian Map of 1414 includes three headlands and an island beyond Norway. On later maps by Danish and Hungarian cartographers, these same headlands are identified as Greenland, Estotiland, and Markland. The singular isle on the East Coast is identified on the maps as "Promontorium Winelandia" which we now know was the northern peninsula of Newfoundland. This isle served as the gateway to a Norse colony called <u>Wineland det Goda</u> located someplace near Nova Scotia or the St. Lawrence Gulf. Bishop Hans Resen constructed a copy of ancient sea charts in 1605 which placed Promontorium Winelandia in the position of Newfoundland at the northeast extremity of the Gulf of St. Lawrence; his map has the region of Nova Scotia indicated as "Norumbega."

Commercial Benefits of The Franciscan Survey

Franciscan maps and gazetteers played a vital role in the growing prosperity of English merchants; they provided a foundation for Portuguese exploration of the Atlantic; and they enabled the trans-Atlantic expeditions of Columbus. Indeed, the map Columbus used to plan his 1492 voyage was derived substantially from the friar's survey. It was this survey that first pinpointed the location of Cipangu (a.k.a. the Antilles) which was the prime objective of the Spanish flotilla.

One of those who seems to have derived great inspiration from the <u>Inventio</u> and perhaps great fortune as well was the English merchant John Day of Bristol. His elder associate, John Jay, Jr., is the very same Bristol shipping magnate who was responsible for sending several expeditions west in search of Brazil each year from 1480 onward. Day was quite familiar with the <u>Inventio</u>, and in fact, he owned his own copy of the manuscript.

Although historians generally stress published reports that the Bristol expeditions never reached Brazil (due to contrary winds and currents), a letter which Day sent Columbus in 1497 reveals that some of the ships had actually reached their objective. The discrepancy between published accounts and personal correspondence probably arose from the tendency of merchants and royalty to regard details of their overseas expeditions as national secrets. After news arrived in England that Spaniards had finally succeeded in sailing to the Caribbean, Day apparently felt that secrecy was no longer imperative, and so he offered to share his knowledge about prior voyages with Columbus.

In his letter, Day mentioned that sailors from Bristol had reached <u>tierra firma</u> (continental lands) and had also discovered <u>Ysla de Brasil</u>—the Isle of Brazil (Morison, 1971, 206). These were two different places: the former being the northern continent in the vicinity of Cabot's "New-Found-Land," and the latter being some mysterious "isle" in the distant, southwestern Atlantic. The name "brazil" appears on the Angelino Dulcert map of 1325 as: <u>insula montonis sive abresil</u> (i.e., "the mountainous isle of brazil"). A Spanish Franciscan mentioned Brazil along with the Azores as one of the mid-Atlantic isles—although he did not suggest that it was actually located near the Azores. John Day noted that vessels from Bristol had sailed to Brazil <u>en otros tiempos</u>, that is "in years past." Their objective was the land of brazilwood trees. We know that the <u>Inventio Fortunatae</u> also dealt with a land of brazilwood trees. Since the fortunes of Columbus were not going very well in 1496, he may have sought to examine the ancient Franciscan's travelog in hopes of locating Brazil and shipping back a cargo of the valuable dyewood. And that is in fact what Columbus did in 1497. He sailed much farther south than on previous voyages to Hispaniola (the Antilles). After his vessel dropped anchor off the coast of Venezuela, Columbus stepped ashore for the first time on the mainland of the New World, and he set his men to work gathering brazilwood (Babcock, 1922, 55).

Columbus probably saw or heard about the <u>Inventio</u> during his travels to Bristol, England, circa 1476. The important knowledge he gained from the friar's manuscript on this occasion concerned large isles in the western Atlantic. These isles offered the potential of serving as waystations on trips to Asia. Columbus also learned that navigable seas and temperate lands in the Polar Regions provided access to Asia across the North Pole. He even experimented with that approach in 1477, and he wrote his own treatise on the feasibility of sailing to Asia across the North Pole.

Another mariner who probably owed a debt of gratitude to Franciscan surveyors was the Venetian, John Cabot (Johan Cabboto), who King Henry VII commissioned to lead western expeditions for England. Cabot's first expedition departed from Bristol in 1494 or 1497 and reportedly headed straight west on a latitude course straight for the Gulf of St. Lawrence. It seems that the more common route for a western voyage took vessels north by compass towards Iceland before heading southwest to Frisland—the direction Columbus had sailed in 1477. We can only speculate that Cabot had access to the <u>Inventio</u> as a consequence of his association with King Henry. We also know that one of his objectives was to find the land of brazilwood trees—which figured so prominently in the friar's travelog and in the voyages of Master Day. At any rate, the accuracy of Cabot's navigation south of the latitude of icebergs leads to the inference that he relied upon more than good luck and dead reckoning when he sailed west from Bristol.

Scientific Minorite
from a 16th century print

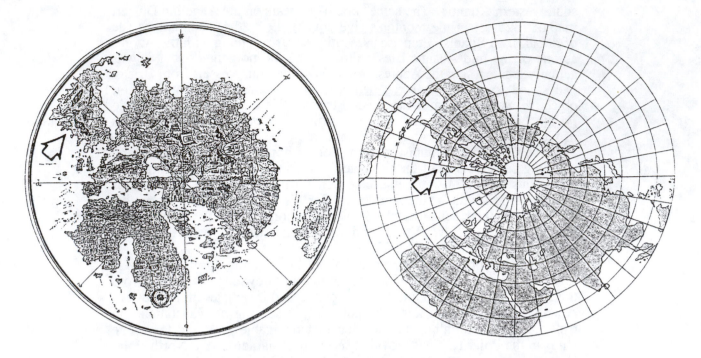

Norveca—The Northern Continent

DeVirga's map (left) compared to a modern stereographic projection of Earth (the Northern Hemisphere centered on the North Pole) reveals the comparatively similar positions of North America and Norveca—the offshoot continent in the northwest quadrant of DeVirga's map. The discrepancies in the two maps resulted from the use of different perspectives (DeVirga's map is centered on the Caspian Sea), different areas of inclusion (DeVirga portrayed both hemispheres on a disc), and different sources of information. DeVirga's map includes the east coast of America as far as Brazil—but it was placed along the top of Europe and Asia because that was the only place that made sense according to current religious and geological beliefs.

Norveca & Europa
from DeVirga's Map

Titles from the Northwestern Quadrant of DeVirga's map indicate that the overseas land was regarded as a Norwegian territory of Europe. Later maps referred to this region as Europe Spetentrionalis (Europe of The North) or simply Hyperborea (Land Beyond The North Wind). The crown over Norveca indicates this is part of the Norse kingdom—Norbega. The closeness of this title to Noribega—the name of a kingdom identified by Giovanni Verrazano along the East Coast of North America in 1524 is probably not coincidental.

source: Thompson (1995); after Destombes (1964)

116

The Norveca Map

England's mysterious friar, Nicholas of Lynn, assured the disdain of orthodox scholars and many of his contemporaries by naming his travelog—the Inventio Fortunatae.   His title blatantly refers to the "Fortunate Isles" of Greco-Roman legend.   Although Classical philosophers had said that these isles were located in the far west across the Atlantic Ocean, Medieval maps identified isles near Africa as the Fortunate Isles—a title that 15th-century geographers applied to the Azores, Canary Islands, and Cape Verde Islands. By choosing the title of a Classical legend, Nicholas expressed his belief that he had visited the same isles that were known to the Romans.

This analogy that Nicholas implied between the region of his survey and ancient legend seems perplexing. If we assume that his travels only took him to regions north of 54°—the so-called "Polar Regions" indicated in Mercator's account, then it doesn't seem to make sense that the friar actually traveled any place besides Arctic seas north of Iceland. However, if we keep in mind that the friar's reference point in the Western Hemisphere was the magnetic pole that is situated more than a thousand miles south of the geographic pole, and if we consider testimony from Ferdinand Colon and Bartholomew Las Casas that the friar had identified lands directly opposite Africa, then it becomes apparent that the friar believed that the lands he found in the north and west were the same ancient lands which Roman sailors reported across the Atlantic. Accordingly, the friar must have believed that Roman tales of voyages across the ocean were fading accounts of actual voyages—not simply "fables" or "fantasies" as orthodox historians have long proclaimed.

Extant accounts of the friar's voyages make no mention of maps— only extensive catalogs or gazetteers of geographical coordinates. Typically, field surveyors merely supplied cosmographers with tables of coordinates and geographical descriptions which sometimes included magnetic bearings and the directions of prevailing winds. These provided the best available reference points for those who used maps for navigation. It was not unusual for cartographers to be artistic sorts of people who were adverse to sailing; while true surveyors enjoyed traveling but often lacked patience for spending long hours with mathematical tables, drawing equipment and calligraphy. Christopher and Bartholomew Colon, Juan De La Cosa, and Martin Behaim were among the few who seemed equally adept at exploration and cartography. Albertin DeVirga was one of those who found his calling in the chart houses of Venice instead of hunkering down in Venetian galleys that ventured out onto the Atlantic Ocean.

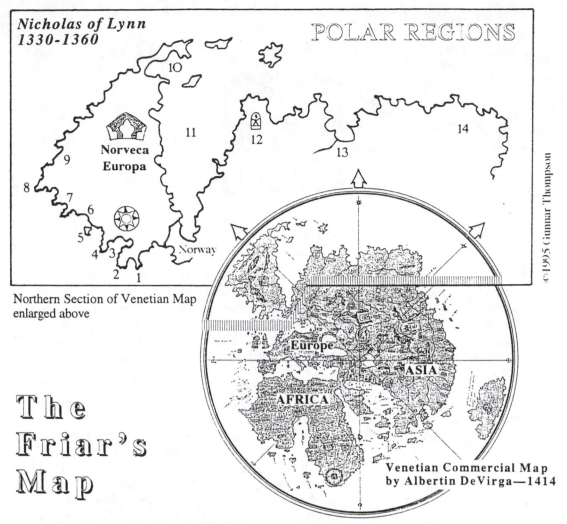

Nicholas of Lynn
1330-1360

Norveca
Europa

Norway

© 1995 Gunnar Thompson

Northern Section of Venetian Map
enlarged above

The Friar's Map

Venetian Commercial Map
by Albertin DeVirga—1414

Polar Regions ca. 1360 A D

Territories which English Franciscans surveyed during the 14th century are shown as
"Norveca Europa" or the Polar Region on a World Commercial Map by Albertin DeVirga (ca.
1414). These territories—representing the east coast of the New World—were shown north
of Europe and Asia in accord with cartographical traditions. Use of the name "Norveca" (or
Norway) to identify the northwestern continent extending beyond Norway shows that the map
was derived by someone such as Nicholas of Lynn who was familiar with the extent of Norse
overseas colonies during the mid-1350's. Greenland (1) is recognizable as a slender
peninsula connected by Arctic lands directly west of Norway. This same pattern is evident on
the Medici Atlas (1351), on a map by Claudius Clavus (1424), and on maps of the North by
Henricus Martellus (1489). Baffinland (2) can be identified by its similarity to "Wildt Lappland"
on Martin Behaim's globe of 1492. A strait (3) corresponding to Hudson's Strait separates
Baffinland from Labrador (4). The friar identified the Magnetic North Pole near Foxe Isle at 66°
North. His *Inventio* tells of islands west of Spain—the Newfoundland archipelago (5)—shown
here as a single isle. This island corresponds to "Promontorium Winlandia" on 16th-century
Danish maps of the north. Nicholas reported forested lands (6) and European habitations (7).
This region is called "The Isle of White People" on Behaim's globe. Hakluyt (1552) identified
the same region as "Norumbega." Nicholas related that he visited deserted towns (9) with
houses and ships built from "huge timbers." Abandonment was most likely a result of bubonic
plague (Black Death) ca. 1350. Nicholas reported isles (10) west of the Azores. These isles
on DeVirga's map correspond to Florida and the Antilles. Beyond these lie the Gulf of Mexico
(11) and the north coast of South America. A symbol for cannibals (12) marks this as the coast
of Venezuela. A gulf at the mouth of a river (13) reveals the first mapping of the Amazon river.
Nicholas traveled as far as a forested land of brasilwood trees—most likely Brazil (14).

In 1414, DeVirga compiled a world map from the latest mariner's charts and gazetteers. The northern section of his map constitutes the only known scientific survey of the Northern Regions and North America completed up to this point in time. Details of this section of the Venetian Map compare so closely with the account of the Inventio Fortunatae that it is reasonable for us to designate this map as having derived from the friar's extended survey between 1330 and 1360 AD. Henceforth, we shall refer to the northern section of the Venetian Map which was apparently derived from the Franciscan survey as the "Norveca Map."

The Northwestern Continent

The northwest quadrant of Albertin DeVirga's 1414 world commercial map has a vast continent extending out to the northwest from Norway. This continent, designated as "Norveca Europa," corresponds in size, position, and outline to early maps of North America. The correspondence is particularly striking on circular maps of Earth that have as their central point the eastern Mediterranean. This region of Palestine or eastern Turkey was a common focal point for mappamonds and early world maps in the portolan tradition.

Norveca's size and location are the first clues that the northwestern land mass represents North America. On the Venetian Map, Norveca is situated northwest of Europe—the same position which North America occupies on a polar projection of the globe as seen in a modern atlas. The Norveca map is the earliest-known example of North Atlantic maps that portray New World continental areas in relatively accurate positions in relationship to Old World continents. This map is based on geographic coordinates, thus lands such as Wineland and Greenland that most Medieval geographers thought were situated due north of Norway are shown close to their actual location west of Norway.

Most Medieval wheel maps indicated various northwestern isles in the approximate location of Norveca. The oldest extant map to show Greenland and Iceland in this location is a Danish T-O map circa 1300. Maps by the English geographer-monk, Ranulf Higden (ca. 1350), show ten isles northwest of Europe—including Thule, Iceland, and Wineland. Even in the time of Ptolemy (ca. 150 AD), there was knowledge of isles and lands to the north. Ptolemy called these lands Thule (probably Iceland), Scandia (Scandinavia), and Hyperborea. Scandia was the size of Scotland on Ptolemy's map—that is, it was only a small fraction of its actual size.

Numerous late Medieval maps include isles that are identified as "habitable lands" near the North Pole. Mainland areas near the pole are often called Hyperborea or Septentrionalis—meaning The North Land. Other variations include Hyperborea Europa, Ultima Thule, Norveca Europa, or just plain Norwegian Territory—as it appears in a map from the Ptolemaic Atlas of 1470. Geographers often referred to these lands as the "Northern Regions" or "Polar Regions"—indicating lands they thought were located near the North Pole. However, we have seen that maps which identify Northern Regions above the Arctic Circle as "habitable lands" resulted from confusion of the Magnetic North Pole of Hudson Bay with the Geographic Pole at the top of the Earth.

The name "Norveca"—that DeVirga gave to the northwestern continent—provides further correlation with territories which ancient geographers believed were situated near the North Pole. Maps by Michael Lok (1582) and Cornelius Judaeus (1593) show territories on circular

119

Northwest Quadrant, DeVirga Map, 1414 AD

Petrus Vestonte Map, 1321 AD
source: Skelton, et al. (1965, f. 2)

Catalan-Este Map, ca. 1450 AD
source: Skelton, et al. (1965, f. 2)

Giovanni Leardo Map, 1452 AD
source: Skelton, et al. (1965, f. 2)

Western Terminus of Norway

The continent of Norveca (North America) begins at the western terminus of Norway as indicated in the section (above) from DeVirga's map. European maps rarely show the western coast of Norway any farther west than the meridian between England and Ireland (as in the Medici maps of 1351). Most often, Norway terminates directly north of Denmark (or Dacia) as seen on the Vesconte Map (1321), the Catalan-Este Map (1450), and the Leardo Map (1452). Thus, we can regard the huge appendage (Norveca) projecting northwest from Norway as a germinal representation of North America. Most cartographers regarded the "Northern Regions" as being contiguous with Europe via a land bridge extending across the North Pole.

120

maps in northwesterly positions relative to Europe—i.e., in the same position occupied by Norveca Europa on the Venetian Map. We see similar names to Norveca associated with a New World region where the French-Italian explorer Giovanni Verrazano identified "white" inhabitants and "Norse villas" in 1521. These names are Norombega and Noribega—both variations of Norse or Germanic names for Northern Settlement. Other spellings for the New World territory include Norvega (a close match to Norveca) and Norumberga. Thus we have established similar geographical positions of territories having similar names. And these territories were identified by 16th-century European cartographers as North America.

In a 1912 review of the Venetian Map, Franz Von Wieser offered his critical assessment that he believed the mysterious Norveca represented a grossly inflated Norway. Indeed, his translation for the rubric "Norveca" was simply Norway. This translation is accurate, however the rubric is found beneath a crown signifying the sovereign realm of Norway. An adjacent label indicates that this territory is part of "Europa." So the complete designation is: The Realm of Norway Europe—here indicated as a land west of the Norwegian homeland—Norway.

Unfortunately, Wieser's assessment was hampered by limited information available in the early decades of the 20th century. We now have sufficient knowledge of mapping traditions during the 14th and 15th centuries to enable us to accurately delineate the borders and positions of adjacent northern territories such as Norway, Finland, Greenland, Baffin Land, Labrador, and Newfoundland. Maps by Vesconte (1321), Leardo (1452), Bianco (1436) and many others confirm the tradition among cartographers that Norway's western border terminated north or northeast of England. These maps show no lands farther west connected to Norway; and they identify the terminus along the shore of the North Sea.

The western coast or terminus of Norway can be identified on the Norveca map by two large bays typically shown northwest of Denmark. The second bay to the west is identified on the Medici Atlas (1351) as the bay of Bergen—Norway's principal west-coast port. These same bays are shown on the Venetian Map east of a slender peninsula that represents the Island of Greenland.

Traditionally, the Island of Greenland was regarded as a narrow peninsula attached to a trans-Arctic land mass called Hyperborea. Maps showing lands connected to the western border of Norway—specifically the Medici Atlas and Medici Marine Atlas of 1351—name the land "Alogia" (or Freehold Land) in reference to the freehold estates of Greenland. Norse historian Fridtjof Nansen (1911, 260) confirmed that the slender peninsula west of Norway on these ancient maps represented the island known in modern times as Greenland. The same pattern of showing the Northern Regions as a transcontinental land bridge connecting Greenland to Norway is seen in the "Nancy Map" by Claudius Clavus (1424) and maps by Jacob Ziegler in 1532 and 1535. Ziegler's 1532 map terminates in the southwest with a land called "Bacallaos." This title (a.k.a. Stockfish Land) most often refers to Newfoundland or a nearby isle in the Gulf of St. Lawrence. A few maps, including those made in accordance with reports from the Cabot expeditions refer to "Bacallaos" as the entire eastern coast of North American mainland. Therefore, Ziegler's map expresses the belief that a northwestern territory known as "Greenland" was contiguous with the North America. It also serves as a caution for historians who might be tempted to assume that

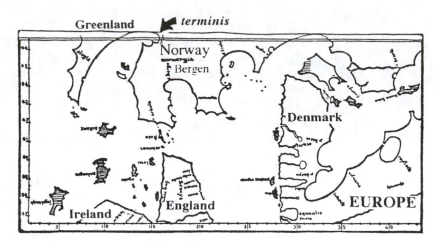

Medici Atlas (1351)
source: Nansen (1911, 260)

Western Terminus of Norway

Most Medieval and Renaissance maps show the west coast of Norway ending north or northeast of Denmark. One of the few exceptions is the Medici map (1351,top) which has Bergen directly north of England. Bergen was the westernmost port of Norway. The northwest section of the Bianco Atlas (1436, center) and the Genoese Map (1457) show Norway's west coast northeast of England. Since we know that the west coast of Norway and thus its western border was northeast of England, lands extenting farther west from the top of Norway must represent either Greenland or some other lands to the west. Finland was traditionally shown east of Gotia on the Baltic Sea.

Lelewel (1857) identified the first peninsula northeast of Norway on the Genoese Map as "Greenland." This was based on his reading of the original label. This is consistent with the Medici Map of 1351 in which the first headland —west— is Greenland (Alogia). But in the case of the Genoese Map, Greenland is northeast of Norway. This follows a tradition in European mapping of showing lands beyond (or west) of Norway above northern Europe. Of course, lands beyond Greenland were also shown above northern Europe or China—and these lands correspond to North American territories such as Baffin Island, Labrador, Newfoundland, and Nova Scotia.

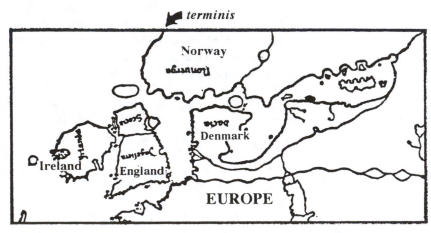

Andrea Bianco Atlas (1436)
source: Nansen (1911, 267)

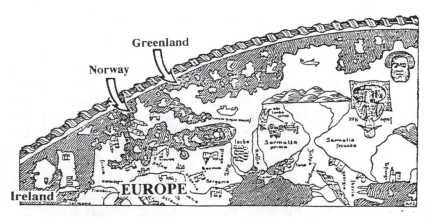

Genoese Map (1457)
source: Nansen (1911, 287)

122

references to "Greenland" in ancient mariners' accounts refer only to an Arctic isle. In fact, numerous references to "Greenland" actually correspond to mainland (North America). Typically, these references include such lands as Labrador and Canada below the Arctic isle.

There are two obvious explanations for the naming of northern Canada and the maritime provinces as "Greenland." First, this is the region where refugees from Greenland Island migrated, and they christened the new land with the name of their homeland—a not uncommon practice. Second, the land had abundant trees—thus it was a "green" land in reference to the vegetation and climate. Third, the name Greenland had become so common by the 15th century as a designation for habitable lands that were presumed to be in the Northern Regions— that any habitable lands to the north were automatically called some version of "Tera Verte" (that is, "green land"). This is the name that the Duke of Moscow gave to the mostly frozen (but marginally habitable) isle of Svalbard—a.k.a. Spitsbergen.

The portrayal of Norveca as a continental-sized land area across the northwest Atlantic Ocean in the approximate location of North America, constitutes prima facie evidence of the New World on a map nearly a century before the "official" discovery of America. The identification of the Norveca continent with North America is confirmed by a comparison of the coastlines on the Norveca map with those of Danish maps of the North Atlantic.

Topography of The Saga Map Tradition

The overall shape of Norveca's land area is similar to a modern map of North America. The gross outline is the same: both have a strait between Labrador and Baffin Land that leads to a huge bay (Hudson Bay); both have a northern section facing the Atlantic that includes major headlands or peninsulas; both have a large island (Newfoundland) midway down the northeast coast; and both end with a peninsula (Florida) which is adjacent to a huge gulf (the Gulf of Mexico).

Norveca's east coast has a distinct series of headlands that characterize the scientific mapping tradition of the North Atlantic. These headlands, which were based on Icelandic sagas dating to the 11th century include: 1) Greenland, 2) Helluland, 3) Markland, 4) Promontorium Winelandia, and 5) Wineland. The Norveca map (which was based on the friar's 1360 gazetteer) marks the beginning of a cartographic tradition that includes the Medici Atlas (1351) and maps by Claudius Clavus (1424—the "Nancy Map"), Sigurdur Stefansson (1570 or 1590), Bishop Hans Resen (1605) and the Hungarian Vinland map of 1599. From 1424 on, all of the maps show the western headlands as extensions of mainland along a trans-Arctic continent. This continent extended from Norway or northern Europe and continued unbroken across the North Atlantic to the Northern Regions in the west.

The first headland—called "Greenland"—is usually portrayed as a narrow peninsula reaching down to about 60° North latitude. Some maps show a fairly accurate coastline of deep fjords, while the Hungarian map portrays Greenland as an island. However, aside from late summer or during periods of particularly cold winters, Greenland and northern Canada are joined to the polar ice cap by a bridge of ice that extends to Norway. Those maps showing a slender peninsula of land for Greenland Island reflect the fact that the east coast is virtually uninhabitable due to coastal ice sheets that extend down from the mountains.

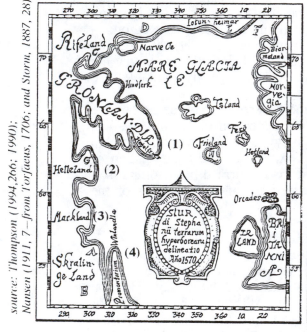

source: Thompson (1994,266; 1990); Nansen (1911, 7—from Torfaeus, 1706; and Storm, 1887, 28)

1) **Gronlandia or Greenland Isl.**
2) **Helluland, Estotiland or Baffin Isl.**
3) **Markland or Southern Labrador**
4) **Prom. Winlandia or Newfoundland**

Geographic Saga Maps

Three very similar copies of ancient sea charts have survived the ravages of time. Shown above are Sigurdur Stefansson's 1590 map and a schematic copy of a map by Christian Fresio (a.k.a, Bishop Resen) which bears the date of 1605. However, the bishop indicated on his map that his "composite map" was based on charts many centuries old. A Hungarian map from Tyrnavia (1599) is very similar to the Stefansson Map—but it has sufficient modifications to identify it as having been derived from a separate, earlier map. Helge Ingstad published a copy in Westward to Vinland (1969). Numerous Western historians have disparaged these maps as vain attempts to "usurp the glory of Columbus," however the fact that they follow the very tradition established by the Albertin DeVirga map establishes their ancestral pedigree beyond any doubt. All these maps show four headlands or peninsulas west of Norway. These are 1) Greenland; 2) Helluland—a.k.a., Estotiland (Baffin Island); 3) Markland (Labrador); and 4) Promontorium Winlandia (Newfoundland). The identification of Promontorium Winlandia as an island—Newfoundland—is fairly common. Paul Chapman (1981) made such an identification; so did Gwyn Jones (1986, 283) and Helge Ingstad (1969). This same sequence of three headlands followed by a major island is seen on the Norveca continent in the Albertin DeVirga Map.

The next headland on the Norveca map corresponds to Icelandic sagas that designate the second headland beyond Norway as Helluland (slab rock land). This land is most often identified as Baffin Island. Some scholars also include the northern half of Labrador because of similar topography. The shape of Baffin Land as a broad headland attached to Greenland is seen on maps derived from the 1492 globe by Martin Behaim. On Behaim's globe, the headland attached to the west of Greenland has a bay and a small peninsula on the northern side adjacent to the North Pole. A similar configuration is also present on the Norveca map. Although modern maps show Davis Strait separating Baffin Land from Greenland, this "strait" was often closed off at the north end by ice. Thus, early maps often refer to the strait as "Davis Gulf." A close correspondence between these two maps and the actual physical shape of the region can be seen by comparing them to a modern atlas. Baffin Island is clearly the region designated "Wildt Lappland" on Behaim's globe, and it is definitely the second headland of Norveca.

The third headland, Markland, was known as a land of trees. Southern Labrador suits the description in the sagas, although some scholars believe Newfoundland was considered part of this territory. Other names for the region included "Estotiland" (a variation of Scotland) and "Skraeling Land" or Land of Savages (i.e., non-Christians). Markland was a common destination for vessels from the Norse settlement on Greenland, as well as Iceland, and Norway. As late as 1347, Icelandic annals reported that a ship from Markland loaded with lumber had crashed upon the western coast. The ship was destined for European markets. The king of Portugal dispatched a vessel to Labrador shortly after Jao Fernandez identified its location circa 1495. Accurate identification of the route to Labrador was important because the Portuguese were in need of lumber. The king's ship was assigned to bring back a cargo of wood and slaves on a round-trip voyage that was expected to take from two-to-three months.

Most scholars, including Paul Chapman (1981) and Gwyn Jones (1986, 117), have identified the fourth headland on the maps, Promontorium Winlandiae, as Newfoundland. The reason why the island is referred to as a "promontory" is because the northeast corner sticks out into coastal waters sufficiently to be regarded as a reliable landmark. The island is situated north of the Gulf of St. Lawrence and across from "Skraelingland"—southern Labrador.

South of Newfoundland is the Gulf of St. Lawrence, and beyond that lies continental land—the "Wineland" of the sagas and Norse geographical texts. Richard Hakluyt identified this area as Norumbega; Verrazano's Norumbeque extended from Nova Scotia to Florida—approximately the same territory labeled "Norveca Europa" on the Norveca map.

DeVirga's map is the first to show headlands beyond Greenland; it is also the earliest extant map having the Saga Map pattern of three headlands followed by an island as a representation of territories northwest of Norway. It is the first map to show the joint relationship of Greenland and Baffin Land joined together as they are most of the year by an ice shelf across Davis Strait. It is the oldest known map to show the vast extent of Norse territories in the New World—here labeled "Norveca Europa." They are shown as a continent in the same relative position as North America on a circular map of Earth. Since there are extant historical accounts of Norse annexation of lands to the (Magnetic) North Pole, there are extant reports of tax collectors spending three years to complete

Northern { Regions {

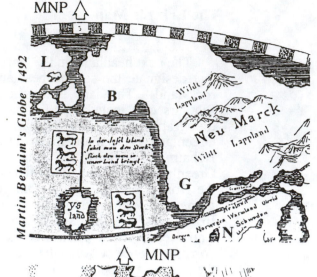

Martin Behaim's Globe 1492

Hammond's Atlas for 1963

DeVirga's Map 1414

Identification of Greenland & Baffin Island
Joint Headlands in North Atlantic Cartography

The Friar's Map (as shown on DeVirga's 1414 rendition—below) is the earliest known map to show Greenland and Baffin Island as adjoining territories. Numerous 16th-century cartographers also showed Greenland and Baffin Island as part of a trans-Arctic land reaching from Europe to North America. In Martin Behaim's version of the Northern Regions (top), Greenland (G) is shown adjoining Baffin Island (B). Baffin Island can be identified on this map by its position relative to Greenland and by its shape: the outline shows one peninsula reaching towards the Magnetic North Pole (MNP) and three humps or peninsulas on the opposite side. This configuration matches nicely with Arctic land areas as they appear in Hammond's Atlas (center). In this case, an ice sheet is shown between the islands as it would appear until late summer. Greenland can also be identified as the first peninsula northwest of Norway on Behaim's globe and on DeVirga's map. Lands west of the adjoining Baffin-Greenland include Labrador (L), Newfoundland (F) and Norveca (North America).

B = Baffin Island
E = England
F = Newfoundland
G = Greenland
I = Iceland
L = Labrador
N = Norway

MNP = Magnetic North Pole

rounds in Norway's western isles, there are port documents and Vatican records showing imports of North American furs to Europe, there are expeditionary reports of white settlements along the East Coast, and there are archeological reports of artifacts and masonry dwellings in the Ohio, Charles, Hudson, and St. Lawrence river valleys—we can conclusively state that DeVirga's Norveca continent is none other than North America. This was a region of extensive Iron Age settlement more than a century before Columbus.

The Norveca map includes the East Coast as far as South America—making it the first map to clearly show New World territories. Among the more pronounced features of this coastline are Florida, the Antilles, and the Gulf of Mexico.

The Southeastern Peninsula & The Origin of Florida

One of the more intriguing elements of the Norveca map is the pronounced appendage reaching out from the northwestern corner and surrounded by three huge isles. Orthodox historians might be tempted to dismiss both Norveca and its appendage as pure fantasies—for no such land exists northwest of Norway. However, many difficulties confronted the map's Venetian creator, Albertin DeVirga, and it is these difficulties that were responsible for the strange shape of his Old World and New World lands. He had to compile his map from gazetteers drawn by numerous surveyors using different points of reference. He had to convert field reports and geographical calculations of the Western Hemisphere and somehow place these lands from the opposite side of the globe alongside Old World continents. And due to religious traditions, he had to center his map on the Holy Lands. Thus, we might be able to appreciate the enormous challenge that confronted him.

There was no way for DeVirga to simultaneously show the approximate shape of Florida and at the same time place it anywhere near its true location on the globe. Modern cartographers have devised a reasonable solution in the form of cylindrical maps—but these are severely distorted at the Polar Regions. Since most people are least interested in that portion of the globe, the distortion causes the least inconvenience. However, DeVirga had to be content with the available technology, so he showed Florida and the adjacent tropics around the Caribbean Sea in what his contemporaries regarded as the "tropical Northern Regions." Like numerous Medieval maps, the Norveca map shows temporal lands (Hyperborea) near the North Pole and across the top of Asia simply because there was no better place to put them on circular maps of the 15th century.

Florida can be identified on the Norveca map by its location at the corner of the northern continent where it is also situated between the Atlantic Ocean and a great gulf—representing the Gulf of Mexico. The three isles represent the Antilles. Although this explanation doubtless seems far-fetched to orthodox skeptics, it will be shown that a tradition of cartography was initiated by this map that leads directly to the accurate placement of Florida on later maps. By the 15th century, globes and elliptical maps enabled cartographers to show land areas from both hemispheres simultaneously and with reasonable accuracy. However, the northern regions on all these maps were considerably distorted (and grossly enlarged) due to the inability to portray converging meridians at the poles.

127

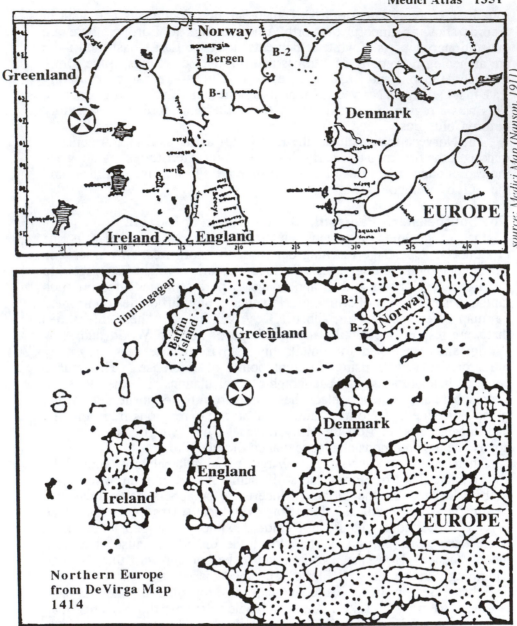

source: Medici Map (Nanson, 1911)

Identification of Greenland on the DeVirga Map

The tip of Greenland is marked by the target symbol on the Medici Map (1351, top) and the DeVirga Map. Greenland can be identified on the Medici Map by its location and name. Here it is called Alogia—referring to the "freehold" lands of Greenland. The narrow peninsula and its location are very similar to a peninsula on the Claudius Clavus Map of 1424 on which the land is called "Gronlandia Provincia." The Medici Map shows two bays (B-1 and B-2) between Denmark and directly north of England. At the top of the western-most bay is the title "Bergen" for the principal western port of Norway. On DeVirga's map and most other maps, Bergen (B-1) is shown on the west coast towards the northeast of England. Thus, Greenland can be identified as the first headland west of Norway. As seen on DeVirga's map, it has the common, narrow peninsular shape; it is situated north of England; and it is shown adjacent to a larger island to the west that represents Baffin Island. These common features of contemporary maps enable us to identify this first headland on DeVirga's map as "Greenland," and we have reasonable assurance that our identification is accurate. This is not a wild guess; it fits with the known traditions of the age.

128

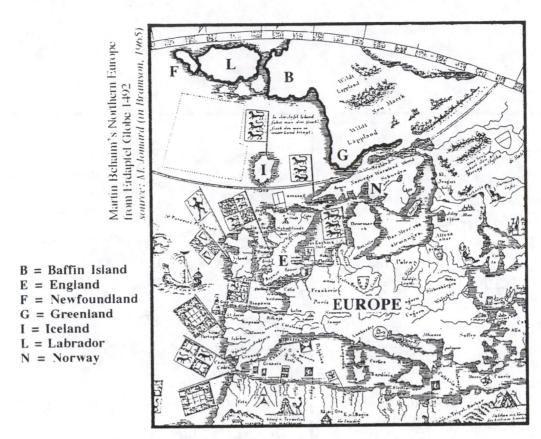

Martin Behaim's Northern Europe
from Erdaptel Globe 1492
source: M. Jomard (in Bramson, 1965)

B = Baffin Island
E = England
F = Newfoundland
G = Greenland
I = Iceland
L = Labrador
N = Norway

Identification of Baffin Island

A section from Martin Behaim's globe (above by M. Jomard 1842) shows a northern territory called "Wildt Lappland." This land corresponds to the combined territories of Greenland (G) in the south near the Arctic Circle and Baffin Island (B) farther north near the North Pole. Greenland can be identified by comparing Behaim's map to the Donis Kort (1468, below) which has "Engronelant" clearly indicated at the top right. It can be seen that the outlines of Scandinavia and Greenland on both maps are identical. Territories on Behaim's map above Norway are oriented towards the Magnetic North Pole which lies directly north of Iceland (I). Baffin Island appears as a broad land with three humps on the bottom and a small peninsula on top. The waterway between Baffin Island and the next land west (Labrador) was called Ginnungagap or the presumed passage between the Atlantic and the source of water at the North Pole. The Donis Kort introduced the practice of showing Greenland with a broad tip; earlier maps had a narrow peninsula.

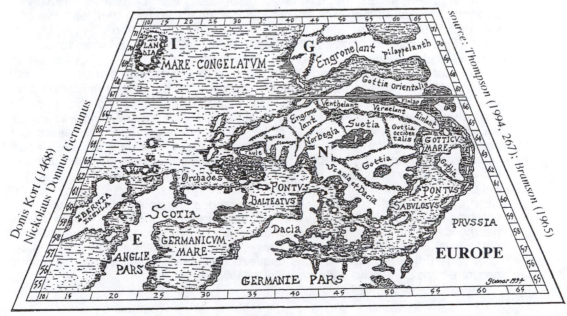

Donis Kort (1468)
Nickolaus Donnus Germanus

source: Thompson (1994, 267); Bramson (1965)

129

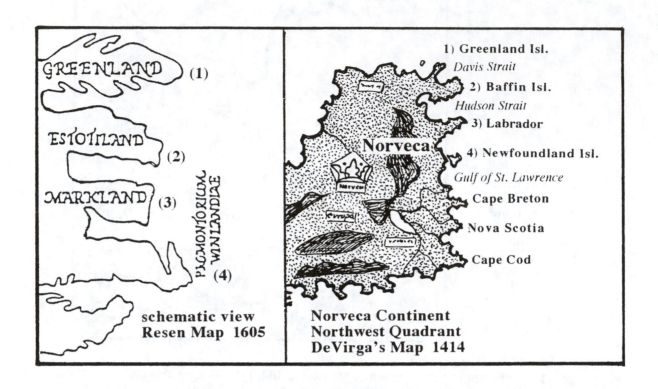

schematic view
Resen Map 1605

**Norveca Continent
Northwest Quadrant
DeVirga's Map 1414**

1) Greenland Isl.
Davis Strait
2) Baffin Isl.
Hudson Strait
3) Labrador
4) Newfoundland Isl.
Gulf of St. Lawrence
Cape Breton
Nova Scotia
Cape Cod

DeVirga's Norveca Continent 1414 AD
Beginning the Tradition of Geographic Saga Maps

Orthodox historians once assumed that Geographic Saga Maps, like those of Sigurdur Stefansson (1590), the Hungarian Vinland Map from Tyrnavia (1599) and the original charts which Bishop Resen used for his map of 1605 were all based on post-Columbian originals. Some believed that the maps were part of a plot to deprive Columbus of the glory for discovering America. Others assumed that the lands represented on the maps were innocently named after lands identified in once-forgotten sagas that somehow resurfaced after Columbus. However, geographic maps of the North Atlantic can now be traced back to at least two pre-Columbian sources: the Medici Maps of 1351 and the Albertin DeVirga Map of 1414. This later map—and possibly the Medici maps—follow the known voyages of the English friar-astronomer, Nicholas of Lynn in the mid-1300's. DeVirga's map shows a large, continental land (the Norveca continent) extending out from Norway in the northwest quadrant. The first headland of this continent is identified as Greenland, and its adjoining headland is identified as Baffin Island—based on its position and size relative to Greenland. In the mid-1300's, Greenland was always shown as a narrow peninsula; maps of the 15th century show Baffin Land as a broad peninsula with a gulf at the top. The third headland we can assume is Labrador as it lies across a great gulf from Baffin Island. This gulf corresponds to Hudson Strait—known to the Norse as Ginnungagap. The fourth headland is an island—in fact the only island on the entire Norveca continent. This island corresponds to Newfoundland—which is the only huge island heading south from Labrador until reaching Cuba. Thus, DeVirga's map has the identical sequence—three peninsular headlands followed by an island—that occurs on all subsequent North Atlantic maps from Scandinavian sources. This is a cartographical tradition spanning the 15th and 16th centuries—i.e., it is unquestionably pre-Columbian, and it is fairly accurate considering the early stages of Atlantic exploration.

130

Norveca—Mirror to The Friar's Itinerary

The travels of the English friar-astronomer, Nicholas of Lynn, have been detailed in the previous chapter. It is evident from Mercator's account of the Flemish writer, Jacob Cnoyen, that friar Nicholas traveled along all of the territories illustrated in the northwest quadrant of the Venetian Commercial Map. As friar Nicholas is the only historic figure prior to the creation of this map who visited the "northern regions" for the purpose of conducting an accurate survey, it is posited that Albertin DeVirga derived the northwest quadrant substantially from the friar's account of his expedition and from the Franciscan gazetteers that were assembled over the span of thirty years. It is also possible that DeVirga's information came from various copies of the Inventio maps and indirect sources that had access to other Franciscan gazetteers.

Martin Behaim attributed part of his globe to contemporary Portuguese explorations. Although modern historians typically attribute only the coast of Africa on his globe to Portuguese sources, we have noted that northern voyages by Dulmo, Scolvus, and Behaim into the Northern Regions are likely sources for information regarding New World lands—which Behaim mistakenly placed in the Arctic Circle. Fridtjoff Nansen deduced that Behaim had derived his knowledge of Scandinavia and Greenland directly from the Inventio Fortunatae (Skelton, 1965, 175). He made the same conclusion regarding the Clavus map of the north in 1424 and a papal letter of 1448 which describe the habitable regions of the north in sufficient detail to confirm an actual visit by someone skilled in scientific cartography.

Richard Hakluyt (1582) leaves no doubt regarding his belief that Nicholas traveled along the East Coast of North America from Greenland to Florida. These travels included visits to coastal villages in a region of the eastern seaboard known as "Norumbega" (i.e., Nova Scotia, Massachusetts, and New York). He also reported that Nicholas traveled as far as the land of brasilwood trees. Such a voyage corresponds to lands shown on the Venetian Commercial Map north of Europe where a distinctive peninsula seems to represent Florida, adjacent isles seem to represent the Antilles, a great gulf is suitably placed for the Gulf of Mexico, and the opposite coast bears the symbol of Gog-Magog representing a Land of Cannibals. Renaissance cartographers placed similar symbols on the north coast of the Mundus Novus (South America) to represent cannibals who attacked unwary sailors. These were the infamous Caribs that Columbus described in the Caribbean Sea.

Thus, Norveca and adjacent territories extend for the entire length of the friar's travels from Greenland to Brazil as they are specified in accounts of the Inventio Fortunatae.

The Temporal Limits of Norse Sovereignty

Icelandic sagas and Catholic geographies including those by Ranulf Higden consistently identify the isles near the North Pole as Greenland, Helluland, Markland, and Wineland. This description is consistent from the discovery voyages of Leif Ericson in 1003 to Higden's Polychronicon in 1325. The isle of Frisland was added by the 11th century; and in 1261, King Haakon of Norway added a new territory with his proclamation of sovereignty over lands from Norway to the North Pole. This region was referred to as Regnii Norwegie the "Realm of Norway" on the 14th-century Andreas Walsperger map and as the realm of "Norveca Europa" on the Norveca map. References to Norse sovereignty in the Polar

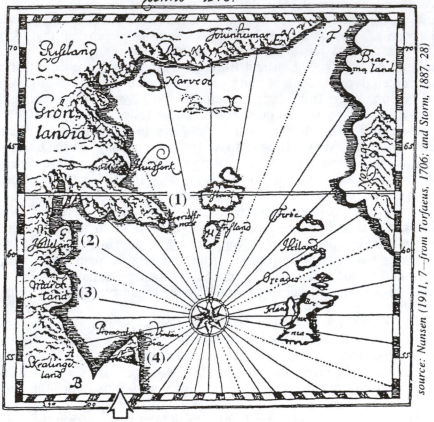

source: Nansen (1911, 7—from Torfaeus, 1706; and Storm, 1887, 28)

Promontorium Vinlandia
or Newfoundland

Geographic Saga Map

A 1590 copy of ancient sea cards or mariner's charts by Sigurdur Stefansson shows the traditional "northern regions" mentioned in Norse sagas. The four headlands are: 1) Gronlandia; 2) Helluland or Estotiland; 3) Markland; and 4) Promontorium Vinlandia—an island now commonly identified as Newfoundland. On this map, Promontorium Vinlandia is shown adjacent to mainland territory here called Skraelingeland and taken to represent southern Labrador. The first mention of these lands can be traced to the sagas of Leif Ericson and Icelandic voyagers from Greenland. Originally, saga maps on sea cards showed a magnetic orientation with headlands situated north of Norway. Here, they are shown in fairly accurate geographical positions—an indication that their placement has been based on celestial observations. The earliest source for such observations can be traced back to an English friar, Nicholas of Lynn. This map follows the tradition established in the Medici Atlas (1351) which shows Greenland as a narrow peninsula northwest of England. The immediate predecessor to this map is the 1424 chart by Claudius Clavus, and before that the 1414 world map by Albertin DeVirga. Most scholars believe this map was done in 1590—presuming the 1570 date to be a copyist's error.

Regions are not often found after 1350—at which time the Black Death devastated Norse colonies and the homeland. Some historians estimate that two-thirds of the population perished. German pirates plundered Norway's coasts thereby severing the few remaining ties to New World colonies. In 1484, Hanseatic pirates massacred forty sailors from Greenland Province—probably from the region of Nova Scotia (Oleson, 1964, 121). The plague and the subsequent disintegration of the Norse realm and the probable collapse of Norveca as a political and military entity places a timeline on the use of terms which identify North America as a Norse territory.

After 1380, Norway came under the rule of Denmark and surrogate Danish kings or regents. From that time onward, the overseas colonies were simply referred to as part of the greater "Greenland Province." Thus, the "Nancy Map" by the Dane, Claudius Clavus, in 1424 simply identifies the land west of Norway as Gronlandia Provincia—meaning "Greenland the Province of Denmark."

From the end of the plagues circa 1410 until invasions by English, Danes, and the Portuguese, the western continent (Norveca) was up for grabs. The Norwegians didn't recover as rapidly from the plague as England and other nations of central Europe because cooler temperatures in northern Europe made Norway's marginal farming areas less productive: less food meant fewer warriors. Meanwhile, England, Denmark, and Portugal recovered and took control of the North Atlantic.

Although DeVirga produced his map in 1414, at which time New World territories were no longer under Norse rule, he used an out-of-date logo (the crown and the name Norveca) to identify the overseas continent. This usage reveals that his source for the northern region was from a mid-14th century gazetteer—produced at a time when Norway still held title to the Northern Regions. Since Nicholas of Lynn was the only historically identified person conducting a survey in the Northern Regions when they were under Norse control, it stands to reason that his gazetteer also identified the Northern Regions as Norveca (or Norse territory), and this out-of-date information was included in the Venetian Map of 1414. The mistake is understandable: the Franciscan gazetteer was still accurate with regards to geographical coordinates—indeed, it was the only reliable source available for the Northern Regions.

The Conspiracy Argument

During the early 1900's, orthodox historians disputed claims that Danish saga maps (such as Bishop Resen's North Atlantic chart) were derived from pre-Columbian traditions of scientific cartography. The argument was made that Scandinavian cartographers were essentially primitive in their knowledge of the North Atlantic and that they did not adopt the Ptolemaic mapping style until the 16th century. Thus, all maps that followed the Ptolemaic principles of mapping—which included most Danish maps—were presumed to have been compiled late in the 16th century. Due to the fact that Resen's map wasn't finished until 1605, and the oldest version of the saga map style was a 17th-century copy of Stefansson's 1590 map, there was insufficient evidence to counter the orthodox argument.

The most scathing attack upon the veracity of Danish documents came from indignant academicians who insisted that Danish claims of pre-Columbian voyages to North America were part of a conspiracy by northern Europeans to steal the glory of Columbus—a southern European (Skelton, et al., 1965, 252, 253).

Academic fantasies of conspiracies will have to be abandoned in order to accommodate new perspectives of history. The contemporaneous existence of the friar's travelog, the Inventio, and the early 15th-century map of Norveca constitute conclusive evidence of a scientific survey of the North Atlantic. The Norveca map has the same configuration of three headlands followed by an island that appeared on 16th-century Danish maps. Is this simply a coincidence? Or is it evidence that Scandinavian cartographers had access to Franciscan sources in England? We know they had access, because Cnoyen's account mentions that the Inventio was known to the Norse king in 1364. By 1380, Norway was under Danish rule; and this is the connection between the Franciscan map and Danish cartography. The Norveca map is clearly pre-Columbian; therefore, the Danish tradition of North Atlantic maps based on scientific principles was also pre-Columbian—even if the Danes, themselves, were not the ones who originally conducted the field survey. If there was a conspiracy to deprive Columbus of his claim to New World discovery, then it stands to reason that the plotting began before Columbus was born.

Franciscan friar
Nidrosia Cathedral
Trondheim, Norway

Friar Nicholas & The North Pole

The concept of a world with two North Poles is something we take for granted. Boy Scouts on Klondike Derby courses and R.O.T.C. cadets on maneuvers learn to compensate for magnetic declination. They know from experience the distinction between the geographic alignment of maps and the direction of magnetic compass needles in the field. The ancients were not so fortunate: according to Classical legends, compass needles pointed toward the Geographic North Pole—site of a huge magnetic mountain. This Greek myth suited most Europeans who lived in a region where magnetic declination was barely noticeable. Seafarers from London to Venice confirmed that compass needles pointed reliably towards Polaris—the pole star—that was situated directly above the northern-most regions of Earth.

Mariners who traveled across the Atlantic or Pacific invariably noticed difficulties with their "magic" pointers. Marco Polo commented on the discrepancy between his compass and the pole star in his travelog of 1298. Nicholas of Lynn noted the discrepancy in 1360; and Columbus observed the problem in 1492. Geographers back in Europe couldn't imagine that the revered Greek scholars of antiquity had erred—so they simply disregarded such critical reports from the field.

Magnetic North and The Location of Northern Lands

Although 15th-century cartographers knew about such northern territories as "Thule," "Albania," "Hyperborea," "Frisland," "Vinland," and "Greenland," they were uncertain of the precise locations. On most maps, Thule is shown southwest of Norway; on other maps it appears north of Norway, north of Russia or even east of India. The apparent confusion of placement and naming was the consequence of conflicting legends and reports from explorers—some of whom relied on celestial navigation, while most used magnetic compasses.

The compass was a boon to seafarers; however it was the nemesis of cartographers. In northern latitudes, the compass is of limited reliability for mapping because of phenomena known as magnetic variation and magnetic deviation (or declination). Above the Equator, compass needles point towards the North Magnetic Pole located above Hudson's Bay. However, this location of Magnetic North is far south of the Geographic North Pole. The amount of declination near Greenland can exceed 50-degrees. North of Norway, the compass needle points North, but the direction of travel is actually west-northwest. Past Greenland, the needle still points towards Magnetic North and Hudson's Bay—although the direction of travel is westerly relative to Europe.

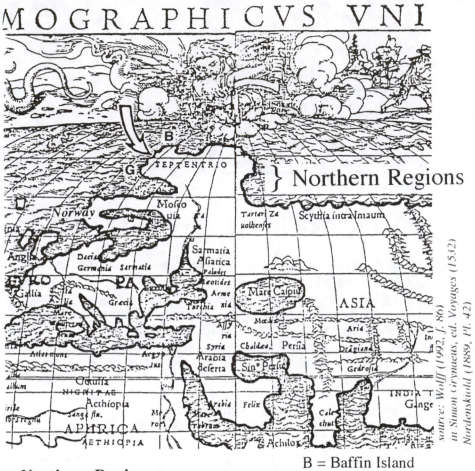

} Northern Regions

*source: Wolff (1992, f. 86)
in Simon Grynaeus, ed. Voyages (1532)
Nordenskiold (1889, Pl. 42)*

B = Baffin Island
G = Greenland Isl.

Northern Regions
or Septentrio Europa

Maps by Hans Holbein and Sebastian Munster (1532, above) and Joachim Von Watt (1534, below) show a huge land extending above Norway and reaching to the North Pole. This land represented the "Northern Regions" which 15th-century travelers believed was their destination when heading due north by compass bearings. Two peninsulas on Von Watt's Map (B & G) represent Baffin Island and Greenland—demonstrating that so-called Northern Regions actually represented lands to the west of Europe.

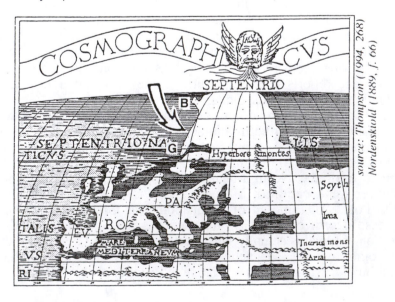

*source: Thompson (1994, 268)
Nordenskiold (1889, f. 66)*

Neither sun nor constellations were of much help to confirm direction of travel, because most voyages occurred in Summer when the sun hovers above the horizon for six months. During this time, the North Star—which was the principle direction-finder for ancient travelers—was concealed by daylight. The result was that sailors using compasses believed they were heading North, when in fact they were voyaging to lands far to the west near the Magnetic North Pole.

Most cartographers and sailors of the 15th and 16th centuries relied on the compass because of its ease of use and presumed reliability. The consequence of this dependence on the compass was the mislocation of western territories which cartographers placed in erroneous locations north of Norway on most 16th-century maps. Greenland was most consistently shown north of Norway when its true position was far west. It is commonly seen in such a location in maps by Donnus Nickolaus Germanus which were based on the Ptolemaic Map of The North by Claudius Clavus circa 1460 (Nansen, 1911). Unlike Donnus Nicolaus, Clavus seemed to be aware of the true position of Greenland to the northwest of Ireland.

Donnus Nicolaus produced a magnetic version of northern lands circa 1466. His map, which placed Greenland north of Norway, was included in a document called Geographia. Some scholars believe the map is a copy of a lost version of north Atlantic lands by Claudius Clavus. Latin editions of the Donnus map were printed in 1468 and 1474. The map was further revised by Danish mapmakers in 1482 and published as the "Donis Kort." Henricus Martellus made his own variation in which Greenland was portrayed northwest of England in the form of a long peninsula. His geographic-based map was printed in Florence circa 1480. A Strassburg magnetic version followed in 1513; and Martin Waldseemuller issued a copy in 1525. These maps which amounted to thousands of copies (made by the new European printing presses) are notable for several reasons: 1) they all bear the archaic Dutch term for Vinland (i.e., "Venthelant") above Norway and adjacent to Greenland; 2) they all show an archaic "Thule" (representing Iceland) south of Norway simultaneously with an island identified as "Iceland" far out in the northwest Atlantic; and 3) they all feature two Greenlands—one adjacent to Norway and another forming a separate peninsula above Norway. With the exception of the geographic-based Martellus map, Greenland was misplaced north of Norway and east of England, when in fact the true position was far to the west. In other words, most of the extant maps placed Greenland Island according to magnetic coordinates.

The Orthodox Argument
—Irreverent, Irrelevant, & Immaterial

In 1912, Austrian scholar Franz Von Wieser decided that the northern section of the Venetian Map was nothing more than a grossly distorted Norway—so he believed there was no purpose for further research on the map. Similarly, the modern-day Italian specialist on Albertin DeVirga, Piero Falchetta (1995), believes that the Norveca region on the Venetian Map is simply a "distorted Scandinavia." This rationale is put forth as a self-evident truth without an explanation as to why a Venetian would portray far-off Scandinavia as big as the continent of Europe. Thus, orthodox historians have conveniently dismissed anything that might compromise their academic heritage; dogma survives unchallenged, while

source: Nordenskiold (1889)

Key:

N   Norway
V   Ventelant
G   Greenland (magnetic)
G2 Grvenlant (geographic)
H   Hyperborea
M   Magnetic Mt.
GP Ginnungagap
B   Baffin Island
L   Labrador
NF Newfoundland

Polar Regions of Johann Ruysch 1508

This is the northern section of a world map by Ruysch circa 1508. Ruysch has a caption on this map between 90° and 70° specifying that the northern region is based on an account in the *Inventio Fortunatae*. There are four lands around the magnetic mountain at the center—which seems to follow Mercator's version of the story of a Flemish traveler who talked with a certain Franciscan surveyor in Bergen. However, this third-hand account hardly enabled Ruysch to construct an accurate map of the region. His version seems more akin to Roman myth. He probably cited the *Inventio* in order to justify this monstrous fabrication. Unfortunately, historians have assumed it is an accurate reference to Nicholas of Lynn and have accordingly condemned the friar as an unreliable source.

The Ruysch map is instructive concerning the location of Greenland on late 15th-century maps and those of the 16th century. On the Norwegian peninsula (**N**) we find "Ventelant" (**V**) near the Arctic Circle. This is an archaic placement for Vinland—which was thought to be "north" of Norway. In like manner, there is a second peninsula above Norway which usually represents Greenland Island (**G**) on most maps of the period. Above this is Hyperborea Europa (**H**) which is a carryover from the Norveca Europa of the Venetian map of 1414 where it was presumed the Hyperboreans lived near the North Pole. Across the vertical ocean or Ginnungagap (**GP**) is a caption that cautions mariners not to rely upon compass bearings as the compass fails in this region. Usually, maps had this caption southwest of Greenland—thus we are on good grounds for identifying the land here called "Grvenlant" as Labrador (**L**). Since most historians have assumed this is simply another frivolous naming—we can understand the controversy over whether the Spanish navigator Fernandez (The Labrador) actually discovered Greenland or Labrador. On the other hand, we know that several cartographers identified North American mainland as "Greenland" so the label for Labrador on this map is not so unusual.

the continent of "Norveca" enters into the twilight zone of fantasy isles which presumably are of no importance to serious scholars.

The blasé attitude of historians towards the Northern Regions stems from misconceptions rooted in 16th-century cartography. One of the titles that Richard Hakluyt (1599, 303) reported for the Inventio was: Inventio Fortunatae qui liber incipet a gradu 54, usque ad polum—that is, "Discovery of The Fortunate Isles which begins at 54° and continues to the pole." Hakluyt found this reference in a letter from Gerhard Mercator to John Dee (Hakluyt, 1599, 101; Quinn, 1974, 107). This wasn't actually the title of the friar's book; it was Mercator's own elaboration of the title that reflected his mistaken belief that the book only dealt with lands between Scotland and the Geographic North Pole. Modern historians assumed that nothing of importance relating to New World discovery occurred within this sub-Arctic region, so they had an excuse for dismissing the Inventio as irrelevant. Regardless of Mercator's contrivance, it becomes readily clear to anyone who reads the extant reports of the friar's travels that the Inventio concerns Arctic, temperate, and tropical regions in the western Atlantic. These regions cover the entire coast of North America and are of great importance to New World discovery.

During the 16th century, several famous cartographers including John Ruysch (1508), Gerhard Mercator (1569), and Cornelius Judaeus (1593) said that the configurations of Polar Regions on their maps were taken from the travelog and gazetteer of the Oxford friar Nicholas of Lynn. The maps portray obviously fictitious rivers and a polar stream, or whirlpool, around the Geographic North Pole. This pole is identified as a magnetic pole in the form of a huge mountain of magnetic stone which served to explain why compass needles pointed north. Classical writers Pliny The Elder and Ptolemy expounded the magnetic-mountain theory in 2nd-century Rome (Hennig, 1953, 319). Mercator's Polar Region has four rivers flowing towards the pole in a cross-shaped pattern corresponding to the cardinal points of a compass. These rivers correspond to the "in-drawing seas" of Classical mythology—although a notation on the map states that this is the configuration reported in the Inventio Fortunatae. The fact that several other 16th-century cartographers name the Inventio as a source for the four-rivers polar configuration certainly invites skepticism and ridicule from modern historians.

Orthodox historians assumed that frigid temperatures in the Arctic and the obvious Classical pedigree of fabulous polar lands on these maps were sufficient grounds to brand the Inventio and its author as frauds (Hennig, 1953, 321). Generous critics surmised that friar Nicholas simply plagiarized his "account" of the Polar Regions from Classical mythology while pretending to sail to the North Pole.

However, written correspondence between English advocate John Dee and Gerardus Mercator tells a much different story. In his 1577 letter, Mercator acknowledged that he had not actually seen the Inventio; his version of the Polar Region was based on a second-hand account from Jacob Cnoyen. Mercator revealed that the only source he had to work from was Cnoyen's recollection of conversations with a priest who had talked to friar Nicholas. He also confirms that the diagram on his map was derived from Classical sources mentioned in the friar's book:

> The Philosophers describe four indraughts of this Ocean sea, in the
> four opposite quarters of the world, from whence many do

North Polar Regions

1. Navigable Polar Sea

Behaim's Version of Inventio Fortunatae—1492

As one of the principal cartographers for Portuguese royalty, Behaim was in a position to have access to the *Inventio Fortunatae* and other Franciscan maps of the Polar Regions. The Polar Region of his globe (as it is portrayed in the Doppelmayer facsimile of 1730), shows five islands that might serve as stepping stones between Europe and Asia. Baffin Island (**B**) and Greenland (**G**) are shown as contiguous land north of England. Across the strait (Ginnungagap) is Labrador (**L**). The second large island (**A**) west from Baffin Island has a legend in German which reads: "Many white people live here." This isle can be identified as Albania—a land of white people that was mentioned in numerous maps and in 13th-century Icelandic sagas. Across the North Pole is a huge, navigable sea—much like the Polar Sea which Columbus said could serve as a route to China. Such lands and a navigable sea correspond to the friar's account of temperate seas near the Magnetic North Pole in *Inventio Fortunatae*.

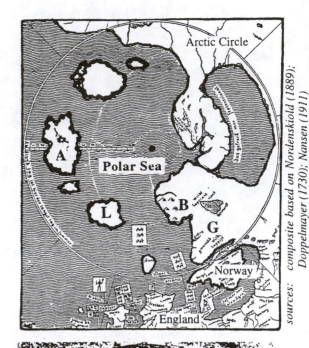

sources: composite based on Nordenskiold (1889); Doppelmayer (1730); Nansen (1911)

2. No Polar Sea

Mercator's Fabulous Polar Regions—1569

Several cartographers, including Johannes Ruysch, Gerhard Mercator, and Cornelius Judaeus, attributed the source of northern sections of their maps or globes to the *Inventio Fortunatae*. However, Mercator's map seems more based on Classical Greco-Roman concepts of the Polar Regions than on the account of the Franciscan survey. This map has is no navigable sea—only four compressed isles of ice surrounding the magnetic mountain of Classical mythology which was presumed to be at the geographic North Pole. Mercator placed a second Magnetic Pole near Siberia in the Strait of Anian to explain the phenomenon of magnetic compass declination. His source for this fantasy might have been Marco Polo who noted the discrepancy between compass north and the position of the pole star.

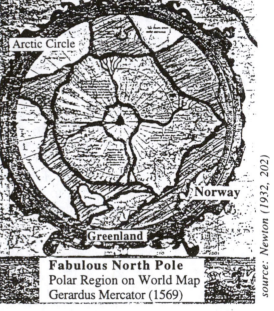

Fabulous North Pole
Polar Region on World Map
Gerardus Mercator (1569)

source: Newton (1932, 202)

3. No Polar Sea

Polar Regions according to Judaeus—1593

Lands that Cornelius Judaeus shows near the Arctic Circle differ substantially from Polar Regions as they were described in the *Inventio*—even though he names the friar's book as his source. This portrayal of the North Pole is essentially an updated version of the Polar Regions as Mercator conceived of them based on Classical sources described in the Cnoyen account as related by John Dee.

source: Nordenskiold (1889)

140

conjecture that as well the flowing of the sea, as the blasts of the wind, have their first original. (Hakluyt, 1599, 100)

Elsewhere in his letter to John Dee, Mercator states that it was a Norse priest and not the friar who told the story of a whirlpool and a magnetic rock at the Geographic North Pole. Farther along in this same letter, Mercator says: "The Minorite (Franciscan friar) had heard that one can see all round it (the magnetic rock) from the sea; and it is black and glistening." Later cartographers, including Mercator, seem to have failed to grasp the distinction between what Nicholas said "he had heard" about the Geographic North Pole and what he saw in the region of the Magnetic North Pole. Although friar Nicholas claims to have traveled to the Polar Regions (that is, the Magnetic North Pole), there is no indication that he described that area—the region of Foxe Basin (at the Magnetic Pole)—in Classical terms. According to the Cnoyen account, Nicholas says that there are four lands near the (magnetic) pole—two of which are habitable. One of these he calls "the healthiest land in all the North." These two habitable lands of the friar's acquaintance are clearly indicated on Behaim's globe of 1492—although they are situated near the Arctic circle. They correspond to Nova Scotia and New York. Behaim's rubric above these isles identifies them as lands occupied by European settlers: Hir findet man weisse volk— that is, "Here live white people."

It is apparent from Jacob Cnoyen's account of the friar's travels that the Minorite was familiar with Classical concepts regarding the Geographic North Pole, and he probably discussed these concepts in his book. However, we must keep in mind that the friar's journey to the Polar Region principally concerned lands that he found in the vicinity of a different "North Pole"—the Magnetic North Pole. In this region of his travels, the friar encountered temperate—even tropical—isles.

The essential problem from the perspective of 14th-century cartography was that geographers had not differentiated between the Geographic North Pole and the Magnetic North Pole, nor had they devised a map projection capable of showing simultaneously the continental layouts of both hemispheres. Indeed, the only way to illustrate lands across the seas from the Old World was to cram them alongside the borders of maps in the form of tiny isles or include them as abstract lands pasted above Europe and Asia. This is the principle reason why Medieval maps have tiny isles scattered around the border, or they have nebulous territories such as Hyperborea, Albania, Amazonia, or Gothia Orientalis infused into the tops of Europe and Asia. There was no other place available on circular maps to show these overseas lands. Orthodox historians, ever quick to deny the intelligence of Medieval mariners, often ridicule the ancients for all the so-called "fabulous lands" scattered along the borders of mappamonds. But this characteristic "failing" of Medieval cartography is more a function of the infancy of mapping technology than it is a symptom of the unfettered Medieval imagination.

There are practical reasons why 16th-century geographers cited the Inventio as the presumed source for information concerning the Geographic North Pole. By the 16th-century, cosmographers had gained sufficient stature as a profession of scientists, and they were understandably concerned with their public image. Their reputation for precision and reliability was essential to assure a growing market for their products. At the same time, they were dependent upon the accuracy of

141

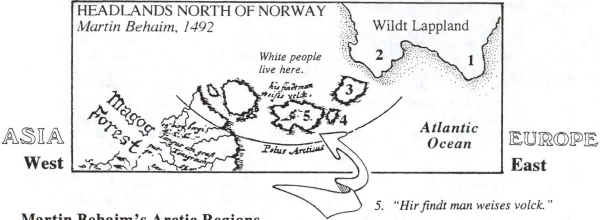

(1) Greenland Isl.
(2) Baffin Land
(3) Labrador
(4) Newfoundland Isl.
(5) Nova Scotia

HEADLANDS NORTH OF NORWAY
Martin Behaim, 1492

White people live here.

Wildt Lappland

ASIA
West

EUROPE
East

Atlantic Ocean

5. *"Hir findt man weises volck."*

Martin Behaim's Arctic Regions & The Saga Map Tradition

Historian Fridtjof Nansen (1911) believed that Martin Behaim based his portrayal the northern regions (or lands above the Arctic Circle) on his 1492 globe to the writings of a 14th-century English friar-astronomer Nicholas of Lynn. Northern regions on Behaim's globe also correspond closely to lands named in Norse sagas: 1) Greenland; 2) Helluland or Baffin Island; 3) Markland or Labrador; and 4) Wineland. Traditionally, Scandinavian maps of the North Atlantic and the 1414 map by Albertin DeVirga show the 4th headland as an island. In the case of Behaim's globe, the fourth headland is a smaller island—so the pattern seems consistent: three large lands followed by an island. These isles correspond to territories that actually extend well below the Arctic Circle and are west of Europe. Magnetic declination is to blame for their mislocation north of Europe and north of the Arctic Circle on Behaim's globe.

According to A.E. Nordenskiold, the globe was accurately copied by J.G. Doppelmayer (1730) but distorted by later reconstructions. Doppelmayer's version shows the fifth Arctic isle (**5**) corresponding to New England or Nova Scotia as a land of "white people." Later copyists changed this caption to read: "white falcons." Incidentally, this region of Nova Scotia corresponds to the territory of Norumbega which 16th-century explorers including Verrazano, Alfonce, and Hakluyt identified on the East Coast near the Gulf of St. Lawrence. Explorers, such as Jacques Cartier and Samuel Champlain reported whites living in this region, and it was here that Portuguese Captain Estevao Gomez captured white slaves in 1524. The similar sequence of isles or headlands on Behaim's globe, on DeVirga's 1414 map, and on Danish saga maps leads to the conclusion that they were all based on a common heritage—the Franciscan survey of the North Atlantic.

Northern Regions from Martin Behaim, 1492 after facsimile by J.G. Doppelmayer, 1730

Portuguese caravel
15th century woodcut
source: Peres (1943)

142

field reports, so they preferred gazetteers based on field surveys using sextants or astrolabes as opposed to the less-reliable compass. New mapping techniques which Arabian and European scholars had recently devised finally enabled the simultaneous mapping of both hemispheres on the same piece of hide or parchment. Cartography had entered the realm of science where precise reference points were required, and only the most-reliable sources were used in map construction.

Unfortunately, cartographers were faced with a conundrum when it came to showing the Polar Regions on their maps. Due to the harsh climate and lack of financial rewards, no competent surveyor had traveled to the Polar Regions since the dubious expeditions of the English friar in the 14th century. It didn't matter that the friar's work was ancient, or that it restated what everybody else had heard from Classical sources. Nicholas was the only available source in the 16th century. The fact that the Polar Regions were described in his Inventio was sufficient basis to give the myth of four-seas and four-lands about the North Pole an aura of contemporary respectability.

On the other hand, Cnoyen's account of the friar's travels—which only Mercator and Ortelius had an opportunity to examine—contained contradictory views of the Polar Regions. The Classical image of frozen wastes surrounded by inaccessible mountains of ice was present—as were the indrawing seas. However, the friar had also reported that the region of the North Pole that he visited was temperate; here, the seas were open and navigable, and two of the nearby land areas were inhabited. Mercator seems to have ignored this temperate image of the North Pole; later cartographers simply accepted Mercator's reference to the Inventio as his source for the Classical version of the Polar Region, and they drew their maps accordingly. For those geographers who believed in scientific theories about Earth's temperature zones and frigid lands surrounding both North and South poles, the fact that Nicholas mentioned Classical theories added the credibility of a highly-respected world traveler. Mercator and his followers made one concession to the friar's conflicting versions of the North Pole: they indicated on their maps that two of the Arctic isles were inhabited. This artifact—derived from confusion over the friar's conflicting reports—has provided modern scholars with unending mirth. How, they wonder, could Renaissance cartographers have been so stupid!

Once more, we are witness to the confusion that resulted from the friar's identification of two poles—while his contemporaries all believed there was only one magnetic pole which was synonymous with the Geographic North Pole.

Only Martin Behaim's globe appears to have been based on the actual Inventio—or at least a gazetteer of longitudes and latitudes that the English friar calculated using an astrolabe. Even Behaim confused the friar's prime reference point—the Magnetic North Pole which he apparently assumed was at the same place as the geographic pole. Otherwise, his globe can be accepted as a fair representation of New World territories in the Northern Regions (from Greenland to Newfoundland) as they may have been described in the Franciscan gazetteer.

The isles on Behaim's globe do not correspond to Classical myth. In fact, they correspond fairly closely to the shapes and locations of actual lands. Greenland and Baffin Land are identifiable directly north of Norway; these are adjacent to four isles towards the southwest— Labrador, Newfoundland, Nova Scotia, and New England. The reason

Source Bramson (1967, f. 21) and Jomard (1862); Thompson (1996)

Polar Regions according to Martin Behaim—1490 to 1492

This version of the northern section on Behaim's globe is from an 1850's drawing by M. Jomard and is thus more reliable than later reconstructions. Like most of his contemporaries, Behaim portrayed Greenland directly north of Norway—so this section betrays that the geographer has relied on compass bearings for the purposes of locating land areas. The lands themselves have remarkably accurate outlines—as far as Greenland (**G**) and Baffin Island (**BI**) are concerned. The accuracy can be verified by comparison to a modern atlas. Here, Behaim has referred to both as "Wildt Lappland" although other copyists have inserted the name "Greenland" for the lower peninsula. This is an understandable substitution—since the outline of the land is identical to maps by Donnus Nickolaus Germanus (1482) that identify this as "Engronelant."

We see on this map a waterway directly north of England and Iceland leading straight to the North Pole, and this conforms very well with Norse traditions of a strait called Ginnungagap leading to the North Pole and the seas beyond. In this case, the pole is in effect a magnetic pole (**MNP**) for lands north of the Arctic Circle. A traveler heading by compass north from Bergen would pass Davis Strait (**D**) and Baffin Island. If the traveler headed "west" at this point, the next land would be Labrador (**L**), followed by Newfoundland (**N**) and then the rest of North America.

why the isles are shown north of the Arctic Circle on Behaim's globe is due to the fact that the friar based his survey on the Magnetic North Pole at Hudson Bay, while Behaim's globe assumes a centerpoint at the Geographic North Pole.

There are many extant reconstructions of Behaim's globe which has suffered through the years from decay and sloppy restoration. The number and shapes of the Polar isles varies considerably from one version to the next. In 1889, Adolf Nordenskiold cautioned his colleagues to use the oldest reconstructed version of Behaim's globe (the one by Doppelmayer in 1730) because subsequent versions were becoming increasingly inaccurate even though they were supposedly based on the original globe that still survives in Nuremberg. Historian Henry Vignaud (1902, 206) also commented on the baffling discrepancies between the many reconstructions of the globe. G.E. Ravenstein issued his highly-acclaimed version in 1908. There is virtually no similarity between the Polar Region of this reconstruction and Behaim's original from the Doppelmayer facsimile. Even Ravenstein was aware of inaccuracies that had crept into the original before he constructed his own version of the globe:

> Ravenstein, who made a very thorough study of the matter, tells us that this globe has been twice retouched or renovated and that the only way to ascertain exactly what was originally delineated is to treat it as a palimpsest (paper mache) and remove the accretions. In particular, he relates the story of an expert geographer who found the draftsmen about to transpose St. Brandan's Island and Antillia; but they yielded to his protest. Of course, it is impossible to be quite certain that these map figures are such and in such place as Behaim intended or that they bear the names he gave. (Babcock, 1922, p. 47)

Nevertheless, orthodox historians have lauded the inaccurate 1908 surrogate as "proof" that the Inventio was a hoax based on mythology (Taylor, 1956). Ravenstein's reconstruction has become the favorite of orthodox historians; it is often illustrated in textbooks; and it was featured in the Encyclopedia Britannica.(1954).

We have seen how the Inventio was misconstrued, how Mercator misidentified Nicholas as the source for his Classical version of the Polar Regions, and how cartographers confused the Magnetic North Pole of the Franciscan survey with the Geographic North Pole. We have noted that historians ridiculed the Inventio because the friar claimed to have reached the North Pole—presumably an obvious impossibility due to the polar climate. However, the Hudson Bay region of the magnetic pole is a temperate land; and it is well within the reach of 14th-century explorers. Furthermore, the friar's achievement of reaching and identifying the magnetic pole was independently confirmed in the Nancy Manuscript by the Dane Claudius Clavus in 1427.

Two Poles—
Impact of The Voyages and Writings of Brother Nicholas

Orthodox historians have assumed that the Inventio Fortunatae dealt exclusively with lands between 54° North (the latitude of Dublin and Labrador) and the North Pole—because this is one of the subtitles reported in Mercator's memoirs. These "northern regions" were beyond the seven climatic zones of Ptolemy and were generally regarded as

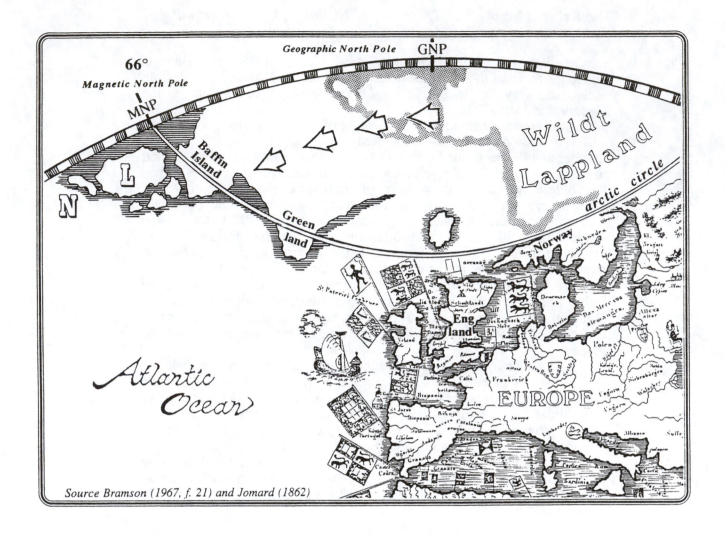

Source Bramson (1967, f. 21) and Jomard (1862)

Behaim's Globe Shows North America ca. 1492

Cartographer Martin Behaim noted that his sources for the 1492 globe included the most recent Portuguese travels. As an employee of Portuguese royalty, he also had access to Franciscan survey maps passed on via English sovereigns to Prince Henry The Navigator. We know from the Nancy Manuscript of 1427 that an anonymous surveyor had identified a second North Pole for the Western Hemisphere; and this North Pole (the magnetic pole) was situated at 66° or at the approximate latitude of the Arctic Circle. If we then slide the Polar Regions as they are portrayed on Behaim's globe to the southwest so that the old North Pole is directly above the Arctic Circle— then we can reconstruct the Polar Regions from the perspective of the Western Hemisphere. The result (above) gives us a remarkably accurate portrayal of the North Atlantic with Greenland and Baffin Island assuming their correct geographical positions northwest of Europe instead of due north as they were originally portrayed on Behaim's globe. This realignment also brings the adjacent northern isles down to the appropriate locations for Labrador (**L**) and Newfoundland (**N**).

If these Polar Regions were simply random fabrications of a novelist, then the accurate outlines and locations would not occur. But as we have seen with the exercise above, the Franciscan map of Polar Regions—as modeled on Behaim's Globe—clearly shows evidence of scientific mapping deep into North America.

Most historians have missed this vital connection due to their reliance on inaccurate reconstructions of Behaim's globe and the tendency to regard anything above the Arctic Circle on old maps as being irrelevant to the cavalcade of American discovery. Indeed, most published versions of the globe entirely cut off the northern section— presumably so as not to confuse readers with irrelevant information. By fiat, they simultaneously eliminate the most important clues to ancient, trans-Atlantic voyages.

uninhabitable—although they included portions of Germany and England. Considering the implication that the <u>Inventio</u> dealt solely with Arctic regions that are uninhabitable, it might on the surface seem reasonable for modern historians to question the relevance of the friar's manuscript and map to the subject of American discovery.

Of course, the serious scholar has to look beyond the surface of titles and innuendoes to comprehend the importance of the Franciscan and his travelog. Such an effort is not likely to occur in the context of professions where loyalty to traditional heroes and ideologies discourage innovative ideas. Historian Hakluyt specifically stated that the <u>Inventio</u> included North American territories known to 16th-century cartographers as Norumbega (in the region of Nova Scotia), and references by Ferdinand Colon and Bertholomew Las Casas specifically mention that the <u>Inventio</u> reported lands west of Spain and Africa—that is, lands which the Romans also called "Fortunate Isles."

Orthodox historians typically ignore such references because the implications are that English sailors as well as Romans frequented North America in ancient times. These same historians have failed to grasp the fact that the friar identified the location of the Magnetic North Pole.

Norse historian Fridtjof Nansen credited Nicholas of Lynn with using his astrolabe to determine the accurate latitude for Bergen, Norway. This city is shown for the first time in an accurate position on the "Nancy Map" by the Dane Claudius Clavus Swart. Although there is no proof that the coordinates for this trading center was established by Nicholas, it seems reasonable to associate the increasing accuracy of North European maps with the growing fraternity of Oxford trained friar-astronomers. Coincidentally, historian Marcel Destombes (1964) expressed his belief that the portrayal of Scandinavian territories on the Venetian Map of 1414 had influenced the configuration of those same areas on the Nancy Map.

The Nancy Map is a fairly accurate representation of the relative positions of Norway, Denmark, England, Greenland, and Iceland. The map is considered to be an extraordinary specimen because of its rather accurate placement of the tip of Greenland near its correct latitude of 60° North; furthermore, the map shows Greenland's east coast in the western Atlantic beyond Ireland. This is regarded as a significant advancement in North Atlantic cartography, because most contemporary maps and many later ones located Greenland in a totally inaccurate position due north of Norway. Clavus didn't break away completely from the conventions of European cartography: his map shows two sets of latitudes. Those of Ptolemy occupy the right margin; those from the Franciscan survey are found on the left.

It seems that friar Nicholas was aware that compass directions in the Western Hemisphere deviated from true geographic north as it was known in Europe. And this is perhaps his most important discovery: the location of the Magnetic North Pole. The <u>Nancy Manuscript</u> (1427) which Clavus wrote to accompany his map of northern lands includes the following passage:

> From this headland (Greenland) an immense country extends eastward as far as Russia. And in its northern parts dwell the infidel Karelians whose territory extends to the north pole towards the Seres (Asia, China or the Far East). In that region, the pole—which to us is in the north—is located at 66°. (after Nansen, 1911, 262)

Clavus does not give his source for this statement, but Nicholas of Lynn is the obvious candidate for the honor. The only way a correct latitude could have been determined given 14th-century technology was for an explorer to find the very doorstep of the magnetic pole. And this is precisely what friar Nicholas claims to have done.

Norwegian historian Fridtjof Nansen notes that the Inventio Fortunata probably included accurate calculations for the southern tip of Greenland, the City of Bergen, and Stavanger Harbor (Nansen, 1911, 261). The Nancy Manuscript has Greenland reaching to 59°15' whereas the correct latitude by modern calculations is 59°46'. Considering the difficulties inherent in surveys and the relatively primitive equipment available in the 14th century, this is a remarkably accurate calculation. If it is true, as Nansen suggests, that the accuracy of latitudes on the Nancy Map reflected measurements borrowed from the Inventio Fortunatae—then Nicholas set forth his belief that the Western Hemisphere had a different North Pole than prevailed in Europe. In other words, there were two poles!

The North Pole of the Western Hemisphere, which Clavus (or Nicholas) located at 66° north, corresponds to the Magnetic North Pole in its earliest estimated position near Hudson Bay. By noting the location of the North Pole on Martin Behaim's 1492 globe, we can estimate the approximate longitude of the pole at the time of the friar's travels. Behaim places the North Pole northwest of Baffin Land in the vicinity of Prince Charles Island in Foxe Basin. This suggests that the geographical coordinates for the magnetic pole in 1360 were about 66° North latitude by 75° West longitude.

The magnetic pole is not stationary but moves within a huge territory of several hundred square miles. Explorer J.C. Ross located the magnetic pole in 1831; at that time, the pole was situated at 71° N latitude 96°W longitude in the Boothia Peninsula of Canada or 1400 miles south of the Geographic North Pole. By the time Roald Amundsen found the pole in 1903, it had shifted several hundred miles north. In 1945, a scientific expedition located the pole at 76°N 102°W. This represents a shift of five degrees north in the span of a century (Encyclopedia Britannica, Vol. 21, 1954, 959). Precisely where the pole was in 1360 is speculative, but the measurement—66°N—given in the Nancy Manuscript is within reasonable limits.

Confirmation that Christian explorers actually found the pole can be deduced from evidence in the Nancy Manuscript. Most scholars, including Nansen (1911, 262) identify the "Karelians" mentioned in the manuscript with "Skraelings" reported in Icelandic sagas. That name referred to native peoples or Indians living in the forest wilderness of Markland—that is, southern Labrador, Newfoundland, and the East Coast south of the Gulf of St. Lawrence. Anthropologists have identified these natives as members of the Abenaki, Delaware, and Beothuk tribes. Farther north, in northern Labrador, there lived people the Norse called pygmies—referring to the Inuit or Eskimo. Archeologists have identified them as the "Dorset" culture. According to the passage quoted above from the Nancy Manuscript, there were people called "Karelians" living near the North Pole—that is the Magnetic North Pole which Clavus (and presumably Nicholas) identified as being situated at latitude 66°N. The location of these inhabitants, at the North Pole, helps to verify that Christian explorers accurately identified the location of the Magnetic Pole—because native peoples (Skraelings or Karelians) do indeed live in that region where the climate is temperate most of the year. If the Nancy Manuscript had mentioned "pygmies" living near the pole, then a region closer to the Arctic Circle would have been indicated—but that was not the case. Thus, Hudson Bay is the region which Clavus and the friar designated for the Magnetic North Pole.

Behaim's Map of Polar Regions

Like most historians, the author at one time believed that a globe which Martin Behaim crafted between 1490 and 1492 was grossly inaccurate. The most commonly available version of this globe, a 1908 reconstruction by G.E. Ravenstein, had eighteen isles in the Arctic Regions beyond Greenland. Since there was no correspondence between this version of the Arctic and reality, there seemed to be no point looking further on the globe for evidence of pre-Columbian voyagers to America across the North Atlantic. That mistaken impression might have endured had it not been for the author's fortuitous encounter with Bo Bramson's book—Danish Maps (1967). One of Bramson's illustrations was a copy of the European section of Behaim's globe by M. Jomard (1862). It was evident from Jomard's version of the globe that the lands portrayed on Behaim's "Erdapfl" globe had shifted over the centuries. It was apparent that subsequent copyists had merely chronicled the sequential decay of the globe in the Nuremberg Museum—as opposed to rendering accurate facsimiles of the original. Suddenly, all of my assumptions about Behaim's globe being based largely on supposition had to be discarded.

It took several months of searching through library stacks to locate a reliable version of Behaim's globe. An oversized volume of Adolph Nordenskiold's Facsimile Atlas of 1889 contained J.G. Doppelmayer's 1730 facsimile map. The Doppelmayer facsimile consisted of two hemispherical views of the 15th-century globe. It was readily apparent that this version differed considerably from Ravenstein's feeble concoction. It was also evident that Behaim's original showed the same sequence of three headlands followed by an island that was typical of Danish saga maps.

By following the coast of "Wildt Lapland" on the Doppelmayer facsimile, the outline of Greenland is clearly discernible. The next headland (Baffin Land) can be identified by its shape: this land has three humps facing magnetic south and a small peninsula facing magnetic north. That pattern corresponds to the physical reality of Baffin Island as seen on a modern atlas. A large island in Behaim's Arctic region can be identified as Labrador by its proximity to Baffin Land and its location southwest across a strait extending between the North Pole and the Atlantic Ocean. Norse sailors regarded this strait—Ginnungagap or Christian's Strait (the modern Hudson Strait)—as a waterway due north from Norway. This is precisely how it is portrayed on archaic 16th-century maps. This due north orientation resulted from the fact that Hudson Strait lies almost due north from Norway by compass bearings, although its actual position is due west. As we have seen in similar cases, inaccuracies inherent in the use of compass bearings in northern seas was to blame for the misconception. The fourth land on Behaim's globe is an island— probably Newfoundland—which can be identified by its relative size and proximity to Labrador. Beyond the island is a larger territory where Behaim has the notation: hir findt mann weises volck (that is, "White people live here"). At least, that is the notation on the facsimile map by J.G. Doppelmayer (1730).

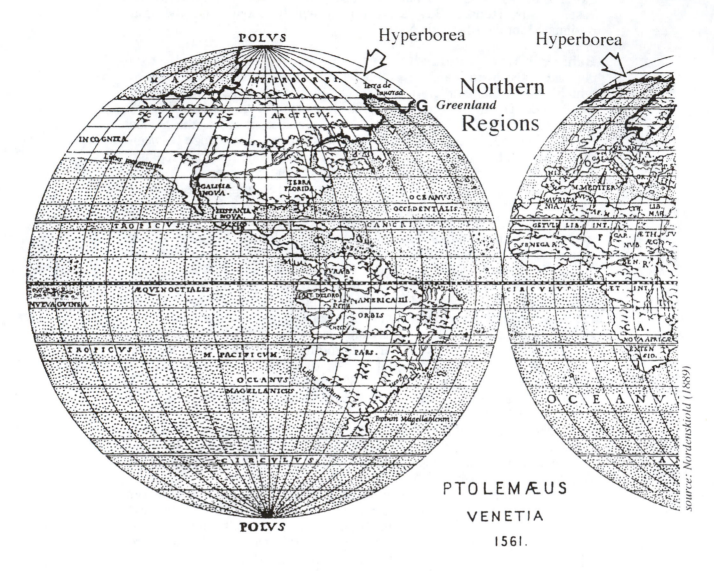

POLVS Hyperborea Hyperborea

Northern

Greenland

Regions

MARE HYPERBOREA

Terra de Iapotad:

G

CIRCVLVS ARCTICVS.

INCOGNITA.

Littus incognitum.

GALICIA NOVA. TERRA FLORIDA.

HISPANIA NOVA. OCEANVS OCCIDENTALIS.

TROPICVS. CANCRI.

VRAB

NVEVA GVINEA. AEQVINOCTIALIS. ALT. DE LORO AMERICA III.

ORBIS

TROPICVS. M. PACIFICVM. PARS.

OCEANVS MAGELLANICVS.

Fretum Magellanicum.

POLVS

CIRCVLVS

PTOLEMÆUS

VENETIA

1561.

source: Nordenskiold (1889)

Hyperborea—The Northern Regions
Ptolemaic Orb, Venice, 1561

Anonymous world map shows "Hyperborea" above North America.
Hyperborea was the Roman designation for a temperate land beyond
Borea—the North Wind. This map has the Northern Region extending
from the top of Europe to Canada. Before the invention of this dual-
hemispherical projection, New World lands were simply assumed to be
an extension of the Northern Regions, thus travelers told tales of
Hyperborea being a temperate land—which is exactly what we should
expect near Hudson Bay (site of the Magnetic North Pole).

150

As A.E. Nordenskiold (1889) pointed out, subsequent copyists changed the shapes of the isles as well as various legends on the original globe. On the G.E. Ravenstein surrogate globe of 1908, the caption reads: "Here they catch white falcons." The importance of the correct notation is that it corresponds to the territory identified on Resen's 1605 map as "Norumbega." This is the same region of Nova Scotia that Richard Hakluyt identified as a 14th-century English colony. It is also the same region where Samuel Champlain reported "white" (European) settlements in the 16th century; and it is the same locale where Portuguese slave ships captured "white" natives for sale in Lisbon.

Although Behaim's chain of northwestern Atlantic isles (including Baffin Land, Iceland, and Greenland) are shown north of the Arctic Circle, the true geographical location of these lands is actually south of the Arctic Circle. This misplacement and the fact that Baffin Land is situated in the vicinity of the Magnetic North Pole reveal that placement of the northern isles resulted from confusion of the Geographic North Pole with the magnetic pole. Indeed, Baffin Land actually was in the vicinity of the magnetic pole at the time friar Nicholas conducted his survey. This confusion of orientation is also evident from Behaim's placement of Greenland directly north of Norway—when in fact the true position of Greenland Island is west-northwest. It is only when a magnetic compass is being used for orientation that Greenland seems to be north relative to Bergen—because the compass needle points toward Greenland (and the Magnetic North Pole beyond in Hudson Bay). In this regard, Behaim's portrayal of the Northern regions follows the pattern of a Magnetic North orientation seen in maps by Donnus Nickolaus Germanus (1482).

If Behaim's northern isles are moved southwest on a schematic map from their location near the Geographic North Pole to their approximate location around the magnetic pole of Hudson Bay (at 66°N), it becomes apparent that "Northern Regions" or "northern isles" on Behaim's globe actually correspond to North American territories south of the Arctic Circle. Once moved to this more-accurate geographical position, the separate "isles" can be interpreted as sections of mainland between the Atlantic and Hudson Bay. Behaim probably worked from several gazetteers that represented sequential surveys of different areas of mainland which were separated by huge rivers, gulfs, and bays. Also, part of his conceptualization of Northern Regions might have been derived from the saga-map tradition of four headlands (or isles) followed by the isle—Newfoundland. Another possibility is that Behaim attempted to improve the accuracy of his globe by plotting coordinates from more-recent (but less reliable) accounts of Portuguese navigators in 1477.

Historians have assumed that northern isles on Behaim's globe were merely examples of the so-called "fabulous islands" which seafarers reported in the North Atlantic. This unfavorable judgment is the result of a lack of information, a failure to distinguish between charts plotted with a magnetic versus a geographic orientation, and dependency upon Ravenstein's inaccurate surrogate globe of 1908.

It is not uncommon to see illustrations of G.E. Ravenstein's 1908 version of the Behaim globe sans everything above the Arctic Circle. Implicit in such illustrations is the belief that the Polar Region couldn't possibly have any relevance to New World discovery. Nothing could be farther from the truth. But who among lay readers can judge the importance of "hidden isles" that are deleted from historical texts or concealed by scholarly ignorance?

151

Were the Polar Isles Stepping Stones to Asia?

Having seen field reports of temperate lands in the Polar Regions and continental lands across the North Atlantic, European geographers were still perplexed about the inhabitants of these lands and their relationship to the empires of Asia. The pattern of Northern isles on Behaim's globe implies that they could serve as stepping stones to Asia. Frigid waters were of no concern—if Behaim's globe serves as a guide to current geographical concepts. His polar sea is a navigable waterway from Greenland to the continent beyond. Columbus believed in the stepping-stone theory: his voyage to the north in 1477 was one of many early attempts to locate a Northwest Passage via the northern isles.

The Norveca map with its portrayal of North American mainland, Florida peninsula, Antilles, and great gulf reveals European knowledge of the North Atlantic that anticipates English, Portuguese, Danish and Venetian explorations during the 15th century. This knowledge, which was preserved in the <u>Inventio Fortunatae</u> and reflected on subsequent "scientific" maps of the Atlantic, influenced the course of history during the dawn of the Renaissance. In spite of the accuracy of Franciscan gazetteers, however, mapping of the Atlantic was still in its infancy: merchants and mariners remained in the dark as to what they might encounter across the western sea. Would sailors have to battle the denizens of Gog-Magog along the way? Would the whirlpools of Norse folklore—the dreaded Maelstrom—suck them to their doom?

Kings, merchants, and geographers were particularly puzzled after wide-spread circulation of <u>Marco Polo's Travels</u> suggested that the land across the Atlantic was Cathay—the great empire of China. Polo claimed that the Spice Islands and golden kingdoms were not far beyond. Ultimately, the incentives proved more of a lure than the dreaded "edge of Earth" was a deterrent. By the late 14th century, merchants of Venice were poised to test the theory that Cathay could be reached by sailing west.

The Description of the Cross-Staff.

This Instrument is of some antiquity in Navigation, and is commonly used at Sea, to take the Altitude of the Sun or Stars, which it performs with sufficient exactness, especially if it be less then 60 degrees, but if it exceed 60, it is not so certain, by reason of the length of the Cross, and the smallness of the graduations on the Staff.

Venice Goes West

As the hub of commerce between Europe and the Orient, Venice was the wealthiest city in Christendom during the 14th century. In more ancient times, she had served as a staging ground for the Crusades; and when it served her ambitions, she bartered transit to the Holy Lands in exchange for the loan of an army. Constantinople and Zara, Yugoslavia, fell to her rented knights; and territories along the Adriatic and Aegean Seas bowed before Venetian fleets. Eastern Mediterranean nations that Venice did not conquer with an army often found themselves dominated by trading houses and financiers who were based in Venice. Genoa (on the west coast of Italy) was a constant competitor for commercial suitors, but the charms and dowry of Venice always prevailed—that is, until after the 15th century. In 1380, her fleets dealt the Genoese navy a crushing defeat in the Battle of Chioggia. Meanwhile, the Venetian army overwhelmed northeastern Italy penetrating west to the Adda river, fighting south to Ravenna, and storming north to the Alps. Croatia was her ally; Crete was her consort—Milan and Florence her handmaidens. She was home to the Templars and the most influential financiers of Europe. By special papal dispensation, Venice played host to Moslem traders and thereby dominated the Asian markets from colonies in Alexandria, Egypt, and La Tana on the Sea of Azof.

Nicolo and Maffeo Polo were only two of many successful overseas merchants who made Venice their home. China was their destination in 1260, and the venture brought such wealth and pleasure that the brothers returned again in 1269 with Nicolo's son Marco in the van. By 1295, they were all back in Venice; and Marco had many fabulous stories to tell of his twenty years in the service of the khan.

It was only due to unfortunate circumstances—that being his capture by a Genoese warship—that led Marco to dictate his memoirs from the unlikely environs of a Genoese jail. Otherwise, his tales of golden pagodas, exotic rituals, and vast cities probably would have passed with him into eternity. Polo's contemporaries mocked his "fabulous" tales; their nickname for him was "Marco Millioni"—in reference to his propensity for using the word "million" when referring to the servants, shops, cities, and ships of Kublai Khan. Polo's very real adventures were so bizarre by the standards of ordinary Venetians that they seemed outright impossible. Given such a climate of doubt, it is unlikely that the prosperous Marco would have bothered writing about his exploits had he not found himself in a situation of acute boredom. Following his death, manuscript copies of Polo's travelog circulated among the aristocracy; when Gutenberg's printing presses transformed the communications

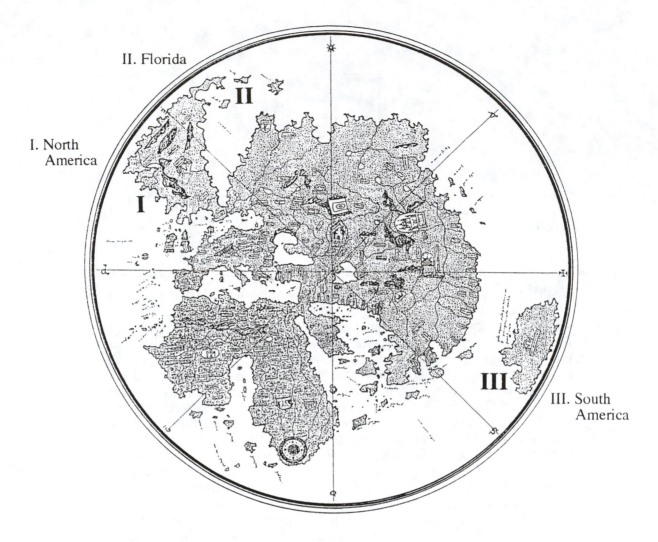

Albertin DeVirga World Map   1414 AD
facsimile

The map has three principle features that betray knowledge of New World territories before Columbus: I.) a triangular-shaped continent reaching northwest from Norway; II.) a long peninsula with three islands at the top of the triangular continent; and III.) an oval-shaped continent southeast of Asia. The triangular-shaped continent is labeled "Norveca" and also "Europa." This land corresponds to a region on other Medieval maps called: "Hyperborea Europa"—Europe of the North Pole; or "Septentrionalis"—the north land. Although historians have generally assumed this to be a mythological or "fabulous" region, substantial evidence confirms that this represents North America. Indeed, it is the earliest cartographic portrayal of North America as a separate continent from Asia. The peninsula extending to the northeast (II) is the earliest representation of Florida—shown here at the edge of a continent above a great gulf which can be identified as the Gulf of Mexico. The three islands adjacent to the peninsula represent the earliest portrayal of the Antilles Islands. The southeastern continent (III), called *Ca-paru sive Java Magna*, represents Peru. This is not the earliest mention of the name Peru on an ancient map. It appears on Roman maps in the Macrobius tradition as "Perusta"—meaning very hot land. (Facsimile by the author.)

154

industry of Europe in the mid-15th century, Polo's <u>Travels</u> became a popular pastime for literate shopkeepers and aspiring explorers like Christopher Colon—later known as "Columbus."

Given the driving spirit that seems to guide successful commerce, it was inevitable that Venetian merchants would extend the tentacles of their empire into the northern outposts of Western Civilization along the Baltic and North Seas. Galley service to Lisbon, Flanders, and England began in 1317 and continued on a regular basis for the next two centuries (Newton, 1932, 29). Sandwich, Southampton, St. Catherine's and London were the principal British ports where Venetian merchants established homes and markets. Such imports as Indian cotton, Chinese silk, china-ware, Malabar ginger, nutmegs, cloves, aloes, camphor, and precious gems dazzled English gentry who sought desperately to escape the hum-drum of bland pudding, itchy woolens, and faux jewelry.

Invariably, Venetian merchants who sailed as far as the British Isles cast their sights even farther north and west. They listened with great interest to stories in Bristol about profitable fishing grounds beyond Iceland and lucrative fur-trapping outposts in Friesland that were frequented by Norse and Hanseatic traders. Marco Polo's tales of Oriental wealth and the nearby Spice Islands also kindled their imaginations. In this era of commercial prosperity, powerful entrepreneurs speculated about untapped opportunities waiting in continents across the Atlantic.

The Book of Secrets

During the early 1300's, the Genoese cartographer Petrus Vesconte produced a series of world maps to accompany a book by his associate Marino Sanudo. The maps are as mysterious as the book which promoted a 1306 crusade to the Holy Lands. Sanudo called his book <u>Liber Secretorum Fidelium Crucis</u>—that is, "Book of Secrets for True Believers in The Cross." Ten manuscript copies of the 700-year-old book have survived—suggesting that the document achieved widespread circulation among European merchants and lords in the 14th century. They are the oldest known <u>mappamonds</u> to employ a matrix of rhumb lines (or compass lines) for use in navigation and are therefore comparable in design to 13th-century portolanos. Vesconte's map is most notable for its portrayal of the Asian coast.

Unlike earlier <u>mappamonds</u>, Vesconte's map lacks biblical anecdotes and the standard Isle of Paradise on the coast of Asia. In its place, there is a schematic coastline with a long peninsula surrounded by islands at the northeast opening of a large gulf. Towards the north, another gulf and the territory of Albania suggest the embryonic concept of New World lands across the Atlantic. It would be tempting to attribute the configuration of the Asian coastline to the inspiration of Marco Polo. However, the location of the isles do not conform to Polo's estimates of the location of Korea and Japan. At 45° north, they are at the correct latitude, however Polo estimated the distance from mainland China to Japan at 1,000 to 1,500 miles—or far greater than the space indicated on Vesconte's map. Although it is premature to suggest that Vesconte and his associates had begun mapping the New World at this early date, it is not speculative to note that his Venetian counterpart, Albertin DeVirga, was doing just that within the century.

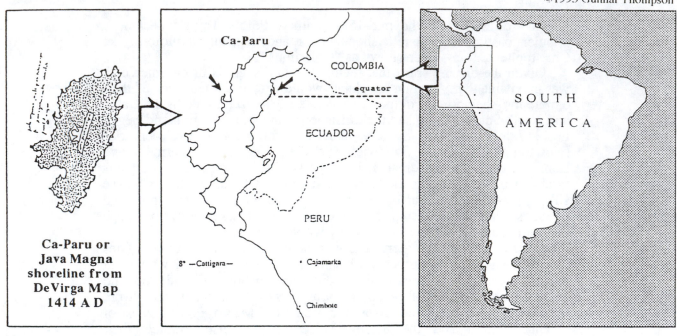

Ca-Paru or Java Magna shoreline from DeVirga Map 1414 AD

Ca-Paru
South America on DeVirga's Map, 1414 AD

A huge island-continent in the southeastern quadrant of Albertin DeVirga's map (1414) is in the approximate position of South America. The west coast of this island is very similar in configuration to the actual coastline between Ecuador and Peru and has a large gulf corresponding to the Gulf of Guayaquil. Coastlines from DeVirga's map (left) and from a modern atlas (Hammond, 1965—right) are compared in the above illustration. Bays and headlands show sufficient correspondence to rule out the most remote possibility of coincidence. Perhaps the most singular feature is a very narrow peninsula near the Equator—at Cojimies, Ecuador (dark arrow). This degree of accuracy could only have been achieved by rather sophisticated surveys by persons skilled in astronomy. Furthermore, there is a tradition from Roman times of a land across the ocean from Asia that has a large bay or gulf at about 3° below the equator. This isle carries the designation: *Caparu sive Java Magna*. Caparu is the equivalent of Peru—the native term for the land. This designation on DeVirga's map confirms that the region was known to Europeans prior to the 16th century. The native Quechua term means: Land of Abundance. This region is identified on 2nd-century Roman maps as Cattigara, on 8th-century Hindu maps as Patala India, on 13th-century Arabian maps as Waq-Waq, and on Spanish maps as Ophir—the legendary land of King Solomon's gold mines. It was here that Francisco Pizarro found hoards of Inca gold in 1533.

156

The Venetian Mercantile Map of The World

During the 14th century, Venetian merchants established strong ties with royalty throughout Europe. They were the principle financiers who funded England's continental wars; they were the middle-men who imported fine silks for the king's table and his wardrobe. As valued servants and consultants, the Venetians had access to royal gossip and intelligence. That intimate relationship is no better demonstrated than by the production of a world mercantile map in 1414 AD.

Venetian cosmographer Albertin DeVirga compiled his map of trading centers from numerous sources including Arabic and English gazetteers. The Northern Regions were based on 14th-century Franciscan surveys; African territories were copied from the Persian geography of Hamd Allah Mustawfi; seacoasts of the Indian Ocean and China Sea were derived from Moslem portolanos; and a distant isle across the Eastern Sea was based on ancient Roman maps. Thus, DeVirga's creation was the most comprehensive and most current world map ever compiled. As the Venetian standard, it was destined to serve the planning and management needs of the leading mercantile families of the Republic.

The exquisitely-crafted parchment document measures 696 cm by 440 cm (approximately 32 inches x 55 inches) and includes a circular map of the world along with a zodiac and two tables of figures—a lunar table and an Easter table (Destombes, 1964). Surrounding the world are decorative motifs that are distinctively Arabic in character. The cosmographer's name, city of origin, and date are inscribed on the parchment—although the last figure of the date is illegible. Most scholars assume a date of 1414, but the actual date could be anywhere from 1410 to 1419. The map shows an elongated Mediterranean Sea which is common in Classical and Medieval maps. Arabia and the Persian Gulf are excessively enlarged; Africa is nearly split into two parts by a gulf on the west coast.

Another map by DeVirga is in the collection of the Bibliotheque Nacional in Paris. This smaller map portrays the Black Sea region in 1409 (Document # Ge. D-7900). Comparison of the style and writing on both maps was sufficient for Austrian historian Franz Von Wieser to verify authenticity of the Venetian Map in 1912.

The Venetian Map portrays Earth as a globe flattened into a disc with Mount Ararat (Eastern Turkey) as the central reference point. This perspective strikes a compromise between European mappamonds and circular Arabian maps. Christian geographers traditionally centered their maps on Jerusalem, while Moslem cartographers used Mecca or Tehran as the focal point of the Known World. The central portion of the Venetian Map is dominated by three continents, Europe, Africa, and Asia which were drawn in accordance with contemporary European and Arabian sources. In addition to this central land mass, there are two additional land areas or continents—one situated in the northwestern quadrant and the other situated in the southeastern quadrant near the edge of the map. The land area in the northwest—"Norveca Europa"—represents the earliest Venetian concept of the New World as a continent situated in the Northern Regions of the North Atlantic. The continent situated in the Pacific east of Asia represents South America.

South America on The Venetian Map

A huge island in the southeastern Pacific bears the rubric: Caparu sive Java Magna. This island occupies the approximate position expected for South America on a circular map. Indeed, it can be identified as South

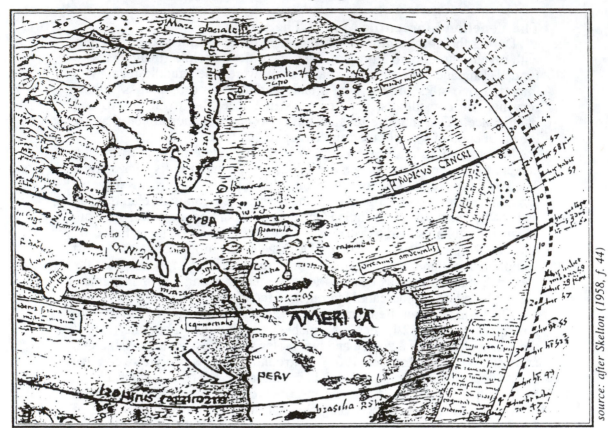

source: after Skelton (1958, f. 44)

Spanish map of 1535

Perusta
Peru

Macrobius map of 440 A D
source: after map in Huntington Library
San Marino, California
source: Kimble (1938)

Source of the Name—Peru

Some writers including the historian Harrisse attribute the naming of Peru to Spanish soldiers under the command of Francisco Pizarro during the invasion of the region in 1531. Presumably, a native told the Spaniards that this was the name of a river—so the Spanish adopted that name for the whole country of the Incas. However, a map by Diego Ribero in 1529—three years before the conquest—already has the region identified as "Peru." In another version, natives are said to have called the west coast Peru—because it was a native Quechua term for "Land of Abundance." As much of the coastal zone is arid, a 5th-century Roman term, *perusta*, must also be advanced as a source for the name of the region. Indeed, this name appears for the northern section of the Antipodes (South America) on maps by the 5th-century Roman cartographer—Macrobius. This early naming of Peru would account for the term "Ca-paru" on DeVirga's 1414 map.

Per   Ophir   **Peru**

America on the basis of its position, name, geographical configuration, and numerous traditions of a land of abundance across the Pacific. The name of this continent, Ca-paru, is the earliest known mention of the native term, peru, on an extant map.

Franz Von Wieser's 1912 critique of the Venetian Map expressed his opinion that the southeastern isle was meant to represent Cipangu (Japan) or Java. Wieser speculated about Japan because the isle was too far west of Malaya to be considered as one of the Indonesian isles. Regardless of the fact that the logo for the isle includes "Java Magna" (Greater Java) as an alternative name, it is too far away from the Asian coast to be regarded as representing any previously identified isle by that name. Japan, on the other hand, might seem more plausible because Marco Polo estimated that Cipangu (Japan) was located 1,000 to 1,500 miles east of China. However, even this option isn't very attractive because the scale of the map suggests that Caparu is actually several thousand miles farther east.

Identifying the isle as Japan must have seemed like the most practical explanation within Wieser's narrow perspective of cartography in which he assumed that New World territories were unknown until after Columbus. However, the position of Caparu is actually too far south and too far east to represent Japan—which is in reality a group of islands off the coast of China. Indeed, the Venetian Map has four islands in about the right position for the Japanese isles. Unfortunately, Wieser's training as an orthodox scholar didn't demand anything beyond making a judgment based on the assumptions of his profession. Had he bothered to compare the outline of the west coast of this island with a map of South America—he would have been forced to consider the inevitable solution to his dilemma: Caparu is South America.

A comparison of the Isle of Caparu with a modern map of South America leaves little room for doubt that the west coast is a close parallel to the shoreline from Ecuador to Peru. In this region, South America has a westward bulge into the Pacific Ocean. This bulge compares favorably in position and size to Caparu. The coast has a series of topographical features which show striking similarity. These include a small peninsula near the equator, two major headlands facing west that are separated by a large gulf—the Gulf of Guayaquil, and a small headland or peninsula at the southern end of the bulge.

The corresponding coastlines are not identical, however this level of similarity is only possible from a society that has developed a highly sophisticated mapping technology. Certainly, 15th-century Europeans did not have this level of accuracy. Indeed, this area of the Venetian Map is more accurate than the outline of Norveca which is obviously from a different source. Chinese explorers or 2nd-century Romans are the most-likely candidates for producing the original gazetteers for Caparu.

According to the 2nd-century Roman geographer Ptolemy, an important city called "Cattigara" was situated beyond the Sinus Magnus (i.e., the Pacific Ocean) along the western shore of "Sinarum regio"—a land that formed the eastern border of the Indian Ocean. This was also at the farthest extremity of the Known World. Cattigara was located south of the equator at about 10° and directly below a huge bay or gulf. In the 15th century, European cartographers identified the southeastern land as India Patalis; by the 16th century, they called it Mondo Novo—the "New World." Eventually, this land was called South America.

Ptolemy's map had two Indias: 1) India intra Ganges; and 2) India extra Ganges. The first was the India most commonly known today as

Benedictus Arias Montanus, 1572

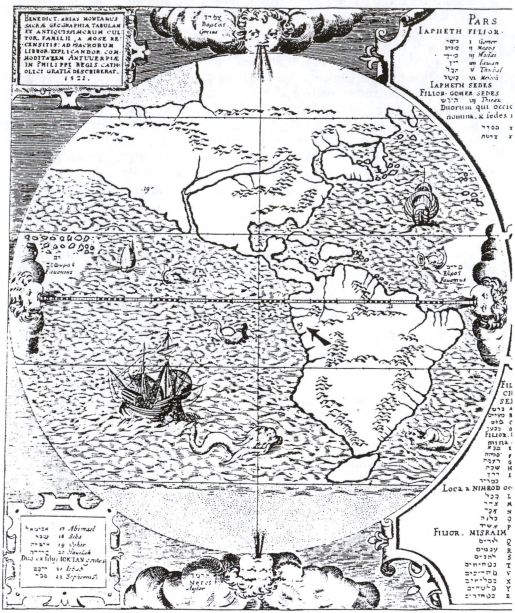

Ophir, Paru & The Source of Solomon's Gold

The Rudimentium Novitiorum (Lubeck, 1475) located the fabled Ophir—source of King Solomon's mines—west of Africa and South of Asia. This position corresponds approximately on the schematic Novitiorum to South America. This location is also indicated on a map by Arias Montanus where the #19 on the coast of Peru (or Paru) is designated as Ophir. If this was indeed the location of the fabled gold mines, we have a rationale for why this distant land was indicated on Roman maps and on DeVirga's map of 1414. It was in this locale that the Spaniard Conquistador Francisco Pizarro encountered the Inca empire whose gold hoards surpassed those of all other nations. And they were promptly appropriated for the Spanish treasury.

source:
Benedictus Arias Montanus
Sacrae Geographiae Tabulam
Antwerp, 1572

160

"India"—the subcontinent. It was situated between the Indus and Ganges rivers. Beyond the Ganges lay the Second India—corresponding to Indo-China and the Malayan archipelago. The southern region of the archipelago including Sumatra and Java was called the "Golden Chersonesus" (or chersonese). East of this archipelago, the <u>Sinus Magnus</u> (or "Great Gulf") separated the Second India from a Third India which was later identified as India Patalis.

Ptolemy's associate, Marinus of Tyre, noted in his geography that Roman merchants reported land to the east of Sabda (Java) after sailing "innumerable days." Marinus believed that the eastern land was situated about 45° or 5,000 miles farther east than the farthest extremity of land on Ptolemy's map. This length approaches the position of South America but still falls about 3,000 miles short. Considering the difficulties sailors had estimating distances and longitude in those days, the region Marinus proposed as the eastern extremity of the Indian Ocean and the Sinus Magnus seems like a fairly reasonable estimate of the actual location of South America. Ibarra-Grasso joins Magellan, Bartholomew Colon, historian Peter Martyr and others in identifying South America as the eastern land of Ptolemaic maps.

An Arabic map by Hamd Allah Mustawfi (1350) is the oldest extant map to show Ptolemy's eastern land in the approximate location of South America. Mustawfi's map shows a land identified as "Waq-Waq" situated far across the Indian Ocean, although the distance is not indicated. On the Florentine Portolano of 1447, the Sinus Magnus was expanded to allow for a larger ocean, however Cathay (China) was inaccurately located at the center of this territory south of the Equator. Henricus Martellus Germanus (1489) misidentified the southern land as Malabar. Martin Behaim (1492) accurately identified the land as India Patalis—the Third India. This was the name that South America was commonly known as throughout India, Indo-China, and Indonesia during the 15th century.

By 1529, Spanish maps designated the west coast of South America as "Peru." This is a Quechua native term meaning "Land of Abundance." The native term is essentially the same as the one inscribed on the Venetian Map a century earlier where "Ca-paru" stands for the southeastern continent. The monk Arias Montanus identified Peru as the location of King Solomon's fabled gold mines. His map of 1572 has the name "Ophir" on the western coast at the approximate location of Cattigara on other maps. It was in this vicinity that Francisco Pizarro encountered the Inca empire whose gold mines were the most prodigious on Earth.

Hindus also knew of the region as "the land of gold." That was one of the definitions associated with India Patala—a distant land across the Indian Ocean. Another name for this territory was "The Land of Abundance." Hindu merchants sailed to the west coast of the distant continents until the maritime invasion of Alphonso DeAlbuquerque effectively terminated trans-Pacific trade in the early 1500's. The presence of maize in India can be traced to trans-Pacific trade. Hundreds of Hoysala-dynasty sculptures show deities holding a variety of corn cobs which University of Oregon Professor Carl Johannessen (1989) and Nehru University Professor Jaweed Ashraf (1995) have conclusively identified as maize. This identification was confirmed by a photographic expedition in 1995 by John Jones representing the Multicultural Discovery Project.

Although it was often misidentified and misplaced on European maps, South America had played a significant role in Old World trade for more

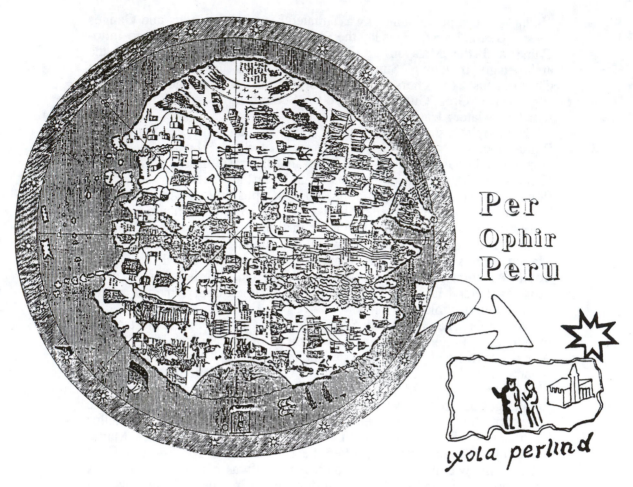

Per
Ophir
Peru

ıxola perlind

Ophir, Peru, and Bianco's 1436 Mappamond

During the 18th century, several historians speculated that Francisco Pizarro and his cohorts had stumbled upon the fabled land of Ophir when they invaded Peru in 1531. Gold and silver hoards shipped back to Spain from this treasure far exceeded anything Europeans had ever seen before—and the mines are still pumping out the ore. Some scholars put forth the theory that the name for King Solomon's gold mines in Ophir was derived from the name that native Peruvians gave to their own land—Peru. Indeed, one version of the ancient Phoenician word Ophir is simply Per—the first syllable of Peru. The name might also have been derived from a Mediterranean word for hot or parched land—and one such Latin word, per-usta, was used to describe the northern sector of Terra Australis or the Antipodes. This land was subsequently identified by Peter Martyr, Columbus, Las Casas, and many others as South America.

Andrea Bianco's 1436 map further clinches the comparison of Ophir with Peru and with the legend "Ca-paru" from the Venetian Commercial Map of 1414. As is the case on the Venetian map, a land situated southeast of Asia on Bianco's map is called "ixola per-lind." This translates as isle of Per land—the Land of Per. Thus, we can realize that the designation of Ca-peru on the Venetian map is not a fluke—it is within the traditions of contemporary cartography. (Note: there is an island in the Banda Sea that is called Biru or Piru. How this fits into the story of Solomon's mines is unknown.)

source: Peres (1943, Pl. 15)

162

than two thousand years. The rubric "Ca-paru" on the southeastern continent of the Venetian Map of 1414 was part of that heritage. This map is the oldest extant map to show South America (Caparu) as a separate continent.

A world map by Francesco Roselli in 1508 has a huge land situated southeast of Asia in the approximate position of Ca-paru on DeVirga's map. This nameless land also has a huge bay in its northwestern coast which approximates the bay of Ca-paru on DeVirga's map and also the Gulf of Guayaquil or Cattigara on Roman maps. On the opposite side of Roselli's map is the extreme border of Mundus Novus (a.k.a., South America). Because the nameless land southeast of Asia is actually the western coast of Roselli's Mundus Novus, the identification of this territory (either on Roselli's map or on DeVirga's map) with the west coast of Peru is confirmed. So, here we can see a fairly accurate portrayal of South America's west coast two decades before Spanish incursions into the region; and we see a vague portrayal of the Pacific Ocean a decade before Magellan. This map also has a fairly accurate portrayal of Antarctica (Portinaro & Knirsch, 1987, Pl. V).

Java Magna is sometimes associated with Australia and sometimes with a huge land east of Asia in the mid-Pacific Ocean. On Bernardo Silvano DaEboli's 1511 map, Java Magna is in the eastern Pacific about 5° west of the coast of South America. This places it in the vicinity of South America on a similar map by Roselli in 1508. Such placement confirms that the land in question often represented the west coast of South America, and it represents another visage of ancient Roman voyages across the Pacific to a huge land with a huge gulf within 10° south of the equator (Portinaro & Knirsch, 1987, Pl. VI).

Venetian Voyagers

Richard Hakluyt's Divers Voyages Touching the Discoverie of America (1582) identified six explorers who preceded Columbus to America. Four of them were Venetians: Marco Polo (1270), the brothers Nicolo and Antonio Zeno (1380), and Nicolaus Conti (1444).

During his long sojourn in the Far East (1270-1292), Marco Polo led an expedition across the Strait of Anian to explore a place known as The Land of Women. His travelog describes a voyage along the west coast of Alaska where the North Pole was ahead (by compass bearing) and the Pole Star was behind him towards the south. This phenomenon, unbeknownst to Polo, was the result of magnetic declination. His unsettling experience of the polar discrepancy could have occurred only along the coast of southern Alaska or British Columbia. His keen observation confirms that Polo's expedition had crossed over the Strait of Anian to the New World. Indeed, this crossing was confirmed by descriptions of his expedition in the travelog. Polo's Pantect map of this journey provides further confirmation of the transoceanic voyage. By the late 16th century, European geographers recognized that the Strait of Anian separated Asia from America; thus, English historian Hakluyt credited Polo with an early voyage along the west coast of North America.

In addition to accounts of historic travelers such as Marco Polo and the Zeno brothers who were apparently well-known to the English aristocracy, there must have been various lowly mariners, priests, and pirates who made their way to the Americas in the van of merchants and fishermen. The Italian Ramusio noted in his Viaggi that a merchant ship sailed on an expedition "to the west" from Crete in 1432. The vessel was

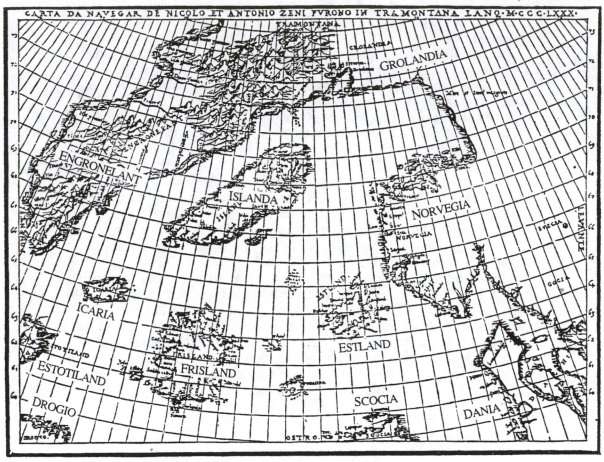

Zeno Map of Northern Regions, Venice 1558

This map is a copy of a late 15th-century or early 16th-century chart. According to the account of the Zeno letters published in Richard Hakluyt's *Diverse Voyages* (1582), the map was simply an antique chart that a descendant of the Venetian explorer Nicolo Zeno happened to have available when the explorer's letters were published. It is probably derived from contemporaneous maps by Nicholas Martellus Germanus, Arabian cartographers, and possibly Norse sources. Although the letters and map were regarded as authentic in the 1500's, later historians denounced the collection as a fraud—largely due to the inclusion of supposedly fictitious islands (Frisland, Icaria, Estland, etc.). These islands were mentioned in the Zeno Tale, and the compiler of the letters, Nicolo Zeno IInd, apparently drew these on the map to illustrate the narrative of his ancestor. Most of these islands were also mentioned in earlier, historical writings—so there is no basis for assuming they are the fantastic creation of Zeno II. Estotiland, Estland, and Drogeo are found in Norse accounts and maps; Frisland was a commonly known land on Arabic maps, and Columbus regarded it as an alternative name for the Icelandic Isles—later identified as Newfoundland. Modern historians have protested that there is no such place as Frisland—but it was probably an archaic term for Newfoundland. The archaic naming took place in the 12th century when Frisian nobles found a "new land" in the "Northern Regions" beyond Iceland.

164

beaten back by contrary winds southwest of Ireland and was forced into the Arctic Circle north of Norway. The ship finally crashed on Rusten Island in the Lofotens, and the crew were rescued by Norwegian fishermen (Newton, 1932, 207). A legend on the Fra Mauro's map says that the shipwreck of the Venetian Pietro Querini on the Norwegian coast occurred in 1431 (Skelton, et al., 1965, 116).

There was another voyage a few years later that came to the attention of historians. In Diverse Voyages, Richard Hakluyt credits the Venetian captain Nicolaus Conti with a voyage to the New World in 1444. Virtually nothing is known of this ancient traveler.

The Zeno Exploits

The New World adventures of two Venetian nobles, Nicolo and Antonio Zeno, are recounted in two somewhat differing books: Giovanni Ramusio's Viaggi (ca. 1574) and Richard Hakluyt's Diverse Voyages (1582). The account originated from the pen of Nicolo Zeno, junior, who found a package of letters from his ancestors that were written while on an extended expedition to the New World circa 1380 or 1390.

Antonio Zeno was a wealthy knight whose storm-driven vessel reached an archipelago of isles in the western sea. Hakluyt leaves no doubt that this archipelago was the country later identified as "Norumbega"—that is, eastern North America near the Gulf of St. Lawrence. Zeno's escapades took him to Friseland, Estotiland, Icaria, Estlande, Grisland, Greenland, and a number of smaller isles including: Bres, Talas, Broas, Iscant, Trans, Mimant, and Dambere. These isles correspond most closely to an archipelago often referred to as the "Icelands" or Icelandic isles on contemporary maps.

The letters told of Zeno's rescue by a local chieftain (Zichmni) who spoke Latin and warred against pirates as well as the Norse king and numerous princes who dominated the area. One of these foreign princes might have been Earl Henry St. Clair of Orkney—a Scottish lord who at various times served Norse and Danish kings. Historical records show that he attended the 1389 coronation of the Danish Queen Margaret who presided over Norway and Sweden. Within the Sinclair family who were descendants of the hereditary earls of the Orkneys, there is a strong tradition that Earl Henry had traveled across the North Atlantic to the Western Continent. The earl's tomb, built circa 1404, contains sculptures of maize plants that could have come only from America, and a rock cliff near Westford, Massachusetts, bears a crude inscription of a knight holding a shield with the heraldic insignia of the St. Clair clan. Henry's travels and battles in the Orkney Islands and Shetlands certainly took him far into the North Atlantic; however, nothing in the ancestral records connects this loyal Celtic lord to the pirate Zichmni (Oleson, 1964, 109).

Zeno's skills as a navigator led to his appointment as an admiral in the continuing conquests of Zichmni's warriors. Before long, the Venetian invited his brother, Nicolo, to come share in the adventure. Nicolo died in Greenland circa 1395; his brother, Antonio returned to Venice sometime before 1406 where he subsequently died. Nicolo's letters to relatives back in Venice were eventually stored in an attic where they were found sixty years later by a youth—Nicolo Zeno II.

According to the letters, each year, fishermen came from northern Europe to harvest salmon and codfish in the islands. In many respects, the tale seems like a fair sampling of other reports from seafarers who visited the "Icelandic Isles" in the western Atlantic: many pirates,

source: Nordenskiold (1889, Pl. 31)

**Ptolemaic Map
Gregorius Reisch
1480**

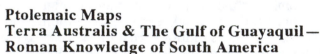

GREGORIUS REISCH, MARGARITA PHILOSOPHICA.

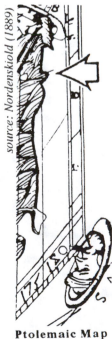

source: Nordenskiold (1889)

**Ptolemaic Map
Bologna, 1477**

*Golden
Chersonese*

Ptolemaic Maps
Terra Australis & The Gulf of Guayaquil—
Roman Knowledge of South America

Roman maps of the 5th century (such as the 440 AD map by Macrobius) show a huge continent below the equator. This land had various names: the Antepodes (Land Opposite the Known World), Terra Altera (the Other World), and Terra Australis (the Southern Continent). Macrobius specified that this land was situated beneath the equator and opposite both Africa and Asia across the ocean. This land was also indicated on maps by Ptolemy dating to the 2nd century but virtually lost to Europeans during the Middle Ages due to religious prejudice against pagan knowledge. Ptolemy's map was re-discovered in 1409 from Arabian sources who had preserved copies of the map. A 15th-century version of this map by Gregorius Reisch (1480) is shown above. Ptolemy described the southern land as Terra Incognita (Unknown Land) running between the tip of Africa and a land east of Asia that he identified as "Sinarum Regio." On the west coast of this eastern land just south of the equator he placed a large gulf and below that a city called "Cattigara." The gulf at 3° south on the Reisch map is shown enlarged (at right); the same gulf at 5° on a similar map from the Bologna edition of Ptolemy is shown enlarged (at left). This gulf corresponds to the Gulf of Guayaquil and the gulf on DeVirga's map showing the continent of Ca-paru.

166

abundant fish, diverse people, and gold deposits. The letters created a sensation in Europe at the time of their publication, and they were generally regarded as authentic for the next two centuries. As a fairly accurate reflection of conditions in the Icelandic Isles during the 14th century, there was no reason to question their authenticity—that is, not until the Zeno account became a serious threat to a cult of historians who promoted a "Columbus was First" historical paradigm.

In modern times, orthodox historians have criticized Ramusio's account on the assumption that the highly-respected Venetian historian had been duped. Presumably, the "letters" were a hoax which Nicolo Zeno concocted in the 16th century in hopes of promoting his own ancestors at the expense of the Genoese Columbus. The hoax theory seemed plausible to orthodox historians who naturally suspected anyone who disagreed with the approved dogma as being guilty of treason. As rationale, they pointed to the traditional rivalry between Genoa and Venice; they noted similarities between Zeno's tale and contemporary accounts of explorers in the New World; and they disputed the authenticity of a so-called Zeno map that some said was "too accurate" for the late 15th century while others criticized its inclusion of so-called "fantasy isles."

Orthodox historians regard the Zeno story as a "proven fraud" written in the 16th-century. The fact that it was widely-regarded as accurate for two centuries seems of little importance. Marco Barbaroso's Discendenze Patrizie (1552) tells of Zeno voyages to the isles of the North Pole and the death of Nicolo, the Elder, following his return to the Orkney Isles circa 1400. Barbaroso's publication preceded the account in Ramusio's Travels (1574) by more than twenty years (Sinclair, 1992, 131). This version is also consistent with 16th-century opinions that the destination of Zeno's expedition was near the North Pole.

Complaints raised against Zeno's story are at best superficial; and deeper investigation shows that they lack substance. Nicolo the Younger was a highly-respected citizen and member of the Council of Ten of the Venetian republic. In 1561, he prepared for Ruscelli's edition of Ptolemy a copy of a map of northern seas which included isles visited by his famous ancestor. The volume entitled The Discovery of the Islands of Frislanda, Eslanda, Engroneland, Estotiland, and Icaria made by two brothers of the Zeno Family was printed by Marcolino at Venice in 1558. Babcock (1922, 130) notes that "Estotiland" in the narrative refers to Newfoundland. The same region corresponds to a territory mentioned in the text of a French map of 1668 as being called Estotiland by the Danes, Nouvelle Bretagne by the English, Canada Septentrionale by the French, and Labrador by the Spanish (Babcock, 1922, 130).

The complete title of the Zeno narrative is rarely included in the writings of modern historians (see for example Ramsay, 1972, 54). This seemingly innocent exclusion in the interests of shortening a title of about thirty words unfortunately eliminates one of the most important clues to the authenticity of the Zeno account. Among the list of isles in the title is the phrase Fatto Sotto il Polo Artico—meaning "situated under the Arctic Pole." Orthodox historians have characterized the Zeno account as a tardy attempt to by nationalistic Venetians to defraud Columbus of his glory as the discoverer of the New World. However, neither Zeno nor the Venetians made such a claim as the account referred to previously known islands of the Polar Regions.

Nicolo II's admission that he had destroyed the letters while a youth and reconstructed their content from memory seems sufficient explanation

167

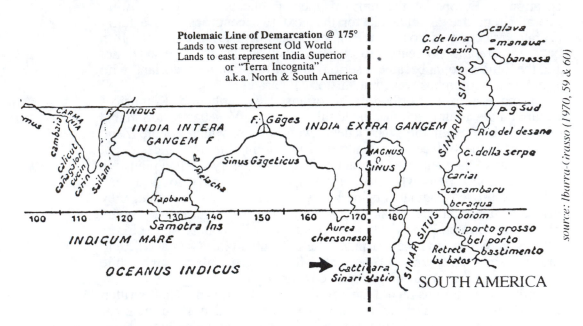

Bartholomew Colon
Terra Australis & The Gulf of Guayaquil—
Roman Knowledge of South America

Two charts by Bartholomew Colon (or a later copyist) confirm Roman knowledge of South America. These charts were made between 1503 and 1505. They clearly show Cattigara as a city on the western shore of South America (here called "Mondo Novo" or New World). These maps were done prior to Spanish voyages onto the Indian Ocean (Oceanus Indicus)—which was the Hindu name for the Pacific. The North Pacific Ocean is shown on Bartholomew's map as the Sinus Magnus. Magellan renamed this as the "Pacific" in 1521. Colon's placement of Cattigara on the west coast of South America clearly shows that Ptolemy's eastern land ("Sinarum Regio") and the land that Behaim identified as India Patala were in fact known lands—the legendary Antipodes or Terra Australis. Historian Peter Martyr also identified the Southern Continent which Columbus called "Alter Orbis" as the Roman Antipodes.

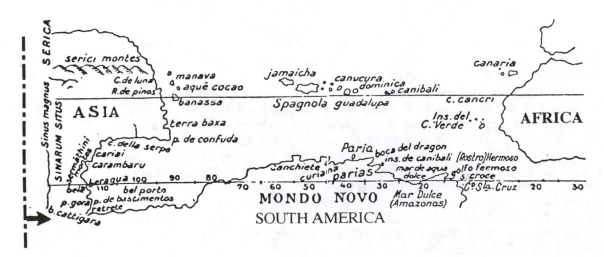

for the brevity and contemporary flavor of his story. In every other respect, it is certainly plausible within the broader context of Venetian voyages into the Atlantic.

One of the complaints which orthodox historians have put forth in support of their hoax theory is that the places where Nicolo Zeno supposedly sailed included "fabulous isles." A number of islands mentioned in the Hakluyt translation—such as Frisland, Talas, Broas, Bres, and Dambere—were featured as an archipelago on the Modena Map of 1350. This map shows the archipelago at the right latitude for Newfoundland. Similar maps, though without the same names, were printed throughout the 15th century. Nevertheless, orthodox historians stressed that the inclusion of "Frisland" in the account was proof of fraud. According to historian John Fiske: "When at length it was proved that no such island exists (meaning Frisland), the reputation of the Zeno narrative was seriously damaged" (Fiske, 1920, Vol. I, 236).

Unlike his associates, John Fisk was among the few who believed the Zeno story was legitimate. He accepted Miller Christy's argument that Greenland on the map had been plotted using magnetic coordinates: "The genuineness of the Zeno narrative is thus conclusively proved by its knowledge of Arctic geography, such as could have been obtained only by a visit to the far North at a time before the Greenland colony had finally lost touch with its mother country" (Fiske, 1920, Vol. I, 239). Indeed, it can be shown that the Zeno chart is very similar to Maps by Martellus circa 1490. Nor is Frisland purely fictional: Columbus, by his own account, visited the isle in 1477. It seems Frisland was an early name for Newfoundland.

The younger Zeno's claim that the land his ancestors visited was "Norse territory" is time-limited knowledge that suggests written testimonial from a place and time that was beyond the knowledge of most Europeans. In effect, Nicolo Senior—a Venetian—was admitting that the New World lands his ancestor sailed to in 1380 were not "new" discoveries, but instead were under Norwegian sovereignty. This is hardly the kind of statement one would expect from a hoaxer whose motive was to promote his own ethnic pride at the expense of the Genoese. Aside from the Venetian Map by Albertin DeVirga (1414), Norwegian territories from Greenland to Wineland were presumably thought to have been located near the North Pole, and contemporary maps showed the Icelandic Isles north of England—not west. Yet Zeno's tale clearly places the Icelandic archipelago at the latitude of salmon spawning areas in Norumbega—i.e., southern Labrador and Newfoundland.

According to Nicolo's own words, the so-called "Zeno Map" was simply an "antique" that happened to be available in the mid-1500's:

> Of these northern parts I thought good to draw the copy of a sea-card which amongst other antiquities I have found in my house. Although it has been rotten through for many years, yet it can still be opened. For those who delight in these things, it may serve to shed some light on the subject and enable the understanding of details that otherwise cannot be so easily conceived. (Hakluyt, 1599)

There is no illusion in Hakluyt's version of the story that the sea-card (or map) was an artifact left by the ancestral Zeno; it was simply an antique which the writer thought might help illustrate his narrative. The map has meridians and portrays Greenland in accordance with late 15th-

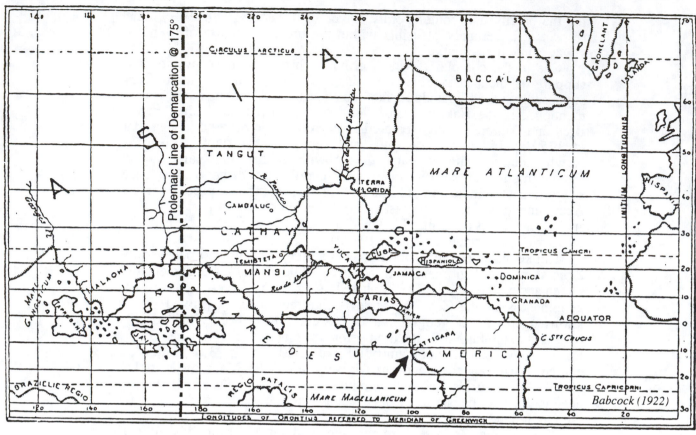

Babcock (1922)

Oroncio Fineo & Roman Knowledge of South America

A globe by Oroncio Fineo (1531) was based on a map by Monachus (1526). The illustration above is a cylindrical projection taken from the globe. Cattigara and the adjacent gulf at 7° is shown on the west coast of "America" which at this time represented the continent now known as South America. Inclusion of the west coast on this map is interesting because the region was presumably unknown to Europeans until after Pizarro's 1533 conquest of the Incas. The Pacific Ocean is identified as "Mare de Sur"—or the Southern Ocean. This map provides further evidence that the western bulge of South America and the Gulf of Guayaquil were known to the Romans—who placed Cattigara on their maps. Archeological evidence confirms Roman visits to a land they called "Terra Australis" or "The Antipodes": scholars have identified Roman-style amphitheaters and an aqueduct near the ancient Peruvian capital of Cuzco. These facilities, built by native laborers in pre-Inca times, confirm Roman cultural diffusion to coastal Peru.

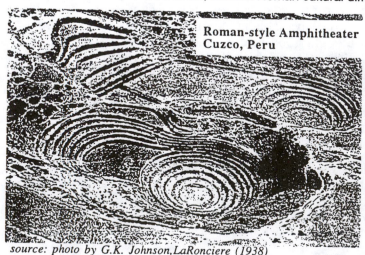

Roman-style Amphitheater Cuzco, Peru

source: photo by G.K. Johnson, LaRonciere (1938)

source: DuPouget (1895, fig. 168)

170

Roman-style Aqueduct Rodadero river, Peru

century maps, so the date of the original is not likely to be earlier than 1460—that is, a century after the Zeno voyage. Historian William Hobbs (1946) believes that the map which has so bothered historians was refined and set into a grid of latitudes and meridians by an engraver who worked for Ramusio. If this is the case—as Hakluyt's account implies—then the map is not a valid complaint against authenticity; therefore, Nicolo's tale must be regarded as lying within the realm of possibility.

Babcock (1922, 139) notes that Zeno could have found all the information he needed for his narrative in the maps and travelogs of "real" explorers on file in European libraries. Indeed, he points out that the basic characteristics of the Zeno map conform to those of known cartographers of an earlier age, such as the maps of Claudius Clavus (1427) or Donnus Nicolaus Germanus (1474). Before these maps were found, some scholars accused Zeno the Younger of totally fabricating a fantasy map of the North Atlantic. Now we know that Zeno's map was actually in good company with authentic maps of the same era, so perhaps the Zeno narrative is not so fraudulent as orthodox historians assumed.

The English advocate, John Dee, was among those who were convinced of the authenticity of the Zeno narrative. He used the story and map as part of his legal argument in 1580 that isles mentioned in the far west, Friseland and Estotiland, were among the places colonized by King Arthur (Newton, 1932, 203). This early colonization was cited as a rationale for English sovereignty over lands from Labrador to Florida. Of course, Dee's known bias towards the British cause implicates him in the conspiracy to dethrone orthodox beliefs.

One might reasonably ask: "If Venetian sailors reached the St. Lawrence Gulf, where are the artifacts?" Not to worry! Venetian artifacts were found: sailors on Miguel Corte-Real's ill-fated expedition of 1502 found a gilded sword hilt and silver trinkets of Venetian manufacture at a native village in Labrador (Fiske, 1920, Vol. II, 19). Most historians conveniently assume that the trinkets and sword are relics of Cabot's voyage to Newfoundland. After all, Cabot was a Venetian expatriate; he could have traded, or lost, such items on his voyage in 1497. But this is simply an assumption; the relics could just as easily have come from a Venetian trading expedition or from the Zeno voyage of 1390.

Croatian Voyages West

According to Croatian archives which Louis Adamic reported in a 1972 publication of Svetu Magazin, several Croatian merchant vessels foundered off the Carolina coast in 1449 (Prazak, 1991). Their intended destination had been China—which they expected to find across the sea from Europe. At least, that was where China (Cathay) was situated on current maps. During the 15th century, ships from Croatia traveled across the Mediterranean and beyond—sometimes independently and sometimes in association with Venetian galleons. Croat vessels built in Ragusa (now Dubrovnik) were referred to as a-ragosa (meaning vessel from Ragusa).

Adamic's search of Croatian archives commenced following conversations with senior citizens who told him of ancestral traditions that Croatians had sailed across the Atlantic in ancient times. The brief account mentioned that three of the five vessels in the expedition were left stranded near Chesapeake Bay; the other two ships sailed back to Dubrovnic. Unfortunately, war with Turkey prevented a relief expedition. Charles Prazak believes the survivors joined the Powhatan tribe and gave their name to Croatan Island.

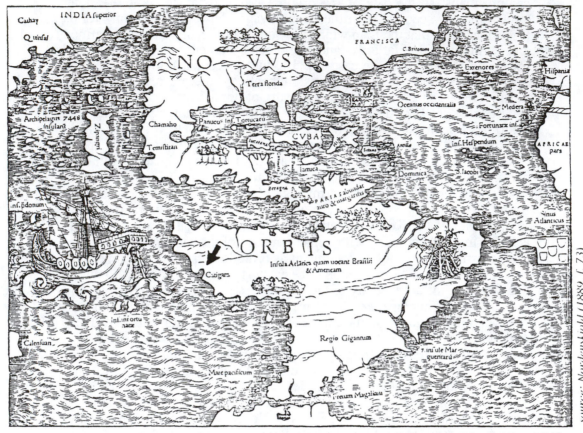

source: Nordenskiold (1889, f. 73)

Sebastian Munster—1540

Terra Australis & The Gulf of Guayaquil— Roman Knowledge of South America

A 16th-century map by Sebastian Munster in the Swiss *Ptolemaic Basileae* atlas (1540) adds more evidence that Ptolemy's Cattigara was a Peruvian city known to 2nd-century Romans. On this map, South America is part of the combined New World (Novus Orbis—Insula Atlantica quam uocant Brasilii & Americam). Cattigara and its adjoining gulf to the north are shown on the west coast at about the right position in the bulge of South America. This is the same bulge that appeared on DeVirga's 1414 map as a semicircular continent southeast of Asia. Roman visits to the New World are confirmed by discovery of artifacts in Mexico and Peru. A carving of a quadrant used in surveying and found in Peru (Ibarra-Grasso, 1970, 178) helps to explain the accuracy of shorelines on Roman maps.

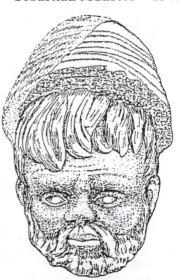

source: Thompson (1994)

Roman Merchant ca. 200 AD
Ceramic sculpture found inside a Mexican pyramid.

source: Ibarra-Grasso (1970)

Old World style Quadrant
Stone sculpture from Peruvian ruins circa 1000 AD.

The crew of a Croatian caravel, <u>Atlante</u>, sailed across the Atlantic Ocean and found land in 1484 (Sinovic, 1991). According to historian Charles Prazak, archives reported in <u>Zajecnicar</u> (December 2, 1979) tell of several Croatian vessels carrying refugees from Turkish invasions who reached the Carolinas near Roanoke Island in 1470. Prazak (1993) and Sinovic (1991, 153) believe that these survivors merged with native Algokian tribes and made significant contributions to their culture and language. They have identified the name of one native tribe, the Croatoans, and an isle in Cape Hatteras, Croatoan Isle, as derivatives of the Croatian language. This isle in the Croatoan territory was given as the destination of survivors of the Lost Roanoake Colony in a message left on a tree circa 1584. Some words and common phrases of the modern-day Croatoan Tribe reflect ancient contributions from Croatia: for example, the word <u>pokosi</u> has the same meaning—to cut grass—in the native and Croatian tongues (Sinovic, 1991, 155).

In the 16th and 17th centuries, explorers encountered distinct ethnic groups in the Carolinas who were known as "Melungeons." These people have distinctly Mediterranean or Iberian physical features which identify them as descendants of early Basque, Portuguese, or Croatian voyagers. Sinovic (1991, 154) notes that: "Both English chroniclers in the expeditions of Raleigh and Grenville in 1584-1586, Arthur Barlowe and John White, describe some of those Indians as having certain European features and being of lighter, yellowish color and reported seeing Indian children with very fine chestnut and auburn hair." Their ancestors might have included survivors of early Croatian shipwrecks, Croatian sailors (a.k.a. Venetian subjects from Dalmatia) accompanying John Cabot whose vessel was lost at sea circa 1498, or Croat-Portuguese colonists from the 16th century. In 1880, historian Hamilton McMillan noted that: "Croatoan Indians have traditions which are tied to the individuals, the owners of the destroyed ships from the past" (Sinovic, 1991, 155).

Stories of Croatian voyages to America are not surprising due to the associated activities of Venetian cartographers, merchants, and explorers with their eastern allies on the Adriatic Sea. The close vicinity of Venice and Croatia and the fact that Croatia was a principality of Venice during much of the 14th and 15th centuries favored mutual knowledge of lands across the Atlantic as well as joint expeditions to any promising market.

Vanishing Venice

Joint Croatian and Venetian mercantile ventures on the North Atlantic had to compete with the rising tide of English, Danish, Portuguese, and Hanseatic fleets which dominated the region. Problems closer to home also drained the resources of Venetian allies in wars with Turkey. Meanwhile, Venetian cartographers gained favor as artisans for Portugal's famed mariner prince, Henry the Navigator.

The Venetian cartographer Andrea Bianco produced a chart in 1448 that has two islands southwest of Cape Verde with the legend <u>icola otenticha xe longa a ponente 1500/ mia</u>—"authentic island lying 1,500 miles to the west." R.A. Skelton (1965, 159) believes this might be a reference to Brazil. Bianco's Atlas of 1436 mentions <u>stocfis</u>—Stock Fish Isle or Newfoundland, and <u>y. Rouercha</u>—Greenland (Skelton, 1965, 175). Venetian physician Giovanni da Fontana wrote (ca. 1450) of the Atlantic Ocean: <u>et ab eius occasu finitur pro parte etiam terra incognita</u>—"in the west it is bounded by unknown land" (Skelton, et al., 1965, 159).

173

During the 1380's, Norse sea power declined and Venetian merchant empires recovered from the Black Death. Venetian merchants were well-aware of the vast potential for commercial exploitation of New World markets. Commodities such as cheap furs, narwhal tusks, whale oil, and wood products were available from natives and settlers who were desperate for European trade goods. So there was great incentive for Venetians to sail across the Atlantic. Distance was not a limiting factor nor was the quality of Venetian ships; nor was the endurance of Venetian crews an issue. After sailing 4,000 miles from Venice to London, the comparatively short trans-Atlantic excursion was not a hindrance to enterprising merchants. Indeed, maps, archives, and artifacts provide cross-confirmation of Venetian voyages. Standard commercial maps, like the one which Albertin DeVirga compiled in 1414, assisted mariners to plan and implement New World voyages.

However, English, Danish, Portuguese, Spanish, and Genoese naval powers took control of the western Mediterranean and the Atlantic. Thus, foreign naval superiority, access to western European ports, and overwhelming commercial competition effectively blocked the continued westward expansion of the Venetian mercantile empire. However, this mid-15th century exclusion from the North Atlantic doesn't diminish the importance of Venetian voyages to New World shores at the dawn of the Age of Exploration.

KEY:

AO = Atlantic Ocean; **C** = China or Sin; **E** = Europe; **G** = Greenland; **H** = India or Hind; **IO** = Indian Ocean; **NA** = North America; **RS** = Red Sea; **SA** = South America; **WA** = West Africa; **WQ** = Waq Waq.

Hamd Allah Mustawfi World Map 1350 AD

American continents are portrayed schematically on this map by Persian cartographer Mustawfi. They are shown as a ring of land surrounding Africa and Eurasia. Waq-Waq (WQ) in the southeast probably represents South America.

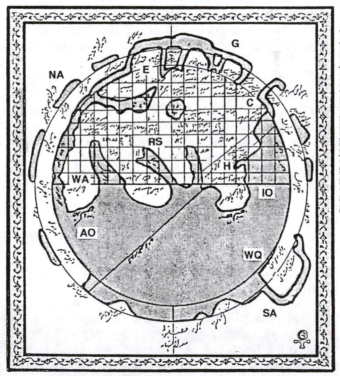

Based on a 17th-century manuscript copy in Munis' *Atlas Tarikh al-Islam* (1987). The map is presently in the British Museum Library in London. 13.M2

Translation with assistance from Professor Fazi Khoury, Far Eastern Studies, University of Washington, and Afifi Durr, Seattle Arabic Language Service.

Atlantic Enigma
—Secret Voyages to Unknown Lands

Beginning with the Franciscan expeditions to North America, there is a continuous cartographic tradition of lands across the Atlantic from Europe that are substantially like North and South America. The Vesconte map of 1306 witnessed the dawn of a New World image consisting of an overseas continent bordered in the north by a bay and in the south by a peninsula and a gulf. The Venetian Map of 1414 added new details by identifying a southern continent which was the source of brasilium. Subsequent maps refined the continental outlines and brought the Atlantic coast into the range of European ships. By the last decade of the 15th century, cartographers showed the mainland coast opposite Europe at about the right distance for modern New England, and the southeastern peninsula came very close to the actual position of Florida. This pattern of increasing accuracy is not attributable to chance—particularly when Portuguese archives attest to voyages across the Atlantic. Columbus participated on one of these ventures—a joint Danish-Portuguese expedition—between 1476 and 1477. One purpose of the voyages was to settle the question of whether the land across the seas was the Cathay of Marco Polo or the Markland wilderness of Norse tradition. This was the great enigma confronting 14th and 15th-century voyagers.

Based on knowledge acquired from the friar's travelog and gazetteers, Portuguese rulers abandoned early-on the concept of a westward approach to the Spice Islands. Instead, they committed the bulk of their resources to the arduous task of building way-stations along the African coast. The accuracy of their maps and their highly-developed geographical knowledge had convinced them that the only feasible approach to Malucca, Madras, and Calicut lay in that direction.

Ibernia Magna & the Voyage of the Spanish Franciscan

During the 15th century, Europe was awash in conflicting nautical charts and stories about lands across the Atlantic. As this period straddled the era of catastrophic plagues, maritime trade wars, and increasing cold in the northern regions, historical accounts were jumbled by sudden changes in regional populations, political alliances, and the naming of territories. Each new conquest resulted in new names and flags—causing great confusion for Christian travelers. Meanwhile, Roger Bacon's urgent plea to his Franciscan Brothers to prepare accurate accounts of overseas nations began to influence the emerging field of geography. Friars set about preparing encyclopedias of territories including the cities and flags of their principal leaders.

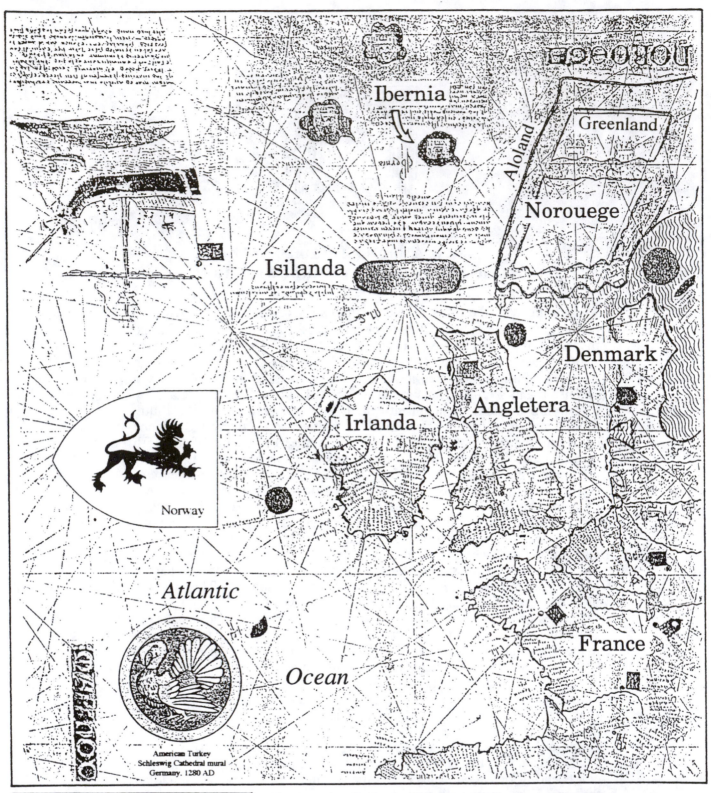

Isilanda

Ibernia

Aloland

Greenland

Norouege

Denmark

Angletera

Irlanda

Norway

Atlantic

Ocean

France

American Turkey
Schleswig Cathedral mural
Germany. 1280 AD

Ibernia

Viladestes Map of Ireland in North America   1413 AD
This map by Mecia Viladestes has two Irelands.   In addition to the regular Ireland ("Irlanda") shown west of England ("Angletera"), there is a second Ireland—here spelled "Ibernia" that is north of Iceland (Isilanda). This Ireland of the north—situated on this map above the Arctic Circle—corresponds to northern isles of North America near the North Magnetic Pole.   It is the same "Ibernia" that a Spanish Franciscan visited ca. 1350 and described in his book, El Libro Del Conocemientos, as a land of the far northwest with trees and fat birds (turkeys).   The friar's description of the Ibernian flag as being the same as the Norwegian flag confirms that this Ibernia is a North American colony because in 1350, Norway had laid claim to all the lands from the Baltic to the Magnetic North Pole.

One of the more prominent geographical encyclopedias from this era was El Libro Del Conoscimiento (or Book of Knowledge) which was compiled by an anonymous Franciscan circa 1350. Four manuscript versions have survived—one in the British Library and two in the National Library at Madrid. As much of the document was quoted in the writings of Pierre Bontier and Jean Le Verrier in 1404, we can be certain of the great antiquity of the original document (Markham, 1912, ix).

According to the friar, he sailed from his home at Seville with the intention of preparing a manual of world travel. The original title of his manuscript suggests the importance that it has for our understanding of Medieval geography. The full title is: "The Book of Knowledge of all the Kingdoms, Lands, and Lordships that are in the World, and the Arms and Devices of Each Land and Lordship, or of the Kings and Lords who Possess Them." This travelog describes what was then known of Asia, Africa, Europe, and isles of the Atlantic Ocean.

Sir Clements Markham prepared an English translation of the most complete version of the travelog for the Hakluyt Society in 1912. Although some historians had speculated that the friar's manuscript might have been derived from accounts of other travelers, Markham noted that several passages contain information that could only have come from direct observation. For the most part, the travelog seems to be highly objective with few instances of fabulous storytelling which were otherwise common in manuscripts of the Middle Ages. The Spanish friar reported most political and geographical details with great accuracy. For example, he mentioned that Denmark and all the lands to the north used the banner of the Norse king—a black lion in a field of gold. This report of the flags of ruling lords in the Northern Regions tallies with Norse claims of sovereignty over all the territories from the Baltic Sea to the Magnetic North Pole. This claim endured from about 1261 to 1380.

The friar mentioned that another isle in the north Atlantic that used the Norse banner was called "Ibernia." Although the common translation for "Ibernia" is Ireland, it is apparent from the friar's account and from contemporary maps that this "Ibernia" does not refer to the Ireland situated west of England. We will refer to this second Ireland as "Great Ireland." This identification of a second Ireland corresponds to the mention of an Irlandah-al-Kabirah or "Great Ireland" in Al-Idrisi's world geography of 1154. Al-Idrisi mentioned that this Great Ireland was somewhere in the North Atlantic beyond Greenland.

In his book, Description of the World, the 12th-century Arabian cosmographer Al-Idrisi described northern territories of the Atlantic: "Between the extremity of Scotland and the extremity of Ireland are needed two days sailing ... from the northern extremity of Scotland to Resland (Friesland) requires three days; and from Resland to Irlandah-al-Kabirah (Ireland The Great) one day" (after Ashe, 1962, 152).   The required sailing times are too short, but the description clearly tells of an Ireland The Great thought to lie across the northwest Atlantic.

Thus, the Arabian geographer believed there were two Irelands: the regular "Irlandah" west of England and a second—Great Ireland. The northern isle corresponds to "Hvitramanland" (Whitemans' Land) or Hibernia Major of Icelandic sagas. Another name for this land in Irish tales is "Irland it Mikla" (Great Ireland). The friar's commentary describes this northern Ireland as a forested isle with fat birds:

> I left Inglaterra (England) in a boat and reached the island of Irlanda (Ireland) which is a short crossing of a mile. They say that

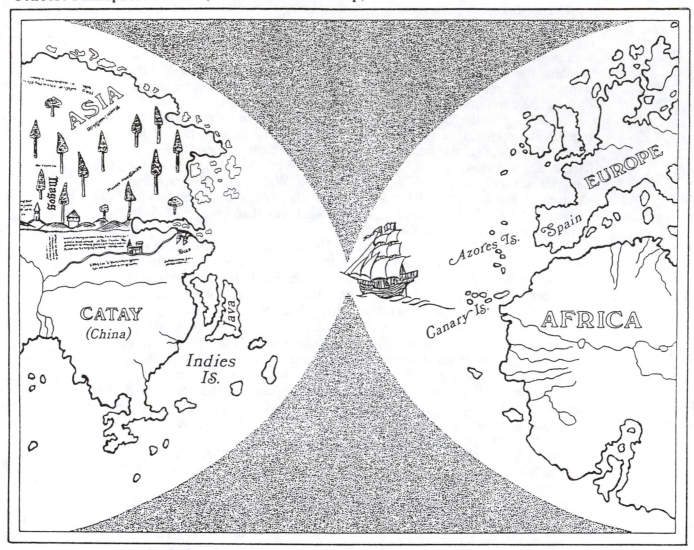

Atlantic Enigma

European geographers were not all in agreement concerning what was across the Atlantic Ocean. They all accepted the fact that there was continental land; the issue was how far away it was and how civilized. Most everybody who was a sailor accepted that there were lands to the north (by compass) that were rich in fish, furs, and lumber. Danes called the region "Greenland Province;" the British called it "Frisland" or the "Icelands;" the Portuguese called the region "Bacalaos." Martin Behaim believed the opposite land—a wilderness—was 2,000 to 3,000 miles distant. Toscanelli and Columbus expressed the belief that the opposite land was the highly-civilized Cathay (China) of Marco Polo. That was the principle motivation for attempting a direct voyage across the central Atlantic. If the overseas continent was Cathay—then merchants could expect to make untold riches by establishing trade. However, if the people of the new lands lacked adequate weapons—then conquest and evangelism were in order. At any event, Europeans were determined to push west.

formerly it was called Ibernia. Know that it is a well-peopled
island with a good climate, and that there are three great cities in it.
The chief one, where they crown the kings, is Estanforda
(Strangford), the others Ymeria (Limerick), Gataforda (Waterford),
Rois (Ros), and Donbelin (Dublin). In this island there is a great
lake, and they say that the lake brings good fortune, because many
enchantments were made on its banks in ancient times. The king of
this island has the same arms as the king of Inglaterra.

Being in Irlanda, I sailed in a ship bound for Spain and went
with those on that ship on the high sea for so long that we arrived
at an island called Eterns (Faeroe?), and another called Artania
(Orkney?), and another called Citilant (Shetland?), and another
called Ibernia (The Ireland of The North). All these islands are in
the part where the sun sets in the month of June (the northwest
Atlantic), and they are all peopled, well supplied, and with a good
climate. In this island of Ibernia there are trees, and the fruit that
they bear are very fat birds. These birds are very good eating
whether boiled or roasted. The men in this island are very long
lived, some living 200 years. They are born and brought up in a
way which makes them unable to die in the island, so that when
they become very weak, they are taken away and die presently. In
this island, there are no snakes nor vipers, nor toads, nor flies, nor
spiders, nor any other venomous things. And the women are very
beautiful though very simple. It is a land where there is not as
much bread as you may want, but a great abundance of meat and
milk. Know that this island is outside the seven climates. The
king of this island has for his device the same flag—gold with a
black lion—as the king of Noruega (Norway).

After this, I departed from the island of Ibernia in a ship and
voyaged so far over the western sea that we sighted the Cape of
Finnisterre (the northwest cape of Spain). (Markham, 1912)

Several passages from this account clearly reveal that the Spanish friar
was not describing the island commonly known as "Ireland" that is
situated west of England. First, the friar tells us that this "Ibernia" is an
isle that he sailed to after visiting Irlanda (Ireland). Second, he mentions
that the isle is north beyond the Faeroes, Orkneys, and Shetlands on the
high seas. Third, he tells us that the isle is located where the sun sets in
June (that is, to the northwest of Europe), and he says that this isle lies
beyond the "Seven Climates" of Ptolemy. Since Ptolemy's climatic zones
barely included the British Isles, we know that the friar's Ibernia (Great
Ireland) was considered a land to the far north. This places Ibernia in the
"Polar Regions" of Medieval geography, and it cautions us to consider the
possibility that Ibernia represents one of the many isles of the temperate
regions near the Magnetic North Pole—i.e., North America. We should
also note that the friar makes no mention of Iceland—suggesting a voyage
somewhat south of the Arctic Circle at the latitude of Labrador, Nova
Scotia, or Newfoundland.

The "fat birds" he mentions probably represent an American game bird
commonly known as the "turkey." The lack of serpents and insects fits
well with America's northeast coast—Labrador or Nova Scotia—at least
in the early months of Spring.

The most telling clue regarding the identity of this northern isle is the
fact that the ruling lord uses the standard of Norway. No true Scotsman

Zaltieri—1566

Vinlanda Infula

Yale Vinland Map—1440

Key:
G Ginnungagap
U Ungava Bay
H Hudson's Bay
R St. Lawrence river
N Nova Scotia
V Vinland
F Florida
B Brazil

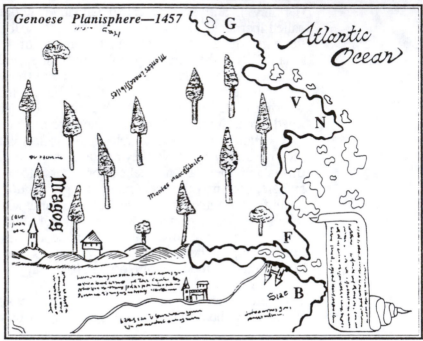

Genoese Planisphere—1457

Atlantic Ocean

Franciscan Map of Wineland—1440 AD

Yale's Vinland Map was acclaimed for showing a somewhat amorphous land called "Vinilanda" (above left) northwest of Europe in the approximate position of New England. The map was compiled by an anonymous Swiss Franciscan, and it fits neatly into the mapping traditions of other Franciscans and cartographers serving Portuguese royalty. Several features of this land are also seen in contemporary charts. The Vinland map has a huge lake and wide river draining towards the northeast. These characteristics immediately suggest the Great Lakes and the St. Lawrence river; and a similar map by Zalteri (1566) has a lake and river—the St. Lorenys—in that location. Two features seen on the Florentine planisphere (1447) and on the nearly identical Genoese planisphere (1457) included a forested continent in the north with a southeastward facing peninsula (Florida) above a huge narrow gulf. This narrow gulf—which represents the Gulf of Mexico—is way too narrow, but that misconception might have resulted from a navigator sailing between Florida and Cuba and mistaking this extended, horizontal coastline for the northern shore of South America. The concept of a huge wilderness forest exemplified in the Genoese map is similar to the accounts in Norse sagas concerning Markland—a land of forests north of Wineland (or Vinland). Andrea Bianco's map of 1436 identifies Basera (Brazil) south of the gulf. This Vinilanda on the Yale map suggests Norse exploration from Labrador to Brazil—the same region indicated for the Franciscan survey in the *Inventio Fortunatae*.

or Irishman would invent such a story—nor is a Spaniard likely to imagine a Norwegian banner flying from the flagpole of an Irish castle. Yet that is exactly what happened to northern isles between 1261 and 1380 when Norse kings claimed sovereignty over all the regions from the Baltic to the (magnetic) North Pole. This identification of the Norse flag as the banner of Ibernia places the isle within or near the Norveca continent (i.e., North America).

Historian Markham (1912, p. 13) assumed that the northern Ireland in the friar's travelog was a mistake of a copyist who used "Ibernia" in place of Iceland. However, several characteristics of the friar's Ibernia do not correlate very well with Iceland: the fat birds, forests, and good climate seem more in keeping with the east coast of North America where "Irland Mikla"—Great Ireland—was known in Icelandic sagas to be situated near Vinland The Good. Furthermore, Iceland was well known to Medieval travelers and clearly marked on contemporary maps so the chances of mistaking Ibernia for Iceland is extremely remote.

A Jewish mapping tradition established in the Mediterranean island of Majorca shows the location of isles north of Iceland and west of Greenland. Due to the fact that this region on the map is the farthest away from the map focus on the Mediterranean, we can assume that the schematic nature of northern isles and their placement has been greatly distorted by distance and the curvature of the Earth's surface. Indeed, it is impossible for an island to be simultaneously north of Iceland and west of Greenland. On these maps, Greenland is shown adjacent to Norway in a position <u>northeast</u> of England. If we use Greenland (or Alogia) as the point of reference, then an isle west of Greenland on the map corresponds to land west or southwest; and this is where Ibernia is placed on the map.

The earliest map from the Majorcan tradition is Angelino Dalorto's map of 1330. He issued a similar map in 1339. Another version, the Catalan Atlas circa 1375, was issued by an anonymous cartographer. The most recent map in this series was the 1413 world map by Mecia Viladestes (DuJourdin et al., 1984, no. 7 & 12). This map has an isle called "Ibernia" north of Iceland and west of Greenland in the North Sea. This isle is in addition to the standard Ireland which is called "Irlanda" and situated in the appropriate location west of England. Thus we see in these maps contemporary portrayals of islands in the approximate locations which were mentioned in the Franciscan travelog—and the naming is also the same. We are therefore certain that the naming of the northern isle as "Ibernia" is accurate and not a mistake as historians have assumed.

By 1380, plagues of the Black Death and harsh winters effectively ended Nordic supremacy in Ibernia (Great Ireland) and elsewhere in Norveca (i.e., eastern North America). The overseas colonies were depopulated at the same time that other European nations began recovering from the effects of the plague. Venetian, Hanseatic, Danish, Portuguese, French, and English voyagers fought for control of North Atlantic isles. New merchant ventures based on fishing or fur-trading overwhelmed the few survivors of old Norse and Irish colonies. New names, such as New Amsterdam, New England, New York, and New Sweden replaced the old territories of York, Norveca, and Norumbega. Ibernia—located either in lower Labrador or Nova Scotia—probably took on the Celtic name "Estotiland" that is seen on 16th-century Danish charts of the North Atlantic. This "Estotiland" is very similar to the word "Escotiland" used to designate lands occupied by the Gaelic (northern Irish) tribe that settled

Eventually, the investment paid off for Portugal; Admiral Vasco Da Gama finally reached Calicut in 1497.

Portugal's apparent preoccupation with the trans-African coastal route to the Orient left the way open for Spain to seek its own share of the spice market by sailing west—straight across the Atlantic. That direction was the shortest approach to the Spice Islands—according to Florentine cosmographer Paolo Toscanelli and his protégé—Cristobol Colon. The cosmographer was convinced that the distance across the Atlantic to Japan was only 3,000 miles; the mainland of India and Cathay was only 1,000 miles farther. Of course, by the time Toscanelli's recommendation reached King John II's minister Fernao Martins in 1474, it was seemingly too late to reverse the Portuguese steamroller that was grinding its way through village and jungle towards South Africa. Orthodox historians offer no clue why it was that Portugal chose the more difficult route without considering the obvious alternative that paid off for Columbus. Instead, Columbus is portrayed as a visionary, while the Portuguese seem like bull-headed autocrats who missed the greatest opportunity of history by failing to adopt Columbus as their champion.

Medieval maps showed clear sailing between Europe and East Asia across the Atlantic. There was some disagreement regarding the size of the world, and a few sailors feared falling off the "edge" of the ocean, monsters, boiling seas, and the legions of Satan lurking beyond sight of land. Nevertheless, the most important issue was simply the width of the Atlantic Ocean. Most maps of the period, including Toscanelli's planisphere (or elliptical map), showed the <u>Oecumene</u> or "Known World" of Europe, Africa, and Asia sufficiently enlarged to occupy most of the globe. At the farthest extremity of Asia was a region variously called "India Superior" (Greater India) or "India Tercera" (the Third India). Many geographers presumed that the Indies Islands—rich in spices and gold—lay east of India Superior or just across the Atlantic from Europe. Presumably, the Portuguese never considered sailing across the Atlantic because contemporary scholars believed the coast of Marco Polo's Asia was nearly 14,000 miles away—too far for a ship to sail without hope of replenishing fresh water and provisions.

Reality paints a different picture: King John I had access to contemporary geographical accounts that accurately delineated the expanse of the Atlantic and the coasts of distant continents. John's heirs continually expanded that base of knowledge by sending expeditions across the Atlantic to verify or improve intelligence concerning overseas lands. Prince Henry's palace at Sagres served as a convention center for cosmographers from across Europe; and it was a repository for the latest maps, gazetteers, and geographical accounts of the planet.

Although planning sessions at Sagres were conducted in secret—as were transoceanic expeditions—copies of maps invariably found their way to the Vatican or to the principal Mediterranean mercantile centers of Genoa and Venice. Cosmographers in Lisbon also had access to royal navigational charts, and copies of Lisbon's maps and globes also circulated in Europe. Only the latest field reports were kept secret; royal decrees merely prohibited the transfer of actual maps out of the country. An Italian emissary lamented "It is impossible to get a chart of the Cabral voyage because the king has decreed the death penalty for anyone sending one abroad" (Kimble, 1938, 202). Otherwise, maps were available to those with proper authorization. Even though Lisbon's map archives burned during massive earthquakes and fires (1531, 1551, 1755), copies

182

north of England. Thus, several writers have speculated that Estotiland is simply a New World variation of the northern Gaelic homeland.

During the 15th century, Bristol merchants might have sailed to a Great Ireland across the North Atlantic. According to Henry Taylor's research on Bristol customs accounts, a number of merchants claimed that the destination of their vessels was Hibernia (Ireland) when in fact they sailed for Newfoundland instead (Wilson, 1991, 69). Whether this was simply a ruse concocted to mislead customs agents or the result of enduring traditions of a Great Ireland across the Atlantic is speculative.

The Portuguese Dilemma

Historical accounts of Europe's Age of Exploration usually begin with Portugal's brilliant explorer, Prince Henry The Navigator whose life spans the years from 1394 to 1460. Due to the fact that Portugal was situated on the Atlantic Ocean, access was limited to Mediterranean ports whose markets included the precious commodities of the Orient. If Portugal could only devise an alternative route that circumvented the stranglehold of Venetian, Genoese, and Moslem merchants, it seemed that the nation would prosper accordingly. Oddly, Prince Henry seemed to be obsessed from the outset by a determination to approach the Spice Islands of India by way of South Africa and the Indian Ocean. This seems like the wrong direction for such an enterprise—if we are to believe the orthodox version of history. Presumably, Europeans thought that India and Cathay were situated across the Atlantic—although the distance was a matter of speculation. If geographers had the location correct, then it would seem reasonable for the Portuguese to at least consider a voyage west to the Orient—as that would have been the shortest route. Even though the Atlantic seemed like a huge ocean—numerous Classical writers and even the esteemed Roger Bacon had claimed that the voyage was relatively short. Besides, there were several huge islands along the way, Antilia and Cipangu, which could serve as waystations. This assessment, which was the substance of the Columbus proposal in 1483, reflected a fairly common appraisal of the extent of the Atlantic Ocean circa 1425. Nevertheless, orthodox historians assure us that King John and his princely son, Henry, decided to take the long way around Africa to India—seemingly without any intelligence about the western Atlantic.

It was an ambitious quest: the voyage to Calicut—the nearest Indian port serving the Spice Islands commercial network—was more than fourteen thousand miles towards the east around the Cape of Bon Esperanza—the Cape of Good Hope at the southern tip of South Africa. Henry undertook his enormous venture in several phases: he designed a new expeditionary vessel called the <u>caravel</u>; he established a college of marine geography at Sagres; and he dispatched expeditions to capture towns along the African coast. These towns were intended to serve as waystations for merchant ships as soon as sea lanes were cleared to India. Henry's optimism, courage, and sheer willpower sustained Portuguese sailors throughout difficult conquests from 1415 to 1460; but the gallant prince died before his navy reached the equator. Slaves and gold taken from Moslem ports essentially paid for Henry's Enterprise of The Indies.

The dream of reaching the Orient lived on: Portugal's King John II resumed the quest in 1481. Numerous fleets sailed south; many vessels were lost at sea; hundreds of brave souls died aboard ships from scurvy, typhoid fever, and malaria. Thousands of natives and many Moslems perished in the attacks; thousands were sent back to Portugal as slaves.

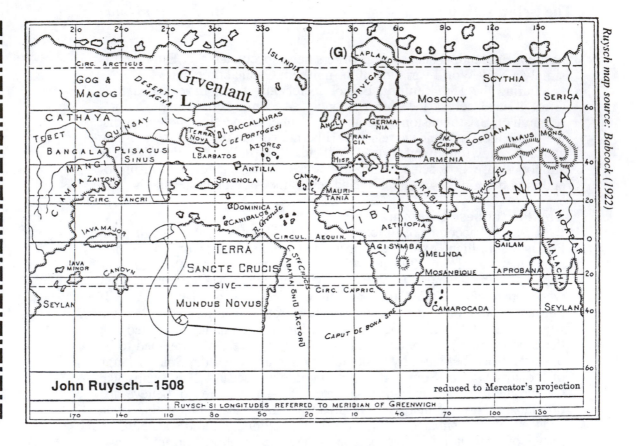

Ruysch map source: Babcock (1922)

John Ruysch—1508

reduced to Mercator's projection

RUYSCH SI LONGITUDES REFERRED TO MERIDIAN OF GREENWICH

Greenland as North America

Johan Ruysch's 1508 map (above) has "Grvenlant" (**L**) as the title for several adjacent territories including Greenland Island, the southeastern region of Baffin Island, and Labrador. An archaic version of Greenland Island (**G**) can be seen on this map directly north of Norway where it is called *lapland*—following a 15th-century concept of the north. Pietro Coppo's 1528 map (below) has a northern continent representing territories from Labrador to Chesapeake Bay—in a pattern similar to the LaCosa map of 1500 AD. He calls this continent *Isola Verde* or Green Isle (**V**). On this map, the customary Island of Greenland is the peninsula (**G**) north of Norway. Coppo's map reflects the 15th-century belief that Greenland was the overseas destination of traders and fishermen that later cartographers called North America.

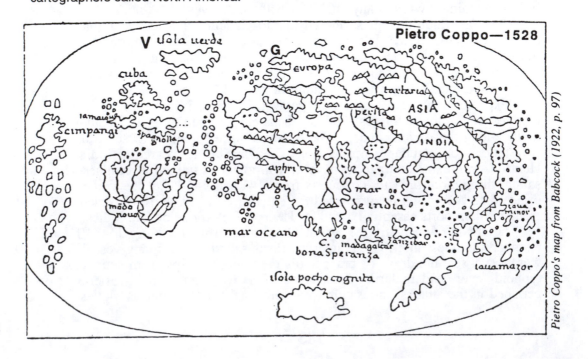

Pietro Coppo—1528

Pietro Coppo's map from Babcock (1922, p. 97)

of the most important maps including a 1490-1492 globe by the Nuremberg expatriate Martin Behaim survived in other European cities.

Far from being closed-minded and dogmatic as they are often portrayed in historical accounts, Portuguese kings were the most enlightened of Europe's monarchs—at least in terms of their geographical understanding. They also benefited from the accumulated knowledge of royal relations: Prince Henry was the great grandson of Edward III of England—the same sovereign who initiated the Franciscan survey of North America. His grandfather, John of Gaunt, was a close friend of the Oxford Franciscan—Nicholas of Lynn. Although it may be speculative to assume that Henry saw a copy of the <u>Inventio</u>, he was certainly close enough to English royalty to hear the stories of Edward's exploits and legends about overseas lands.

Throughout the 15th century, Portuguese explorers continued to improve their knowledge concerning the continental lands across the Atlantic. Although historical accounts of their expeditions are rare, a pattern of increasing awareness of the location and character of the overseas lands is reflected in mariners' accounts and maps. It was not out of fear or ignorance that King John II rejected the Columbus proposal of sailing west to the Indies; the rejection was due to the fact that John already knew what was on the other side.

Early Portuguese & Basque Voyages

Martin Behaim's globe of 1492 identifies the Atlantic isle of Antilia as the 8th-century refuge of Portuguese Christians who escaped the Saracen invasion. The text reports that the refugees, under the direction of an archbishop from Oporto and six minor bishops, brought along their livestock. Behaim, like his contemporary Nicholas Martellus, implied that Antilia was synonymous with an island called Cipangu (Japan) which Marco Polo reported as lying about 1,000 miles east of Asia.

Basques from northeastern Spain were active in North Atlantic fisheries probably by the 11th century. Arabic cartographer Al-Idrisi (1154) identified the region of "Bakargar" north of China, and it was similarly identified on a map by the Florentine Francesco Rosselli in 1492—where it is called "Balor Regio." These names are variants of <u>baccalaos</u>—a Basque-Portuguese word for stockfish or codfish. The name appears on Medieval maps north of China because that was the conventional placement for territories across the North Atlantic that cosmographers believed were north of Marco Polo's Cathay. This "Balor" can be seen to move steadily eastward on Renaissance maps until it crosses over the Strait of Anian (Bering Strait) and eventually merges with the 16th-century territory of Baccalaos just south of Labrador. Basque oral traditions in the 17th century told of the ancestral discovery of Stockfish Land—a.k.a. Newfoundland (Herrmann, 1954, 209).

Natives in the region of the Gulf of St. Lawrence informed John Cabot in 1497 that their name for cod was "baccalaos" and this was also the name they used for their territory (Newton, 1939, 151). Following that identification, most 16th-century maps show an island near the Gulf bearing the name "Baccalaos" or some variation thereof, and lands on the Gaspe Peninsula were soon identified as a Basque fishing colony. Basques in large enough numbers settled along the shores of southeastern Newfoundland that the land was known by the Basque word—<u>bacalaos</u>—for nearly a century. Some scholars suspect that Bristol harbor records from the mid-1400's showing Basque imports of cod and beaver pelts

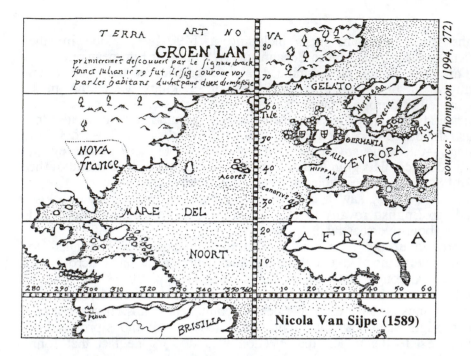

source: Thompson (1994, 272)

Nicola Van Sijpe (1589)

Trans-Arctic Greenland

The northern region of North America appears as a forested land north of Europe on this 1589 map by Nicola Van Sijpe. Trees shown above the Arctic Circle reflect legends about a place the Danes called "Greenland" (i.e., North America) being a temperate and forested land near the North Pole. Such legends still persisted into the 16th century; and they continued to influence cartography.

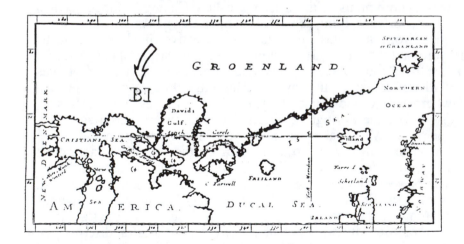

Danish Map of Greenland Province—1650

This Danish chart shows the super-island of Greenland that combines Arctic territories westward across Baffin Island (**BI**) and into Canada. Here, Hudson Bay is identified by the Danish term—Christian's Sea; Hudson Strait is identified as Christian's Strait; and Davis Strait is called David's Gulf.

186

actually represent New World trade from Basque villages along the Gulf of St. Lawrence. Basque whalers had sailed to the seas east of Greenland in the early 15th century; fishing vessels reached Newfoundland by the 1480's (Mowat, 1965, 455).

Portuguese explorers were active in the western Atlantic during the early 15th century. Historian Henry Harrisse gave a detailed accounting of such voyages in The Discovery of North America (1892). Although he freely conceded that many attempts were made in an effort to reach continental lands or the Isle of Seven Cities, he was dubious that any of the expeditions were successful.

In 1427, Prince Henry sent ships to look for the "Lost Islands" of Classical legend—Phoenician isles, Antilia, or the Isle of Seven Cities that was thought to lie in the far-western Atlantic (Sanceau, 1947, 109). Goncalo Velho Cabral led one expedition into the Atlantic in the service of Prince Henry circa 1425. He returned from that voyage without finding any significant isles and convinced that the legends of isles in the western sea were nothing more than myths. However, the prince again dispatched his vassal in search of missing isles, and this time Cabral located the Azores circa 1427. This triumph went unreported in the chronicles of Portugal: historian Elaine Sanceau (1947, 110) observes that "no contemporary writer records the discovery." However, records of Portuguese maritime commissions reveal that Diogo de Sevill scouted the Azores in 1427.

Ferdinand Columbus noted that some Portuguese cartographers believed Antilia (or the Isle of Seven Cities) was located only 200 leagues (600 miles) west of the Azores (Babcock, 1922, p. 72). At this point, there is deep ocean with continental land more than a thousand miles farther west. However, the Spanish often failed to account for the added benefit of favorable currents which added significantly to the actual distance traveled. According to Ferdinand, a Portuguese vessel was driven to the mainland (Antilia) by storms in 1430. Upon returning to Lisbon, the crew reported finding gold in sand taken from the island.

Goncalo Cabral sailed west in 1431; Joao Fernandes sailed frequently between 1431-1486. Fernandes was later identified as a navigator called "the Labrador" who sailed with John Cabot in 1478. His claim to fame rests in telling Cabot the location of Greenland and other territories that became known as Labrador.

Galvano (1555, p. 72) reported an ancient account that a storm-driven Portuguese vessel had reached "the Isle of Seven Cities" in 1447. He noted that there were some Spaniards who believed the western isles were the same lands which were later called the Antilles or New Spain. Galvano's New Spain eventually became Mexico.

Vincent Dias sailed in 1445; and Diego de Tieve's journey began in 1454. Some of these mariners reported lands and gold across the Atlantic. Goncalo Cabral and Fernandes had as their objective the "Isle of Promise" which Brendan of Clonfert visited in the western Atlantic during the 6th century. Harrisse (1892) notes that Goncalo Cabral's 1431 voyage was an effort to find isles indicated on a map (presumably lost) which Dom Pedro obtained in Italy in 1428. Diego de Tieve's original commission stipulated that his royal assignment was to look for Antilia (Newton, 1932, 83). According to Pedro Velasco—a confidant of Columbus—the isle of Antilia had been sighted by a Lusitanian vessel prior to Diego de Tieve's voyage (Harrisse, 1892, 656). Sometime later,

187

Hanseatic Cogs in "Northern Seas"

A mappamond called the "Borgia Chart" (circa 1450) shows Hanseatic cogs in the Arctic Ocean above Europe and Asia. Superficially, this map might seem to reinforce traditional beliefs that Medieval Europeans were totally unaware of the New World continents across the Atlantic. However, this belief is dashed by the name of one of the Arctic ports: "Albania Magna." This Albania (or "White Man's Land") is situated in northeastern Asia—a region that would otherwise be regarded as uninhabitable. Icelandic sagas identified a northern "White Man's Land" (Hvitramannaland) as a land that was formerly known as Irland Mikla—or Great Ireland. The sagas also told of this land being situated beyond Wineland—the Norse colony that some believed was near the North Pole but has since been identified as a region near the St. Lawrence river. Al-Idrisi's 1154 map placed a northern Albania between Norway and Greenland; maps by Gudmundsson and Thordsen in the 16th century located Albania in North America in the vicinity of Nova Scotia.

On this map, the geographic pole is situated roughly between the captions for "Europe" and "Asia." Thus, cogs which seem to be traveling between Norway and China actually represent commerce between Europe and North America—in the temperate regions near the magnetic pole of Hudson's Bay.

source: 19th-century Russian Geography

188

de Tieve was sent west to look for gold, but his storm-tossed ship wound up in Ireland.

King Affonso V granted a patent to Dom Fernao in 1457 to resume the search for isles in the western Atlantic (Harrisse, 1892, 656). According to the historian Las Casas, the papers of Columbus recorded the landing of a Spanish vessel on Antilia circa 1460. Affonso V also commissioned Joao Vogado to govern two isles which he found in the west Atlantic in 1462 (Harrisse, 1892, 656). That same year, Goncalo Fernandez reported an island northwest of the Canaries—possibly Nova Scotia.

During the mid-15th century, Portuguese maps usually identified two large isles midway between Europe and Asia. These were called Santanaxio, which some authors identify as a French word for forest land, and Antilia—a Portuguese term for a small land before (ante) a continent. They first appear on the 1424 Pizzigano Portolan which is also known as Pope Urban's map. Orthodox historians point out that there are no such lands in the mid-Atlantic, so they categorize these isles along with St. Brendan's Isle, Isla Verde, Maida (or Maidens' Land), and Brasil as Medieval fantasies. Renaissance cartographers took a different view by associating newly-discovered isles with ancient lands: an unknown cartographer identified Isabella (Cuba) and Hispaniola (Haiti) as the Antilles on the Cantino Map of 1502.

Some writers place Jao Vaz Corte-Real in Newfoundland by 1464 (Nansen, 1911, 359). Others believed that he sailed with a joint Norse-Danish expedition under command of Didrik Pinning and Johannes Pothorst in 1471. According to a letter written in 1551, the expedition charted continental land across the Atlantic. Jao Vaz Corte-real was a porter until 1474—at which time he suddenly became governor of two islands in the Azores. Cameron (1965, 123) reasons that the promotion followed upon the heels of some important discovery—such as significant lands across the Atlantic. Antono Cordeiro's Historia Insulana (1717), or History of The Azores, informs us that Corte-Real had just returned from a voyage to terra do bacalhao (stockfish-land) by order of the king. Gaspar Fructuoso, historian for the Corte-Real family noted in his book, Saudades da Terra (1590), that: "There landed at Terceyra two noblemen who came from Terra de Baccalaos (Newfoundland) where they had gone to discover by order of the Portuguese king. One calls himself Jao Vaz Corte-Real and the other Alvaro Martins Homen" (Tornoe, 1965, 59).

Orthodox historian Fridtjof Nansen (1911, 359) has called these reports "unhistorical." Nevertheless, the king of Portugal rewarded Joao with the post of Governor of Terceira in the Azores for his discovery of "Stockfish Land"—i.e., Newfoundland (Hermann, 1954, 291). Jao Vaz sailed west again in 1473; a trip to Newfoundland in 1485 ended in disaster. His death in the Azores came in 1496.

The name "Terra Corte-Real" or "Corte-Realis" appears on several 16th and 17-century maps in the region of southern Labrador. One of these, Joan Bleau's 1648 map of Terra Nova, appeared in a book called the Atlas Major (Bleau, 1662). Isolationist historians have assumed that such titles refer to the sons of Jao Vaz who were shipwrecked along Labrador in the early 1500's. However, maps by the Portuguese cartographer Dourado in 1534 have the legend teso de Joao Vaz and baia de Joao Vaz inscribed along the shore of Labrador—as if to say "these lands were found by Jao Vaz." Maps in the Miller Atlas (ca. 1519) indicate the northeastern region of the New World as Terra Corte-Regalis—presumably in honor of discovery voyages which took place before the same area became known as Labrador. Portuguese historians have no doubt that these maps confirm the mainland discovery of their favorite son: a bronze memorial in Lisbon bears the inscription "Jao Vaz Corte-real, Discoverer of America" (Cameron, 1965, 114).

A letter to King Christian III of Denmark referred to the 1473 Luso-Norwegian expedition under the command of Pining and Pothorst (two German captains) who sailed with several ships to "islands and continents in the north."   The expedition was jointly sponsored by the king of Portugal. Jao Vaz Corte-real might have accompanied this voyage.

Ruy Concalves da Camera sought isles in the northwest Atlantic in 1473—according to a patent issued by Affonso V.   In 1474, King Alfonso V awarded to Fernao Telles a patent to discover and govern any lands he might find westward in the Atlantic (Newton, 1932, 83).   The objective of this expedition and many others that followed was to find the "Isle of Seven Cities" (Harrisse, 1892, 657). This long-lost isle was the refuge of Bishop Orporto and seven subordinate bishops who sailed with hundreds of followers and their farm animals to escape the Saracen invasion of 734 AD (Behaim's globe, 1492). Beliefs that this exodus had taken treasure hoards along on their trans-Atlantic flight inspired greedy mariners to risk their lives in futile voyages to the New World.

One mariner, the Dutch captain Antonio Leme, led a Portuguese expedition west from Madeira in 1476. It was claimed that they found three islands west of Terceira. That same year, two Azorean brothers, Jao and Alvaro daFonte, spent a fortune seeking the western isles (Harrisse, 1892, 659).   According to the Columbus Journal, another Madeiran captain petitioned Jao II in 1484 to commission a caravel to take possession of an isle previously located west of the Azores in one of history's numerous unrecorded voyages.

During the early 16th century, cartographers identified lands north of the St. Lawrence river as "Labrador" in tribute to Jao Fernandes—a Portuguese navigator who accompanied John Cabot in 1498. Fernandes was known to his shipmates as "the Labrador" (meaning Land owner or proprietor). According to Newton (1932, 134), the name first was applied to Greenland because Fernandes had told Cabot's pilots about its location before they passed by in 1498—which means that Fernandes had been there some years earlier (Newton, 1936, 134). It is known that Fernandez traveled north in 1492; but he might have been in the area as early as 1431 on an expedition for Prince Henry. The "Greenland" which first bore the name Labrador was not the Arctic isle we commonly think of as Greenland—instead, it was the northeastern coast of North America. Maps of the 16th century commonly show the titles Engroneland and Labrador on the same territory—on continental land of the northwestern Atlantic. Meanwhile, the Arctic isle by that name is safely sequestered north of Norway where it has passed unnoticed by many historians.

The Scolvus Controversy

A Danish-Portuguese expedition sailed from Iceland in 1476 under the command of Johannes Skolp (Scolvus). George Horn, Lelewel, Wyfliet, and Harrisse (1892, 657) characterize the mariner as a Pole in the service of the Danish government. His name is variously spelled Scovvus, Scolno, or Scolvus.

They sailed "north" by compass bearings—in other words in the direction of Hudson Bay. A map by Gemma Frisius (1537) has a notation relating to the voyage written on the Isle of Grocland (or

Groetland) located due west of Greenland. This isle seems to be a relic of earlier days when sailors heading towards the Magnetic North Pole passed between land that seemed by compass bearings to lie due west of Greenland when in actuality it was due south in the location of Labrador. The caption on the Frisius map says that this is the place where "John Scolvus met the Quii people." The Quii are variously designated as Icelandic colonists, the Iro-quois, or natives of the Cree nation. Some maps have the Quii people as Le Quii or Le-Quios (Newton, 1936, 216). Maps by Mercator (1537) and the Nancy globe (1545) refer to quij populi which Trygvvi Oleson (1964, 97) translates as an Icelandic term for "white men." Anthropologist J.R. Tornoe(1965) believes Columbus accompanied the Scolvus voyage as it took place the same year that the Spanish mariner claims to have sailed far north of Iceland. Such a voyage would have brought Columbus to North America 16 years prior to his official discovery of the New World.

Historian Fridtjof Nansen, who was usually skeptical of early North Atlantic voyages, regarded the Scolvus account as accurate—because it was mentioned in several credible sources. He notes an anonymous English account of 1575 in which it is said that "In the north side of this passage, John Scolvus, a pilot of Denmark, was in the year 1476" (Nansen, 1911, 130). Harrisse (1892, 658) observed that: "As to the voyage itself, it is not an impossibility, and we can easily realize that a Danish king should have sent a vessel in the track of the Scandinavian adventurers, whose voyages were yet too recent in 1476 to be forgotten."

The Dutch cartographer Cornelius Wyfliet in 1597 claimed that Scolvus was one of the early explorers of North American—along with Frislandish fishermen and the Zeno brothers. According to Wyfliet, Scolvus "penetrated the northern strait under the very Arctic Circle and arrived at the country of Labrador and Estotiland." Here, Wyfliet not only confirms the Scolvus voyage of 1476, he identifies Labrador and Estotiland as the often misidentified "northern regions." Besides the testimonial on the Frisius map, Scolvus is also mentioned on Michael Lok's map of 1582 which carries the legend "Jac. Scolvus Groetland" on an island west of Greenland. This Groetland is sometimes confused with Baffin Island. However, the name is probably an archaic representation for Great Land or mainland south of Greenland—which would take us again to Labrador. On Mercator's map of 1569, the inhabitants of this island are called "Suedi"—or Swedes.

Historian George Horn also mentioned the Scolvus voyage in Ulysses Peregrinans (1671) where he says: "John Scolvus Polonus discovered under the auspices of Christian I, King of the Danes, the Anian strait and the country Laboratoris in the year 1476" (Nansen, 1911, 132).

Like Wyfliet, Horn has identified Labrador as the Dane's destination—suggesting among other things that, had Columbus been along for the ride, he traveled far into North America. Perhaps, this experience was the inspiration behind a book which Columbus is said to have written describing the feasibility of a trans-polar seaway to Asia. It was mentioned in his son's biography. Some cosmographers believed that the Strait of Anian—which Horn mentions in his brief statement—extended above North America and connected with a passage between Greenland and Labrador. This strait, which we call "Hudson Strait," was known by many names to ancient seafarers: Greenlanders called it Christian's Strait; the Portuguese knew it as The Strait of The Three Bretheren (the Corte-Real brothers); and the old Norse referred to it as

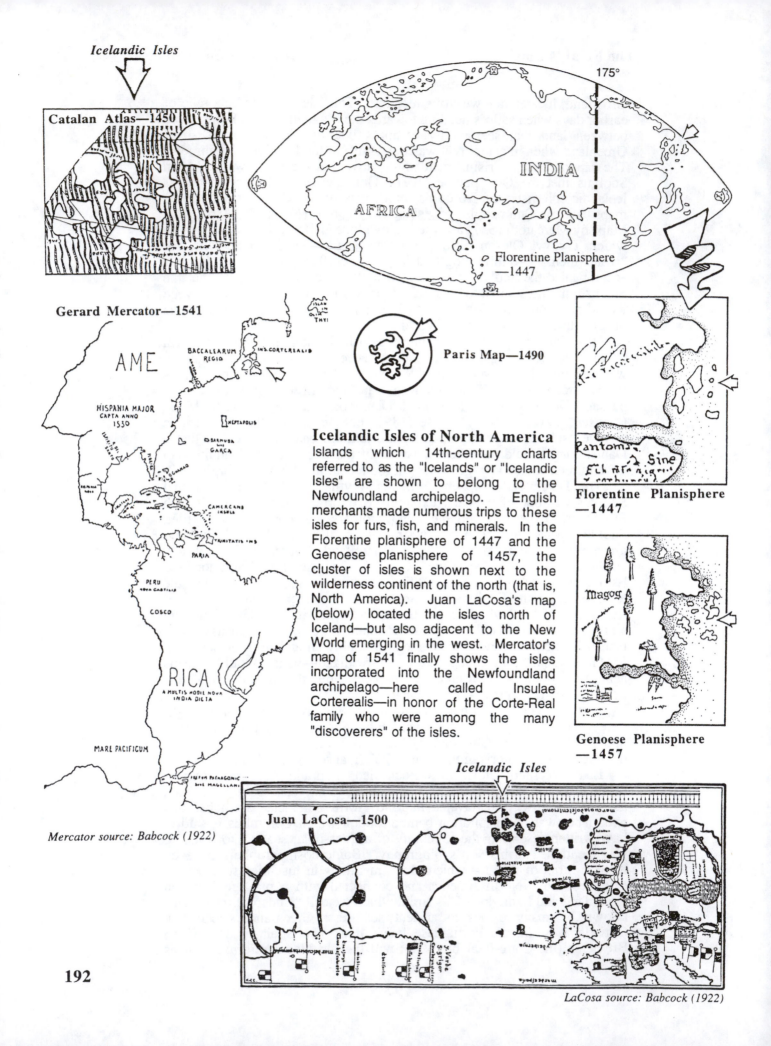

Icelandic Isles

Catalan Atlas—1450

175°

INDIA

AFRICA

Florentine Planisphere
—1447

Gerard Mercator—1541

ISLAN IN OLI AT THYI

AME

BACCALLARUM REGIO

INS.CORTEREALIS

HISPANIA MAJOR
CAPTA ANNO
1530

NEPTAPOLIS

BERMUDA INS GARCA

Paris Map—1490

R. ? Ticircccshil...

CAMERCANB INSBLS

Pantoms
Sine

**Florentine Planisphere
—1447**

TRINITATIS INS

PARIA

PERU
NOVA CASTILIA

COSCO

Magog

RICA
A MULTIS NODIE NOVA
INDIA DICTA

MARE PACIFICUM

Icelandic Isles of North America

Islands which 14th-century charts referred to as the "Icelands" or "Icelandic Isles" are shown to belong to the Newfoundland archipelago. English merchants made numerous trips to these isles for furs, fish, and minerals. In the Florentine planisphere of 1447 and the Genoese planisphere of 1457, the cluster of isles is shown next to the wilderness continent of the north (that is, North America). Juan LaCosa's map (below) located the isles north of Iceland—but also adjacent to the New World emerging in the west. Mercator's map of 1541 finally shows the isles incorporated into the Newfoundland archipelago—here called Insulae Corterealis—in honor of the Corte-Real family who were among the many "discoverers" of the isles.

**Genoese Planisphere
—1457**

FRETUM PATAGONIC INE MAGELLANI

Mercator source: Babcock (1922)

Icelandic Isles

Juan LaCosa—1500

192

LaCosa source: Babcock (1922)

Ginnungagap. A connecting strait between the north Pacific and north Atlantic is indicated on the Frisius map of 1537. Several other maps of the era show a similar trans-Arctic strait which helped to keep alive forlorn hopes of a Northwest Passage to the riches of the Orient.

We have identified five slightly different references to the 1476 Scolvus voyage from seemingly independent sources. Nevertheless, the orthodox Scandinavian historian Gustav Storm thought it impossible that Europeans could have traveled beyond Greenland during the mid-to-late 1400's, so he declared the testimonials on 16th-century maps to be the result of an anti-Columbus conspiracy (Nansen, 1911, 131). Storm believed that later geographers merely repeated a false claim made by their predecessor, and he accused Wyfliet of "inventing" the story about Scolvus in order to disparage Columbus. Fridtjof Nansen effectively quashed Storm's conspiracy theory:

> Storm thought that Wyfliet might have borrowed from Gomara, and himself invented and added the date of 1476 in order to disparage the Spaniards and Portuguese as discoverers; but Storm was not aware that this date, as we have seen, is mentioned in an earlier English source. (Nansen, 1911, 131)

Storm's fantasy of an anti-Columbus conspiracy was thus proven to be erroneous. However, that episode didn't end the diatribe against any explorer who dared to sail west before 1492. Joseph Gardner and his associates in Mysteries of The Ancient Americas (1986) also blasted what they believed were mythical tales of Danish-Portuguese explorers:

> Other accounts of the late 16th century mention the supposed New World voyages of two European pirates, Didrik Pining and Hans Pothorst, and the explorations of a navigator, Johannes Scolvus (Jan of Kolno), who might have come from Poland. So far as is known, such references were produced by writers who wanted to out-Columbus Columbus, after the fact. As American historian Samuel Eliot Morison has written, "Whilst there is no reason to believe that the pirate pair discovered anything, it is possible that Scolvus sailed around Cape Farewell, Greenland, and looked into Davis Strait." (Gardner, 1986, 19)

Morison's quote is demonstrative of the quandary facing serious scholars of American discovery. In most cases, a simple accusation by an "authority" such as Morison is deemed sufficient proof of dishonesty or fraud if it concerns pre-Columbian voyagers. However, in this case, it seems that Columbus "out Columbussed" himself: tales of his own Arctic voyage were found in the margins of a book from the Columbus library.

Columbus Sails The Arctic

Fray Bartholomew De Las Casas' Historia De Las Indias recorded the notes verbatim without any attempt at an explanation—perhaps because the places were common knowledge at the time. Colon gives the year of his voyage as 1477—close enough to the Scolvus expedition to suggest the possibility that he hitched a ride. On the other hand, the destinations he gives in his notes—Island, Frisland, Tile, and Ultima Tile—were also frequented by Bristol merchants; so an independent voyage is equally possible. Colon's notes mention an "island"—which was the current Danish-English term for Iceland; his "Ultra Tile" (or ultima Thule) represents either Greenland or Labrador. He also mentions "the Tile of

193

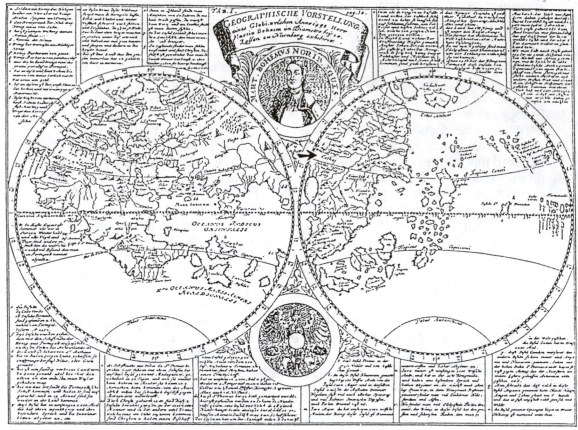

Martin Behaim, Globe   1492

Cathay (China)

Great Gulf

Gulf @ 3°

Behaim's Globe
Terra Australis & The Gulf of Guayaquil —
Roman Knowledge of South America

Martin Behaim's 1492 globe shows South America and the Gulf of Guayaquil at 3°. Location of the gulf at this location follows the Ptolemaic tradition seen on earlier maps. On this map, Cathay (China—arrow) is placed at the top of the Sinus Magnus (Great Gulf). Magellan identified this gulf as the Pacific Ocean—whose size Ptolemy and later copyists vastly underestimated. The east coast of the southern continent (here called "India Patalis") was estimated from Marco Polo's travelog and reports from merchants who sailed on Persian ships to Asia. The inaccurate coastline for South America resulted from the confusion of the southern continent with Malaqua—Malaya. The east coast of the northern continent derived from maritime surveys which extended as far south as the Gulf of Mexico by 1492.

Ptolemy" which his shipmates called "Frislanda." Since neither the Danes nor the English referred to Iceland as Frisland, the "Tile" of Colon's notes seems to refer to an Icelandic Isle—probably in the vicinity of Newfoundland or Nova Scotia. It is in this region that tides are known to vary by 25-feet (or 25 brazas). In the words of Colon:

> I navigated the year of 1477, in the month of February, ultra Tile, island, 100 leagues, whose southern part is distant from the equator 73° and not 63° as some people say, and it is not within the line that includes the West, as Ptolomeo says, but much further west. And to this island, that is as large as England, go the English with merchandise, especially those of Bristol, and at the time that I went there the ocean was not frozen, notwithstanding that there were great tides, such that in some parts two times in the day they would rise 25 brazas and descend others the same in height. It is quite true that the Tile, of Ptolomeo, is where he says, and that it is currently called Frislanda. (from Las Casas, Historia, after Yellen, 1992)

Another Portuguese captain, Alonso Sanches DeHuelva, sailed west in 1479. His voyage probably would have gone unnoticed by history had it not been for a disastrous shipwreck and an encounter with Columbus. Tempests and deadly calms made DeHuelva's return trip from the Caribbean a disaster. Columbus found the stranded captain on a Madeira beach only days before he died from exposure. Whether or not the Spanish mariner actually obtained a log or map from the shipwrecked Portuguese captain is of little consequence. All Columbus really needed to know was that there were significant lands across the sea within reasonable sailing distance: that intelligence could have been gained simply by talking to the dying captain.

The month-or-so that it took for DeHuelva's ship to make the crossing was substantially less than sailors were accustomed to on voyages between Venice and northern ports of the Hanseatic league. Some historians have dismissed the account of DeHuelva—whom they call the "secret pilot"—due to their belief that the tale is merely another misguided attempt to disparage the glory of Columbus. However, the tale was well-known among contemporaries of the Spanish mariner, and it was recorded by both Bartholomew Las Casas and Ferdinand Colon—two biographers who had a personal interest in preserving the reputation of their hero. As far as Ferdinand was concerned, the story was true—but it was irrelevant to the fact that Columbus would have sailed across the Atlantic regardless of what he learned from the pilot. Ferdinand believed that it was his father's God-ordained mission to bring salvation to New World savages, and where the Admiral happened to get his information about lands and seas across the ocean was of little consequence.

Later Portuguese Expeditions

Following a 1483 proposal that Columbus offered to King John II of Portugal, three more expeditions sailed west. Fernao Domingo de Arco of Madeira led the first expedition in 1484. His commission called for him to occupy an isle west of Madeira—presumably Antilia. The only isles in that direction are Haiti and Cuba in the Caribbean Sea. The second expedition was under Fernao Dulmo of the Azores who petitioned John II for a license to search for Antilia and the Isle of Seven Cities also in 1484. Two years later, Dulmo joined into partnership with Joao

Affonso de Estreito (Newton, 1932, 83). A record of the expedition says that a German resident of the Azores was sent as a cosmographer. This description only fits Martin Behaim—a Nuremberg expatriate who had distinguished himself as a Lisbon globemaker before taking up residence in the Azores (Newton, 1932, 83). The third expedition was under Pedro Vasquez De LaFrontera. Martin Alonzo Pinzon was also on the ship which reached as far west as the Sargasso Sea before being forced to turn back (Harrisse, 1892, 660). Las Casas reported that Vincente Diaz, a Genoese merchant and resident of Terceira, also made three trips west between 1484 and 1492. As was true for most of these quasi-secret voyages, nothing is known of the result.

Orthodox historians assume that these voyages were a vain effort to usurp the Columbus concept of sailing west to the Orient; and they assume that neither expedition found land across the Atlantic. Such assumptions add mystique to the 1492 Columbus venture. However, the stock declaration that "nothing was found" is mere speculation. The Portuguese were very secretive about their expeditions and it is not likely that they would have made a claim of discovery even if one had occurred.

What would they have reported that they didn't already know? As it was, their initial impression of the land was that it was a valuable source of furs and fish—though not the Cathay of Marco Polo. Indeed, maps and globes attributable to Portuguese sources—such as Toscanelli's Planisphere of 1457 (a.k.a. the "Genoese Planisphere") and Martin Behaim's globe of 1492—portrayed the northwestern continent across the sea as a wilderness. Some called this wilderness the Magog forest; Martin Behaim called it a "Tartary Wilderness."

Behaim's globe was partially based on his own experience. His voyages certainly took him to the coast of Africa; Portuguese and German historians have suggested that he also sailed to America. The Nuremberg Chronicle for 1493 makes no mention of reports that Cristobol Colon discovered a shortcut to India, however it does mention that Martin Behaim—expatriate of Nuremberg—in company with Jacobus Carnus of Portugal sailed to an overseas land below the Equinotical line. Upon facing east at noon, they observed that their shadows fell to the right or south—thereby confirming that they had sailed past the Equator. In other words, they had crossed the equator and discovered the alter orbis. This "alter orbis"—or "Other World" of Greco-Roman legend, has been identified as the Mundus Novus (New World). The year of this voyage is unknown but was probably between 1480 and 1490. The king of Portugal knighted Behaim in 1484 for his service. During the 19th century, German historians claimed that this passage in the Chronicle was evidence that Behaim had preceded Columbus to the New World—as the only mainland across the Western Sea and also below the Equator is South America.

Orthodox historians have condemned both the entry in the Chronicle and its interpretation as part of a nationalist, German plot. Nineteenth-century historian John Thatcher (1967, 73) assumed that this entry in the Chronicle was an example of Germanic pride interfering with history, and he noted that his contemporary, Harrisse—himself a staunch isolationist, claimed that the entry was made "by a different hand" in the original Latin manuscript. In other words, Harrisse suspected that a German conspiracy was already organized by 1493 in an effort to defraud Columbus of his rightful glory as discoverer of the New World. Historian John Fiske (1920, Vol. I, 423) agreed: "A ridiculous story that he (Martin Behaim) anticipated Columbus in the discovery of America originated in the misunderstanding of an interpolated passage in the Latin text of Schedel's Registrum.(a.k.a. Nuremberg Chronicle, 1493, p. 290)."

Portuguese voyages to the New World's northwest territories were not unknown to Columbus—although he believed like most of his contemporaries that the lands he visited in Labrador (or Frisland) were not in the far west but instead were situated around the North Pole. Sailing to this region was the origin of his belief that the Orient could be reached by sailing across a navigable sea surrounding the North Pole. Some years after his own northern voyage in 1477, Columbus mentioned to his son, Ferdinand, that he knew of a northern land called "Baccalaos" (i.e. "Stockfish Land"). He believed this was the place where two of his associates, Fernao Dulmo and Velasco De Galicia landed on separate voyages in the service of Portugal.

Fernao Dulmo's voyage took place in 1486—the same year given for an inscription on Martin Behaim's 1490-92 globe which mentions that a Portuguese vessel sighted Antilia in the western Atlantic. Some scholars believe Antilia represents Florida or Cuba. Indeed islands near Cuba were named the Antilles shortly after Columbus established colonies in the area.

Testimony by Columbus and accounts of Behaim's travels with the Dulmo expedition confirm that Baccalaos (or Newfoundland) was a well-established trading post and fishery by the time of the Bristol voyages west in the 1480's. The 1486 patent which Jao II granted to Dulmo makes clear that the Portuguese expected to find an unclaimed continent across the Atlantic (Harrisse, 1892, 660). This patent confirms our knowledge that the Portuguese were aware that the land across the Atlantic was not the Cathay of Marco Polo but was instead a wilderness continent as it was portrayed in the contemporary maps by Toscanelli. However, it was not until the officially-authorized voyages of John and Sebastian Cabot in 1497 and 1498 (under the authority of King Henry VII) that Newfoundland was duly entered into the "official" book of discovery as a newly ordained, Christian territory.

Joao Coelho sailed to the Antilles in 1487. His clandestine voyage was revealed during a court hearing in 1514. Coelho appeared on behalf of an associate, Estevao Frois, who was accused of trespassing on Spanish territory. According to his testimony, both he and Frois were part of a Portuguese expedition that preceded the Columbus voyage to the Caribbean. The defense attorney effectively argued that the Treaty of Tordesillas—which Spain and Portugal signed in 1494—allowed passage to those who had sailed to the said territory prior to the date of the treaty.

Portuguese knowledge of the Atlantic was further revealed in 1493 when Portugal challenged Spain over its claim of new discoveries in the western Atlantic. According to a Papal Bull of 1484, Portugal was to be the sole owner of any lands discovered in the ocean. That decree came about after Europe's other Christian nations failed to join in a unified program of world-wide colonialism and evangelism. However, Spain claimed that by another agreement between Christian kingdoms, Portugal had promised to return any refugees who fled across the border. It was hardly coincidental that Spain had just given Jews an ultimatum to flee or face extermination in 1492. By 1493, thousands of Jewish refugees had settled into new lives and new businesses in Portugal. Spain's diplomats insisted that the Jews had departed with millions of dollars worth of gold and jewelry (that is, their own personal property).

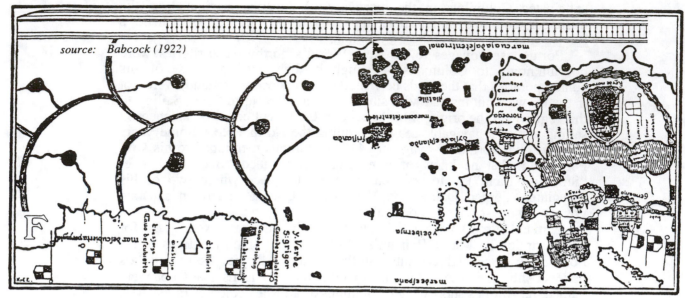

source: *Babcock (1922)*

Isle of Seven Cities—1508

Orthodox historians regard the Juan LaCosa map of 1500 to be the earliest map to include part of the New World mainland found by John Cabot and Columbus. Although the northwestern section of LaCosa's map (shown above) does not identify the land area, historians have assumed that it represents a fictitious, Asian coastline. Sebastian Cabot claimed that expeditions with his father in 1497 and 1498 reached as far as Florida and the Gulf. This coastline is shown on LaCosa's map as a horizontal shore with Florida (**F**) on the far left. A similar coast is featured on the Portolan Atlas of 1508 which identifies the mainland as *septem civitates* or "Seven Cities." This map also identifies the west coast of South America as *Antiglia*—"the ancient land"—suggesting it was known to ancient Roman mariners.

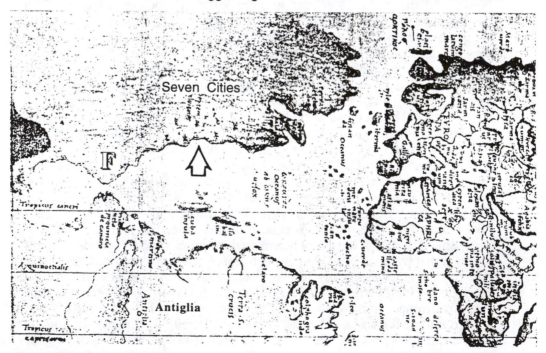

198 **Portolan Atlas of 1508—anonymous**
Egerton Manuscript 2803—British Museum
source: Babcock (1922, fig. 8)
from E.L. Stevenson: Atlas of Portolan Charts, 1911

Thus, Portugal was faced with paying the Catholic Sovereigns millions of dollars and apprehending tens of thousands of refugees—who faced certain death in Spain—or negotiating a settlement (Hakluyt, 1582). The resulting Treaty of Tordesillas granted Spain ownership of new lands discovered in the western Atlantic from a demarcation line or meridian at 370 leagues west of the Cape Verde Islands. Was it merely coincidence that this line of demarcation provided Portugal with future access to Brazil—a land that was not yet "officially" discovered.

According to British intelligence, there was no coincidence: merchant-spy Robert Thorne informed King Henry VIII in a letter dated 1527 that the Portuguese had identified Brazil long before 1492. Thorne's letter stated that: "The King of Portugal had already discovered certain islands that lie against Cape Verde, and also a certain part of the mainland, towards the South, and called it the land of Brazil" (Beeching, 1972, 50).

From Bristol to Brazil

Throughout the Middle Ages, Europeans fantasized about the legendary Irish paradise of Hy-Bresail across the ocean. Geographers believed the land was situated someplace southwest of Ireland—which is where a curious, circular isle appears on ancient maps. The first appearance of Brazil as an identifiable place on a map is on Dalorto's map of 1325. This map has Brazil in the mid-Atlantic Ocean west of Ireland. The isle was included as part of a list of Atlantic isles in Book of The Knowledge by an anonymous Spanish Franciscan in 1350. It was in this book that the isle was said to be situated west of Spain and south of Ireland (Markham, 1912, 22 & 29). The isle's name has various spellings—Bracir, Brexil, Bersil, Berzil, Breasil, and Brazil (Ramsay, 1972, 86).

The origin of the name is illusive. The earliest mention of Brazil has been found in an ancient Irish text, Hardiman's History of Galway, in which "Breasail" was the name of a pagan demigod (Babcock, 1922, p. 50). It may be that the Irish identified Brazil as the overseas paradise of this heroic figure.

By the 12th century, Europeans imported grain (probably corn or maize) that was attributed to the distant isle. Babcock notes that: "The earliest distinctly recognizable mention of brazil as a commodity occurs in a commercial treaty of 1193 between the Duchy of Ferrara, Italy, and a neighboring town or small state which presents grana de Brasill in a long list of merchandise. The same curious phrase, 'Grain of Brazil,' recurs in a quite independent local charta of the same country only five years later" (Babcock, 1922, p. 53). He calls Brazilian grain "a well-established characterization of a known article of trade in the 12th century."

However, the name brazil as a commodity is most closely associated with a dyewood used in the wool industry. At the end of the 13th century, "brazilwood" was listed among the items of an inventory taken on the properties of the Viscount de Leau at Rouen. "Irish wood" (i.e., brazilwood) was used to panel a library in the Louvre in the 1460's (Ashe, 1962, 140). The red dyewood reached France through other ports during the same time period: customs in Hanfleur and in Dieppe levied duties on logs of sapanwood (sapang) which was known as a source of red dye (Chretien, 1993, 203). As the wool industry prospered in England and the Netherlands, red dye also grew in value, and sailors had a strong financial incentive to search for the source of the dyewood.

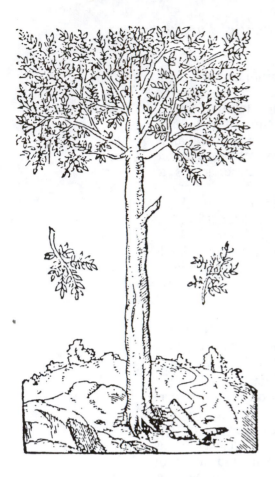

Brazilwood Tree
from Dodoens Stirpium
Antwerp, 1583

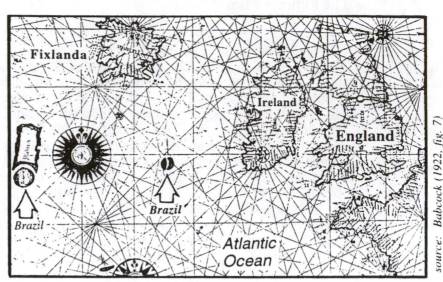

Catalan Map of 1480

Where is Brazil?

Ever since the 14th century, European mariners told tales of an overseas land that was the source of large grain (corn) and a valuable red dyewood called "brazil." Angelino Dulcert's 1325 map has the earliest known cartographical reference—on a circular isle southwest of Ireland. It is called: *insula montonis sive abresil.* The Catalan Map of 1480 (above) introduces two Brazils—one as a bisected circle west of Ireland and a second farther west. The second Brazil is shown directly below a schematic, rectangular isle called *Isla Verde* or "Green Isle"—a.k.a. Greenland. This isle is most likely an early representation of Florida; *fixlanda* to the north probably represents the Newfoundland region.

By the early 16th century, cartographers finally identified the northeastern region of the Mundus Novus (South America) as the source of brazilwood. Thus, the region came to be known as Brazil (**B**)—which was variously spelled: Basera, Prisilia, Bersil, and Brasilia. An early example is the Gregorius Reisch map of 1515.

TYPVS VNIVERSALIS TERRE IVXTA MODERNORVM DISTINCTIONEM ET EXTENSINEM PER REGN

PARIA SEV PRISILIA

MARE INDICVM
Gregorius Reisch map of 1515

200

Babcock reported several historical references to cargoes from Brazil—suggesting that imports from the isle were not uncommon: "Brazil as a commodity figures rather frequently; for example, in the schedules of port dues of Barcelona and other Catalan seaboard towns in the 13th century as compiled by Capmany. Thus in 1221, we find carrega de Brasill, in 1243 caxia de bresil, and somewhat later (1252) cargua de brazil" (Babcock, 1922, 53). Babcock notes that "the word and the thing were not confined to the Mediterranean, for a grant of murage rates of 1312 to the City of Dublin, Ireland, uses the words de brasile venali"—or cargo ship from Brazil. By the mid-14th century, the Black Death swept across Europe devastating most severely the mariners who were at the heart of commerce. The result was that navigational lore concerning the location of the rich, overseas source of brazilwood was lost.

When 15th-century England recovered from the social, intellectual, and cultural impact of the plagues, merchants who heard tales of the rich brazilwood trade commissioned expeditions to search for the lost Brazil. A brief account of only one such expedition has managed to survive. In the Cambridge Itineraria of 1778, it is written that:

> On the 15th of July, 1480, ships belonging to John Jay, junior, of 80 tons burthen, sailed out of Bristol to navigate west of Ireland as far as the island of Brazil. On the 18th of September (1481?), news was received that Thomas Lloyd, the most expert seaman in England, who commanded the expedition, after a navigation of nearly nine months, being storm-beaten, had been compelled to enter a port in Ireland to allow his ships and men to rest ... without having discovered the said island. (Harrisse, 1892, 659)

Most historians take this passage to mean that the expedition was a failure. However, we should take care to "read between the lines" and consider what we know of ancient travel in the North Atlantic. We know, for example, that the typical passage to Iceland was less than two weeks—so a nine-month voyage provided ample time for some kind of commercial activity in ports on some of the many isles and colonies in the western Atlantic. We also know that some 15th-century maps included two Brazils—one west of Ireland (called Hy-Bresail); another to the distant south and the tropical land of brazilwood. If the ships in the 1480 expedition were at sea for nine months—it may well be that they succeeded in finding lands across the Atlantic—even if they failed to overcome the strong Gulf Stream current in their efforts to sail south beyond the great gulf. Indeed, as one or two weeks should have been sufficient to reach Iceland or Greenland, and another two would have taken them to Newfoundland, it seems unlikely that they should have failed to reach some western isle where they had the opportunity to barter for wood, furs, or codfish. We also know that numerous ships that traded illegally with Iceland took their cargoes to outlying ports where they sought to avoid taxation.

Even if the 1480 expedition failed in its objective (Brazil), others surely succeeded. The Spanish minister Pedro DeAyala informed the Catholic Sovereigns in a letter dated 1498 that: "For the last seven years the Bristol people have equipped every year two, three, or four caravels to go in search of the islands of Brazil and the Isle of the Seven Cities" (Harrisse, 1892, 660). And in his letter of 1497 to Columbus, John Day stressed that mariners from Bristol had succeeded in reaching Brazil and the mainland across the Atlantic.

source: Nordenskiold (1889, Pl. 44)

Bacalhos—The Trans-Arctic Continent

A northern land mass reaching out from Europe above Norway reaches across the North Atlantic in the Ptolemaic Basileae edition of 1540. This New World continent was in the tradition of a trans-Arctic land mass dating to Medieval times when it was called Hyperborea, Septentrionalis, or Europe of the North. This is the same territory that in DeVirga's 1414 map is called "Norveca." Here the land is called "Bacalhos"— in accordance with French-Portuguese interests. As the land was shown from a modified geographic (as opposed to magnetic) perspective, New World lands appeared to be within the realm of Portuguese interests as established by the Papal Bull of 1468. Norse power by that time had waned as a consequence of plague and piracy. When John Cabot cruised along the East Coast of North America in 1497, he identified the entire land from the Gulf of St. Lawrence to Florida as "Bacallaos."

202

By the late 15th century, the location of Brazil was no longer in doubt. Babcock (1922, 53) observes that Columbus collected "brazilwood" on his third and fourth voyages along the shore of South America; Cabot expected to find brazilwood in that direction after failing to find it along the coast of North America. Furthermore, the northeastern territory of South America—officially named Terra de Sancte Crucis by Cabral— eventually took on the name "Brazil" because it was the principle source of red dyewood. This renaming of the land infuriated Portuguese authorities who believed the official name was more honorable than the pedestrian "Brazil" which stressed the commercial value of the region. In 1503, Amerigo Vespucci also took on a cargo of brazilwood from the forests of Terra de Sancte Crucis (Fiske, 1920, Vol. II, 170).

Explorers on The Western Fringe—
Frisians, Arabs, Moors, Africans, Jews, Armenians,
Basques, & the French

During the late Middle Ages, the mysterious western lands attracted refugees from the Inquisition; they were also beacons to curious nobles who were bored with the luxuries of palatial estates. Richard Hakluyt identified several ancient explorers in Divers Voyages Touching the Discoverie of America (1582); many tales of Arabian voyagers were reported in Arabic geographical accounts and maps; while others were mentioned in the 14th-century Cnoyen manuscript.

German historian Adam of Bremen is the earliest source for the tale of 11th-century Frisian nobles who sailed to the "northern regions." Frisians are a Germanic people who live along the Baltic Sea near the Netherlands. Their off-shore island habitations are often shown on maps of the Baltic region as the Frisian Islands—but there was another Frisian Island in ancient times situated far out in the Atlantic southwest of Iceland. This so-called "fabulous" island is sometimes called Friesland, Frixlandia, Riesland—or simply Frisland.

Like most Baltic merchants, Frisians were active sailors during the late Middle Ages. In his Descriptio Insularum Aquilonis of 1073, Adam referred to a contemporary voyage of Frisian nobles who left Bremen for the Orkney Islands and then headed toward the North Pole. Adam credits two archbishops for this account. The nobles identified a suitable isle for their colony and set up shop—probably in the vicinity of Newfoundland.

Flemish traveler and chronicler, Jacobus Cnoyen, might have drawn his own version of the Frisian trip from Adam of Bremen, or he could have used independent sources. His brief account says that a group of Frisian nobles simply sailed beyond Iceland to the "northern regions"— which, as we have previously demonstrated, referred to Hudson Bay or lands along the East Coast near Labrador. Cnoyen's account was summarized in Richard Hakluyt's Diverse Voyages (1582) after being taken from a manuscript by Mercator.

In the Geographische Handtbuch by Matthias Quad (1600), the Frisians are described as "kings" who sailed west from Iceland to Frisland—presumably a territory which they renamed in honor of their own homeland. The route of travel by compass bearings would have taken them to Labrador or Newfoundland. In the account by Nicolo Zeno (ca. 1390), Frisland is described as being much larger than Ireland and having a large population with several towns with harbors frequented by European vessels. This account supports the theory that the land was actually mainland—perhaps Labrador, Nova Scotia, or even

Newfoundland. As the centuries passed by and later voyagers came to settle and trade, the name of the place changed to suit the fancy of new owners. Nevertheless, a tiny isle, "Friesland," is commonly seen on charts of the northwest Atlantic dating to the 16th-century—long after everyone had forgotten where the place was located. The name was still current among some mariners at the time of the Columbus voyage north in 1477—as it is one of the places the Spaniard said that he had visited. In Peter Heylyn's Cosmography (1659), Freisland was described as "belonging to the crown of Norway" (Ramsay, 1972, 54).

Arabian geographers were also aware of the Frisian tale and the isle that Frisian nobles named in the northwest Atlantic; the name "Resland" (for Friesland) shows up on Al-Idrisi's silver plate map and wall map of 1154. Portrayed as an isle the size of Ireland, it is located on these maps in the North Atlantic (or "Dark Green Sea") beyond Ireland and Norway.

Al-Idrisi mentioned many isles in the Dark Sea—mostly fabulous isles inhabited by fantastic creatures. Fabulous lands included the Amazon Isles, Sara (the Isle of Alexander the Great), Villuland (the Isle of Illusion), Raka (the Isle of Birds), Kalhan (the Isle of Animal-headed Men), and Al-Gaur (a grassland with oxen). Some of the isles reported in Al-Idrisi's geographical text, such as Shasland (Shetland or Scotland), were very real (Nansen, 1911, 206).

Arabian voyagers traveled across the North Atlantic during the late Middle Ages and early Renaissance. Al-Masudi's Historical Annals of 942 AD tell of a Moorish voyage from Cordova, Spain, under the command of Captain Khashkhash. After an extended voyage west, the ship returned filled with treasures from a land across the sea. What land? Only America lies in that direction. The 12th-century Arabic geographer Al-Idrisi reported a voyage by the Brothers Al-Mugrurim who sailed into the Atlantic out of Lisbon. Their crossing to some overseas land took a month—about the same time it took Columbus to reach the Caribbean in 1492. Al-Idrisi's geography reported the rich fishing grounds of Newfoundland and described the whalebone huts of Labrador's Inuit natives—confirming that voyagers had actually crossed the ocean and had taken stock of the valuable resources of North America.

The anonymous Spanish Franciscan who wrote the Book of Knowledge (circa 1350) told of his travels in the company of Moorish traders who headed west from North Africa. The Moors reached the Azores and Canary Islands before 1350 and substantially ahead of 15th-century Spanish and Portuguese explorers—whom Western historians credit with "discovering" these isles west of Spain. The friar mentioned isles such as Canaria, Tenerife, Porto Santo, and Cuervo—all prior to their "official" discovery. He mentioned the Isle of "La Caridad" which is a possible reference to Al-Kalidat—an Atlantic isle reported in a contemporary Arabian geography. Historian Clements Markham (1912, 22 & 29) assumed that the friar traveled no farther west than the Azores. However, the friar mentions in his travelog the names "Brazil" and "Salvage" which 15th-century Portuguese maps clearly situated west of the Azores. At this point, we can only speculate whether the friar sailed across the mid-Atlantic to the Americas or merely made an early voyage to the Azores and simply repeated legends of fabulous isles to the west.

We know that other Moorish traders went the whole distance. Fra Mauro, a Camaldolese monk from Venice, reported in 1459 that a zoncho de india (identified as an Arabian vessel from India) had headed out into the "Sea of Darkness" (Atlantic Ocean) where it sailed for 40 days before reaching unknown lands.   In 1787, road crews near Cambridge, Massachusetts, dug up a hoard of Arabic coins from the 11th century. These artifacts and inscriptions found in New York and Tennessee confirm that Arabian merchants (probably Moors) reached North America (Thompson, 1994, 294).   These Moorish travelers were probably responsible for the transfer of Mediterranean plants such as figs, oranges, lemons, and almonds to Florida and the Carolinas ahead of the Spaniards.

West Africans sailed across the Atlantic far ahead of the Great Age of Discovery. Arabic historians recorded the oral traditions of African trips as early as the 9th century BC (VanSertima, 1992; Thompson, 1994). During the 14th century, Arab historian Ibn Amir Hajib recorded the account of Sultan Abubakari's Ghanian expeditions across the Atlantic in 1300 AD. His successor, Kankan Musa dispatched several flotillas into the Atlantic on trading and exploratory missions. Although historians acknowledge that these voyages occurred, they often assume that the voyagers were "swallowed up by the ocean." On the contrary, Columbus and his followers reported "Ethiopians"—or blacks—living along the coast of South America. Giovanni Verrazano reported tribes of blacks along the coast of Virginia and the Carolinas in 1521, and 16th-century cartographers recorded the name of an African tribe, the Mocosa, situated north of Virginia. VanSertima (1992, 196) points out that maps of colonial South America bear the names "Almamy" and "Mandinga Bay"— both representing the locations of African tribes. He also notes that Catholic historian Bertholomew Las Casas reported that Columbus and Portuguese King John were aware of trading canoes sailing between Guinea, Africa, and lands across the Atlantic (VanSertima, 1992, 175).

Jews were part of the van of early European trade with North America—which should come as no surprise since they were among the World's most enterprising merchants, and their ancestors were transoceanic sailors as far back as the Phoenicians. Ancient Jewish coins and an inscription from Bat Creek, Tennessee, reveal that North America was a refuge from Roman oppression. It was also a destination for explorers and merchants. Richard Hakluyt (1582) mentioned Benjamin Tudelensis as an explorer who reached Norumbega (North America) in 1178. Apparently, the voyage was still known to Europeans of the 16th century—though Hakluyt's note is the only surviving record.   A Portuguese Jew served as a pilot for the Columbus voyage in 1492, and there is speculation that this was not his first trip across the Atlantic.

Runeologist Richard Nielsen (1994, 3) suggests that Hanseatic merchants based in Lubeck, Germany, sailed to Vinland in North America.   This seems apparent from a 1402 runestone found at Spirit Pond, Maine, that mentions a Vendal (Baltic) ship on a trading voyage to Vinland. Contemporary knowledge of the Vinland colony is confirmed by a mappamond of 1475 and an accompanying geography, the Rudimentium Novitorum, from Lubeck. Several printed versions of the map and geography referred to "Vinlad" or "Winlad"—both references to the Nordic Wineland colony. The presence of decorative panels in the Schleswig Cathedral which feature the distinctive American game bird known as a "turkey" support the thesis that Hanse merchants (or Vendal merchants) traded with settlers in the modern region of New England.

Even Columbus biographer, Bertholomew Las Casas, acknowledged prior voyagers to the isles and mainland of the Caribbean. However, he surmised that they were unimportant in light of the divine mission that Columbus had to save "heathen natives." It was this mission—and not

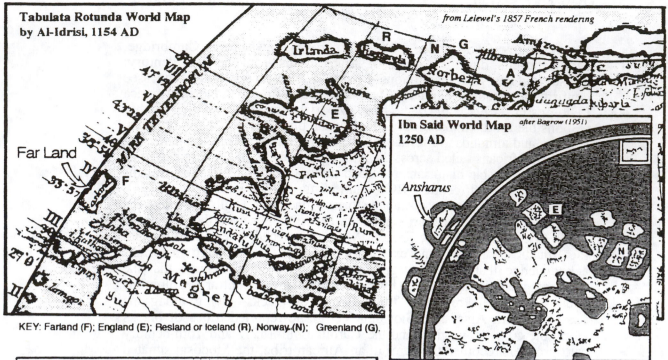

Tabulata Rotunda World Map
by Al-Idrisi, 1154 AD

from Lelewel's 1857 French rendering

Far Land

Ibn Said World Map
1250 AD *after Bagrow (1951)*

Ansharus

KEY: Farland (F); England (E); Resland or Iceland (R), Norway (N); Greenland (G).

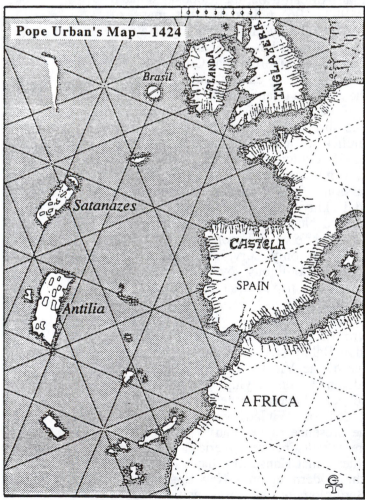

Pope Urban's Map—1424

Brasil

Satanazes

Antilia

CASTELA

SPAIN

AFRICA

Atlantic Isles
Antilia & FarLand

Arabic maps of the 12th century are the oldest evidence of Atlantic isles variously called "Antilia," "FarLand," and "Ansharus." Al-Idrisi's "FarLand" has the same approximate size and location to Antilia on 15th-century Portuguese charts. This location, directly west of Spain is at the latitude of New York—so Arabic renditions such as Ibn Said's "Ansharus" might represent mainland North America. Early Portuguese maps, such as Pope Urban's map of 1424 identify the isle as "Antilia" meaning "isle in front of mainland." This description seems suited to either Cuba and Hispaniola or Japan and the Philippines which have similar positions east of continental land. Caribbean isles were understandably confused with Japan after Marco Polo reported this Asian isle 500 miles east of China. Following the return of Columbus, historian Peter Martyr identified the isle of Hispaniola where the mariner landed as the Antilles of the ancients. Satanazes on Urban's map is thought to represent the forested Markland of Norse tradition.

206

geographical discovery—which Las Casas glorified in his <u>History of The Indies</u>. Columbus was the hero of that influential volume completed in 1563 and published in 1875. Ferdinand Colon mentions that the men sailing with Columbus found a native using an iron frying pan shortly after their arrival on the Island of Guadelupe (Keen, 1975, 112). Thus, he acknowledged the probability of earlier voyagers who sailed to the Caribbean—but they sailed without proper credentials from the king; and they lacked divine endorsement.

French explorers and merchants also took to the seas: Masudi's 10th-century <u>Book of Wonders</u> reported that the king of France sent a ship in search of the Isle of Raka—identified as "an isle of birds" in the Western Sea or Dark Sea (Nansen, 1911, 207). Like many of these early "accounts," all that is reported is a departure to unknown lands; the outcome of the voyage remains speculative. A French manuscript, <u>Description de La Mer Oceane</u>, told the story of a storm-driven vessel that sailed to the Western Continent circa 1480. The French pilot, Saint Jean de Luz, is believed to have related this adventure to Columbus. Some writers believe this "Jean" was the same Juan de La Cosa who later accompanied Columbus to Hispaniola and acquired fame as a navigator and cartographer (Vignaud, 1902, 113). The <u>History of Dieppe</u> carried a report in 1785 concerning a merchant vessel destined for South Africa in 1488. After passing Gibraltar heading south, it was swept out to sea by storms and currents. The vessel, commanded by a Jean Cousin, wound up along the shores of Brazil where the crew took on supplies before returning to France (Fisk, 1892, 150). Historian John Fisk dismissed the account for lack of substantiating evidence and "relegated it to the limbo prepared for learned trifles." A less-judgmental version of Jean Cousin's voyage can be found in <u>Collier's Encyclopedia</u> (1992, Vol. 4, 507).

Many of these precocious explorers found new homes beside natives and earlier colonists. Their descendants of "mixed-blood" constituted the wide assortment of ethnic groups that 16th-century Europeans found when they sailed along the East Coast. Among the people these later explorers mentioned in their chronicles were "white tribes," bronzed natives, Melungeons, and black "Ethiopians."

Early Portuguese Maps

Given the numerous trans-Atlantic voyages undertaken by Portuguese vessels, it is understandable that the Atlantic cartography shows increasing accuracy and correspondence to actual geographical features of the ocean and its isles. A major center for Portuguese cartography during the time of Prince Henry The Navigator (1394-1460) was at the maritime college at Sagres. Henry was assisted in his work at the college by an aging Jew, Jamie Ribes of Majorca (a.k.a. Jafuda Cresques), who was an expert compass crafter and son of the famous cartographer—Abraham Cresques. it was Cresques who had produced a Catalan atlas for King Pedro I (Sanceau, 1947). Maps played a crucial role in Portuguese conquest of the Atlantic and the quest for Oriental markets.

The Portuguese introduced the name "Antilia" into European cartography. The name derives from Portuguese words for isle (<u>hila</u>) and before (<u>ante</u>) to designate an isle before the overseas continent. Antilia appears for the first time on Beccario's map of 1435 as four large isles in the western Atlantic with the designation <u>Insulle a Novo Repte</u>, i.e. the "Newly Reported Isles." (Babcock, 1922, p. 70). This group of isles apparently derives from similarly placed lands on Arabian maps of the

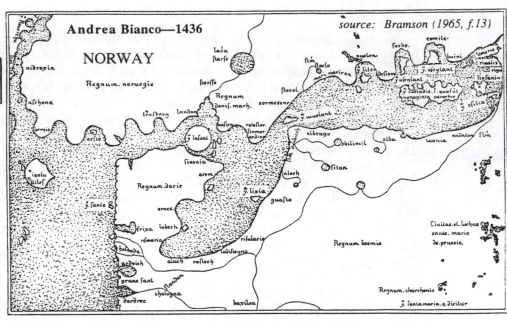

Andrea Bianco—1436

NORWAY

source: Bramson (1965, f.13)

Regnum. noruegie

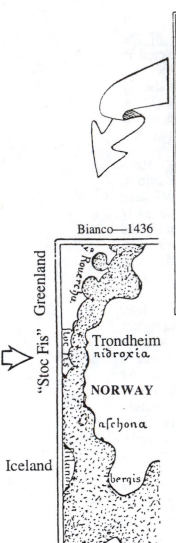

Bianco—1436

Greenland

"Stoc Fis"

Iceland

Trondheim
nidroxia

NORWAY

aſchona

bergis

Bianco's Overseas Lands: "StocFis," Bacalaos, & Brazil

Two maps by cartographer Andrea Bianco reveal Portuguese knowledge of Newfoundland and Brazil. A 1436 chart of the North Atlantic (above) shows a land called "Stoc fis" south of Rouerchu (Greenland). Since Stock Fish referred to the principle maritime harvest of the Grand Banks near Newfoundland, some isle in the vicinity of the Gulf of St. Lawrence seems to be indicated. This combination of lands in the Arctic Isle (66°) with regions farther south near Nova Scotia (45°) is seen in later charts such as the map by Jacob Ziegler in 1532 which has Terra Bacalaos (Stock Fish Land) as the southern region of Greenland Province.

Brazil shows up on Bianco's 1448 Atlantic chart as an unnamed land 1500 miles southwest of Cape Verde, Africa. A caption on the map says *isola otinticha 1500 mia*—that is, "isle authenticated 1500 miles distant." The fact that this land was known to the Portuguese is confirmed by historian Las Casas who says Columbus sailed southwest in 1498 in order to confirm the claim of King Joao who "said that there was *terra firma* to the south" of Hispaniola (Van Sertima, 1992, 176).

Andrea Bianco—1448

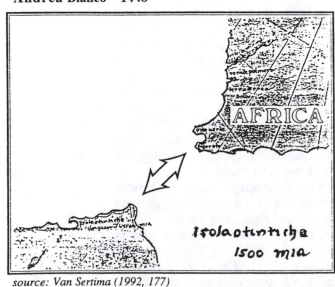

source: Van Sertima (1992, 177)

Margarita Map **after Johann Schoner, 1515**

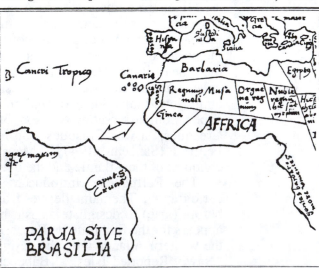

source: Harrisse (1892)

12th century—such as Al-Idrisi's "Farland" and Ibn Said's "Ansharus" on a 1250 AD world map.

Another famous cartographer who recorded Portuguese discoveries for Prince Henry was Andrea Bianco. A notation beside one of the northern isles on the Andrea Bianco map of 1436 designates Stoc fis—or "Stockfish"—which was another name for cod. This is an apparent reference to the salt-fish or baccalaos that were taken along the shores of Newfoundland (Nielsen, 1994,3). Another name used for the same isle and its fish industry was the "Isle of Salt-fish."

English merchants who caught and cured cod along the shores of Newfoundland took along cargoes of salt heading west and returned with the cured fish. Landing on isles or mainland was necessary for the curing process. Historian Ian Wilson (1991, 62) believes that these trans-Atlantic expeditions in the 1480's went unreported in Bristol customs accounts because the sailors had a legitimate claim that they were only on fishing trips and didn't engage in significant trade with the natives.

Bianco's 1448 map identifies mainland southwest of the Cape Verde Isles. A notation on the map reads: has ixola otinticha xe longa a ponente 1500 mia ilha autentica—or "isle authenticated at approximately 1500 leagues west." There can be no mistake about the identity of this isle: a comparison of Bianco's map with early 16th-century charts shows that the "authenticated isle" was situated in the precise location of Brazil.

Secret Maps—The Atlantic Cartography

Several European world maps confirm the increasing accuracy with which Portuguese monarchs viewed the Atlantic and the continents beyond. With the introduction of elliptical mapping based on Ptolemy's 2nd-century canons, cartographers were able to include realistic images of lands from both hemispheres on a single map. During the early 15th century, cartographers portrayed the west coast of "Asia" with characteristics derived from surveys of America. Thus, a Florentine planisphere of 1447 and a Genoese copy of 1457 (the "Genoese Map") have headlands along the northeast coast of what appears to be "Asia" that correspond to Labrador and Nova Scotia. Both maps portray "Asia" (or Farthest India) as two large lands split in the middle by a great gulf. The northern land was shown as a forested wilderness; the south land was designated Cathay. A peninsula at the corner of the gulf looks suspiciously like Florida.

This evolving peninsula can be identified on eight pre-Columbian maps including: the Norveca map (1360); Yale's Vinland Map (1440); the Florentine Planisphere of 1447; the Genoese Planisphere of 1457; Fra Mauro's Map of 1459; two maps by Henricus Martellus Germanus from 1489 and 1490; and Martin Behaim's globe of 1492. Maps by Mauro, Martellus, and Behaim all have the southeastern peninsula (sometimes called "horn of Asia") at or near the Tropic of Cancer—so it is apparent that European explorers had identified the correct latitude of Florida by 1459 (the date of Mauro's map). Since Portuguese explorers sailed into the Atlantic during this time, it is reasonable to attribute the accuracy of Mauro's map as well as the increased accuracy of maps by Toscanelli, Martellus, and Behaim to trans-Atlantic expeditions.

Obscure historical accounts hint that the Portuguese had fairly accurate maps in their possession. According to the 16th-century historian, Antonio Galvano, an associate named Francis DeSosa Tavares had seen a map showing the south African cape and the East Indies in fair accuracy

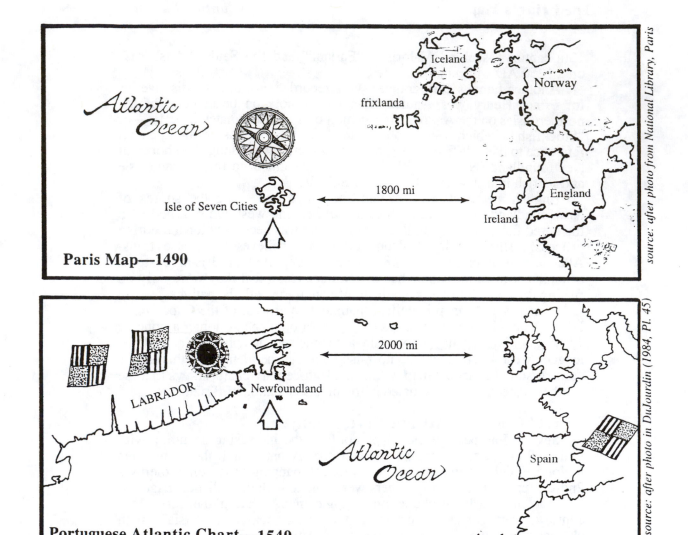

Paris Map—1490

Portuguese Atlantic Chart—1549

Isle of Seven Cities—ca. 1490

Sailors on singular expeditions often saw only a small section of New World shores before returning home. Consequently, maps produced from such ventures are necessarily limited in scope and often create the impression that overseas lands are merely a conglomeration of haphazard isles. It took repeated expeditions by the Cabots, Vespucci, LaCosa, Verrazano, and Cartier to tie the pieces together.

A caption on the Paris Map circa 1490 notes that isles were found directly west of Ireland at about 1800 miles. These isles were called "The Seven Cities"—which was the name of a legendary Portuguese refuge across the Atlantic Ocean. The latitude of these isles (shown on the top map—above) suggests that they represent the Newfoundland archipelago or islands in the Gulf of St. Lawrence. This was the site of 15th-century Portuguese-Danish explorations and 16th-century Portuguese-Basque fishing colonies. As this region was also an objective of Bristol merchants in the 15th century, the Paris Map can be regarded as evidence that some English or Portuguese sailors succeeded in making reaching their objective. Presumably, there was no declaration of discovering a "New World" for the simple reason that the maritime region was already well-known to fishermen and fur traders. The map, which is sometimes attributed to Columbus, reveals a combination of Portuguese and Genoese influence that might be expected of chart-maker Cristobol Colon.

The second map is the northern section of a Portuguese nautical chart of the same region of the North Atlantic—showing the same isles in better detail and clarity. By 1459, it is apparent that the "Seven Cities" of the Paris map actually represent the Newfoundland archipelago—here situated at about 2,000 miles west of Ireland.

210

nearly a century before the Portuguese sailed to India. The map—bearing a date of 1408—was in the possession of Prince Fernando. Modern scholars believe this map might have come from the collection of Marco Polo (Kerr & Eden, 1811, 46). Henry the Navigator also had an early world map showing the southern tip of South America:

> In the year 1428, Don Pedro, the king's eldest son who was a great traveler, went into England, France, and Germany, and thence into the Holy Land and other places, and came home by Italy through Rome and Venice. He is said to have brought a map of the world home with him, in which all parts of the earth were described, by which the enterprises of Don Henry for the discovery were much assisted. In this map, the Straits of Magellan are called the "Dragons-tail," and the Cape of Good Hope—the "Front of Africa" and so of the rest. (Kerr & Eden, 1811, 46)

From these reports of ancient maps, Antonio Galvano was moved to declare that "it appears that there was as much discovered, or more, in ancient times as now" (Kerr & Eden, 1811, 46).

Martin Alonzo Pinzon who sailed with Columbus in 1492 claimed that he had seen a map in the pope's library at the Vatican which showed the continent across the Atlantic. The map could well have been a copy of Toscanelli's 1557 planisphere which was originally sent to the king of Portugal. The Spanish historian Pigafetta noted that King Manuel of Portugal showed Magellan a map by Martin Behaim in 1517 showing the tip of South America and the passage or strait between South America and Antarctica. This is intriguing since Magellan didn't sail on his supposed voyage of discovery until two years later—and Behaim had passed away in 1507. Harrisse (1892, 438) assumed that Behaim simply guessed that there was such a strait: "Behaim doubtless traced, hypothetically, the celebrated strait which Magellan was destined to discover thirteen years later." On the other hand, secret navigators—or ancient maps—could have provided Behaim with the scoop on the Horn of South America and the strait north of Antarctica. Indeed, this strait is indicated on Mustafi's Arabic map in schematic form; it also appears on Roselli's map of 1508.

Francisco Roselli's world map of 1508 has a well-delineated Antarctica shown above the South Pole, and Johan Schoner's globe of 1515 portrayed the Antarctic Isle (called Brasilia Regio) at the tip of South America. Historians have placed discovery of Antarctica at 1818 (Mallery, 1979, 204). However, sections of the continent are present on Roselli's map of 1508, Homem's map of 1513, and the Peri Reis map of 1513. These pre-Magellan portrayals of Antarctica offer confirmation for Portuguese claims that their navigators were aware of the existence of Terra del Fuego (Land of Storms, Fire, or Cold) south of Magellan's route through South America. The modern name for the passage is Magellan's Strait; it was known to Portuguese geographers as "Dragon's Tail" (Fernandez-Armesto, 1991, 77). This name could be a legacy of Arabic geographers who referred to a land in the western Atlantic as "The Dragon's Isle"—perhaps referring to the sovereignty of Asian monarchs (in Cambodia and China) who were known as "Dragon Kings." In China's ancient Shan Hai Ching geography, a map of the overseas continents of North and South America (a.k.a. Fu-Sang) had the shape of a huge dragon encircling the Old World.

Another highly accurate map is Lopo Homem's World Map of 1517. This map which preceded Magellan's voyage by two years shows the

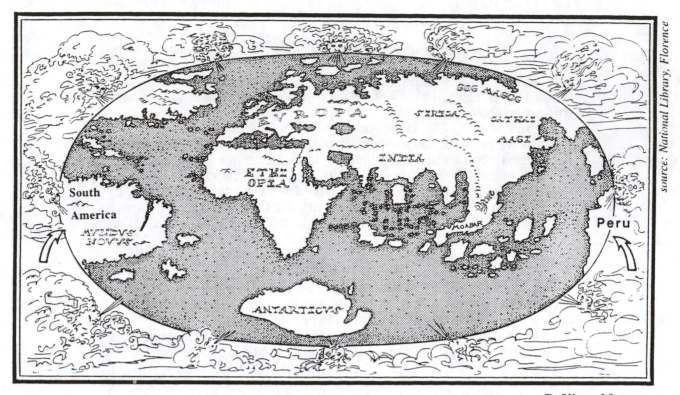

Ancient Lands—Francesco Roselli, 1508

This remarkable map confirms Portuguese claims that royalty had access to maps based on ancient sources. South of Africa is Antarctica—a land that orthodox historians assume was unknown until the 19th century. The map shows an accurate coastline for Peru and Ecuador on a section of South America placed east of Asia. This predates both Magellan's 1520 voyage and Pizarro's 1531 invasion of Peru. The west coast of South America on this map is in a similar position to the coast of Ca-paru—the isle southeast of Asia on the Venetian Commercial map of 1414.

**DeVirga Map
Venice, 1414**

Ca-paru

Lopo Homem's Ancient Lands

Homem's 1519 map predates the 1520 voyage of Magellan and probably influenced his ill-fated attempt to sail around the world. It shows the eastern extremity of the Indian Ocean (later called the Pacific Ocean—**P**) as a relatively short expanse of sea. The narrow passage (**M**) through the Mundus Novus (South America) is where Magellan expected to reach the Indian Ocean. In other words, this passage (later called "Magellan' Strait") was already on the map before he sailed.

The coast of Antarctica is shown below Africa. Southeast of India (or Asia) is Cattigara (**C**)—the province of Peru on Roman maps. The west coast of South America on this map predates the Spanish conquest of Peru in 1531. Southwest of Cattigara is Terra del Fuego (**F**)—the southern extremity of South America.

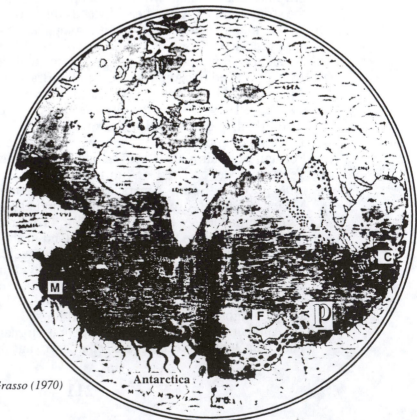

212

source: Ibarra Grasso (1970)

world as it was conceived by Portuguese authorities at a much earlier time. The map already shows the strait which Magellan supposedly explored for the first time in 1520, and it shows Antarctica—which supposedly wasn't discovered until the 18th century. Homem resided in Lisbon where he was known as the king's "Master of Sea Charts."

There is no evidence either from historical accounts or cartography that Portugal conducted a comprehensive survey of the western Atlantic prior to the time of Columbus. Nevertheless, Portuguese cosmographers combined information from Franciscan gazetteers of the 14th century with the most recent accounts of westward voyagers. They also incorporated charts from ancient Roman and Persian sources when these aided in their understanding of overseas territories.

The most important function of Portuguese expeditions into the western Atlantic Ocean during the early 15th century seems to have been the calculation of accurate distances between Europe and the western continents at various latitudes. These served to correct the distortions in the Franciscan survey that had resulted from the lack of common reference points between the Eastern and Western hemispheres. Transoceanic expeditions were necessary to correct the distortions in Franciscan gazetteers due to the lack of accurate timepieces (or chronometers) which enabled the comparison of time between point of departure and point of arrival. Accurate calculation of time intervals was essential to determine longitude of distant shores.

The Franciscan gazetteers were used partially because of their reliability and partially because of their accessibility. Close relationships between English and Portuguese royalty suggest that King John and Prince Henry had access to the latest revisions of the Inventio Fortunatae.

Besides sharing similar concepts regarding the configuration of western Atlantic continents, several key cartographers had personal ties to Portuguese nobility and ultimately to the earliest Franciscan surveyor—Nicholas of Lynn. The mother of King Edward III of England (the king who initiated the Franciscan survey) was of Portuguese ancestry. Edward's father-in-law was Portugal's King Alfonso IV. Edward's granddaughter, through his son John of Gaunt, was wedded to Portugal's King John; she was the mother of Prince Henry the Navigator. Nicholas of Lynn was also a confidant of John of Gaunt and is said to have given the English prince an astrolabe (Holand, 1959). Thus John's grandson, Prince Henry The Navigator, was only one generation removed from the royal favorite—friar Nicholas. Doubtless, he had heard the tales of the friar's journeys across the North Atlantic.

Other Franciscans played long-forgotten roles in the chain of folklore and manuscript maps which transmitted knowledge of the North Atlantic to succeeding generations. R.A. Skelton (1965) identified the anonymous scribe who drafted the Vinland Map of 1440 as a Swiss Franciscan. If this is an accurate identification, the unknown cartographer was indirectly connected to the network of English friars who were knowledgeable about the Franciscan gazetteers. Besides giving a fairly-accurate portrayal of Greenland and Vinilanda (northeastern North America), his map contains one of the earliest portrayals of the East Coast between Florida and Newfoundland. The encouragement that Columbus gained from the Franciscans at La Rabida in 1485 might have been due in part to the common knowledge among brothers of the order concerning prior evangelical missions and mapping in the North Atlantic.

East Asian Coastlines

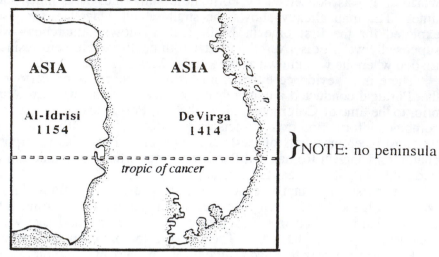

ASIA

Al-Idrisi
1154

ASIA

DeVirga
1414

}NOTE: no peninsula

tropic of cancer

Florida & Medieval Coast of Asia

Medieval wheel maps typically showed the East Asian seacoast as a relatively smooth, curved land—sometimes surmounted by a fortress representing paradise. The prominent exception was Al-Idrisi's 1154 wall map (and the miniature plate of similar design) which has a small peninsula at the Tropic of Cancer. This peninsula represents the port of Canton. Compass charts came into vogue towards the beginning of the 14th century. These circular world maps were precursors of modern maps. Marino Sanudo's map of 1320 (and similar maps by Pietro Vesconte) portray an irregular coast facing the encircling ocean. Sanudo's map has a southeastward facing peninsula with islands above a huge gulf. This might represent the earliest attempt to portray Florida and the Gulf of Mexico, however it is too high up the coast (at 45°) to fit the expected latitude of Florida (tip near the Tropic of Cancer at 27°).

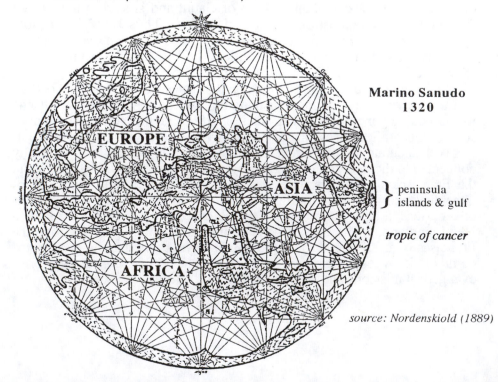

**Marino Sanudo
1320**

EUROPE

ASIA

} peninsula
islands & gulf

tropic of cancer

AFRICA

214

source: Nordenskiold (1889)

Several important cartographers of the 15th century belonged to the "inner circle" of Portuguese royalists who were familiar with the overseas continents. The Venetian Fra Mauro worked under a commission from Prince Henry; he also had the aid of the famous cartographer Andrea Bianco (Skelton, et al., 1965, 125). The Italian cartographer Paolo Toscanelli corresponded with Fernao Martins (the Portuguese minister for King Alfonso V) and also with Columbus. Martin Behaim worked as a Lisbon globemaker and as a navigator for secret Portuguese expeditions into the western Atlantic; and he was probably an associate of Columbus. Henricus Martellus was a close associate of Behaim.

Within this network of cosmographers, royalty, and explorers, there seems to have been a steady exchange of information about the emerging character of lands across the Atlantic. These were real lands of continental proportions—not abstract, imaginary isles of no substance as 19th-century historians have led us to believe. The cosmographers were not all in agreement regarding the location of Cathay; but they all knew the general configuration of the opposite shore; and they knew the approximate distance across the ocean.

Orthodox historians often recite a litany that Portuguese ships sailed west and supposedly returned "without sighting land." On the occasion that they might have sighted land, we are often led to believe that the sailors didn't bother going ashore; and if they happened to land, they didn't have any significant impact on the natives. Supposedly, any lands indicated on 15th-century maps could only represent "fictitious isles floating in the mist of imagination."

On the contrary, if the Portuguese had been such reliable failures as orthodox historians contend, then Europeans would not have had such accurate maps—nor would Columbus have been in the position to declare that he had a map that gave an accurate description of his intended destination and the intervening seas. Furthermore, King John II of Portugal would not have known in advance where to draw the line in his Treaty of Tordesillas, nor would he have been able to advise Columbus in 1493 to look for a continent situated below Hispaniola. It is hardly coincidental that Columbus found such a continent on his voyage of 1498.

In previous chapters, we have followed the journey of friar Nicholas to forested lands west of Greenland, to European colonies, and on to the land of brazilwood trees. Along the way, he passed by a large peninsula (Florida), crossed the Gulf of Mexico, and visited Brazil. The most pronounced features of the lands he passed by are included on the northern section of the Venetian Map of 1414, and they are repeated on subsequent maps by Franciscans and Italian cartographers under contract to Portugal. These features included Hudson Bay, Norveca, Newfoundland, Florida, The Gulf of Mexico, and Brazil.

The Florida peninsula with its adjacent isles—the Antilles—is one of the most pronounced features of the Venetian Map. By rotating the Norveca section of the map to the east (right) that North becomes East, the peninsula of Norveca with its three isles points in a southeasterly direction and has an appearance much like the so-called "horn of Asia" that Ravenstein (1908) noted on Behaim's globe and on maps by Henricus Martellus Germanus 1489-90. We must keep in mind that cartographers commonly placed above Europe and Asia those isles and lands that were situated across the seas to the northeast or northwest. Distortions occurred in polar regions on those maps because cartographers attempted to show within a circular area lands that actually occupied two

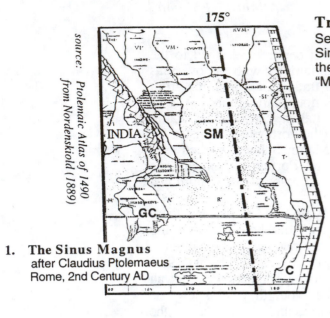

INDIA

SM

GC

C

1. The Sinus Magnus
after Claudius Ptolemaeus
Rome, 2nd Century AD

Transformation of the "Lost" Pacific Ocean

Sequential maps show European concept of the Roman Sinus Magnus expanding to become the Pacific Ocean; while the eastern region of Cattigara expands to become the "Mundus Novus" of Amerigo Vespucci or South America.

1. **Ptolemaic Map (1490)** shows Roman concept of the Pacific or Sinus Magnus (SM) east of the Golden Chersonese (GC) or Indochina. Cattigara (C) represented a merchant city in Peru.

2. **Florentine Planisphere (1447)** shows New world continents attached to the Old World at the previous border of Roman Map at 175°.

3. **Francisco Basso Map (1571)** shows the Sinus Magnus (SM) expanded to form the Pacific Ocean; while the vague, New World continents of the Florentine Planisphere have transformed into the Americas. Cattigara (C) is now on the west coast of Peru. Magellan and Bartholomew Colon identified the Sinus Magnus as the Pacific Ocean.

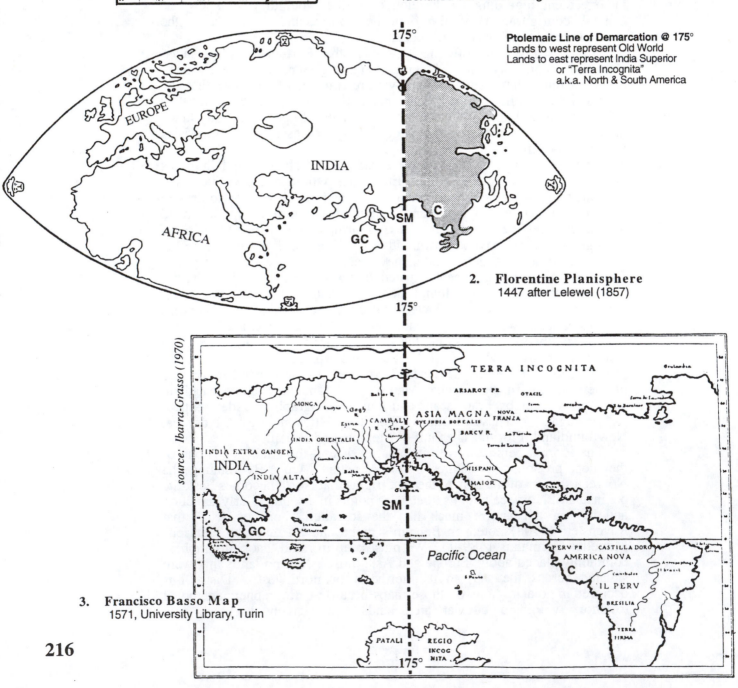

175°

Ptolemaic Line of Demarcation @ 175°
Lands to west represent Old World
Lands to east represent India Superior
or "Terra Incognita"
a.k.a. North & South America

EUROPE

INDIA

AFRICA

SM

GC

C

2. Florentine Planisphere
1447 after Lelewel (1857)

175°

TERRA INCOGNITA

MONGA

CAMBALV

ASIA MAGNA

NOVA FRANZA

INDIA ORIENTALIS

ARSAROT PR

OTACIL

OVE INDIA BORELIS

BARCV R.

INDIA EXTRA GANGEM

INDIA

INDIA ALTA

HISPANIA

MAIOR

SM

GC

Pacific Ocean

PERV PR

CASTILLA DORO

AMERICA NOVA

C

IL PERV

BRESILIA

TERRA FIRMA

PATALI

REGIO INKOG NITA

3. Francisco Basso Map
1571, University Library, Turin

216

175°

hemispheres. The problems inherent in showing polar regions on maps were compounded because it is in this geographical area that Earth's meridians converge and magnetic declination plays its greatest tricks.

From the perspective of the Norveca map turned on its side, the peninsula (Florida) faces southeast; it has three large islands (the Antilles); it is situated above a huge gulf (the Gulf of Mexico); and below it to the south is continental land (South America). This representation of New World lands has all the primary characteristics associated with the East Coast of the United States with Florida projecting toward the southeast. Due to the fact that DeVirga had to locate lands on the Western Hemisphere above Europe, we have no way of telling at what latitude the Norveca peninsula should be located—nor are there any latitudes or meridians on the map to assist in establishing accurate geographical coordinates for the peninsula. The fact that the peninsula and isles occupy a place on the map associated with geographic North may be regarded as a coincidence of distortion and not any suggestion that their climate was frigid or that they were actually located near the Geographic North Pole. Indeed, the design of this map—with tropical lands featured in the polar region—is one explanation why some Renaissance scholars (including Roger Bacon) believed there were temperate lands near the North Pole.

The Vinland map (ca. 1440) was bound with a Franciscan's treatise, the Tartary Relation. This book tells the story of a Franciscan missionary—Giovanni de Plano Carpini—who undertook an overland journey to Tartary in 1215. He returned in 1247. The Vinland map has an inscription telling that it was made to illustrate the Mirror of History written by a contemporary of Giovanni's. Scholars who have studied the Vinland map believe that it was compiled from several other charts made sometime between 1250 and 1440. This time period coincides with the travels of another Franciscan, Nicholas of Lynn, and it spans the time when Franciscans were engaged in mapping the North Atlantic.

During this era of unseasonably warm temperatures in the North Atlantic (9th-14th centuries), travel was presumably much easier as the bays were then more free of ice. Food was easier to find, and larger areas of the isles were cloaked with vegetation—hence the name "Greenland" for an isle that is more commonly covered with ice and virtually uninhabited. It might have been possible—given these favorable conditions—for a Franciscan surveyor to circumnavigate Greenland and produce a relatively accurate portrayal of the island's coastline. A similar outline for Greenland appears northwest of Norway on the Andrea Bianco map of 1436. In both cases, the placement and outline of Greenland reveal that they were charted using geographic as opposed to magnetic coordinates. This confirms that someone trained in use of the astrolabe was responsible for their delineation. It is also possible that the Greenland Island shown on Yale's Vinland Map is intended to show Baffin Island.

When R.A. Skelton and his associates examined the Vinland map in 1958, they were struck by several peculiarities. Besides the insular portrayal of Greenland and the accurate outline of Vinilanda, the coast of Asia was in Skelton's words "unprecedented" in its truncated shape. "There was," he said, "no counterpart in any known cartographic chart" (Skelton, 1965, 120). He assumed that the shoreline was derived from some unknown literary source as there was no relationship to contemporary beliefs regarding the coast of China. A typical Asian coast in Medieval mappamonds had an Isle of Paradise situated along the border

217

of a smoothly-curving continent. However, the Yale Vinland map shows a vertical east coast that ends in a peninsula pointing toward the southeast. This peninsula—most likely derived from a Franciscan gazetteer—represents Florida. Across the gulf below is an extension of Africa with the legend: "Imperia Basera." On 11th-century Arabic maps, this region of Africa has been identified as "Waq-Waq" or South America. This was a geographical contrivance that sought to compromise between conflicting field reports and the realization that a huge continent (the Antipodes) could be reached by sailing west from Africa below the equator. In this case, Basera can be regarded as an Arabic or Persian variation of Brazil.

An elliptical map that Joachim Lelewel (1857) identified as a "Florentine planisphere" (circa 1447) has the Classic form of a tripartite India in which the third India to the west represents the Americas. The map is based on the world as it was conceptualized by Marino de Tyre who believed that the inhabited part of the globe was substantially larger than the estimate given by Ptolemy. Marino also thought the Pacific Ocean (Sinus Magnus) was substantially larger—by about 45°, although that great expanse is barely apparent from the planisphere. In this configuration, the first section is India, the second—Indochina and the Golden Chersonesus, and the third represents North and South America in their most embryonic form—here attached to east Asia.

The Florentine Planisphere calls the northern section of the Third India "Magog"—for a region of barbarians; the southern section is called Cathay (for China). The apparent "Asian" coastline is a fair approximation of the east coast of North and South America with a large gulf (the Gulf of Mexico) separating the upper and lower continental areas. This gulf is somewhat distorted: it is a bit too narrow and it seems a bit too high for the Gulf of Mexico. Nevertheless, the similarity of the coast on the map to the approximate shape of the east coast of the Americas is striking. A peninsula at the southeast corner facing the Atlantic ocean continues the tradition of Florida (a.k.a., the "horn of Asia") seen in the Norveca map and the Vinland map of 1440. We see in this map an attempt to reconcile ancient mapping traditions with more recent mariners' reports and gazetteers. The map is dated to 1447 and thus precedes by ten years a similar map which is often referred to as the Genoese Planisphere (or simply the Genoese Map of 1457).

Both 1447 and 1457 planispheres identify the northern land as a vast wilderness—the forest of Gog-Magog. Neither map gives any indication that this northern area is occupied by a civilization—thus it conforms in character to Icelandic sagas about the forested land of Markland or Greenland. It is definitely not Marco Polo's Cathay. Peninsulas near the top of the northeast coast correspond to Labrador and Nova Scotia.

The southern section on the planispheres represents India Patala with China (Catagum) situated alongside the Sinus Magnus. Here, civilization reigns—for the maps feature legends and symbols of royalty. By showing China adjacent to the Sinus Magnus, cartographers sought to reconcile Marco Polo's claim that China was situated on the Eastern Ocean; while at the same time mariners insisted that the northern land was a vast wilderness. Explorers who sailed past the northern wilderness might have hoped to find Polo's Cathay by heading farther south across the narrow gulf—just as Columbus, Cabot, and Vespucci expressed hopes of finding China in that direction.

Portuguese sovereigns believed that the Florentine and Genoese planispheres provided sufficient grounds for sailing east around the tip of

Africa in their bid to reach the Spice Island trade via Calicut, India. They had already determined through substantial Atlantic exploration that the only feasible route to the spice trade was in that direction. According to the 1452 <u>Chronicle of Guinea</u>, Prince Henry entertained navigators from Greater and Lesser India at Sagres (Newton, 1930, 203). Testimonials from mariners and geographers were sufficient to ascertain that Cathay was situated beside an ocean; they were also sufficient to confirm that Cathay was not located across the Atlantic. Somewhere on Earth, Cathay would be found alongside a missing ocean. It wasn't until the voyages of Balboa, Albuquerque, and Magellan in the 16th century that European geographers began to fathom the whereabouts of the lost Pacific. It didn't help matters that Moslem and Hindu geographers referred to all the waters between the Persian Gulf and South America across the Pacific as "the Indian Ocean." On the planispheres, the missing Pacific was represented by the tiny <u>Sinus Magnus</u>—or "Great Gulf."

Some historians believe the Florentine physician, Paolo Toscanelli, sent a copy of the 1457 Genoese Planisphere to King Alfonse V in 1474 and a similar one to Columbus in 1481. It is apparent from this type of planisphere that Portuguese explorations of the Atlantic—though only vaguely reported in extant documents—were sufficient to delineate the east coast of North and South America. It was on the basis of these voyages that Paolo Toscanelli was able to accurately estimate the distance between the Canary Islands and the isles of the Caribbean at about 3,000 nautical miles. Orthodox historians have assumed that Toscanelli's estimate was the result of a mistaken calculation due to his misreading an Arabic geography. It seems more likely that the Arabic calculation was derived to suit existing knowledge about the size of the Atlantic.

The Franciscan Tradition of Atlantic Isles

Late in the 15th century, cosmographers in Lisbon, Portugal, constructed globes and maps showing the Atlantic and its bordering continents in accordance with the latest surveys and accounts of expeditions. Among those engaged in Lisbon's nautical junta was Martin Behaim (1459-1506), an expatriate from Nuremberg, Germany. His globe of 1490-92 and maps by his close associate Henricus Martellus Germanus circa 1489 are very similar. Their version of the shape of the western Atlantic continents was to some extent based on 14th-century Franciscan surveys and the gazetteers of friar Nicholas.

Martellus and Behaim estimated the distance across the Atlantic between Europe and Asia (or India) at about 4,500 miles; the distance between the Canary Isles in the east and Cipangu in the west was calculated at about 3,000. These "estimates," which must have been influenced by accounts from many Portuguese explorations into the western Atlantic, were fairly accurate. They were also in surprising agreement with the estimated 5,000-mile gap between Europe and Cathay which Roger Bacon and Paolo Toscanelli gave for the expanse of the Atlantic. Toscanelli justified his calculation of the distance by referring to an astronomical measurement called the "short degree." A Medieval Arabian cosmographer, Al-Farghani, had underestimated the distance of an equatorial degree at approximately 57 Arabic miles (Dor-Ner, 1991, 81). When Toscanelli made his calculations using the even shorter length of a Roman mile, the equatorial distance of a degree was set at 45 miles— or 15 miles per-degree less than the actual distance (hence the "short" degree). The net result was that all three cosmographers under-calculated the size of Earth by about 25%. The virtue of this so-called "theoretical calculation" was that it provided a scholarly rationale for the already known distance across the Atlantic.

A Franciscan heritage is apparent from the general shape given to the western Atlantic continents (i.e., India Tercer). Although Behaim did not specifically credit either Franciscans or Nicholas of Lynn as one of his sources, he certainly had access to English Franciscan gazetteers of the North Atlantic while serving as a cartographer and navigator for Portuguese royalty. The shape of the southeast Asian peninsula on the Martellus maps (variously called the Indian Peninsula or the "horn" of Asia) is strikingly similar to the Norveca Peninsula on the Venetian Commercial Map of 1414. We have attributed the earliest configuration of this peninsula to the 14th-century Franciscan survey of the North Atlantic.

It seems that Portuguese cartographers assumed the validity of the Franciscan survey, and they realized that the map coordinates referred to continental lands across the Atlantic as opposed to lands situated only in the Northern Regions. Therefore, the coastline was dropped down from the Arctic (where it appears on the Venetian Map) towards the equator so that it runs on a vertical axis in the approximate position of the East Coast of North America. The close similarity of the southeastern peninsula on the Martellus map and the Venetian Map reveal that the Franciscan version of the western lands was essentially reoriented—as opposed to re-surveyed. Over the passing decades (1414 to 1490), the position of the peninsula was gradually moved on maps from a northwest location toward the southeast. The movement was incremental and deliberate—precisely what we would expect from cartographers adjusting their maps over time to correspond with the increasing accuracy of navigators' observations.

Most Europeans held the opinion that lands across the Atlantic corresponded to the coast of India Superior—as reported by Classical writers such as Pliny The Elder. Most thought Marco Polo's Cathay was situated directly across from Europe. However, Portuguese geographers were not in agreement with "most" Europeans. The German Martellus held the popular view; his associate Behaim disagreed.

Behaim—a Lisbon globe-maker and royal navigator—had access to the latest Portuguese expeditionary reports. He believed that the continent across from Europe was a forested wilderness—much in the tradition of the Norse Markland. He called this wilderness "Tartary." Behaim placed Cathay far to the southwest above the Sinus Magnus (later identified as the Pacific Ocean). At least, that is where it is located on the Doppelmayer facsimile of Behaim's 1492 Erdapfl globe. This represents a fairly-accurate placement considering that Europeans had not yet determined the immense size of the Pacific. Later copyists of Behaim's globe apparently decided on their own that Cathay should be situated along the Atlantic coast of the northern land, and this is where it appears on Ravenstein's 1908 surrogate globe. Since many historians have relied on the 1908 surrogate, they have mistakenly assumed that Behaim was no more knowledgeable about the true location of Cathay than were most of his contemporaries. Obviously, that conclusion is inaccurate.

Both Behaim and Martellus abandoned the archaic mid-Atlantic isle of Antilia in favor of a single isle east of the Florida peninsula. In effect, they assumed that Antilia was synonymous with Polo's Cipangu (Japan). This decision—far from being arbitrary—was probably based on the failure of Portuguese ships sailing a considerable distance across the mid-

Atlantic to find any significant isles west of the Azores. However, some of Behaim's later copyists (including Ravenstein) inserted an isle for Antilia in the mid-Atlantic thereby giving the false impression that Behaim thought there were two separate isles (Nordenskiold, 1889).

As soon as Portuguese mariners established the approximate location of Antilia (Cuba) at about 3,000 miles west of the Canaries on the Tropic of Cancer, cartographers placed the western mainland about 1,500 miles farther west on their maps in accordance with the distance given in <u>Marco Polo's Travels</u> for the distance between China and Japan.

The southern continent, India Patalis, drops off towards the southwest on the Martellus and Behaim versions of the Atlantic. This distorts the size and appearance of the gulf separating the northern and southern continents; and it creates the impression that Patala (South America) is not situated directly south of the Antilles. It seems that this error occurred due to the fact that Portuguese expeditions did not find land immediately south of the Antilles where it was first expected. Portuguese voyages up to 1490 had only confirmed the distance to the shores of the northern continent, the southeastern peninsula (Florida), and Antilia—which is why they are accurately portrayed on Behaim's globe. Indeed, Behaim's southeastern peninsula reaches down to the Tropic of Cancer—which is very close to the actual latitude of Florida; as for longitude, Behaim's southeastern peninsula is only about 1,000 miles too far west from the actual longitude of Florida. This level of precision was not achieved by subsequent cartographers until Mercator's map of 1569.

Sometime between 1490 and 1493, Portuguese vessels in the western Atlantic succeeded in locating the northern coast of South America. These expeditions (coming right before or during the Columbus voyage in 1492) explain why King John II of Portugal admonished the Spanish mariner to look for continental land directly south of the Antilles. It further explains why Portugal demanded the concession of access to lands 370 leagues west of the Cape Verde Islands in the Treaty of Tordesillas in 1494. This treaty gave Portugal access to Brazil. Columbus stated in his ship's log on the way to Venezuela in 1498 that he sought to confirm the king of Portugal's belief that a continent was situated south of the Antilles. In a journal entry of 1498, Columbus says that he sailed south to determine "what had been the intention of Don Joao II of Portugal who had said that to the south (of Hispaniola) there was mainland" (Randles, 1990, 58).

The Columbus Map

It is well known that Columbus brought copies of the latest navigational charts of the Atlantic along on his epic voyage. Although the mariner's 1492 Atlantic map has not survived, historians are fairly confident that they know what it looked like. It was probably quite similar to the latest versions of Atlantic charts currently being produced in Lisbon—the same city where Columbus had worked as a cartographer.

The map was probably a composite from ancient travelogs and recent surveys. Marco Polo had given a glowing account of Japan—an isle of golden pagodas situated about 1,500 miles east of Cathay. He also praised the Indies Islands (or Spice Islands) which included an island of gold called "Iocathe" that was located several hundred miles east of Java. This isle was inhabited by pagan natives who were armed only with spears and arrows. Toscanelli's planisphere placed Java on the Tropic of Cancer. Behaim's globe had Japan at the same latitude. It is easy to see why Columbus was inspired to sail west: the route across the Atlantic to

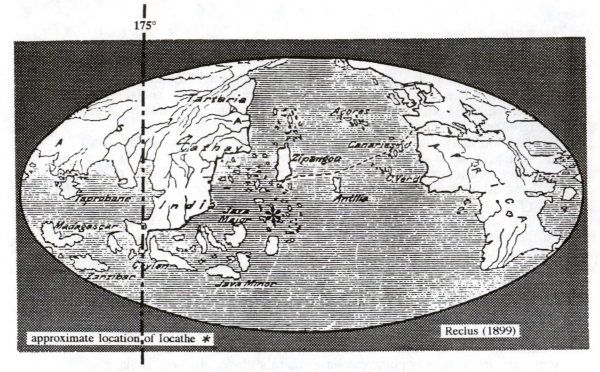

175°

approximate location of Iocathe *

Reclus (1899)

Columbus Map—Enterprise of The Indies

These are two hypothetical versions of maps Columbus might have used to sell his idea of finding a shortcut to the Indies Islands—a.k.a. the Spice Islands. He called this his "Enterprise of The Indies;" the goal was to sail west across the Atlantic to the Spice Islands south of Japan—a.k.a. "Cipangu." An alternative objective suggested by Marco Polo was an isle called "Iocathe" (*above). This isle was supposed to be situated several hundred miles east of Java; it was rich in gold and poorly defended.

Historians attribute this kind of map to Paolo Toscanelli who is said to have corresponded with Columbus in 1474; however, they are not unlike maps that chart-maker Columbus would have seen in Lisbon as late as 1490; and they have a lot in common with maps by Lisbon cartographers Henricus Martellus and Martin Behaim who were likely Columbus associates.

The Columbus map showed mainland (North America) at the right distance from Europe—about 3,000 miles. It showed the Antilles at the right location near the Tropic of Cancer. Lacking is South America which the Portuguese had not yet completely charted. The fact that Columbus declared in his ship's log that he had found land where he expected it to be located attests to the accuracy of his charts. Indeed, these charts represented the culmination of more than a century of English and Portuguese expeditions into the Atlantic Ocean.

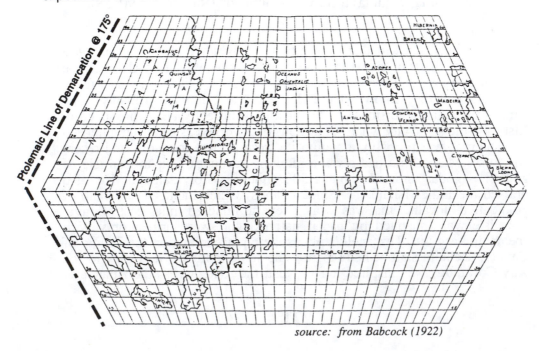

source: from Babcock (1922)

some exotic isle—be it Japan, Java, Antilia, or the Indies Islands was a mere 2,400 miles. Any ship sailing due west from the Canary Islands was bound to run smack into a land of gold. Thus, Columbus conceived of his "Enterprise of The Indies" as a voyage to the wealthy and poorly defended isles of the Far East.

Historian Arthur Newton noted the striking similarity between the geographical ideas of Columbus and those of Martin Behaim:

> We are uncertain of the geographical ideas of Columbus before 1492, but there is no doubt about those of Behaim, for they are fully set forth upon his globe. The two men were certainly in Lisbon at the same time and mixing in the same circles, and it is highly probable that they met. Bartholomew Colon must certainly have known Behaim, for he remained in Lisbon longer than his brother and was probably there as late as 1488. There is an extraordinary similarity between the erroneous geographical ideas of Behaim, as set out upon his globe of 1492, and those of Columbus which he expounded fully in 1498 but undoubtedly held earlier. It is impossible to say whether they were independent or which had the priority, but the essential feature of both was the idea of the comparative narrowness of the Ocean Sea and the possibility of reaching the Far East by sailing to the west. (Newton, 1932, 91).

The accuracy of the map that Columbus used on his voyage in 1492 was not coincidental. Most historians believe that Spain's aspiring admiral had a map that was similar in most respects to the geographical concepts embodied in Behaim's globe and the maps of Martellus. Indeed, the route Columbus chose to sail across the Atlantic can be plotted on Behaim's globe based on the ship's log from the Santa Maria, and the resulting track leads directly from the Canaries to the isle of Cipangu/Antilia (Garrett, 1986). Columbus found land where he expected it to be, and he attributed that success to the accuracy of his maps. Had he doubted their validity or reliability, he probably wouldn't have risked his life on the Atlantic crossing. His faith in those charts was confirmed repeatedly during subsequent voyages. Historian Zvi Dor-Ner (1991, 83) observed that:

> The twenty-inch globe constructed at Nuremberg by Martin Behaim represented the last, best attempt at understanding the distributions of land and water on the earth before Columbus set out upon his enterprise. Behaim's globe, in fact, showed the world as Columbus believed it to be.

Although other regions on maps by Martellus and Behaim were deficient, the relative accuracy of lands bordering the Atlantic resulted from the successive improvements made on charts produced by recent expeditions. Portuguese authorities tried to keep secret the results of those voyages, but copies of sea charts were smuggled to the mercantile and mapping centers of Genoa, Florence, and Venice. The result was that reasonably accurate maps were available to most European sailors.

Both Behaim and Martellus showed the northern continent with a southwestward projecting peninsula corresponding to Florida. They identified the peninsula as part of India Superior. This same peninsula was shown on Toscanelli's map—but it was too far north—at the latitude of central Spain or about 40°. Behaim and Martellus brought the peninsula down to the correct latitude just north of the Tropic of Cancer—practically due west of the Canary Isles. When Columbus landed on Cuba, he believed he had reached this peninsula of India Superior—thus he believed he had reached his destination of the Indies.

Toscanelli's estimate of 3,000 miles for the distance across the Atlantic is particularly amazing as it was right on the mark. Columbus estimated the distance before he sailed at about 2,400; then he sailed an additional 400 miles before reaching a small isle east of Florida. After cruising another 100 miles southwest, his ships finally reached the shores of Cuba. The total distance of the voyage—about 3,000 miles—was precisely what Toscanelli had predicted. Columbus noted in his log that he had found land precisely where he expected to reach Cipangu (Japan or Antilia); he also noted that this expectation was due to the fact that this was the location where land was shown on maps and globes he had seen. It says in the Columbus log that when he reached Cuba: he took a reading of the heavens with his astrolabe and declared that "On the maps and globes I have seen, Cipangu is located in these regions" (Garrett, 1986).

Historians find great mirth in Admiral Christopher's conviction that he found Cipangu (a.k.a., Antilia) in the West Indies—when the "real" Cipangu (Japan) was on the opposite side of the globe. However, it was not Columbus but Portuguese geographers who had confused the widely-separated isles (Japan and Antilia); the Spanish mariner simply verified his location by the accuracy of his charts. The names given to the land areas were erroneous, but the relative positions of the isle and adjacent mainland must be regarded as fairly accurate. Historian Henry Vignaud (1902, 210) points out that Columbus simply compensated for the erroneous titles used by geographers by giving his own names to the islands:

> From his son we learn that it was Haiti (or Hispaniola) Columbus took for Cipangu. Columbus himself confirms this in the first lines of his will drawn up in 1498; and from a legend on Ruysch's map of 1507 we see that even at so late a period, the belief existed that Haiti was Cipangu. It should be observed that on the map of Bartholomew Colon (discovered by Wieser), a map which joins Asia to South America, and whose first leaf represents the maritime expanse between the western extremities of the Old World and its eastern boundaries, Cipangu does not appear at all—while Hispaniola fills the place it should occupy. . . . When Columbus returned from his first voyage, Ruy de Pina wrote that he had come back from the discovery of Cipangu. It is therefore well-established that Columbus thought he had found Cipangu at the very spot where the letter to Martins, and consequently the map which had accompanied it, declared it to be.

"At the very spot"—Vignaud says of the location of an isle Columbus expected to find. Such a voyage on the seas of reality hardly supports the theory prevalent among orthodox historians that the successful landfall in the Caribbean was an "accident;" nor was the landfall a fortuitous coincidence. Columbus sailed toward a "real" island near the Tropic of Cancer. It was not Columbus but several contemporary geographers who had gotten the name wrong. Some called the isle "Cipangu"—others called it "Antilia"—until Columbus named the isles "Hispaniola" (Haiti) and "Isabella" (Cuba).

In the long run, geographical tradition prevailed: isles of the Caribbean are still known collectively as "The Antilles."

Historian Peter Martyr reviewed details of the Columbus voyage shortly after the mariner's return. He deduced that Columbus had reached isles known to the ancients as Antilia:

> Turning, therefore, the sterns of his ships toward the east, he (Columbus) assumed that he had found Ophir, whither Solomon's ships sailed for gold. But, the descriptions of the cosmographers well-considered, it seems that both these and the other islands adjoining are the islands of Antillia." (Pietro Martyr d'Anghiera, The Decades of The New World or West India, in Babcock, 1922, 145).

Martyr's reference to "descriptions of cosmographers," pertains to accounts of the isles which are no longer extant. On the Cantino map of 1502, the isles found by Columbus (Hispaniola and Isabella) are labeled as Has Antilhas. The map is now in the Biblioteca Estense at Modena (Fiske, 1920, Vol. II, 21). Caneiro's 1502 map names the West Indies islands discovered by Columbus as: Antilhas del Rey de Castella—that is, the "Antiles belonging to the king of Castille." Another Spanish map of 1518 uses the similar designation Antilhas de Castela—"the Antilles of Castile" (Babcock, 1922, 147).

In his treatise on New World voyages Discoveries of The World (1555), Antonio Galvano noted historical reports of a western voyage undertaken by Carthaginian merchants in 590 BC. The lands they reached were called "Antilles"—which Galvano identified as the "New Spain" of Columbus (that is, Cuba and Hispaniola). Galvano also noted that his contemporaries had argued over the existence of the legendary isles: "All those historians who formerly wrote concerning the Antilles, as of doubtful and uncertain existence, now plainly allow them to be the same with New Spain and the West Indies" (Kerr & Eden, 1811, 34). In this not-so-subtle manner, ancient geographical sources remind us that Columbus arrived at islands which had appeared on mariners' charts more than a century before the Columbus voyage of 1492; and they were known since Roman times.

The accuracy of Portuguese maps was not surpassed until the mid-1500's. Indeed, some of the early maps of the Caribbean following the Columbus voyage are actually less accurate than Behaim's 1492 version of the Asian coastline. A map by Benedetto Bordone in 1528 showed Florida reaching down from Labrador, while Cuba was placed directly north of Hispaniola above the Tropic of Cancer. Cuba is actually located south of the Tropic. Even Waldseemuller's map of 1507 has Florida and Cuba situated far north of the Tropic of Cancer—an error of 20°. Thus, Behaim's eastern coastline and peninsula are more accurately portrayed than are Florida and Cuba on many post-Columbian maps of the New World. Not until Mercator's world map of 1569 does the New World really take on a reasonably accurate appearance that finally surpasses the accuracy of Behaim's globe—which was in all likelihood an offspring of the English Franciscan survey.

Florida
on ancient maps

after M. Harrisse (1883); source: Babcock (1922, p. 75)

Atlantic Ocean

← Florida

tropic of cancer

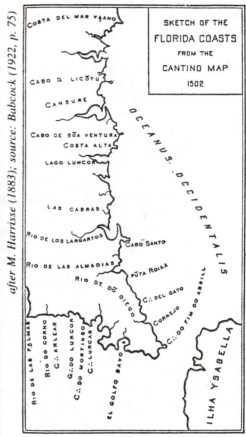

SKETCH OF THE
FLORIDA COASTS
FROM THE
CANTINO MAP
1502

COSTA DEL MAR VSANO

CABO D. LICOTU

CANSURE

CABO DE BOA VENTURA
COSTA ALTA

LAGO LUNCOR

LAS CABRAS

RIO DE LOS LARGARTOS
CABO SANTO

RIO DE LAS ALMADIAS
PUTA ROIXA

RIO DE DO DIEGO
C.: DEL GATO
CORNEJO
C.: DO FIM DO ABRIL

OCEANUS OCCIDENTALIS

RIO DE LAS PALMAS
RIO DO CORNO
C.: ARLEAR
G.: DO LUNCON
C.: DO MORTINHO
C.: LURCAR
EL GOLFO BAVO

ILHA YSABELLA

Terra Florida
Cantino Map of 1502

Early Explorers in Florida

Historians Babcock (1922, 74), Harrisse (1892), and many others have noted that early portrayals of the land area eventually called *Terra Florida* (above, right) were far too accurate to justify claims that the territory was virtually unknown until after Ponce DeLeon officially landed on the coast in 1513. One example of this accuracy can be seen on the Albert Cantino map of 1502 which shows the unnamed peninsula opposite the west coast of Cuba (here called *Ilha Ysabella*). Candidates for early explorers in the region include Nicholas of Lynn (ca. 1330), John and Sebastian Cabot (1480-98), and Amerigo Vespucci (1497).

The principal characteristics of Florida on maps from 1414 to 1492 are the following: 1) a prominent peninsula; 2) projects from mainland in southeasterly direction; 3) situated at the northeast corner of a huge gulf; 4) large islands situated at tip; 5) faces Atlantic Ocean; and 6) tip is located near Tropic of Cancer.

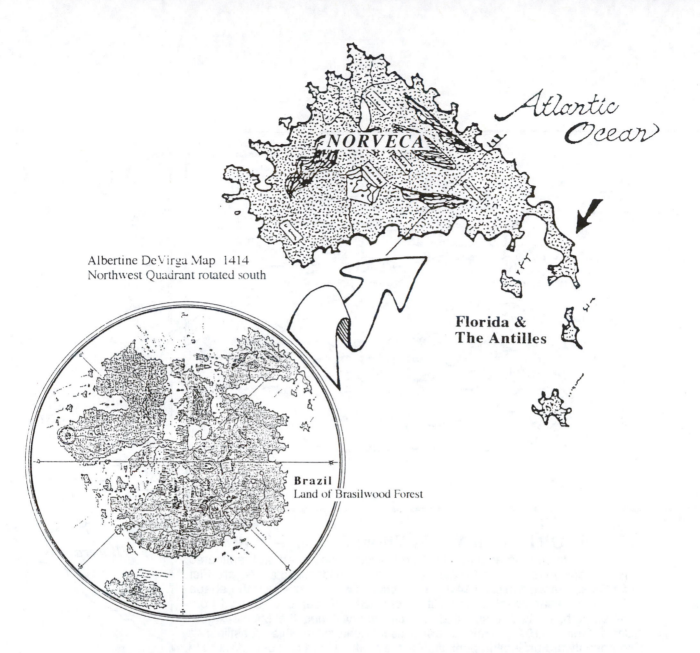

Atlantic Ocean

ˋNORVECAˊ

Albertine DeVirga Map 1414
Northwest Quadrant rotated south

**Florida &
The Antilles**

Brazil
Land of Brasilwood Forest

(A)   FLORIDA on DeVirga's Map—1414 AD

During the Middle Ages, it was customary for Europeans to place isles representing lands across the Atlantic along the northern border of their maps. Sometimes, these overseas land areas were incorporated into the top of Norway, Russia, or China—as in the case of Gottia Orientalis and Albania of the Far East. The map by Albertin DeVirga has a peninsula in the far north attached to the Norveca continent which is identified as North America on the basis of headlands shown along the North Atlantic coast. This peninsula is identified on the basis of its location at the corner of Norveca (North America) above a huge gulf corresponding to the Gulf of Mexico. This peninsula has large islands at the tip—corresponding to the Antilles. Across the gulf is the northeast coast of South America. It is not presumptuous to consider that Europeans traveled this far: according to an account by John Dee, friar Nicholas of Lynn traveled as far as the land of Brasilwood trees—i.e., Brazil (Newton, 1932, 205).

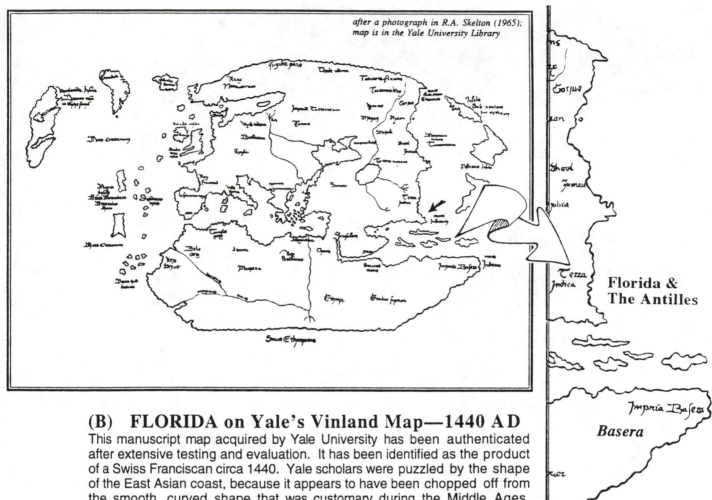

**Florida &
The Antilles**

Basera

(B) FLORIDA on Yale's Vinland Map—1440 A D

This manuscript map acquired by Yale University has been authenticated after extensive testing and evaluation. It has been identified as the product of a Swiss Franciscan circa 1440. Yale scholars were puzzled by the shape of the East Asian coast, because it appears to have been chopped off from the smooth, curved shape that was customary during the Middle Ages. David Quinn (1974) noticed an unusual feature of this coastline: a southeastward projecting peninsula at the southeastern corner of Asia. He called this the "Horn of Asia"—a term which Ravenstein used in his 1908 book (*Martin Behaim*) in reference to a similar Asian peninsula on a map by Henricus Martellus (ca. 1490). However, the unusual coastline of Asia with this protruding "horn" actually represents an early version of the coast of North America. This peninsula, or horn, has all the major geographical characteristics identified for Florida with the exception that it is a bit too high. At approximately 38° it is almost the right height for Korea—however, we know it is not intended to represent Korea because it is located at the southeast corner of the continent. Korea, on the other hand is located midway along the Asian coast.

The map's anonymous creator has identified the land directly south of the "horn" and across the gulf as "Basera"—which is a fairly close equivalent to Brazil. On the Yale map, Basera is connected to the tip of Africa—although this tip projects far east. In this respect, the map can be regarded as an archaic representation of the old Norse concept of Vinland being connected to Africa. This follows a similar map by Andrea Bianco in 1436. This placement leaves Basera across from west Africa—which also happens to be the actual location of Brazil relative to this map.

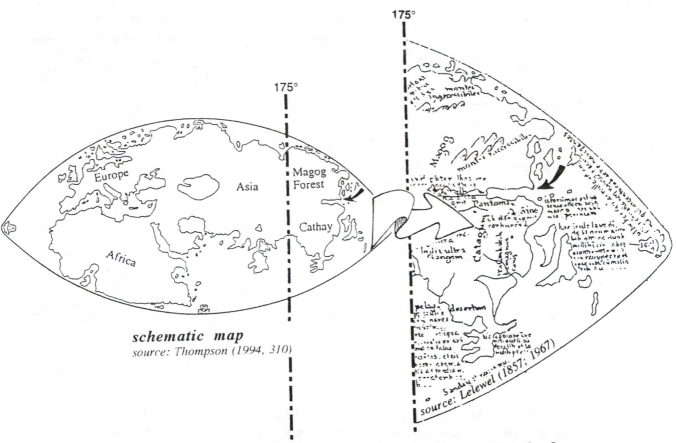

175°

175°

schematic map
source: Thompson (1994, 310)

Europe

Asia

Magog
Forest

Cathay

Africa

source: Lelewel (1857; 1967)

(C) FLORIDA on the Florentine Planisphere —1447 A D

This anonymous map shows an East Asian coastline that approximates North and South America. The only precedents for such a coastline are the map by DeVirga and the Yale Vinland map. The coast is divided midway by a long gulf corresponding to the Gulf of Mexico. Below this gulf is continental land—here referred to as "Cathay." On a similar map by Martin Behaim, the southern land is referred to as Patala or the Third India. This land was subsequently identified by Columbus, Peter Martyr, and Bartholomew Colon as the Antipodes of Classical Legend. Other names for this territory were "Terra Australis" (The Southern Continent) and "Alter Orbis" (The Other World). The northern land, called "Magog," represents a forested wilderness (as can be judged by comparison to the very similar Genoese Map of 1457). This northern land corresponds to the North American wilderness which the Norse called "Markland"—a land of forests. Portrayal of the northern land across from Europe as a forest not only corresponds to physical reality, it reveals that such cosmographers as Toscanelli were skeptical about claims current in Europe that Cathay (China) was situated across the Atlantic. The southeastern peninsula (Florida) is present though in a very compressed form.

Ptolemaic Line of Demarcation @ 175°
Lands to west represent Old World
Lands to east represent India Superior
or "Terra Incognita"
a.k.a. North & South America

229

source: after a portolan in Imago Mundi (Destombes: 1964, Pl. 34)

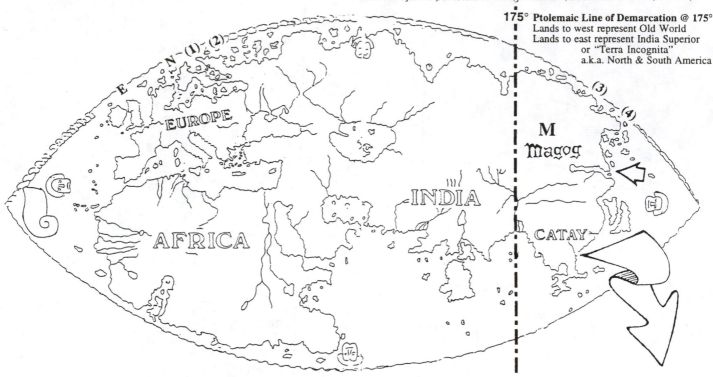

175° Ptolemaic Line of Demarcation @ 175°
Lands to west represent Old World
Lands to east represent India Superior
or "Terra Incognita"
a.k.a. North & South America

(D)   FLORIDA on The Genoese Planisphere—1457 AD

This map, based primarily on the Florentine Planisphere of 1447, is commonly known as "the Genoese Map." Some writers believe it is identical to the map that Paolo Toscanelli sent to Columbus and the king of Portugal. We are concerned primarily with the coast of Northeast Asia—presumed to lie across the Atlantic from Europe. This map follows the Magnetic Saga Map tradition: peninsulas northeast of England represent Norway (N), Greenland (1), and Baffin Land (2). Northern seas between the opposite ends of Europe and Asia represent Ginnungagap or Hudson Strait. On the northeast coast of what is presumed to be Asia (right side), there are two headlands: probably representing Labrador (3) and Vinland (4). This map shows the northern continent as the Magog forest; Cathay was situated far to the south near the Sinus Magnus. The Magog forest corresponds to the Norse Markland. A group of seven isles off the east coast correspond to the Icelandic Isles—a destination of English fishermen—perhaps first charted by Nicholas of Lynn. The southeastern peninsula fits all the characteristics expected of Florida except that it is a bit too far north (at 44°). Since Toscanelli accurately estimated the width of the Atlantic Ocean at about 3,000 miles, we can assume that the peninsula is situated at the approximate longitude of Florida.

E = England
M = Magog
     Forest
N = Norway
1 = Greenland
2 = Baffin Land
3 = Labrador
4 = Vineland

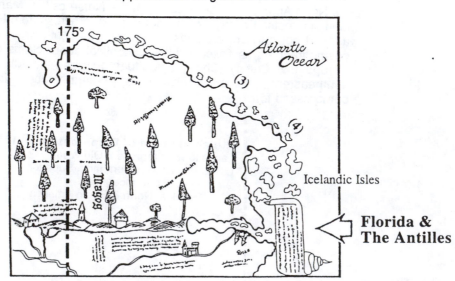

230

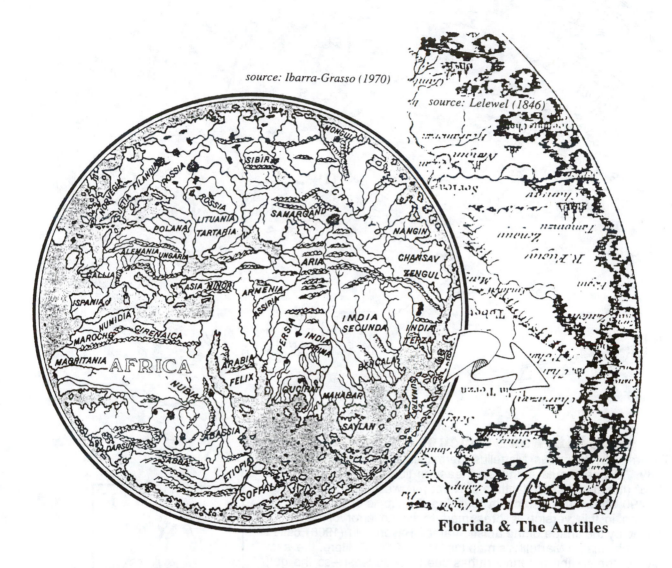

source: Ibarra-Grasso (1970)

source: Lelewel (1846)

Florida & The Antilles

(E) FLORIDA on Fra Mauro's Map—1459 A D

Mauro's map represents an attempt to combine traditional cosmological ideas with Ptolemaic precision. In this map, we find a fairly close representation of Florida— here called *India Terza*—the Third India. The map has no reference points that would enable an estimation of the distance across the ocean between Europe and Asia. Thus, there is no way to determine the presumed longitude for this peninsula. However, the latitude can be determined by comparing the position with known landmarks in Europe and Africa. It appears that Mauro has placed the peninsula at the proper latitude for Florida (about 26°). Since there is no peninsula at that latitude in Asia, we can assume that some mariner had accurately determined the location of the tip of Florida by celestial measurement.

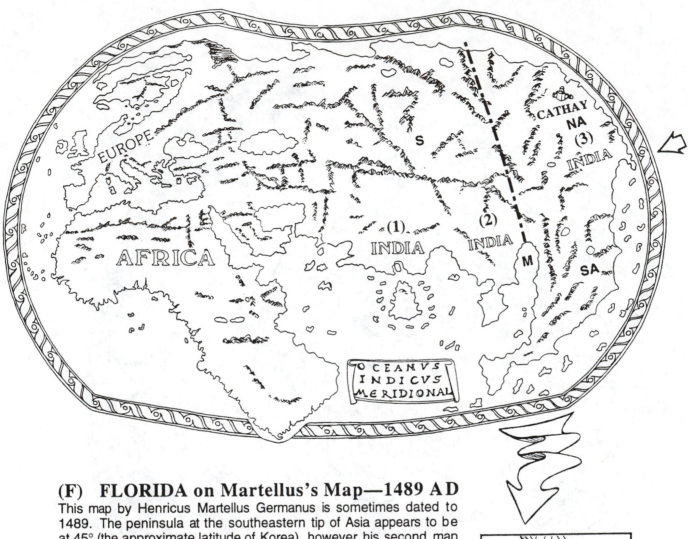

source: after a photograph in Bagrow (1964)
British Museum Add. MS 15670

(F) FLORIDA on Martellus's Map—1489 A D

This map by Henricus Martellus Germanus is sometimes dated to 1489. The peninsula at the southeastern tip of Asia appears to be at 45° (the approximate latitude of Korea), however his second map of 1490 shows the peninsula touching the Tropic of Cancer. The position in this version is presumed to be an error of distortion caused by the shape of the artistic frame. Ravenstein (1908) called this peninsula on Martellus's map the "Horn of Asia." Here, the east coast of the southern continent has been moved west—so the gulf has been eliminated by the expanding border of the southern ocean. When Amerigo Vespucci traveled south of Cuba and found land in 1497, he assumed it was a "New World" because contemporary maps didn't show land in that locality.

This map shows three Indias—as most Europeans thought of Asia only as the region of Asia Minor or Persia that was in the realm of Alexander the Great. The first India represents the subcontinent; the second is Indochina; and the third was an extension of land beyond the border of Ptolemy's map to represent the lands said to lie beyond Serica (S—China). These lands were eventually identified as North America (NA) and South America (SA). Martellus mistakenly placed Cathay (Ming China) on the east coast of India Terza (the 3rd India) in accordance with the writings of Marco Polo who said Cathay was located on the coast of a great ocean. That ocean was the Sinus Magnus (M).

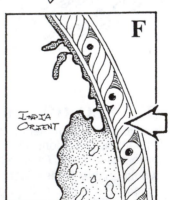

**Horn of Asia
a.k.a. Florida**

Ptolemaic Line of Demarcation @ 175°
Lands to west represent Old World
Lands to east represent India Superior

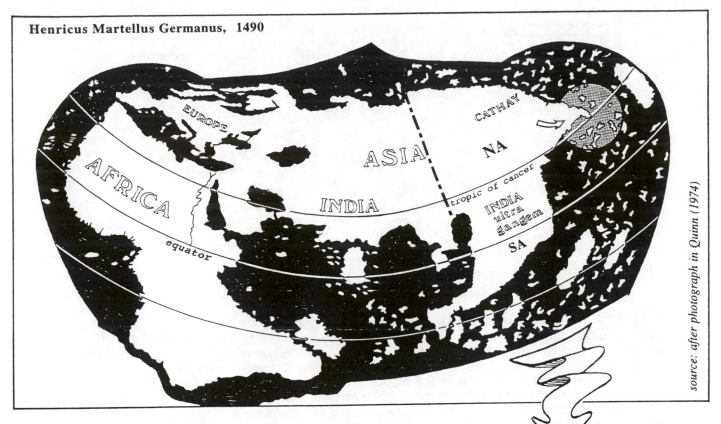

source: after photograph in Quinn (1974)

(G) FLORIDA on Martellus's Map—1490

Henricus Martellus Germanus produced a second, more-accurate map in 1490 complete with curving lines of latitude. Like Mauro's map of 1459, the second Martellus map shows the southeastern peninsula at the correct latitude for Florida—at about 27°. The tip almost touches the Tropic of Cancer—which is the latitude of Key West. Martellus shows Cipangu (Japan) as a huge island at the extreme eastern edge of the map. Some of his contemporaries, including Peter Martyr, believed this "Cipangu" was actually the Antilles—a name used in modern times to represent all the isles of the Caribbean. Columbus called the land "Isabella;" later, the native name—Cuba—gained favor.

The northern land (North America—**NA**) is called India Orient or East India on this map. Cathay (Ming China) was erroneously placed at the northeastern coast. As was the case with his previous map, no land is shown directly below the southeastern peninsula. However, mainland is indicated to the southwest. This is the same land which Bartholomew Colon later identified as the Antipodes (South America—**SA**) only it is here shown too far west relative to Europe. Martellus estimated the distance from Europe to Cipangu at about 3,000 miles and the distance from Cipangu to Asia at an additional 1,500 miles in accordance with Marco Polo's travelog.

Ptolemaic Line of Demarcation @ 175°
Lands to west represent Old World
Lands to east represent India Superior
    or "Terra Incognita"
    a.k.a. North & South America

India Orient

Cipangu

G

Florida on Modern Atlas

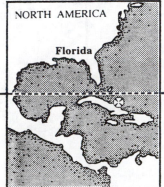

NORTH AMERICA

Florida

tropic of cancer

cross symbol ⊗
marks Columbus
landing

233

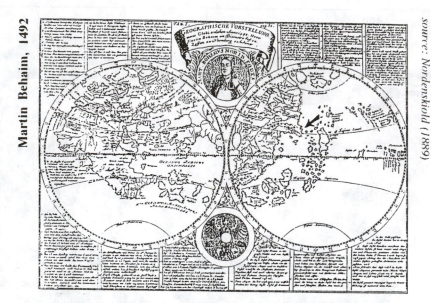

Martin Behaim, 1492

globe facsimile by J.G. Doppelmayer (1730)
source: Nordenskiold (1889)

(H) FLORIDA on Behaim's Globe—1492 AD

Lisbon globe-maker, explorer, and Nuremberg expatriate, Martin Behaim, constructed a globe in 1492 that historians generally regard as the current state of geographical knowledge at the time of Columbus. Since Columbus frequented Lisbon where he had also been in the mapping business, this seems like a fair assumption. Like Martellus, Behaim made a fairly accurate estimate of the distance between the Canary Islands and the Caribbean island that some called Antilia and others called Cipangu (Japan). However, his map indicated that another 1,000 miles lay between this island and Asian mainland. He followed the Genoese Map tradition by characterizing the northern region as a wilderness of forests. His Cathay was located to the far southwest near the Sinus Magnus (or Pacific Ocean). At least, the J.G. Doppelmayer version of Behaim done in 1730 has Cathay in that location. Later copyists seem to have moved Cathay to the northeast coast where it appears on so-called copies of Behaim in the early 20th century (see Ravenstein, 1908, for example). Behaim's globe comes the closest to placing the Asian peninsula at the right location for Florida. It is situated at about the right latitude (it actually crosses the Tropic of Cancer slightly) and it is about 1,000 miles too far west. By the standards of 15th-century navigation, this placement is nothing-less-than incredible. Certainly, it can not be explained by fortuitous circumstance. When Columbus reached the Caribbean using a map and globe that must have been similar to this one, he declared that he had found Cipangu (Cuba) precisely where the charts had said it should be— that is directly on the Tropic of Cancer about 3,000 miles due west of the Canary Islands. Later, when he traveled along the southern coast of Cuba in 1494, he insisted this was the coast of the very same peninsula (Horn of Asia or Florida) that appeared on all the contemporary charts. Unfortunately, he was just a little too far south—so he missed Florida by a few days' sail.

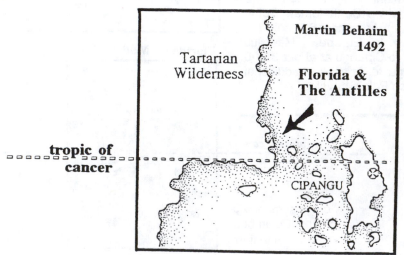

Martin Behaim
1492

Florida &
The Antilles

Tartarian
Wilderness

tropic of
cancer

CIPANGU

target symbol marks Columbus
landing in Cuba in 1492

234

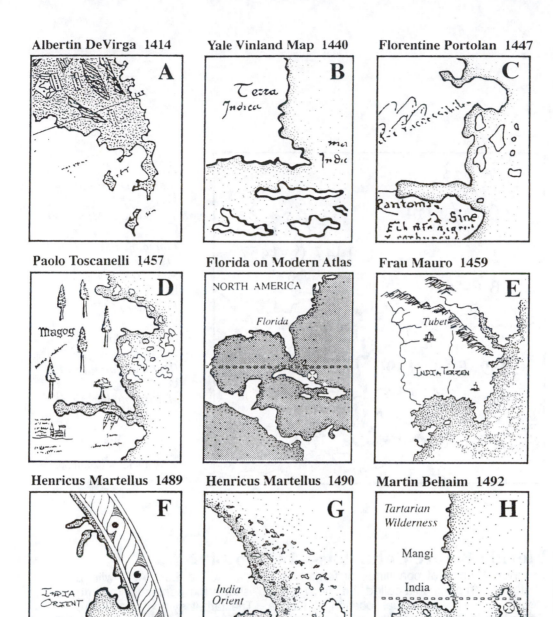

Albertin DeVirga 1414 — **A**

Yale Vinland Map 1440 — **B**
Terra Indica / mar Indic

Florentine Portolan 1447 — **C**
Pantoms... + Sine

Paolo Toscanelli 1457 — **D**
Magog

Florida on Modern Atlas
NORTH AMERICA / Florida

Frau Mauro 1459 — **E**
Tubet / INDIA TERZEN

Henricus Martellus 1489 — **F**
INDIA ORIENT

Henricus Martellus 1490 — **G**
India Orient

Martin Behaim 1492 — **H**
Tartarian Wilderness / Mangi / India / CIPANGU

Florida Before Columbus—1414 to 1492

Numerous maps available to Medieval mariners showed the relative position of Florida in ancient times. The earliest version—a map by the English Franciscan, Nicholas of Lynn ca. 1380—survives in a later copy by the Venetian cosmographer Albertin DeVirga (1414). Many cartographers had access to the friar's manuscript and surveys which he called *The Inventio Fortunatae*. This book is frequently referenced as a map source as late as the 16th century. Variations of the original survey appeared with modifications from 1414 through the mid-1500's. These maps showing an Asian peninsula having the right characteristics for Florida (a southeastward tending peninsula adjacent to an enormous gulf with large isles in the western Atlantic) confirm that European knowledge of the North American peninsula was widespread and enduring—although most Europeans erred in believing the overseas land was either Asia or connected to Asia. Some referred to the region as "Farthest India" or "India Superior"—names used by Classical scholars; others mistakenly believed it was the Asian coast identified by Marco Polo. The Lisbon globe-maker, Martin Behaim, was content to call the northern continent the "Tartary Wilderness." Toscanelli's estimate of the distance across the ocean—some 3,000 miles—and his wilderness coastline approximating the actual position of Florida are too accurate for mere coincidence.

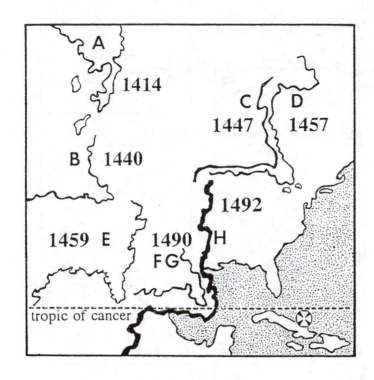

A.
Albertin DeVirga 1414
B.
Yale Vinland Map 1440
C.
Florentine Planisphere 1447
D.
Paolo Toscanelli 1457
E.
Fra Mauro 1459
F.
Henricus Martellus 1490
G.
Henricus Martellus 1490
H.
Martin Behaim 1492

target shows Columbus
landing in Cuba, 1492

Florida Before Columbus—1414 to 1492

Composite chart of coastlines of territory presumed to be East Asia with a southeastern peninsula called the "horn of Asia" shows the peninsula moving steadily towards the actual location of Florida. The target symbol marks the Columbus landing site on the coast of Cuba in 1492. At this location, he took celestial measurements using an astrolabe, and he wrote in his ship's log that he had reached land where he expected to find Cipangu (Japan): "On the globes which I saw and in the paintings of mappamonds, it (Japan) is in this vicinity." Wilbur Garrett, Editor of National Geographic (1986), noted that Columbus had sailed approximately 3,000 miles to the place where Martin Behaim's globe showed the location of Japan. Behaim's coastline from his globe of 1492 (H) is indicated by the heavy black line at the center of the illustration. Behaim's peninsula was about 1,000 miles too far west—which isn't that far off from the true position of Florida. The real coast of Asia is another 12,000 miles farther west. Historians generally assume that Columbus reached this land purely by accident. However, the fact that European cartographers sequentially modified the location of the southeastern peninsula and its adjacent isle (Cuba or Antilia) reveals that Columbus reached lands that had already been identified in physical reality—and he knew where to find them— due west from the Canary Isles along the Tropic of Cancer for about 3,000 miles. We know that there were many Portuguese voyages into the Atlantic during the 15th century. Historians typically assume that they didn't amount to anything. But the fact is that maps betray the navigational successes of those voyages in spite of a secrecy policy which cloaked Portuguese expeditions.

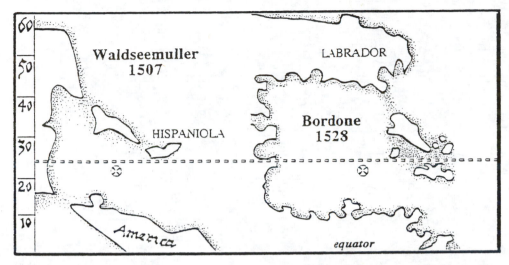

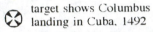

target shows Columbus
landing in Cuba, 1492

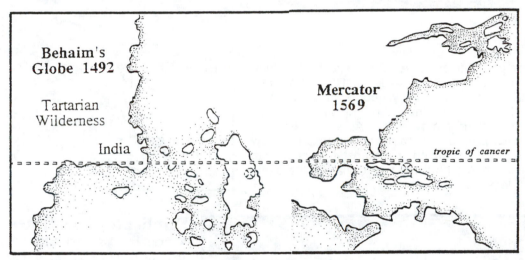

Precision Mapping of Pre-Columbian Navigators

The accuracy of early Portuguese navigators in the western Atlantic is apparent from this chart comparing maps by Martin Waldseemuller (1507) and Bordone (1528) with the 1492 masterpiece globe of Martin Behaim. Using the target symbol as a reference for the geographical location of the Columbus landing in Cuba, it can be seen that Behaim's globe was more accurate with regards to placement of the peninsula (Florida) and the major island (Cuba/Japan). Waldseemuller's map has Florida located 20° too far north; Bordone's map has Florida as a peninsula reaching down from Labrador; both maps show Cuba north of the Tropic of Cancer when its true position is actually south of the line. Gerhard Mercator's map of 1569 is the most accurate up to the mid-16th century. Thus, we can see that the pre-Columbian navigators and cartographers achieved a higher degree of accuracy than many of those who followed the Spanish admiral. Such accuracy must have resulted from actual voyages and measurements—not from mere speculation or fancy.

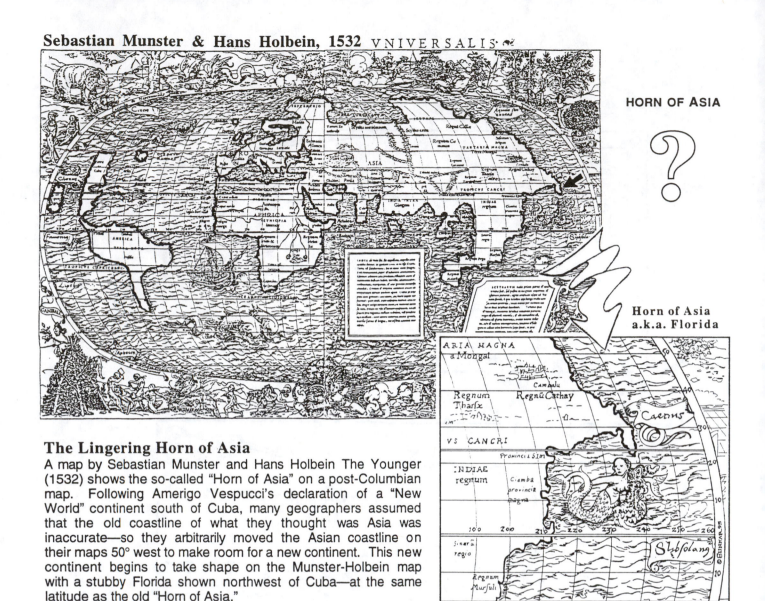

HORN OF ASIA

?

Horn of Asia
a.k.a. Florida

The Lingering Horn of Asia

A map by Sebastian Munster and Hans Holbein The Younger (1532) shows the so-called "Horn of Asia" on a post-Columbian map. Following Amerigo Vespucci's declaration of a "New World" continent south of Cuba, many geographers assumed that the old coastline of what they thought was Asia was inaccurate—so they arbitrarily moved the Asian coastline on their maps 50° west to make room for a new continent. This new continent begins to take shape on the Munster-Holbein map with a stubby Florida shown northwest of Cuba—at the same latitude as the old "Horn of Asia."

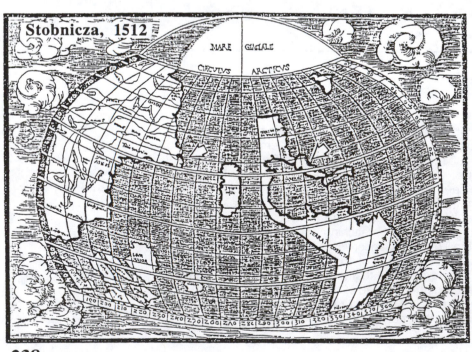

Duplicate Coastlines

A map by Joannes Stobnicza in 1512 (left) shows similar and parallel coastlines of India Superior and the New World. In this case, the Asian "Horn" and the new "Florida" are at the same latitude and have similar shapes—so it is easy to tell that navigators were simply surveying the same place twice! Indeed, the old survey was equally as accurate as the new one. These maps helped create the illusion that Cathay could be reached by sailing via a "Northwest Passage."

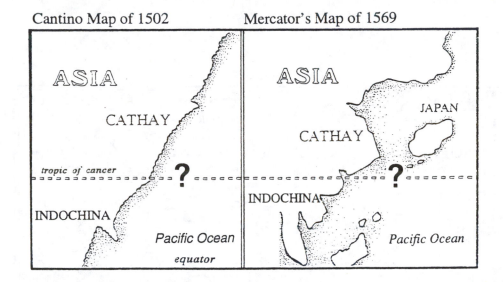

Cantino Map of 1502   Mercator's Map of 1569

Where Is The Horn of Asia?

The mysterious "Horn of Asia" vanished from maps just as soon as Europeans began charting the coast of Asia. It would seem that the "Horn" was only a figment of someone's imagination—unless it actually was meant to represent Florida. The idea of creating an Asian peninsula with all the characteristics of Florida certainly wasn't the result of Marco Polo's travelog, nor was it an attempt to show Korea which was much farther north than the Tropic of Cancer. As we can see from the Cantino Map of 1502 and Mercator's 1569 map, there is no significant peninsula in Asia at the Tropic of Cancer. In all the world there is only one major peninsula located right above the Tropic of Cancer—projecting towards the southeast into the Atlantic Ocean. That peninsula always has been Florida—in spite of the fact that some 15th-century geographers believed that the northern mainland was Asia.

Johan Schoner's 1515 Map

This German map is believed to be a copy of a map which Martin Behaim prepared circa 1500. The map is important because it shows the tip of South America at the accurate latitude for the Strait of Magellan—which supposedly wasn't discovered until 1519-1520. The map also shows Antarctica—also supposedly unknown at the time. The map indicates either knowledge gained from secret voyages or the legacy of ancient Roman mariners. Behaim's map gained him temporary fame for "discovering" the Mundus Novus—or New World of South America.

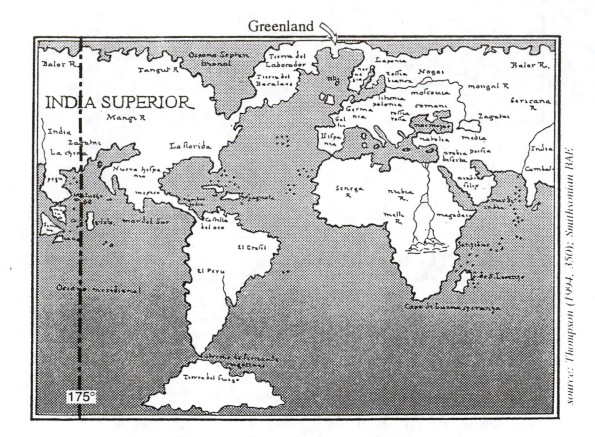

Greenland

INDIA SUPERIOR

175°

source: Thompson (1984, 350); Smithsonian BAE

HYPERBOREA—The Trans-Hemispheric Continent

The popular geographical concept of a trans-hemispheric continent seems to have originated with Albertin DeVirga's 1414 map which is the first to show such a land. This theme dominated charts of the North Atlantic until the late 1500's as numerous explorers searched in vain for a gap in the lands and a northwest passage to Asia. A map by J. Gastaldi (1548) expressed the Ptolemaic concept that the New World was actually an extension of Asia called "India Superior." This concept was in vogue long before the Columbus voyage, and it gave rise to the belief that the Spanish mariner had reached India—hence the name—Indians—for the native peoples. This map is also attributed to an atlas—the Strassburg Ptolemy. Greenland is shown in this map in a magnetic position relative to England. Terra del Labrador and Baccalaos (Newfoundland) correspond to regions called "Greenland" on maps by Martin Waldseemuller and Henricus Martellus Germanus.

- - - - - - - - - - - - - - - - - - - -

Ptolemaic Line of Demarcation @ 175°
Lands to west represent Old World
Lands to east represent India Superior
        or "Terra Incognita"
        a.k.a. North & South America

Invention of A New World

The Roman Seneca, English geographer Roger Bacon, Pierre D'Ailly, Martin Behaim, Henricus Martellus, and Columbus all referred to the land across the Atlantic as "India." Following the lead of German cartographer Martin Waldseemuller in 1507 and the Flemish expatriate, Gerhard Kramer (Mercator), the name "America" gradually replaced that of India Occidentalis on maps of the new world. During the transition in naming, maps often carry a dual designation of "India or America" for the convenience of readers who may be more familiar with the archaic term for the overseas continents. This dual designation is apparent on maps in the Venetian Atlas of 1650 (Portinaro & Knirsch, 1987, Pl. LXXIII). A map showing the Americas bears the title: America sive Indiae Occidentalis—that is, "America also known as The India of the West." North America was called "India Superior" or "Upper India" on the Henricus Martellus map of 1489; South America has the title India Meridionalis or "Southern India." On the planisphere by Nicolas Desliens (1541), the northern continent bears the title: La Novuelle Terre Franceze ("New Land of the French"); while the southern continent is called Terre Firme des Indes Occidentalles—Continent of the West Indies.

We can see in these examples from cartography that lands across the Atlantic from Europe were commonly known since Roman times as "the Indias." It was only for a relatively brief period in the early 1500's that Vespucci's designation of a "New World" for the southern continent became a popular name for Terra Firma across the Atlantic. The term "New Found Land" used to designate isles or mainland in the north had been in use since the Nordic designation of Nyaland or "New Land" in the 13th century. As historian Ian Wilson points out, the term "New Found Land" or "New Land" was applied to most of North America—not just the isle of Newfoundland (Wilson, 1991, 99).

This terminology—referring to territory that was supposedly "new"— was revived by modern historians to characterize their belief that North and South America were totally unknown until the Columbus voyage of 1492. However, as we have seen, this designation of a "new world" comprising both North and South America was actually a brief fantasy of Renaissance philosophers and entrepreneurs. Likewise, the assumption on the part of modern historians that the Americas were "virgin territories" at the time of the Columbus landing can be regarded as a modern fairytale.

Initially, the phrase "New World" referred only to South America. Europeans expected to find a continent in the north across the Atlantic—so there was nothing "new" about sailing to Cathay. Finding a southern continent was a different story. When Martellus and Behaim placed the southern continent (India Patalis) too far west, they created the illusion that there was no significant land directly south of Cuba. Columbus found mainland in that location in 1498—but he failed to declare his discovery of a new land (possibly because the king of Portugal previously told him where to find it). Instead, Columbus speculated that he had reached either the "Alter Orbis" of the ancients or or a biblical paradise.

Amerigo Vespucci—an observant Renaissance scholar—was among the first to risk being branded as a heretic when he boldly declared the presence of a separate continent. Vespucci called the southern continent a Mundus Novus or "New World" in a 1502 letter to Lorenzo DeMedici. He believed it was "new" because several ancient philosophers had denied that such a continent could exist or if it did exist that it was uninhabited. Eleven Latin editions of this letter were published by 1504 and eight

source: Fletcher & Kipling, School History of England
after a photo in Spence (1996, 187)

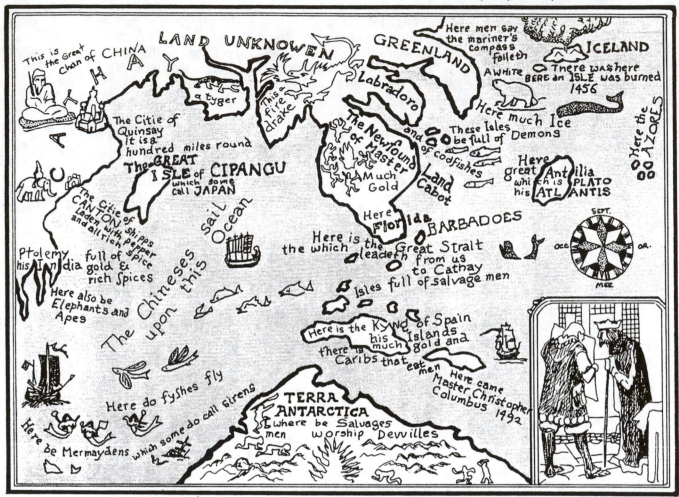

This is a map of AMERICA (and the Way to CHINA as Men believed it to be) which an old PILOT shewed to King HENRY VII in the year 1500

Oxford Map, ca. 1500

This controversial map appeared in a 19th-century text called "School History of England." However, it is largely ignored by orthodox historians. It purports to be a copy of a map that an "old pilot" showed King Henry VII in 1500. As the pilot is not identified—nor is the cartographer—the source of the map is unknown; thus it is of questionable origins. Also, the map names "Florida" which presumably wasn't discovered until 1513. On the other hand, we know the peninsula appears as early as the Norveca map of 1360, and it is clearly delineated on Behaim's globe of 1492 and the Cantino map of 1502—so perhaps Ponce DeLeon simply coined the name "Florida." In this case, the name might have been added by a later copyist. Otherwise, the map appears as we would expect for British sources at the start of the century. John Cabot's "Newfound Land" is shown as the mainland later called North America—lending support to Sebastian Cabot's claim that the 1497 expedition reached mainland west of the isle now called "Newfoundland." This isle is identified as "Land of Codfishes." In the mid-Atlantic is Antilia—which the mapmaker calls Plato's "Atlantis." The Gulf of Mexico is characterized as the "Great Strait" on the way to Cathay—which is how Sebastian viewed the Caribbean Sea. The southern continent (South America) is here called "Antarctica." This was a Greek designation for the land opposite the Arctic—that is, a southern continent. By using this name, the mapmaker suggests that the continent was not a "new world" but simply the southern continent known to the ancients as the antipodes.

242

German versions were in circulation by 1506 (Fiske, 1920, Vol. II, 113). The term Mundus Novus was first placed on maps in lieu of Brazil; Waldseemuller changed the name to America to honor Amerigo Vespucci—the person who discovered the Quarta Pars or Fourth Part of Earth (a.k.a., the Antipodes, Terra Australis, or The Southern Continent). Mercator's map of 1541 was the first to name both northern and southern continents "America." Las Casas returned from New Spain in 1547—by which time Vespucci's name as discoverer of the Antipodal land was more popular than the name of Columbus. Las Casas protested that the continents should be renamed "Colomba" in honor of God's chosen messenger of salvation—but it was too late to turn the tide of popular geography (Fiske, 1920, Vol. II, 158). With the publication of Mercator's widely-circulated maps, the name America was firmly welded into the consciousness of Europeans.

The "New World" concept had one other patron—Sebastian Cabot. Historians have long been confused over the young Cabot's seemingly peculiar behavior during the early 16th century. It seems that Sebastian toured Europe lecturing to audiences and writing treatises about his discovery of the "New World." Since Sebastian was a lowly officer on his father's ship in 1494, 1497 and 1498 when the elder Cabot, Johan, led expeditions across the Atlantic, it seems odd that the son would seek to usurp his father's glory. However, appearances can be deceptive: it now looks as though modern historians are completely confused about what actually took place. A 15th-century portrait of Sebastian bears the caption: "Sebastian Cabot—English son of the Venetian Johan Cabot—who first invented the New Worlds in the service of Henry VII—King of England." The phrase "invented the New Worlds" refers to Sebastian's conclusion—after traveling with his father on several voyages—that the distant land (later Labrador, New England, and the eastern coast of North America) was not Cathay as some had believed but a new, western continent. This is essentially the same conclusion that Amerigo Vespucci reached several years later with regard to the southern continent.

Vespucci, like Sebastian, first sailed in the service of a captain who reached new lands without realizing what they were. Both Vespucci and Sebastian were younger, better-educated and perhaps more-innovative men who realized—and in a sense "invented"—the existence of a New World. So, we can see from what Sebastian said that he never denied his father's achievement of finding new isles that were once presumed to be on the way to China. As these isles were already known to English fishermen, that wasn't really much of an intellectual achievement. In that regard, the realization that overseas lands represented an undeveloped or "new" land represented a significantly important intellectual achievement. Sebastian's self-promotion as the "inventor" (or discoverer) of the New World was simply an English effort to rectify what he felt was a gross historical error: the early 16th-century attention that was being given to Amerigo Vespucci as the one who first realized the existence of a Mundus Novus—or new world.

Both Sebastian's and John Cabot's claims to discovery seem to have been forgotten as a result of subsequent, historical revelations: since Cabot identified the region he found as "Bacalaos"—it was apparent that he had not discovered Cathay—merely a place already known to the Basques and Portuguese. By the time that Hakluyt enumerated his evidence for prior English settlements in the region of Norumbega, it was clear that Cabot's expeditions hadn't discovered anything that was really new. Meanwhile, Waldseemuller (quite accidentally) and Mercator (quite deliberately) gave credit for New World discovery to Amerigo Vespucci. Due to the widespread circulation of Vespucci's writings dealing with his travels in the new continents, he was better known as the "discoverer" even though Sebastian Cabot probably realized the existence of an overseas continent at an earlier time.

According to John Fisk, "when Columbus died, the fact that a New World had been discovered by him had not yet begun to dawn upon his mind, or upon the mind of any voyager or any writer" (Fiske, 1920, Vol. I, 515). It was not until a medallion was struck in 1535 to commemorate the Columbus expedition that the words "New World" became associated with Columbus. Fisk notes that:

> At no time during the life of Columbus, nor for some years after his death, did anybody use the phrase 'New World' with conscious reference to <u>his</u> discoveries. At the time of his death, their true significance had not yet begun to dawn upon the mind of any voyager or any writer. It was supposed that he had found a new route to the Indies by sailing west, and that in the course of this achievement, he had discovered some new islands and a bit of Terra Firma of more-or-less doubtful commercial value. (Fiske, 1920, Vol. I, 514)

King Ferdinand's role in demoting the legacy of Columbus was documented in several court cases. Columbus's heirs demanded that the king bestow upon them the titles and royalties he promised Columbus for "discovering new lands." However, Ferdinand's attorney countered that Columbus hadn't found any "new lands," because the lands were previously known to the Portuguese as <u>Antilia</u>. The 16th-century historian Gonzalo Fernandez wrote in his <u>Historia Natural De Las Indias</u> that Iberians (Spaniards) once had settlements in the New World as a result of Phoenician voyages. Consequently, he supported the king's position that the Spanish mariner—Columbus—had only found lands previously known to Spain (Thompson, 1994, 356).

The resulting transformation of geographical thinking and the popular illusion that Vespucci created with his letter announcing discovery of a virgin continent awaiting European exploitation earned him the glory of having two continents named in his honor. Within a few years—after Columbus, Cabot, and Vespucci had all passed away—European philosophers expounded upon the "New World" concept to identify all the lands in the Western Hemisphere; here was as a divine challenge and opportunity to expand European Civilization. Eventually, the names "America" and "New World" became synonymous with continents in the Western Hemisphere that were ripe for development. As far as Renaissance Europeans were concerned, the New World represented not only untamed wilderness and vast resources—but also free real estate.

It was the way Renaissance Europeans thought about the world that changed most dramatically as a result of expanding exploration, trade, and migration across the Atlantic. Numerous Old World voyagers had sailed to America in ancient times; they had changed the land and cultures in many ways; but none of them had the audacity to claim ownership of the entire hemisphere. It was this boldness and thoroughness of an entirely new breed of Europeans—the entrepreneurs and conquerors—who invented the New World to suit their dreams of wealth and grandeur.

This concept became the creed of modern, orthodox historians.

The Fruits of Norumbega

Historian Richard Hakluyt was among the earliest Europeans to identify the New World of Portuguese and Spanish discoveries as the site of an ancient English colony. In 1582, Hakluyt set forth his argument that King Arthur was the inspiration behind a long-lost settlement in the Polar Regions. Hakluyt identified this land as "Norumbaga"—a salmon-rich, temperate land in the vicinity of Nova Scotia. In defense of this extreme proposition, he marshaled accounts from what were at the time highly-respected authorities: Nicholas of Lynn, Giovanni Verrazano, the Italian Ramusio, and John Cabot.

Was Hakluyt biased when he wrote his book <u>Diverse Voyages Touching on The Discovery of America</u>?

Certainly, he was committed to the English cause, however that does not necessarily mean that his writings are inaccurate. In his book, Hakluyt presented evidence of early English, French, Italian, and Spanish mariners who sailed to the Western Continents. Therefore, his perspective wasn't exclusively British, although it was part of an effort to build a legal case for his homeland. England needed the tolerance—if not the approval of Catholic nations—in order to allow British explorations and trade in the New World. By demonstrating that English subjects had traveled across the Atlantic and settled on the shores of the New World, Hakluyt sought to justify a variance to papal bulls which granted access solely to Spanish and Portuguese sovereigns. Until such dispensation was secured, English expeditions often included Portuguese navigators in the dual role of envoys. Centuries after Hakluyt's book was published, orthodox historians—who were by no means without their own biases—declared all of his sources "spurious" or "irrelevant."

Regardless of the academic controversy over who discovered America, colonial accounts verify that native societies were by no means "virgin" entities when John Cabot arrived in the 1480's or 1490's—depending on the version of "history" you prefer (True, 1956, 14). When European entrepreneurs streamed across the Atlantic in search of Cathay, they found unexpected faces among the crowds waiting along the shores. Trappers carried bows and arrows in the native fashion; but some were white skinned, others black, or bronze. Some spoke Welsh, Old Norse, or Latin; many had a language built up from many bits and that served well the interests of French, English, and Dutch trading companies.

Cabot's Discovery

The orthodox version of English discovery in the North Atlantic traditionally begins with the unsuccessful attempt of Thomas Lloyd

Cornelius Judaeus
(1593)
source: Wolff (1992); Nordenskiold (1889, 95, Pl. 48)
In Speculum Orbis Terrae, Antwerp, 1593

Norveca, Noribega, and The Northern Regions

The Northern Hemisphere from a world may by Cornelius Judaeus (1593) shows North America in a northwesterly position relative to Norway. The territory of Noribega (arrow) occupies the approximate position of Norveca on the DeVirga map of 1414. During the 15th century, the overseas lands of the North Atlantic were referred to as the "Northern Regions." The northeast coast of North America is here portrayed as a series of headlands or peninsulas which was a characteristic of North Atlantic Saga Maps as well as DeVirga's map.

246

(Thloyde) to find Brazil in 1480. According to orthodox historians, Lloyd's ship returned to Bristol after being buffeted by contrary winds for "nine weeks" (Wilson, 1991, 59). However, failure to reach Brazil doesn't necessarily mean that the voyage was not profitable. Under normal conditions, one week would have sufficed to reach Iceland; another four days would have brought Greenland or Labrador into view (Davies, 1966, 220; Mallery and Harrison, 1979, 66). Successful voyages between Bristol and Newfoundland were in fact confirmed by correspondence between John Day and Columbus.

The "nine weeks" that orthodox historians quote for public consumption isn't actually the way the account was written in the original document. According to the Cambridge Itineraria by the antiquary William Worcestre, the voyage actually took "nine months!" Historian Arthur Newton (1936) cites a 1778 copy of the Itineraria as the earliest extant version of the original document. In a voyage of nine months, sailors had sufficient time to trade with natives in Labrador, take their cargo to a clandestine port in Ireland, and return to Bristol with an empty ship and no taxes to pay. If they were actually headed for Brazil, they had to sail against the Gulf Stream, and they would have needed to cross the Gulf of Mexico. Perhaps there was a hurricane in the Caribbean? All that is definitely known of the expedition is that contrary winds prevented the ship from reaching Brazil.

The point is that some historians can't conceive of a voyage into the Atlantic lasting nine months—so they have assumed that the "nine months" reported in the Itineraria is the mistake of a copyist who put down "months" when the original document presumably said "weeks." But that is only an assumption on the part of historians who apparently feel compelled to revise historical accounts in order to make the "evidence" fit their own pet theories. There is no valid reason for making such an assumption.

Accounts of the Cabot expeditions inform us that the Venetian expatriate thought he might find the land of brazilwood trees directly opposite Ireland across the Atlantic. This expectation might have resulted from erroneous reports by fishermen who sailed to the region of Newfoundland, or it could have resulted from Cabot's misreading of the Inventio Fortunatae. The friar's book was certainly widely-known and available in London; merchant John Day (a.k.a. Hugh Say) offered to send a copy to Columbus (Skelton, 1965, 179). Since the book was about regions north of 54°, the southern extremity at 54° might have seemed like a reasonable place to look for the land of brazilwood trees. This latitude happens to correspond to the location of Newfoundland.

Historians have assumed that the report of Lloyd's failure is indicative of futile English attempts to cross the Atlantic; and it is not uncommon to read orthodox versions of history which resume with John Cabot's post-Columbian ventures in 1496, 1497, and 1498. Cabot returned from the first attempt without reaching his objective. Again, contrary winds were invoked to justify the failure. A qualified "success" came in 1497 when Cabot's twenty-man crew on the brigantine Matthew reached Cape Breton Island. Cabot proclaimed this: Prima Tier Vista or "First Land Seen." Nowhere in the scanty accounts from Cabot's expedition is there any indication that he believed this was the isle of brazilwood trees.

A letter which John Day wrote in 1497 clearly states that Bristol sailors reached "Brazil" prior to Cabot's voyage although no precise date or location was mentioned:

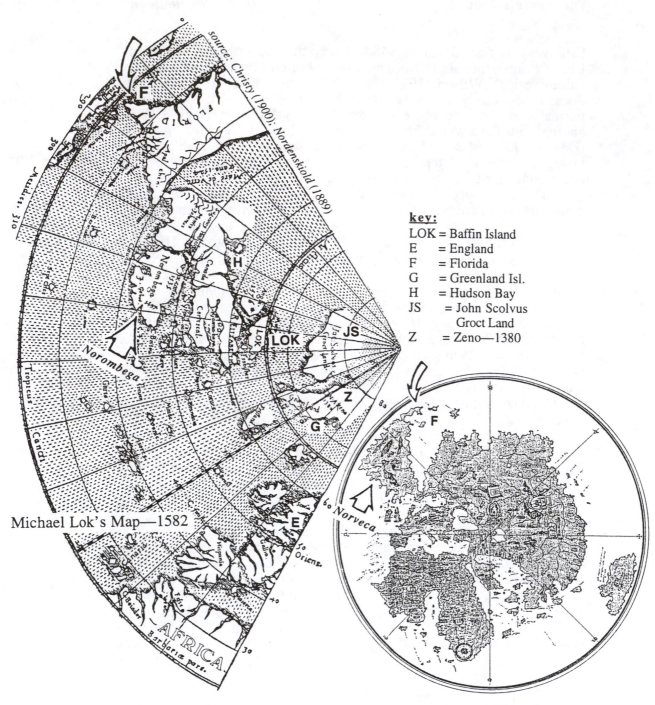

key:

LOK = Baffin Island
E   = England
F   = Florida
G   = Greenland Isl.
H   = Hudson Bay
JS = John Scolvus
      Groct Land
Z   = Zeno—1380

Michael Lok's Map—1582

DeVirga Map, 1414 AD

Norveca and Norombega

Placement of Norombega on circular map by Michael Lok (1582) shows similarity to location of the Norveca continent on DeVirga's map (right). The northeast coast on Lok's map has a similar appearance to earlier Saga Maps which show the northeast as a series of headlands projecting out into the North Atlantic. Frisland (south of Greenland) is actually in the place where Greenland should be located. The territory of Cortereal is southern Labrador; Norombega occupies lands from Nova Scotia to New York. Lok identifies northern Greenland as the site of the Zeno expedition in 1380—nearly ten years before most historians believe the voyage occurred. Note the location of Florida on both maps seemingly north of Europe.

It is considered certain that the cape of the said land was found and discovered in the past by the men from Bristol who found Brazil as your Lordship (Columbus) well knows. It was called the Island of Brazil and it is assumed and believed to be the mainland that the men of Bristol found. (Sharp, 1991, 42)

Although it is tempting to assume that Newfoundland was identified as Brazil, this is by no means clear from the letter. There were two similarly-named territories—one the land of "Hy-Bresail" (a so-called "paradise" near Newfoundland or Nova Scotia), and the other "Brazil" (the land of tropical brazilwood trees in South America).

There are more tantalizing clues concerning early English voyages: a letter which Pedro Ayala sent in 1498 to the Catholic Sovereigns of Spain reported that Bristol merchants had sailed west each year since 1490—although nothing was known regarding their success or failure. In 1527, English merchant Robert Thorne wrote a letter in which he claims his father (also Robert Thorne) and the Bristol merchant Hugh Elliot were the discoverers of Newfoundland. John Dee, Queen Elizabeth's personal geographer and advocate, claimed that Thorne and Elliot had reached Newfoundland in 1494—a date that Sebastian Cabot also claimed for his father's unpublished discovery. That date is also confirmed on the "Paris Map" of 1544. The landfall was not publicly announced due to apprehensions that the land might have been previously known to Europeans—although not officially "discovered" in the sense of being declared property of a Christian king. It was also evident to Cabot and his cohorts that this wilderness they sailed along could not possibly be the Cathay which Marco Polo described as a thriving mercantile civilization with thousands of ships and golden pagodas.

There is some disagreement among historians when the Cabot expedition first sailed, where it landed, and what the place was called. Historian Timothy Jacobson (1991, 49) says that King Henry VII named the point of landing—"New Isle." He adds that "within a few years Newfoundland seems to have taken hold." On the other hand, it is quite possible that the region referred to as New Found Land was the same "Nyaland" or "New Land" which the Norse explorer Landa Rolf identified centuries earlier.

Newton (1932) believes Cabot first landed at Cape Breton north of Nova Scotia. Jacobson (1991, 49) has the landing on Newfoundland—which he believes is verified by "navigational details" in John Day's letter to Columbus. John Fiske (1920, Vol. II, 10) believes that "St. John" refers to Prince Edward Island across the Gulf of St. Lawrence to the south of Newfoundland. He notes that two earlier charts from Seville (in 1527 and 1529) as well as the testimony of Robert Thorne in 1527 suggest that the "prima tierra vista" was on the coast of Labrador.

A map engraved in Flanders circa 1544 and said to be from an original by Sebastian Cabot has the caption prima tiera vista (or Land First Seen) beside Cape Breton. This naming of Cape Breton as the Land First Seen is contrary to popular beliefs that the Cabots first landed on the shores of Newfoundland in 1497. Another caption on the 1544 map says that the landing occurred on June 24th, 1494; a nearby island was named "St. John." It should be noted that this map is most in accord with Sebastian's own testimony that his father's ship passed the New World isle (New Found Land) that is closest to Ireland on their way back to the British

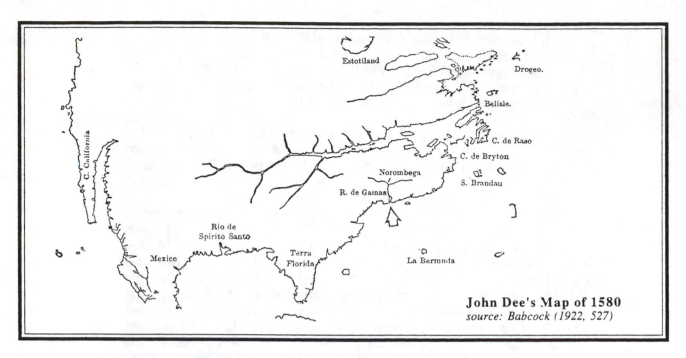

Norumbega on the Grand River

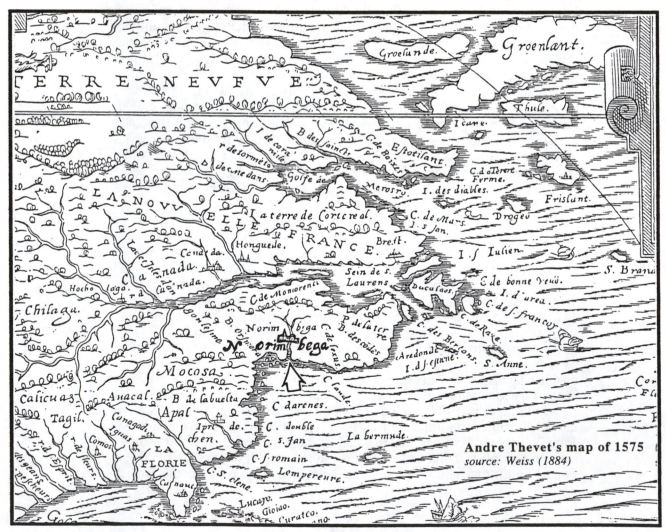

Isles at the end of their voyage. In other words, they passed by Newfoundland last—making Newfoundland the land "last seen."

Newton (1932, 136) believes the Cabots sailed as far south as Chesapeake Bay in 1498 to latitude 36°N. Sebastian's testimony of the voyage was that their ships reached the parallel across from the Strait of Gibraltar which would place the voyagers between 36° and 38°. A copy of their journal and a map of their travels was sent to Spain at the request of Columbus, and it is believed that this record was the source for the northern half of a map by Juan LaCosa in 1502. Some orthodox historians regard this map as the earliest to show New World mainland beyond Hispaniola (Nansen, 1911, 311). On this map, Hispaniola is portrayed as an isle near the continent of Asia; the entire northeast coast reaching from Florida to Labrador features a picket-fence of English flags and the caption: Mar descubierta por ingles—"Sea discovered by the English." The continental land, which Cabot characterized as a wilderness, was identified as the mainland of Terra Nova or "New Land." This naming of "New Land" as a continent seems to confirm Sebastian's claim to priority in the identification of a "New World" across from Europe. A map from Oxford University (ca. 1500) has the words "New Found Land of Master Cabot" inscribed across mainland between Labrador and Florida—confirming that Cabot's voyage was principally south of the isle called Newfoundland.

An account published in Peter Martyr's 1515 journal tells of Sebastian's 1498 voyage reaching the latitude of Gibraltar and passing by the western edge of Cuba—which would have taken the expedition into the Gulf of Mexico (Fiske, 1920, Vol. II, 15). In spite of this cartographical and historical evidence of English voyages along the East Coast prior to 1502, some writers contend that Sebastian Cabot couldn't possibly have sailed that far south until much later.

John Cabot's 1497 voyage established the compass bearings and map for a direct sailing route between England and Newfoundland. This route enabled English trawlers to circumvent taxation in Iceland and made it possible for merchants to bring fish directly from the source instead of having to pay for processing in Iceland. Cabot might not have realized that his compatriots were already sailing to this attractive destination; indeed, he was looking for a "bigger fish"—the Chinese Cathay which he believed Columbus had not yet found. With luck, he hoped to beat Columbus to this prize and the Spice Islands which lay beyond. His voyage (or the voyage of his son) in 1498 established that the northern continent stretched continuously from Labrador to Florida—a land he called "Baccalaos" after a native term for the abundant fish found along the coast. But it was not Cathay.

John Cabot's use of the term "baccalaos" to identify the New World mainland has caused considerable controversy. The word baccalaos was commonly used for the same kind of fish by Portuguese and Spanish sailors. That name was also common knowledge among English sailors who had frequent contact with the Portuguese. Columbus also identified an isle beyond Iceland as "Baccalaos." Given the familiarity his contemporaries had with the source of codfish, explorer John Cabot must have concluded that his quest for Cathay and Brazil had only taken him to Icelandic isles already frequented by European brigantines and trawlers.

Cabot's report that the mainland across from England was the very same territory called Bacalaos that Bristol fishermen had known about for ages probably didn't win him any friends among his creditors who had

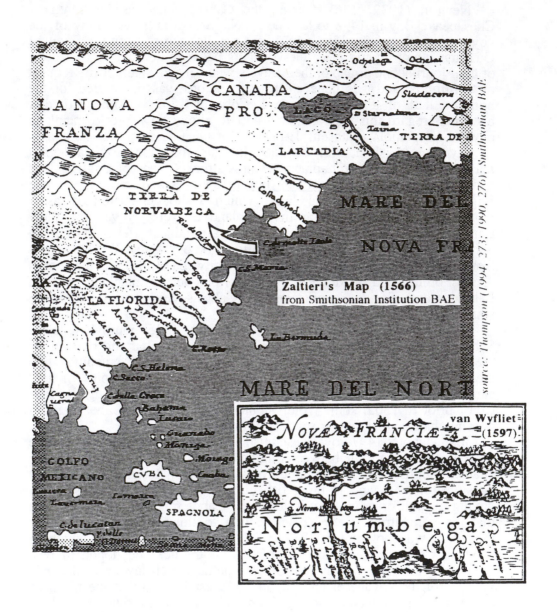

source: Thompson (1994, 273; 1990, 276); Smithsonian BAE

Zaltieri's Map (1566)
from Smithsonian Institution BAE

van Wyfliet (1597)

Norumbega

Most 16th-century maps designate a region between the Gulf of St. Lawrence and Florida as "Norumbega." According to French explorer Giovanni Verrazano, the territory was named by its inhabitants as Norumbega. Explorers identified many different tribes and a variety of ethnic groups in this area, so it is unlikely that a single name or political organization applied to the entire Eastern seaboard. Richard Hakluyt designated lands from the Hudson river to the Gulf of St. Lawrence as Morumbega, and it is in this region that most explorers identified "white" aboriginals. This region is so identified as a "land of whites" on Behaim's 1492 globe. A city called Norombega on many maps probably represents a major trading city; the explorer Alfonce claimed the French had constructed a fortress in this location.

hoped for a shipment of gold or silk from China. However, cartographers quickly plastered the name on their maps. The American mainland was called <u>Terra de Bacalhos</u> (i.e., Stockfish Land) on the Ptolemaic Basileae Map of 1540. In the "Cosmographia Petri Apiani" by Gemma Frisius (1551), the entire continent of North America was identified as <u>Baccalearum</u>.

Orthodox historians have not overlooked the implications of the word—baccalaos—as evidence of pre-Columbian voyages to America. Arthur Newton (1932, 151) took the 16th-century historian Peter Martyr to task for his careless digression from approved scholarship:

> Peter Martyr gives further details of the Cabot voyage. He relates that the term <u>baccalaos</u> is used because the waters swarm with fish like tunnies, which he says, incorrectly, the natives call by this name.

Newton was premature in assuming that Cabot made a mistake and that Martyr's account was "incorrect." Indeed, the mariner's English-bred son, Sebastian, confirmed the accuracy of Martyr's account. His caption on the Paris Map of 1544 states that the greatest number of fish taken near Newfoundland are called <u>baccallaos</u> (True, 1956, 16).

Peter Martyr was not the only historian of his era to innocently relate what was common knowledge about native culture and subsequently disrupt the sanctified dogma of approved scholarship. The Spanish historian Gomara also reported that the natives called their land "Bacalaos." His 1555 <u>History of The Indies</u> says that: "The Brytons and Frenche men are accustomed to take fish in the coasts of these lands, where is found great plenty of Tunnies which the inhabitants call Baccalaos, where of the land was so named" (Fiske, 1920, Vol. II, 21).

Sebastian Cabot offered his services to Spain in 1512; by 1548, he was back in England. His contemporaries claimed that he had "entered the Northwest Passage and seen the Pacific." This claim probably reflects a voyage into Hudson Strait and Hudson Bay—which was initially confused with the Pacific Ocean (Brebner, 1933, 94). In a 1550 letter to Ramusio, Sebastian claimed that he had sailed northwest on the 1509 voyage at the latitude of 67.5°N where he found an open sea (Hudson Bay or possibly Davis Strait near Baffin Bay) which he believed might extend all the way west to Cathay. However, mutinous sailors forced the expedition to turn back (Brebner, 1933, 94). Geographers of his own age studied his narratives and maps and concluded that Sebastian had found the northwest passage. These maps and narratives (now lost) inspired Humphrey Gilbert's 1660's expedition in search of a northwest passage. Some scholars assume that Sebastian's 1509 expedition took his vessel northeast to Denmark Strait—but this theory is not supported by Ramusio's transcript of the letter.

Verrazano's Folly

Giovanni Verrazano revealed the great ethnic diversity of native tribes and identified Old World plants that had crossed the Atlantic to America in ancient times. He also "sinned" in the eyes of orthodox historians by revealing the name of an Old World colony that was still thriving when he sailed along the coast in 1527.

Most 16th-century maps and many 17th-century maps of North America show a region in the northeast designated as "Norumbega." How and when this name originated has been the subject of lingering controversy. Verrazano passed by the East Coast in 1524 and on two subsequent occasions (Hakluyt, 1582). Sometime after his first voyage, he sent a letter to the king of France informing him that "Nurumbega" (a.k.a., Norombeque) was the name which the people of the region gave to their country. In Ramusio's <u>Discorso</u> (1539 or 1556) it states that:

> The country of Nurumbega stretches westward from beyond Cape Breton some 500 leagues to west by southwest to the land of Florida. ... The land is called by its people Nurumbega. (Stromsted, 1974, 143)

The name "Norumbega" was first brought to the attention of European cartographers when the word "oranbega" appeared on a map of the East Coast prepared by Giovanni Verrazano's brother, Gerolamo in 1529. Another cartographer, Vesconte Maggiolo, indicated the presence of a "Norman Villa" in the vicinity of Chesapeake Bay on his 1527 map of the East Coast. This mention of a "Norman Villa" implied the presence of Norse habitations in the same region identified in the letter as Norumbega.

The location of Norumbega seems to have been transient: most 16th-century maps identified New York or Nova Scotia as the region; sometimes the territory is shown extending from New York to Virginia.

After several explorers reported a thriving city of fur-traders somewhere in the northeast, cartographers added a fortress city called "Norombega" to maps of North America. Most identified a town on the Hudson river (or Rio Grande) as the city of "Norombega"; others favored the Charles river in Massachusetts as a site for the mysterious metropolis. The French navigator Alfonce (a.k.a., Jean Fontaneau) reported a Norombegue river and a cape by the same name in the vicinity of St. John's river on the Bay of Fundy, Nova Scotia; and he said that the French had constructed a fortress on this river (Stromsted, 1974,150). He reported that "There is a fine people at this city and they have furs of many animals." Geographer Andre Thevet visited the "city" in 1556 and reported that it was situated on one of the world's most beautiful rivers. English sailor David Ingram trekked through the region in 1569, and he reported farms, fur-traders, and people riding horseback. In 1583, a trader named Ballinger reported a "city" with houses and an active market—someplace in New England.

Eben Horsford (1892) theorized that the name "Norumbega" was simply a phonetic variation of the current name of Norway—which in Medieval times was variously called "Norbegia," "Norobega," "Norveca," and "Noroveg." According to Horsford, Grimm's law of phonetic variation renders Norombega into several variants of the name for Norway, such as: "Norvega," "Noruega," and "Norwega" (Scottish Geographical Society, 1894, 102). Horsford believes that the letter "m" was added to "Nor-bega" by Algonkian speakers who had difficulty pronouncing "b" without preceding it with "m" as in the Algonkian expression "m-Boston." This peculiarity of speech, Horsford notes, is also a characteristic of Greek sailors and immigrants.

There are at least 25 different spellings for this New World nation or city on ancient maps. The 14th Annual Report of the Society of American Ethnology and Archeology (1892) gives "Norvega" and "Normbega" as two common versions of the name (Anderson, 1995, 1). A map by Solis in 1598 has "Norveg" marked in the region of New Brunswick and "Noruega" for a city on the Rio Grande or Hudson river (Stromsted, 1974, 146). Two other versions on 16th-century maps are "Noruega" and "Nova Noruega" (Ramsay, 1972, 145). The 18th-century Swedish historian Thormod Torfaeus (<u>Historia Vinlandiae Antiquae</u>, 1705) regarded Norumberga to be a variation of Norway—which was sometimes spelled "Norouvega." Thus he believed that the name was evidence of Norse settlements in America. Richard Hakluyt (1582) has an unusual spelling of the American colony as "Morumbega." Other spellings include Norimberga and Norbega. Norimberga is close to the spelling of a 15th-century German province—Norimberge (the modern Nuremberg). This version seems appealing as a possible legacy of Vendal or Hanseatic merchants which have historical connections to ancient colonies along the East Coast. Another version, "Norbega," is very close to the name "Norveca" used on the Venetian Commercial Map of 1414 to represent Norwegian territory in North America. Other candidates for the source of the name include Northumbria (an Anglo-Saxon kingdom in England), Nordhan-bygda (a Norse word for "northern village") and Normoria—the name of an old Norse province. It is equally plausible that the region had several similar names which explorers and historians later confused.

Pierre Grignon of Dieppe wrote a treatise on French explorations, <u>Recherches sur les Voyages et Decouvertes des Navigateurs Normands</u> (1535), which mentioned that Verrazano had taken possession of the region for the king of France and named it New France—although the natives called it by the name of "Norumbega" (Ramsay, 1972, 176). Jean Alfonce, the chief navigator for Jacques Cartier, charted the "Cape of Norumbegue" in the region of Cape Cod; he located the "River of Norumbegue" about seventy-five miles west and noted that there was a city of Norumbega that was noted for many kinds of pelts. Ramsay (1972, 182) has the native river spelled "nolumbeka" which also stands for the native Abnaki tribe in the same region.

Some isolationists posit quaint anecdotes or native words meaning "quiet streams," or a French expression <u>Que enorme berge</u>—"What great cliffs!" <u>Terra de Enorme Berge</u> even served as a title for a French book on the region near the Hudson River. In spite of these creative explanations for the name "Norumbega," the preponderance of evidence favors an Old English or Germanic source.

It was not until 1604 that French explorer Samuel Champlain commenced his search for the illusive frontier city. He sailed as far south as Cape Cod—which was probably not quite far enough to be certain that he had found the right location. He reported no evidence of Norombega City on the Penobscott river in Maine—although he did identify a native tribe that had a similar name—the "Norm-bega." This tribal name is loosely translated "tribe of the still waters between rapids." The English called them the Norridgewock; a French map of 1734 identifies them as the "Nation des Norumbeag." English troops attacked and dispersed the tribe in 1724 (Schroder, 1995, 7). Shortly after Champlain returned to France, his lieutenant, Marc Lescarbot, declared that the tales of Norumbega were nothing but mere "fables."

Was Champlain's failure proof that Norumbega did not exist? We have to keep in mind that as a French agent in search of an English colony, there was not much incentive for a successful outcome. Prior to Champlain's trip, Richard Hakluyt had identified Norumbega as proof of ancient English settlements in the New World. Meanwhile, France and England were locked in a contest of colonial expansion and commercial

Mixed Blood—Early European Natives

source: Alabama Dept. Archives

Creek Chief MacIntosh, ca. 1800

source: Smithsonian Institution BAE

Creek Chief Menewa, ca. 1800

source: Rakel (1894, 725)

Labrador Eskimos, ca. 1850

domination. Thus, we can conclude that neither Champlain nor Hakluyt were beyond the influence of nationalism in their respective writings.

Some writers have criticized Champlain for "sailing up the wrong river," however it probably didn't matter what river he sailed. By this point in time—the early 17th century—Europeans of many nationalities were treading along native pathways and encroaching upon native hunting grounds. The economics of fur-trapping and fur-trading with European companies established new alliances and disrupted old ones. Diseases and warfare altered the ethnic and cultural landscape; within a few years new European names such as New York, New Amsterdam, New Sweden, and New England replaced the names of native territories. Eventually, the fading boundaries of the ancient confederacy of Norumbega were lost in the ever-flowing river of "progress" as the frontiers of European settlements moved steadily westward. Therefore, it is not surprising that a map by Urbano Monti (1589) places the vanishing colony west of the Great Lakes in the region of Iowa or Minnesota.

There is some evidence that the name "Norumbega" was familiar to Renaissance Europeans. English poet John Milton wrote of the "stormy gusts of ice and hail" that came from "the north of Norumbega." His haunting words imply that his contemporaries remembered some vague legend of a romantic land near the North Pole. That poetic image mirrored ancient legends of King Arthur's lost colonies and the far-off Avalon. According to Richard Hakluyt, that mystical kingdom had been rediscovered in the western land of Norumbega.

West Friesland—Still On The Map in 1578

Another "lost colony" of the northeast coast was on the isle of Friesland. In Peter Heylyn's Cosmography (1659), Frislandia is described as "belonging to the crown of Norway" (Ramsay, 1972, 54). This isle was described in the Zeno narrative as having a large population with several towns with harbors frequented by European vessels. Columbus claimed to have visited this place in 1477. By then it was already in decline due to a cooler climate and epidemics. The next mention of a visit to the region—in 1524—tells of a land inhabited only by natives—but they were "white" natives. In 1542, French navigator Jean Fontaneau described an island (possibly Newfoundland) with white natives; he called this isle "Frixland" (Stromsted, 1974,150).

On his 1578 voyage, Frobisher claimed that he visited the same isle. His ship's log says that they sailed 14 days west of Ireland without any mention of sighting icebergs—so their vessel was probably far to the south of the standard, Icelandic route. They came upon a land that Frobisher called "West Friesland" (probably Labrador). He found a "good harbor" where the log reports that native boats were seen. Going ashore at a native village, they found a box of iron nails which they regarded as evidence of prior native trade with "civil people" (Beeching, 1972, 199). This was not such a desolate sort of wilderness as we might expect if the expedition had landed on the Arctic isle of Greenland far away to the north. Indeed, the captain noted in his log with regards to minerals and furs that: "This country, no doubt, promises good hope of great commodity and riches." From thence, they sailed toward Frobisher's Straits (Hudson Straits?) where they encountered northern ice floes. Historians have assumed that Frobisher's vessel wandered somewhere in the North Atlantic west of Greenland—but that assumption does not correlate with the account given in the ship's log.

Moorehead (1910)

from Rayner's Mound
Piqua, Ohio 1890

Burial Tablets
These tablets excavated from a native burial mound have writing from a pre-Colonial alphabet. They are evidence of literate people occupying the Ohio valley *prior* to the 16th century.
9.11

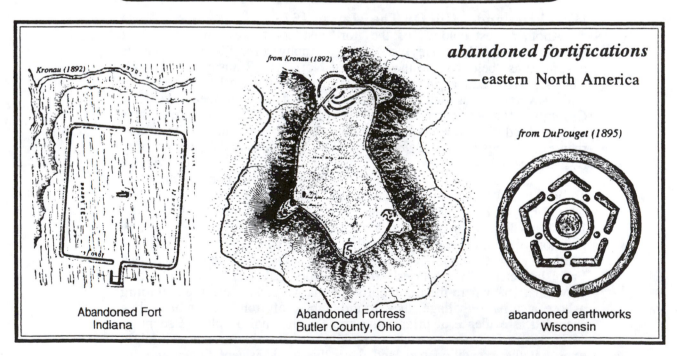

abandoned fortifications
—eastern North America

Kronau (1892)

from Kronau (1892)

from DuPouget (1895)

Abandoned Fort
Indiana

Abandoned Fortress
Butler County, Ohio

abandoned earthworks
Wisconsin

Abandoned Fortifications
During the 17th and 18th centuries, frontiersmen found ruins of ancient fortifications along the Ohio and St. Lawrence river valleys. These ancient forts were encompassed by moats or trenches and palisades. Although natives often built stockades around their villages, they didn't dig earthworks. The reason is natives didn't use shovels. However, North Europeans typically built moats around their fortifications. The presence of earthworks and iron-smelting furnaces inside many of the abandoned forts confirms the ruins are those of ancient European settlements.

Ethnic Diversity in Pre-Colonial America

Accounts from 16th-century explorers reveal an astonishing ethnic diversity among the New World's native peoples. Columbus called the inhabitants "Indians"—but there were many kinds of Indians: black, white, bronze—and every imaginable mixture. Columbus mentioned "white" natives on Hispaniola in 1493. He reported "almost white" natives on a ship in the Gulf of Paria between Trinidad and Venezuela in 1498 on his third voyage (Hope, 1988, 156).

Gaspar Corte-Real's voyage to Labrador in 1500 led to one of the earliest accounts of whites in that region. Damiam de Goes reported the encounter in Chronica do Felicissimo Rei dom Emanuel (Lisbon, 1566). Like many of his contemporaries, he identified the northeast coast of the New World as Terra Verde or "Greenland":

> He named the land Terra Verde. The people are very barbaric and wild, almost like those of Sancta Cruz, except that they are at first white, but become so weather-beaten from the cold that they lose their whiteness with age. (Nansen, 1911, 366)

Verrazano reported white tribes interspersed with blacks and bronze-colored peoples during his voyages along the East Coast from 1524 to 1545. He identified one tribe with exceptionally white skin (piu bianchi) on Rhode Island. His journal of 1524 mentioned "white natives" of the Narangansett Bay tribe of New Jersey (Holland, 1956, 256; Chapman, 1981, 69). Jacques Cartier reported a distinctly "white tribe" in Nova Scotia. Natives told French Canadian Governor Sieur DeRoverbal about whites living in the nation of Saguenay in the west in 1542. DeRoverbal described some Iroquois as "very white but they paint their skin for fear of heat and sunburning" (Mallery, 1979, 170). That same year, French navigator Jean Fontaneau reported that Frixland (Newfoundland) was "inhabited by very white people who were subjects of the King of Denmark" (Stromsted, 1974,150). Samuel Champlain reported white natives in eastern Canada during his 1604 excursion (Wahlgren, 1986, 125; Stromstead, 1974). In 1698, French Jesuit Pierre Charleviox saw bearded natives with blond hair in Labrador. Frontier explorer George Rogers Clark reported in his Journal of 1779 an encounter with tall, blond warriors living in the wilderness. Colonial artist John Trumbull commented in 1790 that Creek natives were very similar to Europeans in facial features; this occurred during portrait sessions for two native chiefs (Josephy, 1961; Thompson, 1994, 168). Another artist, Gilbert Stuart, painted Mohawk natives who had very light skin. They appear to be descendants of mixed native and Anglo origins.

Richard Hakluyt (1582) was convinced that the residents of Norumbega were descendants of Europeans. His judgment was based on an episode in which John Cabot brought three native slaves to England, dressed them in European clothes, and for his own amusement introduced them to his associates as English citizens. The masquerade lasted until someone asked a question and realized that Cabot's stooges had no comprehension of the King's English. Likewise, Thomas Jefferson observed that some of the natives near the capitol in Washington, D.C., were virtually indistinguishable from Europeans: "Dress them in European clothing," said Jefferson, "and they cannot be distinguished from Englishmen" (Hope, 1988, 167). English colonists reported that natives of the Lenape-Renawauk (a New Jersey Delaware tribe) were much like Europeans in appearance.

Norman Villas

Several Nordic structures have been identified on ancient maps and in ruins found along the East Coast of North America. An ancient stone tower—modeled after 14th-century Catholic lavabos—still stands in Newport, Rhode Island. On his map—below—Verrazano reported a territory called Norumbega (spelled Oranbega on this map—1) with longhouses in New England (2) and the Carolinas (3). These are called "Norman villas" on the Vesconte Maggiolo map of 1527. An inland sea—perhaps a fictitious extension of Hudson Bay—served to separate French from Spanish territories (4). Archeologists Eben Horsford, Arlington Mallery, and Thomas Lee excavated numerous remains of longhouses in the northeast.

Old Stone Tower
Newport, R.I.

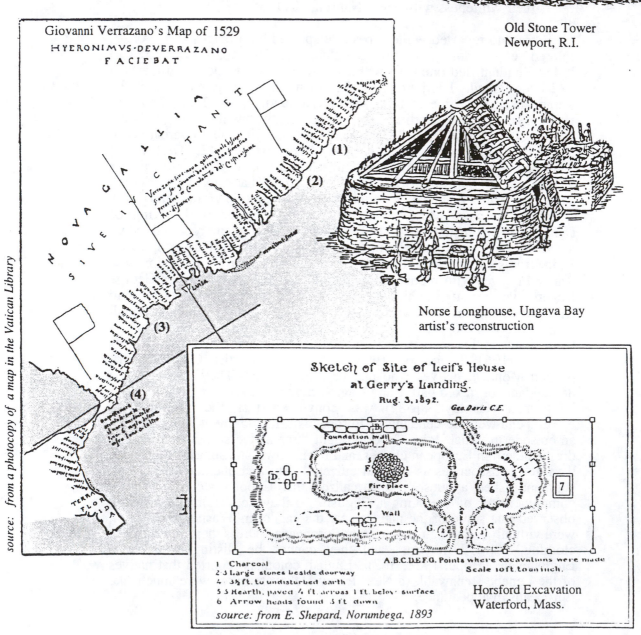

Giovanni Verrazano's Map of 1529

HYERONIMVS·DEVERRAZANO
FACIEBAT

source: from a photocopy of a map in the Vatican Library

Norse Longhouse, Ungava Bay
artist's reconstruction

Sketch of Site of Leif's House
at Gerry's Landing.
Aug. 3, 1892.   Geo. Davis C.E.

1 Charcoal
2-3 Large stones beside doorway
4 3½ ft. to undisturbed earth
5-5 Hearth, paved 4 ft. across 1 ft. below surface
6 Arrow heads found 3 ft. down

A.B.C.D.E.F.G. Points where excavations were made
Scale 10ft. to an inch.

source: from E. Shepard, Norumbega, 1893

Horsford Excavation
Waterford, Mass.

260

Native physical appearance as seen in ancient portraits, early photographs, and so-called "full-blooded" descendants has led Arlington Mallery (1951, 168) and others to suggest that the Iroquois included a mixed native and Scandinavian ethnic heritage. Therefore, it is not surprising that some Lenapes and Algonkians reported legends that their ancestors had come from a land across the Atlantic (Stromsted, 1974, 55 & 116). The Micmac natives had a tradition that grassy mounds near St. Peters in Nova Scotia concealed the remains of white settlers who had occupied the region prior to the arrival of Champlain (Sinclair, 1992, 137). According to French settlers in Louisbourg, Nova Scotia, the harbor was known to the earliest immigrants in that region as Porte aux Anglais—("Port of The English"). Wilson (1991, 181) suspects that this name is a relic of ancient voyagers from Bristol.

Portugal's entry into the world-wide evangelistic movement earned a monopoly over access to Atlantic colonies by virtue of a papal bull in 1484. This decree, which was reinforced by the Treaty of Tordesillas, gave holy blessing to Portuguese raids along the East Coast of North America (in Norumbega and Greenland). The goal of the raids was to remove natural resources—in the form of native slaves—whom the pope had declared to be Portuguese property. Portuguese cavalier Estevao Gomez reported white-skinned people living beside more-Asiatic natives in the northeast territories of Labrador and Baccalaos. This area included Newfoundland and Labrador along the northern portion of the St. Lawrence Gulf. Another contemporary name for this region of North American mainland was "Greenland" or "Greenland Province." Historian Peter Martyr reported in 1524 that Gomez filled his ships with slaves "of both races" (natives and whites) which he captured for sale in Lisbon (Newton, 1932, 172).

Historian Richard Eden translated Gomara's account of the same region in 1555 as follows: "The newe lande of Baccalaos is a coulde region, whose inhabytantes are idolators and praye to the sonne and moone and dyvers idoles. They are whyte people" (Fiske, 1920, Vol. II, 22).

In 1577, Master Dionise Settle of the Frobisher expedition to Baffin Island reported meeting three natives whom he called "crafty villains with a white skin" (Hakluyt in Hawke, 1972, 24). Of the other natives, Settle said: "their color is not much unlike the sunburnt countryman who laboreth daily in the sun." He noted that they used arrows with tips made of "stone or iron" and leather boats made from deerskins. These boats were the size of dories that carried up to twenty men; they were propelled by means of sails, oars, and paddles. "They have some iron," he said "whereof they make arrowheads, knives, and darts" (Hawke, 1972, 28).

Champlain heard native tales of whites living near Hudson's Bay in 1616 (Brebner, 1933, 156). The native reports were sufficiently realistic that Champlain actually expected to find white settlers which he believed were the long-sought residents of Cathay. Natives referred to the whites as the mistigoche—or "the white boat men." Hjalmar Holand (1940, 85) believes these "white boat men" were descendants of immigrants from the Western Settlement of Greenland. In 1930, James Dodd found evidence of ancient Norse explorers in Ontario. Norse remains from a site near Lake Nipigon included a sword, axe, shield handle, and pieces of iron armor. Although Dodd's discovery was initially met with criticism and disdain, the validity of the artifacts were confirmed after a lengthy investigation conducted by J.W. Curran, editor of the Sault Ste. Marie

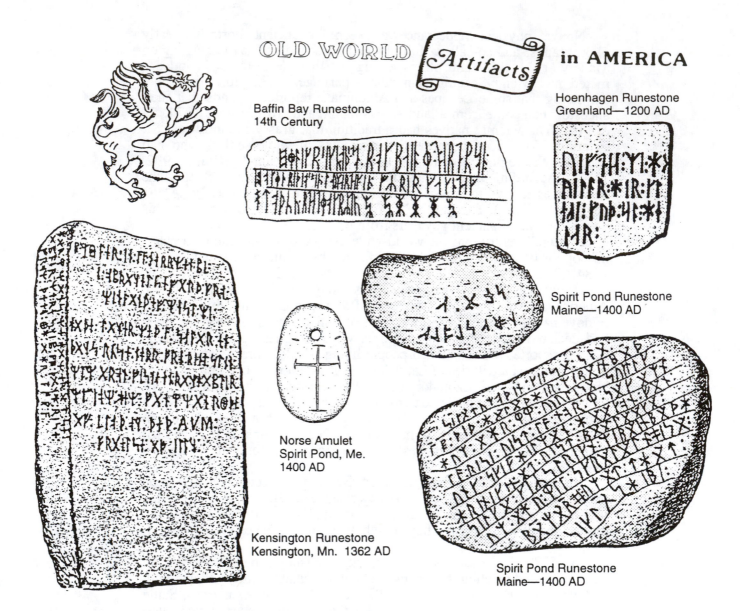

OLD WORLD *Artifacts* in AMERICA

Baffin Bay Runestone
14th Century

Hoenhagen Runestone
Greenland—1200 AD

Spirit Pond Runestone
Maine—1400 AD

Norse Amulet
Spirit Pond, Me.
1400 AD

Kensington Runestone
Kensington, Mn. 1362 AD

Spirit Pond Runestone
Maine—1400 AD

Norse Inscriptions in America

The Kensington Runestone—once branded a "hoax" by orthodox historians—has now been exonerated by the most exhaustive study of ancient runic inscriptions. The presence of this monument to a group of explorers from the Vinland colony should not seem surprising. Indeed, the English friar Nicholas of Lynn made five trips to the region of the magnetic North Pole between 1360 to 1365—this according to testimony in the writings of Gerhard Mercator. The pole was situated in Christian Bay—or Hudson Bay which lies at the mouth of the Nelson river. This river was a principal fur trading route during the 18th century deep into Canada and Minnesota—to the same region where the runestone was carved in 1362. As this date falls at a time when the Paul Knutson expedition from Norway had been dispatched to search for "lost" Christian colonies in the New Land, some scholars believe the Kensington memorial stone is a relic from that expedition.

Broadsword
Lake Nipigon, Ontario

Besides gathering eight court affidavits and conducting extensive interviews and a field visit to the site where the remains were uncovered, Curran found out that Professor McIlwraith of the Toronto Museum had also found remains of iron armor at the site.

The explorer Nicholas Tunes found two types of natives in Baffin Land on his 1656 expedition: the Inuit (or Eskimo) and bands of another sort who were tall and blond. John Franklin described the blond Eskimos as people who "differed little from Europeans" (Herrmann, 1954, 264). In 1837, Arctic explorers Dease and Simpson reported seeing an Eskimo who "might almost have been a Scandinavian" (Herrmann, 1954, 264). Ethnographer Franz Boas in the 1800's reported Eskimo traditions of tall blond people called the "Tunit." Robert Gathorne-Hardy and Wilfred Grenfell reported "blond Eskimos" in Labrador, and Vilhjalmur Stefansson reported blue-eyed natives near the Moose River in Ontario (Holand, 1940, 85). Stefansson declared in a 1910 report that he found bands of "lost Scandinavians" living near the Eskimo on Victoria Island (Herrmann, 1954, 264). Photographs of "Labrador Eskimos" taken during the 19th century show striking facial similarities to Norwegians.

Historian Alexander von Humboldt believed that the Tuscarora tribe of northeast America bore signs of intermingling with ancient Europeans. He noted in his writings "the whitish, often blue-eyed nation of the Tuscarora" (Herrmann, 1954, 175).

Early explorers found evidence of Black voyagers—both Moors of Iberia and West Africans—who traveled to the western continents ahead of the 16th-century European conquest. Verrazano's first encounter with African natives in America came as his ship passed by the Carolina coast. Near Roanoke Island, natives rescued a sailor who had fallen from a dory, and Verrazano observed: "The color of these people is black (neri), not very different from that of Ethiopians" (Weise, 1884, 311; Huyghe, 1992, 191). Ivan VanSertima (1992) identified the African Mocosa tribe on 16th-century charts of the Carolinas. Andre Thevet's map of 1575 shows the location of the Mocosa tribe between Virginia and Norumbega along the East Coast (Weiss, 1884). This French map is partially based on Verrazano's exploration.

Alfonse Quatrefages, anthropology professor at the Museum of Natural History in Paris, identified the Jamassi tribe of Florida as a native population of Africans. Native author Dhyani Ywahoo reported in Voices of Our Ancestors (1987) that blacks settlers were known to his ancestors: "Our elders told me that long before the white men made their appearance upon the shores of Turtle Island, other visitors had come. In the great long time ago, the black people came from Africa."

Diocese of Greenland

One European institution, the Holy Roman Church, remained faithful to the memory—if not the survivors—of 14th-century Norveca. Following the decline of Norwegian sea power in the 15th century, the ravages of bubonic plague, the onset of cooler climates, and the arrival of The Little Ice Age, Norumbega became increasingly more isolated from Europe. Meanwhile, settlers on Greenland Island fled south to avoid starvation and insufferable winters. Historical accounts tell of decreasing mercantile contacts between the Isle of Engroneland (Greenland of the North) and Europe. The island was largely deserted by the start of the 16th century, although Norse refugees and a mixture of various European ethnic groups prospered in isolated communities alongside native tribes on

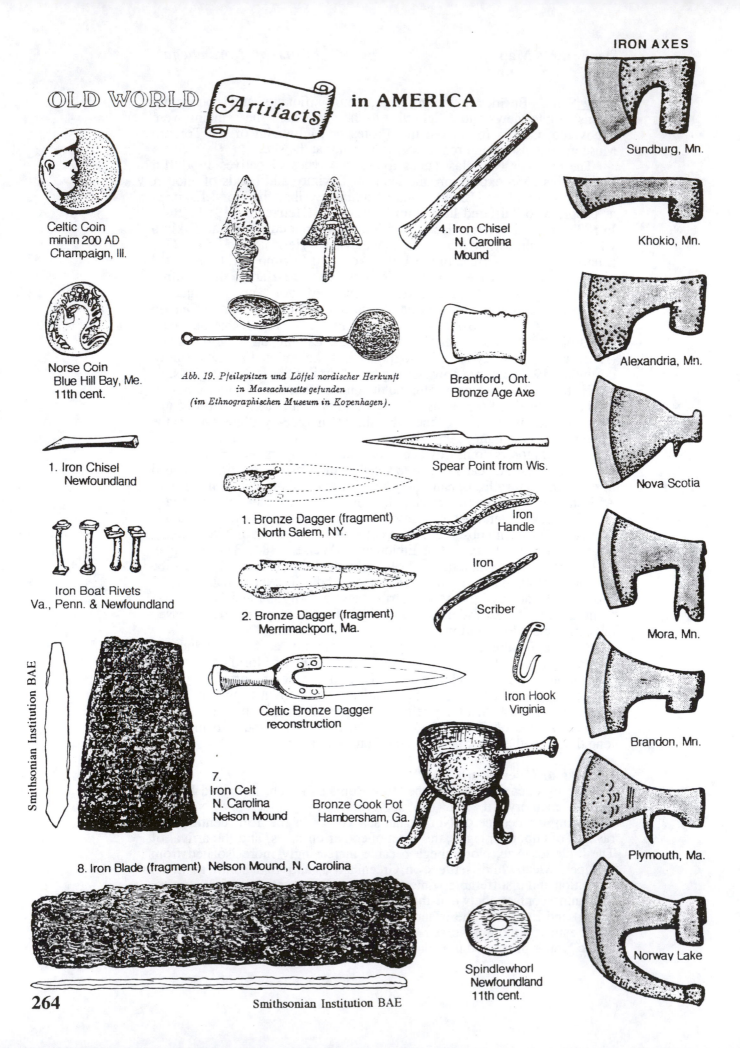

OLD WORLD Artifacts in AMERICA

IRON AXES

Sundburg, Mn.

Khokio, Mn.

Alexandria, Mn.

Nova Scotia

Mora, Mn.

Brandon, Mn.

Plymouth, Ma.

Norway Lake

Celtic Coin
minim 200 AD
Champaign, Ill.

Norse Coin
Blue Hill Bay, Me.
11th cent.

Abb. 19. Pfeilspitzen und Löffel nordischer Herkunft in Massachusetts gefunden (im Ethnographischen Museum in Kopenhagen).

4. Iron Chisel
N. Carolina
Mound

Brantford, Ont.
Bronze Age Axe

Spear Point from Wis.

1. Iron Chisel
Newfoundland

1. Bronze Dagger (fragment)
North Salem, NY.

Iron
Handle

Iron
Scriber

Iron Boat Rivets
Va., Penn. & Newfoundland

2. Bronze Dagger (fragment)
Merrimackport, Ma.

Iron Hook
Virginia

Smithsonian Institution BAE

Celtic Bronze Dagger
reconstruction

7.
Iron Celt
N. Carolina
Nelson Mound

Bronze Cook Pot
Hambersham, Ga.

8. Iron Blade (fragment) Nelson Mound, N. Carolina

Spindlewhorl
Newfoundland
11th cent.

264

the North American mainland from Labrador to the Carolinas. This region, for several decades, was known by its adopted name "Greenland"—which is the name it was known by when Jao Fernandez reached Labrador circa 1492.

Jacob Ziegler's 1532 map of the North Atlantic identified the southern coast of Gronlandia as "Bacallaos"—which was the Portuguese name for Stock Fish Land (a.k.a. Newfoundland). In other words, his "Gronlandia" extended all the way from the Arctic isle as far as Newfoundland. This was probably the same American shore identified in Bishop Gisle Oddson's report as the destination of the inhabitants of Greenland's Western Settlement who had fled "to America" in the 14th century (Ingstad, 1969, 94). Refugees in the Gulf of St. Lawrence region may well have referred to their new home as "Greenland"—thus confusing Renaissance geographers about the identity of new lands.

The relative prosperity of these settlers and their communities was not unknown to church authorities nor to the merchants that occasionally braved the Atlantic tempests. Hanseatic ships, cogs from Bristol, and Venetian galleys were among sporadic visitors. However, as all these visitors sailed by compass bearings—the common belief was that this "Greenland," or "Norumbega," or "New Land" was situated near the North Pole. Archaic maps by Donnus Nickolaus Germanus (1482) show "Engronelant" in this position directly north of Norway and consequently northeast of England. As far as Europeans were concerned, this Engronelant was an Old World colony situated above Europe on the fringe of Arctic lands—the Hyperborea of ancient Roman legend. Although a few competent explorers and geographers must have guessed that Greenland was in the west, the prevailing notion was that it was a northern territory. It wasn't until voyages by Cabot, Verrazano, Cartier, Hudson, Champlain, and Davis established the coastlines of northwest territories that geographers realized that the "Greenland" once thought to be situated above Norway was synonymous with North America. That realization is reflected in 16th-century maps that refer to Labrador or even North America as "Greenland."

During the 14th century, North America was known to Europeans as "Greenland Province," "Isla Verde," or "The Green Isle." It was shown as a continent called "Isla Verde" on a 1528 world map by Pietro Coppo. Many orthodox scholars regard Isla Verde as a "fictitious" island—in spite of Coppo's brilliant deduction that it was a generic term for North America. Historical references presumed to be about the Arctic Island of Greenland often refer to continental lands (i.e., North America); this mistake concerning the true identity of the continental Greenland is often apparent from the nature of the materials being discussed—such as forests (or lumber), white falcons, and exotic furs.

The archbishop's records from 14th-century Bergen mentioned that Greenland contained "black bear, marten, deer, and huge forests." All of these actually were present on the Canadian mainland farther west and not on Greenland Island. Several scholars have noted that Medieval references to a land called "Greenland" referred collectively to all the Northern Regions—Wineland, Markland, Nyaland, and the Island of Greenland (Nielsen, 1994, 8; Thompson, 1994, 267). The Icelandic annals of 1328-1372 informs us that Bishop Alf of Greenland was ordained in 1365—confirming that Catholic congregations were still thriving at that time (Holand, 1940, 143).

Newfoundland Cod Fishery
17th cent engraving
from LaRonciere (1938)

Harvest from The Sea

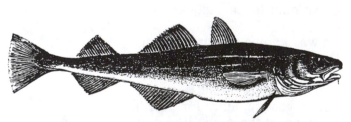

Newfoundland cod
a.k.a. stockfish, bacalaos
source: Nordenskiold (1881)

Extrema America or Terra Nova
17th-Century Dutch Map Title
from printed map by Joan Blau, Amsterdam, 1648
note mariners and codfish

Whaling Factory
Red Bay, Labrador
British Library

As Greenland was a popular name for temperate as well as Arctic lands, some confusion regarding the naming and habitation of northern isles was inevitable. In a 1493 letter written on behalf of Martin Behaim to the king of Portugal, Dr. Monetarius mentioned that the Duke of Moscow "had discovered some years back the great island of Greenland, the coast of which stretches more than 300 leagues, and where there are still numerous colonies of the Duke's subjects" (Ravenstein, 1908). As Moscow was part of the Hanseatic League, the "Greenland" Monetarius refers to might have been the same Isla Verde frequented by Hanseatic merchants in the western Atlantic. This Isla Verde was one of several unidentified isles of the Newfoundland archipelago. Ramsay (1972, 200) believes this was a reference to colonies on Spitsbergen (actually north of Russia) which was settled by the czar's subjects circa 1435. Indeed, Spitsbergen does show up on some 16th-century maps as "Terra Verte" or Green Land. On the other hand, Behaim's 1492 globe has Greenland Island labeled as "Wildt Lapland" and makes no mention of Green Land north of Russia. So we can't be sure what territory the letter was about.

The Arctic island we think of as "Greenland" seems to have been largely depopulated—but not deserted—between 1450 and 1550. Jon Groenlendingr, an Icelandic merchant, visited the site of the Eastern Settlement in 1540. According to Groenlendingr's testimony, his men found the body of a recently-murdered Norse villager, but they didn't find any living residents. Those who fled the settlement might have taken refuge with Inuit natives out of the false belief that Jon and his crew were pirates. Native traditions reveal that the Inuit had given succor to the settlers on similar occasions. At any rate, the settlement was abandoned shortly after Jon's visit.

By the time explorer John Davis visited Greenland Island in 1585, there was no sign of the old settlement: the inhabitants had all fled south, joined with Inuit tribes, or they had perished. Nevertheless, a native trading post still remained in business: in 1586, John Davis picked up a load of sealskins from a location given as "Greenland." This account demonstrates that English sailors still knew the location of trading posts on the Arctic isle (Beeching, 1972, 303). The isle is clearly shown on 16th-century Danish maps and on Waldseemuller's world map of 1516.

Church authorities in Rome must have known of the declining prosperity in the northern isle of Engroneland—if for no other reason than the tithe due to the Church treasury must have fallen with the temperature. However, it seems that the Diocese of Greenland Province (that is, North America) was regarded as a significant Church territory clear up to the Reformation. Pope Alexander VI appointed a new bishop to the Greenland Diocese—the Benedictine Mathias—in 1492. This appointment came on the heels of an appeal from Danish King Christian II who was concerned about the consequences of leaving the bishop's seat unfilled. Pope Leo X appointed Vincentius Pedersen Kampe (Erik Valkendorf) as the successor to Mathias in 1520. Christian II promised to convey Vincentius to Greenland in one of his own vessels, however there is no record that the new bishop ever reached his congregation, nor is it clear which "Greenland" was intended as the destination. The mission was aborted when the Protestant Reformation swept through northern Europe. By 1536, the Catholic Church was outlawed in Danish territories—including Norway and its former, western Atlantic colonies.

Meanwhile, there was a growing need for clergy in Mexico. Millions of New World natives were awaiting salvation and European clothes. The

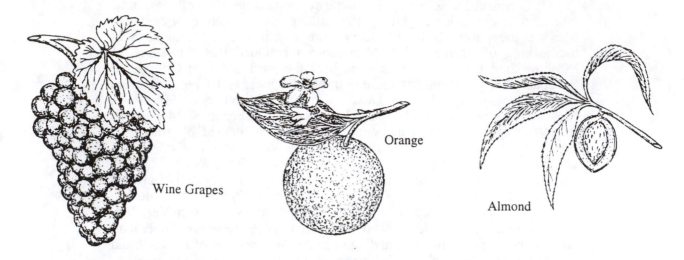

Wine Grapes

Orange

Almond

Apple

Fruits of Norumbega

During the 16th century, European explorers reported an amazing cornucopia of food plants growing in the New World. Cartier reported apples and grapes along the northeast coast. Verrazano reported oranges and almonds north of Florida and grapes near the St. Lawrence Gulf. Champlain also found grapes. Columbus reportedly found rhubarb on Hispaniola. The amazing aspect about all these fruits is that they were originally Old World plants. Apparently, ancient voyagers had carried them across the oceans long before the arrival of English, French, and Spanish colonists.

Two New World plants, pumpkins and potatoes, seem to have arrived in the Old World prior to the 16th century. Herbalists called pumpkins "a Turkish plant;" they called potatoes an import from "Norumbega."

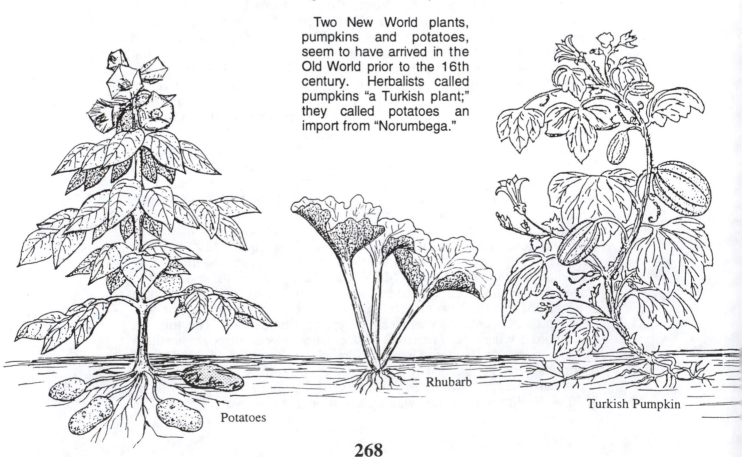

Potatoes

Rhubarb

Turkish Pumpkin

river of gold and silver that poured from the region called "New India" or "New Spain" funded construction of spectacular cathedrals in countries still loyal to the Catholic Faith. Popes and cardinals naturally turned their eyes away from the "Northern Regions" and focused their attention on Mexico, Peru, and the East Indies where they expected the greatest rewards in gold and souls.

Catholic geographers who kept a record of the frontiers of world evangelism also lost interest in lands which many still believed were situated near the North Pole. Babcock (1922, 95) notes that Adam of Bremen's mention of Greenland being located "opposite the mountains of Sueda, or the Riphean range" place it directly north of Norway—which is where it is located on most early 16th-century maps. This placement confirms the equation of Greenland with the Roman Hyperborea and helps explain why Europeans failed to draw a mental connection between Greenland Province (North America) and the rest of the so-called "New World" until the late 16th century. Pope Nicholas V (1448) referred to Greenland as "an island north of Norway" (Ramsay, 1972, 199). Paulo Forlani's 1565 map has Greenland as an island next to the North Pole which follows somewhat the position on Behaim's globe (Portinaro & Knirsch, 1987, 95). Pierre Desceliers' 1550 planisphere shows Greenland as contiguous with northern Norway. On this map, Greenland has a temperate climate, bears, and elephants (Portinaro & Knirsch, 1987, Pl. XXVII). It is also shown as a long peninsula of land north of Norway on maps by Nicolas Desliens circa 1566 (Portinaro & Knirsch, 1987, Pl. XLII & XLIII). Girolamo Verrazano's map of 1529 (in DuJourdin et al., 1984) has Greenland as a peninsula located directly north of Norway with proportions very similar to those of Donnus Nickolaus Germanus (1482).

During the mid-1500's, Catholic authorities focused their attention on Hispaniola, Mexico, and the <u>Mundus Novus</u> or "New World"—which was the early name for South America. Aside from Ponce DeLeon's excursion into Florida, North America and Greenland Province were virtually ignored. Three decades after the Columbus voyage, Church fathers celebrated Columbus as the discoverer of a "New World." It would still be another twenty years before geographers realized that the lands which Columbus, Cortes, and Pizarro had conquered were actually connected to continental lands farther north. These were the same lands that Medieval geographers believed were located near the North Pole. As John Cabot, Juan LaCosa, and Giovanni Verrazano finally confirmed, Mexico and Florida were contiguous with Greenland Province and Leif's old Wineland colony—they were all part of North America.

Danish priests who were more familiar with northern waters abandoned early the notion that Greenland and Vinland were situated near the North Pole. Yet there remained confusion over terminology regarding what territories were part of the Arctic island—Greenland—and what isles were to be regarded as territories of Northeastern America. Nicolay's 1506 map identified Newfoundland as "Verde" (or Green Isle), Coppo's 1528 map used "Isola Verde" for the northern continent, and Zaltieri's 1566 map had "Verde" close to Cape Race, Newfoundland. Babcock (1922, 98) notes that both Nicolay and Zaltieri were familiar with the common designation of the North Atlantic island of "Groenland," yet they still chose to apply the name Greenland to continental land and to numerous "green isles" of the Atlantic. He speculates that this naming of

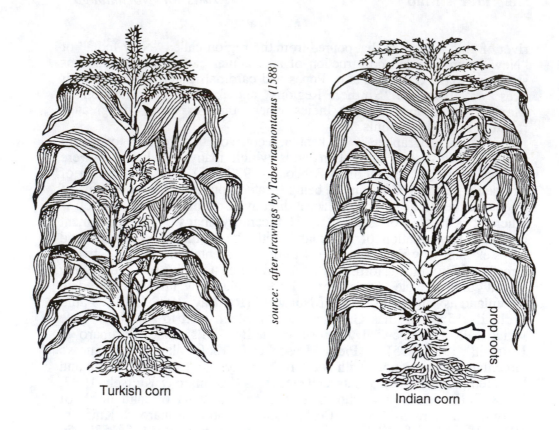

source: after drawings by Tabernaemontanus (1588)

Turkish corn

Indian corn

prop roots

American Grains in Europe

Orthodox historians tell us that Columbus brought native American maize to Europe, but they usually overlook the article by Peter Martyr comparing Indian corn to a variety already growing near Seville. This was the Roman grain that so impressed Pliny the Elder. One variety of corn used to feed animals reached Scandinavia by the 15th century. Another variety, grano de brazil, was imported to Italy.

The grain was known as "Welsh corn" in England; elsewhere, Europeans called it "Turkish corn"—assuming it was an import from Turkey. In 1588, the plant taxonomist Tabernaemontanus noted two kinds of corn in Europe: Turkish corn brought by Moslem traders and Indian corn brought from the New World. The taxonomist identified Indian corn by a second set of roots on the stem called "prop roots."

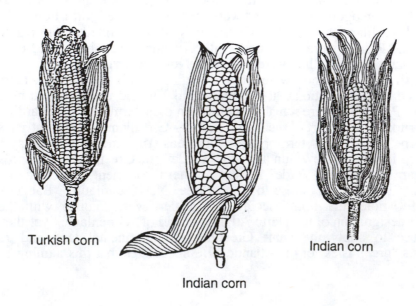

Turkish corn

Indian corn

Indian corn

"fanciful" isles and continental land was simply a reference to the luxuriant vegetation.

Bishop Thorlaksson's map of the North Atlantic drew a distinction between the North American region of Labrador that had been called "Greenland" on 16th-century maps and the Arctic peninsula that he believed should carry the title alone. His own map of 1606 identifies Labrador as America extrema vertis Gronlandiam—that is, "the extremity of America as opposed to Greenland" (in Babcock, 1922, 98).

Remnants of Greenland's congregations passed on part of their heritage. One of the first missionaries to visit the Micmac natives of Gaspe, Father LeClercq, reported in his Relation de la Gaspesie that the Indians had a certain veneration for the cross (Holand, 1940, 76). Had Columbus only pressed on a bit farther to the northwest when he sailed in 1492, he might have been able to attend Catholic Mass with Bishop Mathias on the continent he was later honored with "discovering."

New World Cornucopia

Several writers have speculated that North American imports were vital to the survival of north Europeans during the Middle Ages; they were equally important to Renaissance societies. Certainly, the northern countries took a substantial amount of fish from the Newfoundland Banks as early as the 14th century. Maize, potatoes, and tobacco also crossed the sea. Cameron (1965, 124) notes that the yearly value of stockfish which Portugal took from the Grand Banks amounted to over $4 million—a sum more than twice the value of South American treasure imported to Spain.

During the 14th and 15th centuries, Europeans benefited from imports of ivory and furs from North America. Kings enjoyed the sport of falconeering—courtesy of imported falcons which traders brought from Labrador. Leif Ericson is said to have brought timbers back from Greenland for use in his Bergen house; Irish traders imported brasilwood used in French palaces. English aristocrats puffed away on pipes filled with American tobacco. And peasants in the British Isles tended potatoes in their gardens.

The orthodox version of history tells us that Norse explorers abandoned attempts to trade with natives after several skirmishes forced them to withdraw to Greenland. However, we know that isn't true because records in Bergen tell of a continuous flow of taxes-in-natura from Greenland which were paid in the form of pelts—and these were taken from the hides of black bears, beavers, and foxes of North America.

The importance of this trade both to the natives and to Europeans was an enduring link between the hemispheres. Richard Hakluyt predicted that furs, timber, and potash from Norumbega would make England independent of Baltic merchants. These, he predicted would be the "real source of wealth in the New World" (Beeching, 1972, 17). He quoted with satisfaction the case of a French merchant from Rouen who sold in France for 440 crowns a parcel of furs that were purchased in Maine for 40 crowns—an eight-fold profit margin!

Historian John Brebner (1933, 116) notes that: "In 1534 near Chaleur Bay, the Indians fairly besieged Cartier's company in their anxiety to trade (furs for iron tools)." Jacques Cartier reported that "The savages showed a marvelously great pleasure in possessing and obtaining these iron wares and other commodities ... they bartered all they had to such an extent that all went back naked without anything on them" (in Brebner, 1933, 117).

Tobacco

Native American with Cigar
from Andre Thevet (1558)

Nicotina rustica—tobacco
Dodoens Herbal (1553)

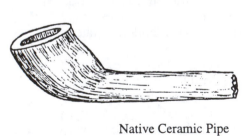

Native Ceramic Pipe
*New Jersey Mound
Smithsonian Report (1875)*

Danish Ceramic Pipe
Irish mound—1000 AD

Elizabethan Gentleman with Pipe
*from Tobacco by Anthony Chute
1595*

272

Even after several skirmishes with natives in 1609, Dutch sailors found "an exceedingly lucrative fur trade" with tribes located along the Hudson river (Brebner, 1933, 223).

Norumbega's merchants brought Indian corn (or maize) to Baltic ports. Botanist John Finnan, author of <u>Maize in The Great Herbals</u> (1950, 182), implicated Norsemen in the transport of a "northern flint" variety of maize to Europe circa 1000 AD:

> How a northern flint type might have reached Europe at such an early date can only be guessed. It is known that the northern flints described by Brown and Anderson were widespread in eastern North America in pre-Columbian times. According to legend, two Norsemen, Karlsefni and Thorfin, in the years 1002 and 1006 AD, brought back ears of corn to Europe from what is now Massachusetts.

The Irish got their first potatoes from the vessels and merchants of Norumbega. Gerard's <u>Herbal</u> of 1597 mentions that potatoes were a product of Virginia and also a crop of Norumbega (Thompson, 1994, 210). This indigenous American plant that became a mainstay of the Irish diet was a native food that Irish settlers adopted in their new habitat (Ibernia) and eventually shipped back to the homeland. Colonial land developers and mercantile agents such as Walter Raleigh transported potatoes and tobacco to English ports as a way of making a meager return for their investments. Historians invariably gave these post-Columbian promoters credit for being the "first" imports—out of a mistaken belief that earlier imports were "impossible."

Northern Flint was not the earliest maize to reach Europe in the ships of ancient travelers. Writing in the 16th century, Joseph DeAcosta observed that a maize-like plant was known to the ancients: "That millet that Pliny writes to come from the Indies into Italy, ten years before he did write it, hath some resemblance unto mays (maize) for that it is a grain, as he says, that grows in reeds and covers itself with the leaf, and hath the top like hairs, being very fertile; all which things agree not with millet" (Markham, 1880, 231). This "Indian mays" that Pliny wrote about in the 1st century was a marginal crop in Spain up to the time of Columbus—at which time Peter Martyr compared it to grain which the mariner brought back from the Antilles (Haiti).

Tobacco reached European ports sporadically—as early as Roman times. The Dutch botanist, Rembert Dodoens (1516-1585), published the earliest-known illustration of American tobacco (<u>Nicotina rustica</u>) in his 1553 herbal—<u>Trium Priorum</u>. At that time, Dodoens did not specify this plant as a New World species because he believed that tobacco was known to ancient Romans as "yellow henbane." Tobacco historian Sarah Dickson (1954) believed that Dodoens was mistaken in this belief due to the fact that he had only verbal descriptions of the plant in books by Pliny The Elder and his Roman contemporaries to serve as references:

> Like his contemporaries, Dodoens relied heavily on ancient authorities: Galen, Pliny, and especially Diosorides, the Greek physician who accompanied the Roman armies on their campaigns in the 1st century of our era. The <u>materia medica</u> written by the last has survived 2,000 years, while much of the work of such classic writers as Sappho, Menander, Livy, Cicero <u>et al</u>, has disappeared. ... Dioscorides has a lengthy description of three kinds of henbane, and he is faithfully followed by Dodoens. He calls these black,

Native Fur Traders
16th cent engraving

source: after 16th-century drawing by DeBry source: New York Public Library

European Furrier Shop
In The Middle Ages

Fur Imports from The St. Lawrence Gulf Region

Church records of the 13th century tell of beaver, ermine, wolverine, and black bear pelts being imported from Greenland to pay the Crusader's tax (Gibson, 1974, 173). These pelts actually represent animal skins taken from mainland territories of North America as the animals were not present on the Arctic island of Greenland. By the 15th century, Basque merchants imported beaver pelts to Bristol—according to harbor records. These accounts probably represent New World imports from the region of the Gulf of St. Lawrence.

When the French explorer Jacques Cartier visited the region in 1535, he reported that the natives were friendly and anxious to trade their furs for iron implements. Henry Hudson also found friendly natives anxious to trade furs for iron tools when he sailed up the Rio Grande (later the Hudson river). And Champlain organized and promoted the fur industry along the St. Lawrence during the early decades of the 17th century. New World furs were a boon to northern Europeans who had a shortage of pelts due to rising human populations.

American Brown Bear
after S. Cabot 1544

274

white, and yellow. It is the last which Dodoens illustrates with the woodcut of the small tobacco, which also has a yellowish flower. It is easy to understand how the herbalist, who had never seen the type described by his ancient authority, should believe that he had in the tobacco plant an example of this kind of henbane. (Dickson, 1954, 34)

The German botanist Fuchs reported in his 1543 herbal that Romans knew of three kinds of henbane; the Swedish botanist Carolus Linnaeus (1707-1778) described five kinds of henbane known to Mediterranean cultures (Dickson, 1954, p. 35). Since Roman times, herbs like tobacco were commonly smoked in small quantities in clay pipes, and these pipes are often found in Roman-era archeological sites in Great Britain. One archeologist even reported the smell of nicotine still present in one of these pipes (Thompson, 1994, 184). Although Europeans heard reports of Native Americans smoking rolled weeds (cigars), it was not until late in the 16th century that herbalists began distinguishing a New World henbane as a new kind of tobacco. It was not the smoking of tobacco (or henbane) that astonished Europeans so much as the fact that native Americans simply rolled up a huge leaf and stuck it directly in their mouths. Such a practice was regarded as gross if not "uncivilized."

Tobacco was not mentioned in <u>Dos Libros</u> which the Spanish herbalist Monardes published in 1565. The fact that it wasn't mentioned supports the theory that American tobacco wasn't regarded at that time as anything significantly different from what was already available in Europe. That same year, Europeans were treated to Benzoni's <u>Historia Del Mondo Nuovo</u> which gave some details of tobacco use in the New World, and it is only after this date that herbalists began mentioning the medicinal properties of New World tobacco as being unique from those of common, Old World henbanes.

Scholars familiar with the ancient traditions of smoking in Persia and India are struck by the fact that native Americans used an Old World name for the indigenous tobacco. In Andre Thevet's book on New World cultures—<u>Les Singularitez de la France Antarctique</u> (1557)—a woodcut illustration shows a native holding a burning cigar which the caption refers to his cigar as a <u>tammaraka</u>. This word is similar to the ancient Sanskrit word <u>tamrakouta</u> which is believed to be the root for Persian words for tobacco including: <u>tubbaq</u>, <u>tavak</u>, and <u>tambak</u> (Thompson, 1994, 300). Several accounts of early explorers tell of natives from the West Indies to California calling the plant "tabaco" or "tabah" (Dickson, 1954, p. 133). The term "nicotine" was not applied to the plant until after the French merchant Nicot imported a Brazilian variety in 1560.

Francis Drake brought stores of a West Indian tobacco to England in 1586. Although this is the date traditionally given for arrival of the plant in the British Isles, the presence of Roman ceramic pipes in ancient ruins along with Pliny's description of yellow henbane as a Roman medicinal suggest that tobacco smoking was known in ancient England.

English writer Edmund Howes reported that the merchant John Hawkins imported tobacco in 1565, and William Harrison (1573) observed that: "In these days, the taking-in of the smoke of the Indian herb called 'tobaco' by an instrument formed like a little ladle, whereby it passes from the mouth into the head and stomach is greatly taken up and used in England against rewmes (rheumatism) and some other diseases engendered in the loins and inward parts and not without effect"

Transoceanic Imports

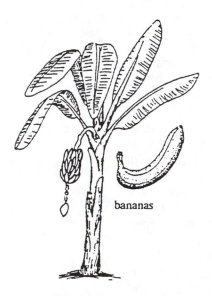

bananas

source: Courtesy of Rare Books and Manuscripts Division, The New York Public Library, Astor, Lenox and Tilden Found.

mamei. guaiaua. guanauma. platane.

Benxoni's History of The New World

Bananas

There are numerous testimonials reporting how Columbus brought bananas back from the New World as proof that his expedition had reached the Orient—since bananas were regarded as an Old World fruit. Early explorers also reported finding bananas growing in the Americas, and illustrators such as Girolamo Benzoni called the banana (or plantane) a New World fruit in his book *Historia del Mundi Novo* (1572).

American Turkey
Schleswig mural
Germany, 1280 AD

source: Schleswig Turkey—after a photograph in Hope (1983, 19)

Turkeys

Norse merchants reported carrying turkeys on their voyages (Gibson, 1974, 173). Examples of these American game birds were painted on decorative medallions in the Schleswig Cathedral circa 1280 AD. Europeans called the bird a "turkey" due to the belief that it was imported by Moslem merchants of the Middle East.

source: Moslem Turkey—Thompson (1994)

Moslem Turkey
16th century painting

(Dickson, 1954, p. 132). As this historical account predates Drake's travels across the Atlantic, unidentified voyagers must be credited with bringing tobacco to England. Although Francis Drake and Walter Raleigh were not responsible for the "first" introduction of the plant, they can be credited with establishing a sustainable market for this New World drug.

Gudmundur Kamban noticed paintings of turkeys—the quintessential American game bird—on 13th-century decorative panels inside the Schleswig cathedral. Hjalmar Holland (1940, 78) believes these were made after Norse or Hanseatic cogs brought the birds back from the East Coast of North America. That is a likely explanation since Richard Nielsen has identified a rune text in Maine telling of a Lubeck (Vendal) ship in the region of Norumbega circa 1400 AD. And the travelog of a Spanish Franciscan (circa 1350) tells of a visit to Ibernia—or Great Ireland in the west—where he saw "fat birds."

Old World Imports

The exchange of plants and animals went both directions. Cloth, iron tools, glass beads, and jars traveled westward on ships from several European and African cities. Such artifacts have been found during archeological excavations of native burial mounds and villages. Typically, archeologists have assumed that such artifacts identify a ruin as "Colonial" without bothering to get confirmation from radio-carbon dating. Thus, John Fiske declares: "As for the mounds which are scattered in such profusion over the country west of the Alleghenies, there are some which have been built by Indians since the arrival of white men in America and which contain knives and trinkets of European manufacture" (Fiske, 1920, Vol. I, 142). Sadly, the credo of "no European artifacts before Columbus" is merely a false assumption that has led to innumerable mistakes in the interpretation of archeological sites.

Paul Herrmann (1954, 285) noted an extended record of Norse and European artifacts that antiquarians found in the New England region:

> Long before the possibility of a Viking colony on American soil had been seriously considered, ancient Norse weapons and utensils, such as spoons, arrowheads, silver-work, etc., were taken from pre-Columbian graves in the region of Middlesborough and Four Corners in Massachusetts; and as early as 1892, when he published his great book on America, the German Americanist, Rudolf Cronau, expressed the opinion that lasting cultural influences must have been exercised on eastern America by the Greenland Norsemen.

Anne Ingstad (1982, 36) reported a domesticated pig bone in the refuse of an excavated longhouse at the Newfoundland site at L'Anse Aux Meadows (radio-carbon date circa 1000 AD). This confirms that Norwegians brought along pigs on their travels from Europe. Pigs were adopted into native farming practices to such an extent that later European colonists assumed that they were indigenous animals. Thomas Jefferson was among those who believed that Native Americans raised pigs. His book, Notes on the State of Virginia (1788) called the "Chochon de Inde" (or "Indian pig") one of the native quadrupeds of America. He differentiated this domesticated animal from the wild "pecari" on his chart comparing "Quadrupeds of Europe and America" (Wayne, 1979, Plate 2).

Immigrants from Greenland Island also brought the common mainstays of farming life: horses, cattle, sheep, goats, chickens, dogs and cats. They were not the "first" to bring horses. The Icelandic Eyrbyggia Saga (1250) reported that Bjorn of Iceland saw Irish inhabitants riding horseback in "Hvitramannaland"—a territory situated near Wineland. Winnipeg natives told French explorers that white settlers with horses had occupied the region in ancient times, and the explorer Pierre Gaultier reported tales of a band of white people with horses that had settled in the far west. Natives called this band the "Ouachipounnes."

Some native tribes maintain that they had horses before the great European invasion of the 16th century; and this claim seems corroborated by tales of frontier scouts who reported seeing horses in native villages. In Tennessee, the native horse was called the "Chicasaw." Antiquarians found pre-Colonial wagon fittings in New York and horse skulls in several native burial mounds in Wisconsin and Michigan (Thompson, 1994, 199, 322). There is also evidence of feral horses roaming the frontier near English and French colonies. Edmund Ruffin's Sketches of Lower North Carolina (1861) refers to the "dwarfish native breed" of the Core Banks. Orville Hope (1988, 4) believes this is the first mention of small, wild horses still found along the islands of Chesapeake Bay. These horses are similar to north European farm animals which Celtic and Nordic farmers brought along on their voyages to America.

When Baron DeLahontan invaded Seneca villages in 1687 during the French & Indian War, he noted that the natives were excellent farmers who raised numerous European animals: "In all these villages," the baron wrote in his journal, "we found plenty of horses, black cattle, foul, and hogs" (Howard, 1965, 29).

Arabian sailors brought back pineapples from the Caribbean and left behind orchards of almonds and oranges. Although historians traditionally credit Spaniards at St. Augustine with bringing the first oranges to Florida in 1565, Ramusio's Discurso (1539) includes a report from Captain Giovanni Verrazano saying that oranges and almonds were already growing along the East Coast when his ships passed by in 1524. Verrazano, Cartier, and Champlain all reported grapes growing near the St. Lawrence Gulf—the same region that was known to Norsemen as "Wineland." On his travels in Mexico, English merchant Henry Hawks observed (circa 1567) several "indigenous fruits." These included such Old World varieties as oranges, lemons, and guavas, (Hawke, 1972, 145). He observed that:

> There are many kinds of fruits of the country which are very good as plantains (bananas), sapotes, guavas, pinas, aluacatas (avocados), tunas (prickly pears), mammees, lemons, oranges, walnuts—very small with little meat on them, grapes—which the Spaniards brought into the country, and also wild grapes—which are of the country and are very small, quinces, peaches, figs, and but few apples—which are very small, and no pears, but there are melons and calabashes. (Hawke, 1972, 149)

On his voyage to the St. Lawrence Gulf in 1535, Jacques Cartier reported in his journal passing an island called "Brest" and an island of birds near a passage called White Sands. They made port at Brest after sailing through a region of "Islettes" in 51°55'N latitude. Among the local plants, he identified pea-sized millet (maize), figs—which the natives called asconda, cashewnuts, apples—which the natives called honesta, and beans (Florio, 1966, 21). Most botanists regard figs and apples as Old World plants. On the mainland, the explorers found "great store of

278

vines—all as full of grapes as could be" (Florio, 1966, 46). Grapes are also regarded as an Old World fruit. Old World grapes and apples in America can be dated to Roman if not Celtic times. Figs, oranges, and almonds are most likely Arabian imports from the time when Moors traveled west from Lisbon and Morocco in the 10th century.

The World Plague

Commerce declined considerably during the late 1300's with the world-wide epidemic of bubonic plague. Although historians once assumed that no Old World diseases reached the Americas until after Columbus, it is now evident that all the worlds major diseases had spread across the seas (Thompson, 1994, 170, 209, 280). Bubonic plague struck Europe in 1347. Significantly, it reached Iceland in 1346 two years before Norway—which is surprising due to the close contact between Bergen and Icelandic merchants (Mallery, 1951, 160). The disease killed more than half of the population in Europe; the impact on European settlements in America was probably even more catastrophic. Fleas carried in furs were the primary agents of infection, and since the furs were carried from North American trappers to Europe, the disease probably spread in that direction as well. A pneumonic strain of the disease spread with influenza. It was particularly virulent and may have exterminated entire settlements in northern regions where settlers huddled together out of cold and fear of attack.

Historians have long assumed that the 1347 epidemic originated in Central Asia and spread by some unknown ship to Sicily or Cyprus before seaborne commerce and rats infected all of Europe (Burke, 1985, 55). The earliest extant report of where the 14th-century epidemic originated comes from the writings of an Arabic scholar, Ibn Al-Wardi (Dohs, 1977, 40). According to Al-Wardi—writing just before his death from the disease in 1349, the Black Death originated in "the Land of Darkness." Arabic geographers regarded this Land of Darkness as the same place Classical philosophers had in mind when they wrote of a land where the sun was hidden for three months during the winter—that is, lands in the "northern regions." Such an origin—or multiple origins— would explain why the plague struck Iceland before reaching England or Norway. It might also shed light on prohibitions that the clergy put forth against westward voyages across the Atlantic—known to Arabs and many Europeans by the foreboding title: "the Sea of Darkness."

Historians once assumed that the name of the epidemic—Black Death—referred to the color of spots on the bodies of those who were infected; but that name wasn't applied to the 14th-century plague until many generations after it had occurred. Black Death might also refer to the place of origin—the "Land of Darkness."

Arlington Mallery, a maverick antiquarian who excavated countless archeological sites in the Eastern United States, noticed several ancient fortresses with huge mass burial pits like those described in plague-torn Europe. These were places where the deceased were interred in haste without customary burial offerings. Mallery (1951, 165) described how plague could have effectively wiped out early European colonies in America. In the wake of cultural disintegration that followed the epidemic, North American coastal areas were more vulnerable to new European colonization than they would have been a century earlier.

Lingua Norumbegia

European languages provided a bridge of understanding for early explorers. Nicolo Zeno reported his encounter with a Latin-speaking pirate in the Newfoundland archipelago in 1390 (Hakluyt, 1582). All along the Carolinas, explorers and colonists reported contacts with Welsh-speaking natives—some of whom claimed that their ancestors had arrived from overseas many generations in the past (Anderson, 1992; Mallery, 1951; Fell, 1989). Walter Raleigh's History of the World (1614) noted that natives used Welsh words (Gardner, 1986, 34). Ethnologists identified Norwegian words common in Iroquois speech; the Nordic trickster god—Loki—also found his way into native lore. And in the Dutch colony of New Amsterdam, settlers relied on a Norwegian translator, Cornelius Sand, to negotiate with the natives of Manhattan—presumably because they understood Norse words (Anderson, 1992).

Leif's Lair on The Charles

The supposed "trump" of orthodox historians concerning the location of Norse, Irish, and Welsh settlements in pre-Colonial America is the presumed lack of archeological evidence. Of course the longhouse foundations which the Ingstads found on Newfoundland confirm Nordic visits to the region but do not establish occupation of the region for a significant time. Medieval maps, on the other hand, confirm long-standing knowledge of North American colonies in such places as Ibernia Magna (a.k.a. "Great Ireland"), Albania, Vinilanda, Norveca, Bacalaos, and Greenland Province. Likewise, historical accounts of Irland Mikla, Vinland, and the Icelandic Isles verify trans-Atlantic voyages to North American outposts. But what about artifacts?

There is even substantial archeological evidence of pre-Colonial European occupation, although orthodox historians tend to dismiss such evidence with disdain or with a judgment that it couldn't possibly be important. This has been the case with respect to a Norse coin from King Olaf Kyrre's reign (1066-80) that was found on an Indian settlement in Maine (Roesdahl, 1987, 275). The orthodox rationale why the artifact is "not important" is the presumption that it was simply a "trade item" that passed among the natives and did not substantiate Norse habitation nor travel in the region. Likewise, Roesdahl calls the Kensington artifact a "fake runestone"; other artifacts are either "fakes" or result of "misidentification" (Roesdahl, 1987, 276). Such "scholarly" dismissals have resulted in a failure to examine substantial evidence of ancient European occupation of North America's East Coast region.

Like Champlain, historian-archeologist Eben Horsford (1892) searched along the Penobscott river for remains of the ancient city of Norumbega. In the mid-1880's he shifted his attention from the Penobscott to the Charles river in Massachusetts. There, he found ancient remains of what he called a "fort" at the confluence of Stony brook and the Charles river; he also found the site of ancient stone-and-earthen "wharves" as well as the remains of several ancient dams. At Watertown, Horsford and a crew of volunteer archeologists excavated the stone-and-earthen foundations of several longhouses. His daughter, Cornelia, excavated several graves which were attributed to ancient European settlers. Horsford concluded that they had found the location of Leif Ericson's homestead, the Vinland seat of Bishop Erik Gnupsson in 1121, and the site of the illusive city—Norombega.

Among the artifacts which Cornelia found near Wayland, Massachusetts, was a rectangular implement about four-inches long made of a vitreous substance which she suspected was obsidian. The artifact was indeed peculiar for the region of the East Coast because obsidian does not occur naturally in the United States east of the Rocky Mountains. This artifact was also similar to obsidian artifacts found in ancient sites in Iceland where the material is referred to as "Icelandic agate." Analysis of the artifact at Harvard University Museum confirmed that it was obsidian. Other artifacts found at Middleboro, Massachusetts, included bone eating utensils and arrowpoints of stone and iron made in the Nordic fashion.

In a review of Horsford's site report, the Scottish Geographical Society (1894, 102) observed that the excavations were thorough and supported the author's claim that Watertown was the site of an ancient European settlement: "Professor Horsford's conclusions were accepted by the American Geographical Society at a special session held at Watertown in 1889, and he was then congratulated on his discovery." Of course not everyone agreed with Horsford. Without mentioning any specific evidence, historian Samuel Morison (1971, 67) ridiculed Horsford's research with the admonition that: Horsford could find Norse ruins in "every Colonial ditch or paved cow-yard."

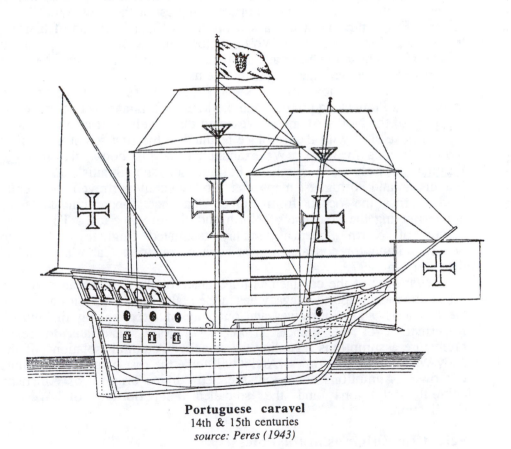

Portuguese caravel
14th & 15th centuries
source: Peres (1943)

The Friar's Legacy

Historians once credited Portugal's Prince Henry The Navigator with initiating the Great Age of Discovery. Now, it seems, European discovery of the New World began at a much earlier time—certainly back to the days of the Phoenicians, Celts, and pagan tribes of the British Isles. The heritage of those voyagers was nearly smothered as a result of religious oppression and plagues during the Dark Ages. It was revived in fragments during the Renaissance—and then smothered, once again, in the backwash of 16th-century European conquest of the New World. By the time Eruocentric academicians wrote the "official" version of history, the requiem for ancient New World exploration was nearly complete. It was at this point that The Friar's Map came out of hiding; now the issue of America's true heritage is again before us.

We have seen how Roger Bacon's idea of scientific cartography inspired his Franciscan brothers and the king of England to undertake the mapping of the North Atlantic. We noted the travels of friar Nicholas of Lynn whose skill with the astrolabe resulted in the first scientific map of North America in 1360. We examined how his book, the Inventio Fortunatae, influenced English, Portuguese, and Spanish explorers. Franciscan and Portuguese maps after 1360 typically portrayed continental lands across the ocean from Europe that had topographical details approximating the coastline of North and South America. The friars' survey of North America certainly facilitated English voyages to Newfoundland for cod and furs in advance of John Cabot's "official" discovery in 1497.

Regardless of the commercial importance of the Franciscan mapping effort, the most important legacy lies in the realm of metaphysics and what we can learn about ourselves and our way of experiencing the world. Resurrection of the Franciscan map will force historians to reject premature assumptions regarding the so-called "cultural isolation" of the New World in ancient times. And it will force the rest of us to reexamine our own assumptions about the so-called "divine origins" of American cultural institutions and the so-called "superiority" of Western Civilization.

Scientific Enigmas at the Poles

As both priest and Oxford graduate, friar Nicholas inherited two conflicting intellectual traditions. His life straddled the waning rule of Medieval Church authority and the waxing of scientific endeavors that kindled the Renaissance. The Church—as custodian of Roman tradition—stressed humility and faith in doctrine; science demanded open-

282

mindedness and a boldness to challenge the unknown. How were these divergent philosophies to be reconciled?

At Oxford, Nicholas walked in the footsteps of great empiricists—the foremost of his era being Roger Bacon (1214-1294) who is counted as one of the early champions of the scientific method. He was also a Franciscan and a person who, on occasion, challenged orthodoxy. His views on nature and geography so infuriated Church authorities that he was arrested and imprisoned as a heretic from 1278 to 1292. Modern biographers think it amusing that Bacon speculated on temperate lands near the North Pole. It was a lingering controversy that must have caused Bacon and his contemporaries great mental anguish and occasional mirth. The same issue preoccupied the life of friar Nicholas.

Since the days of the Romans, scientists had argued with philosophers over the nature of lands at the poles. One Classical tradition, inherited from geographical philosophers, held that habitation at the poles was impossible due to extreme cold. This view had been thoroughly examined in theoretical models whose construction was a mental exercise which amused philosophers. Roman sailors probably helped confirm scientific hypotheses when they found increasing icebergs and cold weather near the geographical poles. Simultaneously, the geographers held that a huge magnetic stone at the North Pole was the explanation for the phenomenon of the ever-reliable compass needle pointing north. This belief resulted from an exercise of "logic." Since it was known that iron was magnetized by rubbing it with a lodestone, a process of deduction led to the conclusion that compass needles pointed north because the North Pole was the location of a huge mountain of the same material. Accordingly, this logical or "scientific" model of Earth gave Classical geography the semblance of mathematical perfection which was highly valued in Roman and Greek society.

Opposing this so-called "scientific model" was another group of philosophers and empiricists which we might call the "Dreamers." They claimed that sailors who traveled to the Polar Regions had observed arcadian lands, orchards, and vineyards. Arrogant "scientists" regarded the dreamers as a mob of dangerous imbeciles.

Both sides in the controversy claimed empirical proof; both sides concluded that their opponents were dead wrong. Early Renaissance scientists who often came from monastic orders and the merchant class tended to side with the theory that Earth had climatic zones; meanwhile the Church sided with a more miraculous view of the world and held that in God's kingdom "all things were possible." The conflict between Church and Science had begun.

During the Middle Ages, most philosophers were not very well informed about the real world. Many spent their days in monasteries where they relied on deductive reasoning to resolve the uncertainties of nature. The important concerns of the day centered on biblical prophesy and scripture—not upon practical matters of geography and medicine. Likewise, those who traveled most often—the soldiers, sailors, and mendicant friars—also viewed their world through the tinted spectacles of superstition and dogma. In spite of their exposure to the real world, they were not the most-reliable observers of natural phenomena. The chasm between experience and knowledge was transformed by the scientific curriculum which Roger Bacon devised for Oxford University. This curriculum changed the way people viewed the world by combining religious education with scientific knowledge. Thus, Brother Nicholas

Science versus Orthodoxy in The Middle Ages

Medieval religion did not escape the rising tide of science and technology. In this illustration from the 14th-century Holkham Bible, God is shown measuring creation by use of a compass. Other English bibles had similar illustrations. Historian Anthony Blunt (1938) identified the compass as a symbol for science. The popularity of such a symbol reflects the rising importance of Natural Law and the scientific method as part of the curriculum at Oxford University. Roger Bacon was a champion of that curriculum; and his leadership played a key role in the practice of surveying and astronomy as it was taught at Merton College—a branch of Oxford University. Nicholas of Lynn, also an Oxford scholar, contributed to the popularity of surveying by writing a book on the use of astrolabes. Thus, in England, science and religion came to be regarded as complimentary forces. Although this reconciliation was tested by the Inquisition and by frequent conflicts with Roman authorities, a solid foundation was established for the teaching of science as part of religious philosophy. Even in the 18th century, the poet-artist William Blake looked back to Edwardian English sources for inspiration: his painting, "Ancient of Days," shows God measuring creation using a compass.

source: Blunt (journal of the Warburg & Courtland Inst., 2-1938, 53-63)
Holkham Bible: after photograph in Paul Johnson (1973)

acquired training at Oxford that enabled him to examine the world using scientific equipment; while at the same time he appreciated the miraculous powers of nature and the importance of faith.

Nicholas seems to have been the first to resolve the controversy over the nature of the Polar Regions in a statement included in Caludius Clavus' Nancy Manuscript of 1427. The friar realized that opposing theorists on the issue of polar climates had failed to consider a third possibility: that there were two different north poles. He arrived at this breakthrough discovery because of his ability to conceive of something the authorities of his era called "impossible." In other words, though a man of science, friar Nicholas was also a dreamer.

Although 15th-century cosmographers seem to have been largely ignorant of the difference between the magnetic and geographic poles, this knowledge seems to have become common knowledge by the early 16th century. A map by the 16th-century cartographer, Pedro Finel, has two scales of latitude on his North Atlantic maps of 1504 to account for magnetic declination. The Ruysch map of 1508 bears a notation in the northwest Atlantic that the compass is unreliable in this region. Charts by Burrus and Athanasius (1632), Kircher (1643), and Edmund Halley (1683) also indicate magnetic variation in the North Atlantic. The first observance of this phenomenon is one of the so-called achievements of Columbus, however we know that friar Nicholas had identified the magnetic pole as a feature of the Western hemisphere that was separate from the geographic pole. This identification of two poles—and the consequent phenomenon of magnetic declination—assures us that Nicholas deserves credit for this scientific discovery. Until now, this is one of many achievements which orthodox historians have erroneously credited to Columbus.

Nicholas was also the first person of historic record to reach the Magnetic North Pole. Historians have also awarded credit for this achievement to more recent explorers: James Ross and William Peary reached the region of the magnetic pole in 1818 near Lancaster Sound—nearly five centuries after friar Nicholas. Most of the attention of scholars and the public seems to have focused upon the quest to reach the Geographic North Pole—a competition which challenged Arctic explorers from Norway, Denmark, England, and the United States. Lieutenant Robert E. Peary, a civil engineer with the U.S. Navy, announced that he reached the geographic pole on April 6th, 1908. However, that claim was contested by Norwegians on behalf of Roald Amundsen who found the geographic pole a few weeks later—but in a slightly different location. Modern scientists now believe that Peary's instruments were inaccurately calibrated—so he probably missed the mark by several miles.

James Ross has been credited with discovering Antarctica in 1841—a feat he accomplished while looking for the Magnetic South Pole. Historian Ian Cameron (1965, 220) acknowledges that merchants who passed by the southern continent referred to the unknown land as "Terra Incognita" prior to the English expedition—so they already knew where it was located. A physician on the Ross expedition, Robert McCormick, called the ice-bound territory a "newly-found land" and proposed that henceforth it would be known as: "The Great New Southern Continent." However, this title had little appeal to geographers. Most people referred to the "newly found" land as "Antarctica"—which was derived from an old Greek word—antarktikos (literally "land opposite the northern region of polar bears"). This reemergence of Classical terminology for a

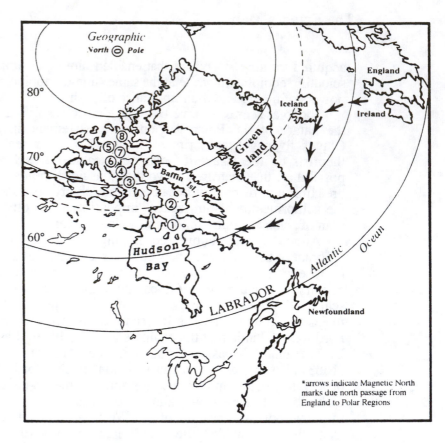

Table of   MNP Coordinates

1)	Roman era	?	?
2)	1330	66°	
3)	1831	71°	96°
4)	1903	north shift	
5)	1945	76°	102°
6)	1959	74°	101°
7)	1963	75°	98°
8)	1980	77°	102°

*arrows indicate Magnetic North
marks due north passage from
England to Polar Regions

Migrating North Magnetic Pole

Over the years, the magnetic pole has shifted towards the north. Medieval maps showing Greenland and Hudson Strait directly north of Norway by compass bearings suggest that the pole was situated in the northern part of Hudson Bay circa 1000 AD. By the time Franciscan surveyors arrived on the scene, the pole was close to the Arctic Circle west of Baffin Island—at least that was where an unidentified friar reported the pole (at 66°) in the Nancy Manuscript of 1427. Subsequent scientific reports tell of the pole shifting farther north—but it is still over 1,000 miles south of Geographic North. A world map of magnetic declination (below) shows that the highest degree of compass error occurs west of Greenland and north of Hudson Bay—site of the magnetic pole.

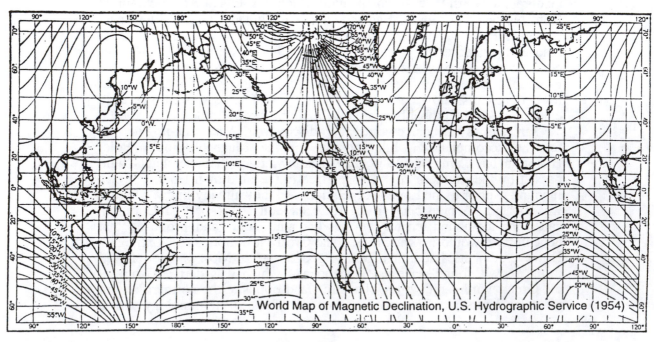

World Map of Magnetic Declination, U.S. Hydrographic Service (1954)

southern continent is not surprising: the land was known to Romans and Egyptians; Roselli accurately named the region on his map of 1508.

Gerhard Macerator's 1569 map had two Magnetic North Poles. One was in the location of the Geographic North Pole; a second was placed northeast of Asia above the Strait of Anian (now the Bering Strait) at 75°N latitude and almost 180° west of Ptolemy's Prime Meridian (at the Canary Isles). Mercator's symbol for the magnetic pole, a mountain island, is similar to the "magnetic mountain" which most of his contemporaries placed at the Geographic North Pole. Placement of a second Magnetic North Pole near Siberia was intended to explain the phenomenon of magnetic compass declination from true north. This second magnetic pole might have been an effort to reconcile the magnetic declination that Marco Polo observed northeast of China. On his expedition to the Anian Region (which we now know was the Pacific coast of British Columbia), Polo observed that his compass needle pointed to a region <u>east</u> of the Pole Star.

Mercator wrote to Hakluyt at Oxford in 1580 supporting the proposal of sailing above Russia to reach Cathay. He had two concerns about prior voyages via the northwest passage (Davis Strait): it took sailors near the "pole of the loadstone" (magnetic pole) and it froze over every year threatening to trap and crush unwary ships. Mercator noted that:

> A more hard and difficult passage I think it to be this way which is now attempted by the west, for it is nearer to the pole of the loadstone, to the which I think it not safe to approach. And because the loadstone hath another pole than that of the world, the nearer you come unto it, the more the needle of the compass doth vary from the north, sometimes to the west, and sometimes to the east, according as a man is to the eastward or the westward of that meridian. (Beeching, 1972, 209)

Dark Seas—Brighter Horizons

There have been two "dark seas" that have encumbered the quest for knowledge of our planet: one was a Medieval phantasm that afflicted European sailors; the other is a dark sea of orthodoxy that has blinded modern scholars to the contributions of non-Europeans in the process of discovery. When Albert Figdor found an important map in Croatia in 1911, leading European scholars realized that the map was complied from Arabian sources. This led to a biased judgment regarding the value of the map, so it was relegated to the attic of history. There it stayed until I rediscovered the document in 1994. What will change, now that the Friar's Map is out of hiding?

R. Buckminster Fuller (1992, 1) believed that human society is held captive by ancient belief systems:

> The Dark Ages still reign over all humanity, and the depth and persistence of this domination are only now becoming clear. This Dark Ages prison has no steel bars, no chains or locks. Instead, it is locked by misorientation and built of misinformation. ... We are powerfully imprisoned in these Dark Ages simply by the terms in which we have been conditioned to think.

Fuller concluded his rather dismal appraisal of the human condition with the bold admonition that humanitarians seek effective ways to expose false belief systems. He believed that such exposure would lead to an environment of clear-thinking that societies need in order to cope with the obstacles facing human survival.:

after an illustration
by William Bleau in
The Light of Navigation
England, 1612

Renaissance Cosmology

Scenes like this one were infrequent during the 13th century but commonplace by the 16th century. At the center, an explorer-navigator explains his rationale for the location of lands in the Polar Region—based on personal experience and the information from available charts. He uses two globes, one celestial and one terrestrial. Plotting geographical coordinates required field measurements of the locations of constellations of the zodiac which corresponded to latitudes. Longitudes were estimated from sun dials, nocturnals, and hour glasses—which were the only devices capable of measuring elapsed time from established geographical reference points. Navigational tables showing eclipses and other celestial phenomena helped field surveyors estimate their location. The compass, circular astrolabes (left) and the cross staff (right) were also used to determine the angle of constellations relative to the Geographic North Pole.

Mapping by the Stars

Celestial and terrestrial globes illustrate the corresponding points of reference between stars and places on Terra Firma (Earth). This illustration appeared in a book by Petrus Apianus in 1524. Plotting these points on the flat surface of a rectangular map resulted in gross distortions of land areas.

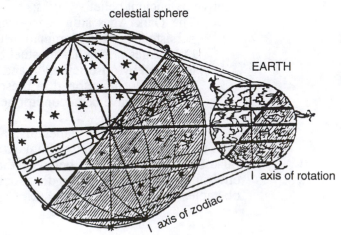

celestial sphere

EARTH

I axis of rotation

I axis of zodiac

source: Nordenskiold (1889)

288

Misorientation, wrong beliefs, and conditioned fixations are escapable only when that which is physically and metaphysically true becomes experimentally provable and comprehensible. The untrue is rendered spontaneously obsolete only by the demonstration of that which is true. (Fuller, 1992, 1)

According to Fuller, overspecialization was endangering the ability of human societies to adapt to changing environments and changing realities. Given this perspective, it might be possible for us to understand how myopic specializations of historians and their devotion to archaic beliefs (that is, "sacred cows" of academia) have delayed the emergence of a truly global history of discovery.

Back in 1961, Edmundo O'Gorman wrote a book about the antiquated thinking of orthodox historians. He called this book The Invention of America. O'Gorman outlined how Eurocentric historians contrived a racist rationale for white supremacy in American society. Although the historians had no conscious intention of achieving such a hideous creation, it was nevertheless the result of writing history within the narrow context of Eurocentric society. In the traditional context of American History—as it is interpreted by orthodox historians—incongruities of history involving pre-Columbian voyagers are described as "insignificant events," or "outright frauds." Presumably, some misguided malcontent is always eager to rob Columbus of his rightful glory. That rationale serves as a smokescreen to conceal the true reason for preserving the orthodox version of history: and that is the perpetuation of institutionalized racism and white superiority.

White Christian European males, we are told, were not only the "first" to discover America: supposedly, "they were the only people capable of making the discovery." We are told that racist message again-and-again in classrooms, in history books, in official U.S. holidays, in museum exhibits, parades, statues, and movies. Eurocentric values and perspectives dominate the view of orthodox historians: thus, American historian John Hale declared—as truth—his preposterous assumption that only 15th-century Europeans were capable of sailing to the New World:

> Renaissance Europe, alone among maritime communities of the world, possessed both seaworthy ships and skillful mariners. Here then, is one explanation why the impetus for exploration came from the European nations that looked out into the Atlantic. (Hale, 1966, 14)

From Hale's perspective (as the descendant and heir of European conquest), the achievement of Columbus was evidence of a race having superior mental and cultural endowment: "Alone of civilized peoples, Europeans of the Renaissance had the technical and psychological equipment and the economic background to carry out a sustained program of exploration" (Hale, 1966, 20). As a spokesperson for orthodoxy, Hale provided justification for why other ethnic groups had failed to reach out across the oceans to discover the New World. In his book, Age of Exploration, Hale claimed that Polynesian outriggers depended on favorable winds—so Polynesians were supposedly unable to undertake deliberate voyages of discovery beyond the confines of prevailing winds; Arab dhows had sewn planks—so they couldn't possibly withstand the rigors of ocean waves. Chinese junks, he wrongly assumed, depended on rowers—making them unsuitable for long-distance voyaging on the

289

open ocean. Thus, he concluded that Chinese mariners always finished second in competition with superior Europeans. Although his assumptions were false, his standing as a "dean" of academia assured that his books—and theories—reached a large and trusting audience.

Nigel Davies (1986, 244) held a similar belief concerning the impossibility of pre-Columbian voyagers to America. He concluded in his book Voyagers to the New World that: "Only the Vikings are known to have visited America before Columbus, and L'Anse aux Meadows bears witness to their arrival; however, Viking influence on the North American Indian was nil." Davies characterized the Chinese as poor sailors with flimsy vessels: "If the Chinese shrank from braving the short crossing from Korea to southern Japan, the mere contemplation of a vast journey to America in ill-suited craft would have been whimsical" (120).

Whimsical indeed! Marco Polo's 13th-century account of Chinese ships and crews emphasized that they easily surpassed those of Christian Europe. Furthermore, the voyages of Chinese admiral Cheng Ho and his fleet of giant junks from the China Sea to Ethiopia in 1405 is well documented. Ho's vessels carried horses for the Chinese cavalry as well as thousands of infantry to intimidate the potentates of ports they visited along the way. Cheng Ho's ships returned bearing trade goods and African animals (including a giraffe) for the khan's zoo. This round-trip voyage—nearly a century before Columbus—was over 12,000 miles.

In a popular text written to accompany a National Geographic television series, Zvi Dor-Ner (1991) had his own rationale for why the white European champion, Columbus, succeeded where all others supposedly had failed. The Chinese, he fairly noted, had excellent ships; however, it was their own pride that supposedly caused them to shun world exploration. According to Dor-Ner (1991, 14): "A centralized decision, made in Beijing, stopped the whole civilization from venturing and exploring." The Arabs, he said, also had fine ships—but they were content with their insular trading empire on the Indian Ocean, and they felt no need to expand into fringe markets. "Why should they outfit risky voyages of exploration to realms that might not pay nearly as handsome a dividend?" asks Dor-Ner (1991, 23). "One thing was different about Columbus's voyage," says Dor-Ner (1991, 71): "Once he returned, no one forgot America was there." Although Dor-Ner is correct that the Ming Chinese outlawed contact beyond their borders (in hopes of preventing epidemics and cultural decay), he has failed to realize that Asians had traveled to the Americas in earlier centuries—as far back as 10,000 BC.

At one time, the story of Christian superiority, God-ordained discovery, and "manifest destiny" were taught as cultural truisms in the United States. As American society became more enlightened, political leaders were forced to pass legislation that guaranteed equal participation and equal representation in society. In the context of a society that was becoming increasingly more humanitarian and egalitarian, the custodians of dogma were forced to invent new methods and rationales to preserve their sanctified institutions of racism and bigotry. They adopted for that purpose the rising popularity and institutions of science and scholarship.

Originally, the United States was a loosely-associated federation of independent and ethnically-divergent states. Foreign wars with Spain and England, as well as the on-going frontier wars with native inhabitants helped to reinforce a national identity. There was a growing market for nationalist literature—which was filled by such romantic writers as

Washington Irving who promoted Columbus as a national hero. So strong was this sanctified and religiously-sanctioned hero that anyone who mentioned the possibility that someone else might have preceded Columbus was regarded as a traitor with respect to true American values. Likewise, those who stressed that the native peoples were civilized and in no need of "being discovered," were treated with disdain by orthodox scholars. That nationalistic mentality still lies at the very core of mainstream American values as they are taught in the public school system and reinforced by parades, holidays, movies, and popular literature.

Anglo-American males (being the majority in population, in political representation, and in economic control) also have a mythology that supports the theme of white male superiority. That mythology has been cloaked in scientific jargon and professed by academics as though it were scientific fact. On the contrary, the jingoistic mythology professed in academia constitutes a fraud that robs the society of its multicultural heritage. It threatens the very future of a new society built upon the principles of equality and synergy.

The false history we are taught in schools robs us of the lessons of our ancestors. Historians stress the glamour of Columbus who sought a shortcut to the riches of the Orient; thus, easily-found gold and conquest are taught as highly-rewarded values. Most American scholars have missed the drama and enterprise of pioneers who built up the codfish and fur trade of the North Atlantic. These imports had arguably more importance for European cultural development than the gold of Mexico and Peru. However, historians have helped to create a mythology that reinforces blind obedience to dogma and the concept of divine approval of orthodox American heroes. They have created a fictitious "Columbus" and rewarded him for his loyalty to doctrine by boldly proclaiming him the single person who "united the previously isolated peoples of the Old World and the New World." By proclaiming this mythological event, historians have missed the tragedy, suffering, and teamwork that was essential for building the foundation of American society.

Over the past 500 years, Western scholars have described the era of European global conquest as a romantic drama. Technophiles called this brutal period of history "progress;" Colonial real estate speculators called it "manifest destiny;" and religious fundamentalists insisted that "divine inspiration" and "racial superiority" were behind European triumphs in the New World. The philosophical foundation behind such rhetoric was the Eurocentric belief that God had chosen a loyal servant—Christopher Columbus—to spearhead a Western Crusade. The mariner's holy mandate—so we are told—was to bring the gospel of salvation to "heathen" inhabitants of the New World. Presumably, that mandate entitled a single ethnic group—white males—with perpetual rights and privileges reflecting their superior status.

Orthodox academicians added scientific justification for the Columbian superhero by proclaiming that Columbus was "first" to bring Western civilization, religion, plants, and animals across the ocean. He was equally glorified for returning to the Old World bearing the fruits of New World agriculture. This mythical cultural transformation, which some called the great "Columbian Exchange of 1492," or the "Great Encounter," etc., provided a convenient and simplistic story to bolster belief in the superiority of European civilization. Few Western scholars have here-to-fore questioned the validity of this orthodox interpretation of history. Indeed, the uncompromising power of religious values and

291

academic nepotism have combined to stifle most criticism. And they culminated in massive, national centennial celebrations of Western technology, conquest, and Columbus in 1892 and 1992. Meanwhile, scholars have trained their subordinates and millions of children in obedience to the dogmas of approved scholastic tradition. The result has been the promulgation of an educational system in America which has promoted institutionalized racism and covertly welded our spirits to Medieval values.

In order to protect vested interests, the custodians of orthodoxy invented a bastardized form of "science" that really wasn't scientific at all. Enlightened thinkers who came close to the truth were branded as heretics and expelled from the academic community. Those who found artifacts that challenged established beliefs were called "hoaxers." Those who tested the ability of ancient mariners to sail across the oceans were described as "non-scientific adventurers." The strategy was to first ignore those who challenged the Columbus myth; next to scandalize their views by calling them "unscientific"; and finally to invoke the aura of academic authority by declaring contrary information "irrelevant" or "insignificant."

With this book on the Franciscan map, academic beliefs have been exposed as falsehoods; orthodox claims been exposed as frauds. As our brief summary of North Atlantic voyages and the Franciscan survey have demonstrated, the sum of previously ignored "incidents" of contact between Europeans and native peoples constitutes an enormous and profound impact on the early history of America. Contact between the hemispheres influenced the course of events in the Old World as well as the New World: diseases, plants, and animals were carried between the hemispheres—sometimes to the benefit and sometimes to the detriment of societies on both sides of the planet. The impact of transoceanic migration and cultural diffusion were certainly not post-Columbian phenomena.

In the rapidly-changing world of the 20th-century, history provides a facade of stability and certainty. We cling to our beliefs about the past; we celebrate our national heroes; we erect statues and monuments, declare national holidays, and educate our children—all in a desperate effort to affirm religious and cultural beliefs. But truth has a way of shattering dogma and eroding facades. Regardless of decades of ignorance and indoctrination, we are now confronted with the reality that the New World was pretty well known to many Europeans and non-Europeans before the 16th century.

We have arrived at a new threshold of discovery. There was plenty of evidence of Old World travelers reaching America in times of yore—even before we found the Venetian Map of 1414 and identified the section from the friar's gazetteer of 1360. But in this authentic Franciscan-Venetian document, we have reliable, physical evidence that historians have long claimed couldn't possibly exist. I believe we have what an English shipwright would call a "clincher"—meaning an iron-hard device that brings together separate pieces of the hull to make them watertight.

We now have proof that the Northern Regions (a.k.a., Polar Regions or Hyperborea) were indeed North American territories on Old Roman, Medieval, and Renaissance maps. We can finally appreciate the profound significance of a scientific mapping tradition in the North Atlantic that began with Roger Bacon in 1266. The Franciscan maps from 1360 to 1440 serve as a cartographical and a temporal bridge between the Medici Atlas of 1351 and the 16th-century maps of Sigurdur Stefansson and Bishop Hans Resen. We have established beyond any doubt that knowledge of the seaway from northern Europe to America via Iceland and Greenland was current during the time of Columbus. We have identified Florida and the Antilles on eight pre-Columbian maps with many more sure to follow as soon as European map collectors reevaluate the importance of antique documents that have been locked away in vaults for private amusement and the profit of investors. We can finally accept the claim of mariner Columbus in 1492 that he actually had a map of his intended destination.

As a result of our encounter with Nicholas of Lynn and the <u>Inventio Fortunatae,</u> we now have the opportunity to nurture the creation of a more truthful and more relevant history of New World exploration. We can—and we must—place our heritage in a global perspective.

Old dogmas will fall as historians begin telling the true story of multi-ethnic voyages and migrations over the past ten millennia. These voyages extended from beyond Phoenician times through the Middle Ages—revealing that the so-called "Age of Discovery" as it has been portrayed by orthodox, Western historians is largely make-believe. American discovery was actually an ongoing cavalcade of voyages and discoveries spanning several millennia and it included mariners from all the world's major civilizations. This was truly a <u>global</u> effort and a <u>global</u> accomplishment. Nostalgia is no longer a "whites only" affair; we can all be proud of our enterprising and curious ancestors.

This ultimate realization of our multicultural heritage—and our common destiny—is the friar's enduring legacy.

Bon Voyage . . .

after Bible Moralisee, Oxford Bodleian Ms. 270b

BIBLIOGRAPHY

Anderson, W.R., Ed. "Well-Kept Secret," in *Vikingship*, Vol. 31 (1), 1995, Chicago, Leif Ericson Society, page 1.

Armstrong, Richard. *The Discoverers.* New York: Praeger, 1968.

Ashe, Geoffrey. *Land To The West—St. Brendan's Voyage to America.* London: Collins, 1962; New York: Viking, 1962. .

Ashraf, Jaweed. *Maize In India—Introduction or Indigenous?* New Delhi: 1995.

Assiniwi, Bernard. *Historie des Indiens du Haut et du Bas Canada.* Montreal: Editions Lemeac, 1973.

Babcock, William H. *Legendary Islands of The Atlantic—A Study in Medieval Geography.* Research Series No. 8. New York: American Geographical Society, 1922.

Bagrow, Leo, & R.A. Skelton. *Meister der Kartographie.* Berlin: Safari Verlag, 1944.

Bagrow, Leo. *History of Cartography.* Chicago: Precedent, 1951; and Cambridge: Harvard University Press, 1964.

Bailey, James. *The God Kings And The Titans.* New York: St. Martin's Press, 1973.

Beach, S.A. *The Apple.* New York: 1905.

Beeching, Jack (Ed.). *Richard Hakluyt—Voyages and Discoveries.* London: Penguin Books, 1972.

Boutet, Michel-Gerald. *The Celtic Connection.* Santa Barbara: Stonehenge Viewpoint (No. 107), 1996.

Bradford, Ernle. *Christopher Columbus.* New York: Viking Press, 1973.

Bramson, Bo. *Gamle Danmarkskort.* Copenhagen: Pederson's Forlag, 1965.

Brebner, John B. *The Explorers of North America—1492-1806.* New York: Meridian Books, 1933 (1955).

Brown, Lloyd. *Map Making.* Boston: Little Brown, 1960.

Brown, Lloyd. *The Story of Maps.* New York: Dover, 1949.

Burke, James. *The Day The Universe Changed.* Boston: Little, Brown & Company, 1985.

Burke, Robert B. (Translator). *The Opus Majus of Roger Bacon.* Vol. I. Philadelphia: University of Pennsylvania Press, 1928.

Cahill, Tom, et al. "The Vinland Map Revisited, New Compositional Evidence on its Inks and Parchment," in *Analytical Chemistry*, Vol. 59, 829-33.

Cameron, Ian. *Lodestone And Evening Star—The Saga of Exploration by Sea.* London: Hodder and Stoughton, 1965.

Chapman, Paul. *Columbus The Man.* Columbus: ISAC Press, 1992.

Chapman, Paul. *Discovering Columbus.* Columbus: ISAC Press, 1992.

Chapman, Paul. *The Norse Discovery of America.* Atlanta: One Candle Press, 1981.

Chretien, Luc. "Viking Expedition," in *Rolex Awards for Excellence*, 1993.

Christy, Miller. *The Silver Map of The World.* 1900.

Colliers. "Brazil," in *Colliers' Encyclopedia*, Vol. 4, p. 507, 1992.

Covey, Cyclone. *Calalus.* New York: Vantage Press, 1975.

Cummings, W.P., R.A. Skelton & D.B. Quinn. *The Discovery of North America.* London: Elek Press, 1971.

Davies, Arthur. "The English Coasts on the Map of Juan de la Cosa," in *Imago Mundi*, Vol. 13, 1956, 26-29.

Deacon, Richard. *Maddock and The Discovery of America.* New York: George Braziller, 1966.

Deaux, George. *The Black Death.* New York: Weybright & Talley, 1969.

Destombes, Marcel, Editor-in-Chief. *Mappemondes AD 1200-1500; Imago Mundi Supplement IV: A Review of Early Cartography.* Amsterdam: N. Israel, 1964.

Dickson, Sarah A. *Panacea or Precious Bane—Tobacco in 16th-Century Literature.* New York: New York Public Library, 1954.

Dols, Michael W. *The Black Death in The Middle East.* Princeton: University Press, 1977.

Dor-Ner, Zvi. *Columbus and the Age of Discovery.* New York: William Morrow and Company, 1991.

DuJourdin, Michel M., Monique LaRonciere, M. Azard, I. Raynaud-Nguyen, & M. Vannereau. *Sea Charts of the Early Explorers—13th to 17th Century.* London: Thames & Hudson, 1984.

Falchetta, Piero. "Marinai, mercanti, cartografi, pittori. Ricerche sulla cartografia nautica a Venezia, sec. XIV-XV," in *Ateneo Veneto*, September, 1995.

Fell, Barry. *America B.C.* New York: Simon & Schuster, 1989.

Fell, Barry. *Bronze Age America.* Boston: Little, Brown & Co., 1982.

Fingerhut, Eugene R. *Explorers of Pre-Columbian America?* Claremont, Ca.: Regina Books, 1994.

Fisher, Joseph. *The Discoveries of the Norsemen in America with Special Relation to their Early Cartological Representation.* London: 1903.

Fiske, John. *The Discovery of America—With Some Account of Ancient America and The Spanish Conquest.* Two volumes. Boston: Houghton Mifflin, 1892 (1920).

Florio, John. Translation from Italian in 1580. *Navigations to Newe Fraunce—by Jacques Cartier.* Reprint. Ann Arbor: University Microfilms, 1966.

Franklin, Wayne. *Discoverers, Explorers, Settlers—The diligent Writers of Early America.* Chicago: University of Chicago Press, 1979.

Fuller, R. Buckminster. *Cosmography.* New York: MacMillan Publishing Co., 1992.

Gardner, Joseph L., Ed. *Mysteries of The Ancient Americas.* Pleasantville, NY: Readers Digest Association, 1986.

Garrett, Wilbur. "Columbus Track on Behaim's Globe," in *National Geographic*, November, 1986.

Gibson, Frances. *The Seafarers: Pre-Columbian Voyages to America.* Philadelphia: Dorrance & Co., 1974.

Goetzmann, William H., and Glyndwr Williams. *The Atlas of North American Exploration.* New York: Prentice Hall, 1992.

Gordon, Cyrus. *Before Columbus.* New York: Crown, 1971.

Goss, John. *The Mapping of North America.* Seacaucus, NY: Wellfleet Press, 1990.

Gregy, Charles T. *Plague!* New York: Charles Scribner's Sons, 1978.

Hakluyt, Richard. *Divers Voyages—Touching the Discoverie of America.* Ann Arbor: University Microfilms, 1582 (reprint 1966).

Hakluyt, Richard. *Principle Navigations—Voyages, Traffiques & Discoveries of The English Nation.* Toronto: Dent & Sons, 1909, 1927 (original Ms. ca. 1600).

Hale, John R. *Age of Exploration.* New York: Time-Life Books, 1966.

Hall, Robert A., Jr. *The Kensington Rune-Stone—Authentic And Important.* Ithaca, New York: Jupiter Press, 1994.

Hansen, Keld, Ed. *Viking Voyages to North America.* Roskilde, Denmark: The Viking Ship Museum, 1993.

Harley, J.B, and David Woodward. *The History of Cartography*, Vols. I, II, III. Chicago: University Press, 1987.

Harrisse, Henry. *The Discovery of North America.* Amsterdam: N. Israel, 1961 (1892).

Harvey, P.D. *Medieval Maps.* London: The British Library, 1991.

Hawke, David F. Ed. *Hakluyt's Voyages to The New World.* (By Richard Hakluyt). New York: Bobbs-Merrill, 1972.

Hennig, Richard. *Terrae Incognitae.* Leiden: E.J. Brill, 1953.

Hennig, Richard. *Von Ratselhaften Landen.* Munich: Delphin Verlag, 1925.

Hermann, Paul. *Conquest By Man.* New York: Harper & Bros., 1954.

Heyerdahl, Thor. *Early Man and The Ocean.* Garden City: Doubleday, 1979.

Hobbs, William. "The Zeno Map Revisited," in *Imago Mundi*, Vol. 3, 1946.

Holand, Hjalmar R. *Norse Discoveries & Explorations In America 982-1362.* New York: Dover Publications, 1940, 1968.

Holand, Hjalmar R. "The Testimony of Nicholas of Lynn," Chapter 9 in *A Holy Mission to Minnesota 600 Years Ago.* Alexandra, MN: Runestone Museum Foundation, 1959.

Holmes, George. *The Later Middle Ages—1272-1485.* New York: W.W. Norton, 1962.

Hope, Orville L. *6000 Years of Seafaring.* Gastonia, NC: Hope Associates, 1988.

Horsford, Eben N. *Leif's House in Vineland.* Boston: Damrell & Upham, 1893.

Horsford, Eben N. *The Discovery of the Ancient City of Norumbega.* Boston: Author, 1890.

Horsford, Eben N. *The Landfall of Leif Erikson AD 1000 And the Site of the Houses in Vineland.* Boston: Damrell & Upham, 1892.

Howard, Robert W. *The Horse In America.* Chicago: Follett Publishing Co., 1965.

Huyghe, Patrick. *Columbus Was Last.* New York: Hyperion, 1992.

Bibliography

Ibarra Grasso, Dick. "Cuatro Viajes Transpacificos Precolombinos en la Historia y el Folklore," in *Revista Argentian*, (1) June 1991. —*La representacion de America en Mapas romanos de tiempos de Cristo.* Buenos Aires: Eddiciones Ibarra Grasso, 1970. —Communication with the author, 1994.

Ingstad, Anna S. "The Norse Settlement of L' Anse aux Meadows, Newfoundland," in *Guralnick*, 1982.

Ingstad, Anne S. *The Discovery of a Norse Settlement in America.* Oslo: Universitetsforlaget, 1977.

Ingstad, Helge. "The Discovery of A Norse Settlement in America," in *Guralnick*, 1982.

Jacobson, Timothy. *Discovering America—Journeys in Search of The New World.* Toronto: Key Porter Books, 1991.

Johannessen, Carl, & Anne Parker. "Maize Ears Sculptured in 12th & 13th Century AD India as Indicators of Pre-Columbian Diffusion," in *Economic Botany*, 43 (2), 1989.

Jones, Gwyn. *The Norse Atlantic Saga.* New York: Oxford University Press, 1986.

Jones, John. "Maize on Hindu Temples," from Expedition to India. Seattle: Argonauts OTMI, 1995.

Josephy, Alvin M. Jr., Ed. *The American Heritage Book of Indians.* New York: American Heritage, 1961.

Keay, John. *World Exploration.* London: Hamlyn, 1991.

Keen, Benjamin (Translator & Editor). *The Life of The Admiral Christopher Columbus—By His Son Ferdinand.* New Brunswick: Rutgers University Press, 1975.

Kennedy, Brent. *The Melungeons.* Macon, GA: Mercer University Press, 1994.

Kerr, Robert F. and F. Eden. "Summary Deduction of the Discoveries of the World by Antonio Galvano (1555)," in *A general History and Collection of Voyages and Travels.* Vol. II. Edinburgh: William Blackwood, 1811.

Khoury, Fazi. Far Eastern Languages, University of Washington, Seattle. Communication with the author, 1992.

Kimble, George H. *Geography in The Middle Ages.* London: Methuen, 1938.

LaRonciere, Charles. *Historie de la Decouverte de la Terre.* Paris: Larousse, 1938.

Lee, Thomas E. "Norsemen in Ungava, Quebec, Canada," in *The Journal of Indo-European Studies*, Vol. 2 (2), Summer 1994, 187-202.

Lehner, Ernst. *How They Saw The World.* New York: Tudor Press, 1966.

Lelewel, Joachim. *Geographie Du Moyen Age.* Brussels: C.J. Pilliet, 1857. Reprint: Meridian Publishing Co., Amsterdam, 1967.

Lunde, Paul. "The Middle East in The Age of Discovery," in *Aramco World*, 43 (3), June 1992.

Lutz, Edward. "Roger Bacon's Contribution to Knowledge," in *Franciscan Studies*, No. 17, June 1936.

Magnusson, Magnus. *Vikings.* New York: Dutton, 1980.

Mallery, Arlington & Mary Roberts Harrison. *The Rediscovery of Lost America.* New York: E.P. Dutton, 1951, 1979.

Mallery, Arlington. *Lost America—The Story of An Iron Age Civilization Prior to Columbus.* Washington, D.C.: Overlook Co., 1951.

Marcus, G.J. *The Conquest of The North Atlantic.* New York: Oxford University Press, 1981.

Markham, Clements R., Ed. *The Natural & Moral History of The Indies—by Father Joseph de Acosta.* (Vol. I, reprinted from the English translation by Edward Grimston, 1604). London: Hakluyt Society, 1880.

Markham, Clements, Ed. *Book of The Knowledge.* London: Hakluyt Society, 1912.

Mascarenhas, Barreto. *The Portuguese Columbus.* New York: St. Martins, 1992.

McCrone, Walter. "The Vinland Map," in *Analytical Chemistry*, Vol. 60, 1988, 1009-18.

McGlone, William R., and Philip M. Leonard. *Ancient Celtic America.* Fresno: Panorama West Books, 1986.

Meyers, A.R. *England in The Late Middle Ages.* New York: Penguin, 1982 (1952).

Moreland, Carl, & David Bannister. *Antique Maps.* Oxford: Phaidon, 1986.

Morison, Samuel E. *Admiral of The Ocean Sea.* Boston: Little, Brown & Co., 1942.

Morison, Samuel E. *The European Discovery of America: The Northern Voyages AD 500-1600.* New York: Oxford University Press, 1971.

Mowat, Farley. *West Viking: The Ancient Norse in Greenland and North America.* Toronto: McClelland & Stewart, 1990 (Little, Brown & Co., 1965).

Myers, A. R. *England In The Late Middle Ages.* New York: Penguin Books, 1952 (1982).

Nansen, Fridtjof. *In Northern Mists*, Vols. I & II. New York: AMS Press, 1911 (AMS Reprints, 1961).

Newton, Arthur P. *The Great Age of Discovery.* Freeport, New York: Books for Libraries Press, 1932 (1969).

Newton, Arthur. *Travel & Travellers of the Middle Ages.* New York: Kopf, 1930.

Nielsen, Richard. "Evidence of Medieval Scandinavian Exploration of North America," in *Proceedings*, Chacmool Conference, Calgary, 1994.

Nielsen, Richard. "The Spirit Pond Runestones," in *Epigraphic Society Occasional Papers*, Vol. 22, 92-113, 1993.

Nohl, Johannes. *The Black Death: A Chronicle of The Plague.* London: Unwin Books, reprint 1961 (1882).

Nordenskiold, Adolf E. *Facsimile Atlas.* Stockholm: Royal Library, 1889 (Kraus Reprints, New York, 1961).

Odddson, Gisle. "Annalium in Islandia Farrago," in *Islendica*, Vol. 10 (2), 1917.

Oleson, Tryggvi J. *Early Voyages And Northern Approaches 1000-1632.* New York: Oxford University Press, 1964.

Peres, Damiao. *Historia Dos Descobrimentos Portugueses.* Porto: Portucalense Editora, 1943.

Pohl, Frederick J. *Atlantic Crossings Before Columbus.* New York: W.W. Norton, 1961.

Poole, Austin L. *Medieval England.* Oxford: The Clarendon Press, 1958.

Portinaro, Pierluigi, and Franco Knirsch. *The Cartography of North America 1500-1800.* New York: Crown Publishers & Crescent Books, 1987.

Portner, Rudolf. *Die Eikinger-Saga.* Dusseldorf: Econ Verlag, 1971.

Prazak, Charles. "Were Croatians in the Carolinas before Columbus?" *Caralogue*, Summer 1993.

Prazak, Charles. "Early Croatians in South Carolina," in *Carologue*, 1993.

Price, Robert. *Johnny Appleseed.* Bloomington: Indiana University Press, 1954.

Priest, Josiah. *American Antiquities And Discoveries in The West.* Albany: Hoffman & White, 1834.

Prytz, Kare. *Westward Before Columbus.* Oslo: Norsk Maritimt Forlag, 1991.

Quinn, David Beers. *England And The Discovery of America, 1481-1620.* New York: Alfred Knopf, 1974.

Ramsay, Raymond H. *No Longer On The Map—Discovering Places That Never Were.* New York: Viking Press, 1972.

Randles, W.G. "The Evaluation of Columbus' India Project," in *Imago Mundi*, Vol. 42, 1990, pages 50-58.

Ravenstein, G.E. *Martin Behaim His Life & Globe.* London: 1908.

Rienits, Rex & Thea. *The Voyages of Columbus.* New York: Crescent Books, 1989 (1970).

Roesdahl, Else. *The Vikings.* New York: Penguin Books, 1991 (1987).

Roukema, E. "A Discovery of Yucatan prior to 1503," in *Imago Mundi*, Vol. 13, 1956, 30-37.

Sanceau, Elaine. *Henry The Navigator—The story of a Great Prince And His Times.* New York: Norton, Inc., 1947.

Sauer, Carl. O. *Northern Mists.* San Francisco: Turtle Island Foundation, 1968.

Schroeder, Wilhelm. "Report From Hamberg," in *Vikingship*, Vol. 31 (3), 1995.

Scottish Geographical Society. *Scottish Geographical Magazine*, 1894, Vol. 10, pp. 101-103.

Seers, A. Waddingham. *The Story of Early English Travel & Discovery.* London: George Harrap & Co. Ltd., 1923.

Sharp, J.J. *Discovery in The North Atlantic.* Halifax: Nimbus, 1991.

Shepard, Elizabeth G. *Norumbega and Vinland.* Boston: Damrell & Uphom, 1893.

Shirley, Rodney. *Mapping of The World.* London: Holland Press, 1984.

Sinclair, Andrew. *The Sword And The Grail.* New York: Crown Publishers, 1994.

Sinovic, Vincent. *Columbus—Debunking of a Legend.* New York: Rivercross, 1991.

Skelton, Raleigh A. *Explorers' Maps.* New York: Praeger, 1958.

Skelton, Raleigh. A., Thomas Marston, and George Painter. *The Vinland Map and The Tartar Relation.* New Haven: Yale University Press, 1965.

Stacy, John. *History of County of Norfolk.* (Vol. I) Norfolk: 1829.

Stooke, Philip J. "Mappaemundi and The Mirror in The Moon," in *Cartographica*, Vol. 29 (2), Summer 1992, 20-30.

Stromsted, Astri A. *Ancient Pioneers.* New York: Erik Friis, 1974.

Synge, Margaret. *A Book of Discovery.* Edinburgh: Thomas Nelson, 1962.

Taylor, Eva G. R. "A Letter Dated 1577 from Mercator to John Dee," in *Imago Mundi,* Vol. 13, 1956, 56-68.

Thacher, John B. *Christopher Columbus—His Life, His Work, His Remains.* Vol. II (reprint). New York: AMS Press, 1967.

Thompson, Gunnar. *American Discovery—Our Multicultural Heritage.* Seattle: Argonauts, 1994 (1992).

Tooley, R.V. *Maps & Mapmakers.* New York: Bonanza, 1935.

Torfaeus, Thormodus. *Historia Vinlandiae antiquae (1705); Historia Gronlandiae antiquae.* Copenhagen, 1706.

Towe, Kenneth. "The Vinland Map—Still a Forgery," in *Accounts of Chemical Research,* Vol. 23, 1990.

Tragaer, James. *The Peoples Chronology.* New York: Holt, Reinhart & Winston, 1979.

Tronoe, J.KR. *Columbus In The Arctic.* Oslo: Broggers Boktrykkeri, 1965.

True, David O. "Cabot Explorations in North America," in *Imago Mundi,* Vol. 13, 1956, 11-25.

Van Sertima, Ivan, Ed. *African Presence in Early America.* New Brunswick: Transaction Publishers, 1992.

Vignaud, Henry. *The Letter and Chart of Toscanelli.* London: Sands & Co., 1902.

Vinner, Max. "The Sea-worthiness of the Merchant Vessel and The Mysterious Vinland Map," in Hansen, 1993.

Von Wieser, Franz R. *Die Weltcarte des Albertin deVirga.* Innsbruck: H. Schwick, 1912.

Wahlgren, Erik. *The Vikings and America.* London: Thames & Hudson, 1986.

Weise, Arthur. *Discoveries of America.* New York: G.P. Putnam's Sons, 1884.

Wilson, Ian. *The Columbus Myth: Did Men from Bristol Reach America Before Columbus?* New York: Simon & Schuster, 1991.

Winge, Herluf. "Greenland Taxes to The Medieval Church," in *Meddelelser om Gronland,* Vol. 21, p. 322, 1902.

Winter, Heinrich. "The Viking Compass," in *Mariner's Mirror,* Vol. 23, p. 102, January 1937.

Wolff, Hans, Ed. *America: Early Maps of the New World.* Munich: Prestel, 1992.

Yellen, Nathan. "Colon's 1477 Voyage to the New World—Bay of Fundy," in *Vikingship,* Vol. 27 & 28, 1991 & 1992.

Ywahoo, Dhyani. *Voices of Our Ancestors.* Boston: Shambala, 1987.

Ziegler, Philip. *The Black Death.* London: Collins, 1969.

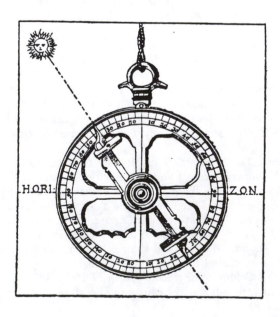

INDEX

Ruysch, John 93 (reference to Inventio), 138 (map), 184 (map)

S

saga map 38-40, 56 (Resen's map; Hungarian map), 122 (Stefansson map), 123-130 (tradition starts with Franciscans), 132 (compared to Norveca map), 142 (compared to Behaim's globe)

sailing routes 37 (Bergen to Iceland to Greenland), 60 (Eastern to Western settlements vis. Bardeson),

Salvagia 112 (forest land; Markland), 187

Sanudo, M. Florida map 214

Schedel's Map (1493) 50

Schoner, J. Behaim's map of Magellan Strait and South America 239

Schoolcraft, H. 30 (native tales of whites)

scientific god 284, 293

Scolvus (Skolp), J. 189 (voyage)

Sea of Darkness 17, 287

sea card 40 (Norse map), see Resen M and Norveca map

sea monster pirates 86, North Atlantic 86

Septentrionalis (Polar Regions) 34, see Hyperborea and Polar Regions

Seven Cities 184-185 (isle of), 198 (map), 210 (1490 map), M 210

ships Norse 40, Medieval 86, Portuguese 142

Sinus Magnus 22, 159, 168 (Colon's map), 215-217 (map of Pacific), see Ptolemaic Meridian

Skelton, R.A. 68, Yale VM 213-17

skraeling 3, 59 (in Clavus report), 88,

Southern Continent 27 (Peru), 170 (on Fineo map)

Spanish Franciscan 81, 174-175, 176 (turkey)

Stefansson Map of 1590 124 (map), 132 (second version of map)

Stooke, P. 12

T

Thordsen, E. 28 (map),

Thule 47 (Iceland),

tobacco 272-5

Toscanelli, P. 225

Treaty of Tordesillas 101, 215

turkey 176 (in Ibernia), 177 (Spanish Franciscan), 274-77

U

Ultima Thule 47

V

Van Sijpe, N. 51 (Greenland in Canada), 186 (map)

Venetian Commercial Map 2 (map), 155 (map)

Venthelant Donis M 54

Verrazano, G. 41 (grapes), 119 (white natives), 249, M 260, 254-5

Vesconte, Petrus 120 (map)

Vespucci, A. 239 (New World)

Viladestes Map 176 (Great Ireland or Ibernia)

Vinland & The Church 53,

Vinland 33, 40, 48, 53 (in the sagas & historical accounts), 57 (location in Polychronicon), 57 (location near Africa), 64-66 (location northwest of Europe),

Vinland Maps 56 (Resen map; Hungarian map), 63, 64 (Higden maps), 64-5 (spelling of Finland confused with Vinland), 66 (maps in Rudimentium Novitiorum & Augsburg), Yale VM 68 & 217

Vinland archaic Danish Vin-i-landa 54, 68, 90

Von Watt, J. 136 (map of Hyperborea)

Von Wieser, F. 10-13, 119, 157 (Caparu or Java Magna)

Voyage of Maeldun 27

W

Waldseemuller, M. 52 (geographic map of Greenland)

Welsh voyages 30-31,

Western Settlement (Greenland) 43 (demise— pirates)

white Indians slavery 261, 263

William Rubruk 81

Wineland (Vinland) 35, 40 (on Sea Card),

Wycliffe, John 80 (Inquisition)

Y

Yale Vinland Map (1440) 64 (Higden's spelling of Win-i-land), 65 (spelling of Finland confused with Vinland), 67-69, 68 (map), 69 (Taylor claims fraud due to Greenland as island), 70 (maps of Greenland as an island), 71 (McCrone claim of fraud), 72 (horn of Asia), 180 (map comparison), 226 (Florida)

Z

Zalteri M 18, 252

Zeno, Nicolo Ist 43 (pirate wars), 44 isles, 46 (Icelandic Isles), 61 (account by Ramusio), 98 (Frisland), 161-169, 164 (map), Lok 248

Ziegler, Jacob 49, 110 (map includes Newfoundland with Greenland), 265

zonal maps 19, 24 (map)

Author's Sketch

Gunnar is a native of Seattle where he was born in 1946. His parents, Florence and Roy Thompson, were the first generation of Norse and Germanic immigrants one of whom married into a Delaware tribe. His father was a mechanical engineer and Boy Scout leader who introduced him to the skills of mechanical drawing and construction; his mother was a prominent public health nurse who founded the Illinois Nursing Association. He graduated *Magna Cum Laude* from the University of Illinois-Urbana in 1968 with High Distinction in Anthropology, and he began a fellowship at the University of Wisconsin.

His diverse ethnic background and multicultural interests led him to support the creation of an African-American student center as well as efforts to expand tutorial services for disadvantaged students at the University of Wisconsin. His commitment to promoting creative education and minority access to the American dream soon led to conflicts with hide-bound administrators. When he expressed interest in the heretical subject of pre-Columbian cultural diffusion, orthodox anthropology professors abruptly ended his graduate studies with a "terminal" Master's Degree. Undaunted, he soon found a more-promising career in rehabilitation counseling. He earned a Ph.D. at Madison in 1979.

Gunnar's quest for truth crosses many disciplinary boundaries as he searches for answers to the challenges that confront modern society. A multi-talented individual, he has written several books on pre-Columbian voyages including *Nu Sun* and the highly popular *American Discovery—Our Multicultural Heritage.* His writings on public policy, multi-national economics, and creative education have anticipated many of the major social and economic developments of the past decade. He is a master multi-media artist; he holds a U.S. patent in ceramics.

The author is concerned that a Eurocentric bias in American education contributes to widespread social denial regarding economic and educational disadvantages. Hopefully, our children will dare to face social and economic inequities that past generations have ignored. With due consideration for the difficult challenges that lie ahead, this book is the author's gift to the children of the future. One day, they will know our true heritage and our common destiny.